From Marx to Hegel and Back

Also available from Bloomsbury

Marx: An Introduction, Michel Henry

The Bloomsbury Companion to Marx, ed. by Andrew Pendakis, Imre Szeman, and Jeff Diamanti

Aesthetic Marx, ed. by Samir Gandesha and Johan F. Hartle

Hegel and Resistance: History, Politics and Dialectics, ed. by Bart Zantvoort and Rebecca Comay

Hegel, Logic and Speculation, ed. by Paolo Diego Bubbio, Alessandro De Cesaris, Maurizio Pagano, and Hager Weslati

Hegel on Possibility: Modality, Perfection, and Dialectics, Nahum Brown (forthcoming)

From Marx to Hegel and Back

Capitalism, Critique, and Utopia

Edited by Victoria Fareld and Hannes Kuch

BLOOMSBURY ACADEMIC
LONDON • NEW YORK • OXFORD • NEW DELHI • SYDNEY

BLOOMSBURY ACADEMIC
Bloomsbury Publishing Plc
50 Bedford Square, London, WC1B 3DP, UK
1385 Broadway, New York, NY 10018, USA
29 Earlsfort Terrace, Dublin 2, Ireland

BLOOMSBURY, BLOOMSBURY ACADEMIC and the Diana logo are trademarks
of Bloomsbury Publishing Plc

First published in Great Britain 2020
This paperback edition published in 2021

Copyright © Victoria Fareld, Hannes Kuch, and Contributors 2020

Victoria Fareld and Hannes Kuch have asserted their right under the Copyright,
Designs and Patents Act, 1988, to be identified as Editors of this work.

For legal purposes the Acknowledgements on p. ix constitute an extension
of this copyright page.

Cover image © Camilla Pentti

All rights reserved. No part of this publication may be reproduced or transmitted
in any form or by any means, electronic or mechanical, including photocopying,
recording, or any information storage or retrieval system, without prior
permission in writing from the publishers.

Bloomsbury Publishing Plc does not have any control over, or responsibility for,
any third-party websites referred to or in this book. All internet addresses given
in this book were correct at the time of going to press. The author and publisher
regret any inconvenience caused if addresses have changed or sites have ceased
to exist, but can accept no responsibility for any such changes.

A catalogue record for this book is available from the British Library.

A catalog record for this book is available from the Library of Congress.

ISBN: HB: 978-1-3500-8267-0
PB: 978-1-3502-6099-3
ePDF: 978-1-3500-8268-7
eBook: 978-1-3500-8269-4

Typeset by Integra Software Services Pvt. Ltd.

To find out more about our authors and books visit www.bloomsbury.com
and sign up for our newsletters.

Contents

Contributors		vi
Acknowledgments		ix
1	From Marx to Hegel and Back: Toward a Helical Approach *Victoria Fareld and Hannes Kuch*	1

Part 1 Reassessing the Legacy of Hegel and Marx

2	Hegel and Marx: A Reassessment after One Century *Axel Honneth*	37
3	Hegel, Marx, and Presentism *Emmanuel Renault*	55
4	Property and Freedom in Kant, Hegel, and Marx *Jacob Blumenfeld*	73
5	I, the Revolution, Speak: Lenin's Speculative (Hegelian) Style *Frank Ruda*	91

Part 2 Capitalism and Critique

6	Critique in Hegel and Marx *Rocío Zambrana*	109
7	Hegel and Marx on 'Spiritual Life' as a Criterion for Social Critique *Frederick Neuhouser*	125
8	Abstract Labor and Recognition *Sven Ellmers*	141
9	Love Will Tear Us Apart: Marx and Hegel on the Materiality of Erotic Bonds *Federica Gregoratto*	161

Part 3 Postcapitalism and Utopia

10	Marx's 'Hegelian' Critique of Utopia *David Leopold*	179
11	Where Are We Developing the Requirements for a New Society? The Dialectic of Today's Capitalism from a Hegelian-Marxist Perspective *Eva Bockenheimer*	197
12	Social Freedom beyond Capitalism: Three Alternatives *Hannes Kuch*	213
13	Honneth's Democratic *Sittlichkeit* and Market Socialism *Michael Nance*	235
Index		253

Contributors

Jacob Blumenfeld earned his PhD in 2018 from the New School for Social Research, with a dissertation on the concept of property in German Idealism. He edited and contributed to *The Anarchist Turn* (Pluto Press, 2013), co-translated *Communism for Kids* (MIT Press, 2017), and recently published *All Things Are Nothing to Me* (Zero Books, 2018). His popular writings have appeared in the *New York Times*, *Viewpoint Magazine*, and the *Brooklyn Rail*. His academic writings have appeared in the *Hegel Bulletin*, *Journal of the British Society for Phenomenology*, *Historical Materialism*, and more. He lives in Berlin.

Eva Bockenheimer holds a doctoral degree from the Ruhr University Bochum. Her thesis examined the conception of gender and the family in Hegel's thought. Her research interests include the philosophy of Hegel, Marx, and Marxism; concepts of sex, gender, and the family; and theories on the future of work and social transformation. She works as a lecturer in educational institutions of several German trade unions and is currently writing an *Introduction to Dialectics*. Her publications include *Hegels Familien- und Geschlechtertheorie* (2013), *Work Hard Play Hard* (editor, 2014), and the article "Hegel and Marx on Family and Gender-Relations" (forthcoming, *Hegel Bulletin*).

Sven Ellmers is Assistant Professor at the Carl von Ossietzky *University* of *Oldenburg*. His research interests include German Idealism and Marx, morality of markets, and normative foundations of critical social theory. Among his publications are *Freiheit und Wirtschaft. Theorie der bürgerlichen Gesellschaft nach Hegel* (Transcript 2015); *Korporation und Sittlichkeit. Zur Aktualität von Hegels Theorie der bürgerlichen Gesellschaft*, co-edited with Steffen Herrmann (Fink, 2017); Sven Ellmers, "'Der Narzissmus wird gesellschaftsfähig.' Subjektivierungspraktiken der Marktwirtschaft" (*Allgemeine Zeitschrift für Philosophie* 44, no. 1, 2019).

Victoria Fareld is Associate Professor of Intellectual History at Stockholm University. She earned her PhD in 2007 with a work on recognition, vulnerability, and exposure in contemporary political philosophy in light of Hegel's philosophy and German Idealism. Her current research focuses on time, ethics, memory, and historical justice. Among her recent publications are "Coming to Terms with the Present: Exploring the Chrononormativity of Historical Time", *Rethinking Historical Time: New Approaches to Presentism* (Bloomsbury 2019)," History, Justice and the Time of the Imprescriptible", *The Ethos of History* (Berghahn Books 2018); "(In) Between the Living and the Dead: New Perspectives on Time in History", *History Compass* 14, no. 9, 2016; "Ressentiment as Moral Imperative: Jean Améry's Nietzschean Revaluation of Victim Morality", *Re-Thinking Ressentiment* (Transcript 2016).

Federica Gregoratto is a lecturer in social and political philosophy at the University of St. Gallen (Switzerland). She has published on the philosophy of love and sex, critical theory (especially Habermas and Adorno), pragmatism (especially Dewey and Addams), recognition and power theories, debt-guilt debates, and feminism. She is working on a book on erotic love as a social space of power, freedom, and transformation. Among her most recent publications connected to this project are: "The Ambiguity of Love. Beauvoir, Honneth and Arendt on the Relation between Recognition, Power and Violence" (*Critical Horizons*, 2018), and "Love Is a Losing Game: Power and Exploitation in Romantic Relationships" (*The Journal of Political Power*, 2017).

Axel Honneth is Jack C. Weinstein Professor for the Humanities in the Department of Philosophy at Columbia University. He was Director of the Institute for Social Research, Goethe-Universität Frankfurt, and Professor of Social Philosophy, Goethe-Universität Frankfurt. His research interests include social philosophy and the logic of social sciences; the theory of recognition; Critical Theory. Among his publications are *The Pathologies of Individual Freedom: Hegel's Social Theory* (Princeton University Press, 2010); *Freedom's Right: The Social Foundations of Democratic Life* (Polity, 2014); *The Idea of Socialism: Towards a Renewal* (Polity, 2017).

Hannes Kuch leads the research project "Economy and Social Freedom" at the Department of Philosophy, Goethe-University Frankfurt. His research interests include social and political philosophy, with a focus on nineteenth-century philosophy, the philosophy of the market, and social aspects of the philosophy of language. Among his publications are *Humiliation, Degradation, Dehumanization: Human Dignity Violated* (as a co-editor; Springer, 2010); "Real Utopias, Reciprocity, and Concern for Others" (*Philosophy and Social Criticism*, 2016); "The Market, Competition, and Structural Exploitation" (*Constellations*, forthcoming).

David Leopold is Associate Professor of Political Theory at the University of Oxford, and is also the John Milton Fellow at Mansfield College, Oxford. He has written widely on aspects of socialism, methods in political theory, and utopianism. He has produced scholarly editions of Max Stirner's *The Ego and Its Own* (Cambridge University Press, 2000), of William Morris's *News From Nowhere* (Oxford University Press, 2003), and is the author of *The Young Karl Marx: German Philosophy, the Modern State, and Human Flourishing* (Cambridge University Press, 2007).

Michael Nance is Assistant Professor of Philosophy at the University of Maryland, Baltimore County, and Alexander von Humboldt Research Fellow at the Goethe-Universität, Frankfurt. His research focuses on social, political, and legal philosophy in Kant and post-Kantian Idealism. Recent publications include "Property and Economic Planning in Fichte's Contractualism", *European Journal of Philosophy*, 2019; "Freedom, Coercion, and the Relation of Right", in *Fichte's* Foundations of Natural Right: A Critical Guide, ed. Gabriel Gottlieb (Cambridge University Press, 2016); and "Hegel's Jena Practical Philosophy", in *The Oxford Handbook of Hegel*, ed. Dean Moyar (Oxford University Press, 2017).

Frederick Neuhouser is Professor of Philosophy at Barnard College, Columbia University (New York), specializing in German Idealism and social and political philosophy. He is the author of four books: *Rousseau's Critique of Inequality* (Cambridge University Press, 2014), *Rousseau's Theodicy of Self-Love* (Oxford University Press, 2008), *Foundations of Hegel's Social Theory* (Harvard University Press, 2000), and *Fichte's Theory of Subjectivity* (Cambridge University Press, 1990). Much of his recent work has focused on the topics of recognition and *amour-propre*, but he is currently working on a project on social ontology and social pathology in nineteenth- and twentieth-century thought.

Emmanuel Renault is Professor of Philosophy in Paris Nanterre University. He has published mainly on Hegel, Marx, and on past and present critical theory. His books written or translated in English are: *Social Suffering* (Rowman & Littlefield, 2017), *Marx and Critical Theory* (Brill, 2018), *The Return of Work in Critical Theory* (Columbia University Press, 2018), and *The Experience of Injustice* (Columbia University Press, 2019).

Frank Ruda is Senior Lecturer in Philosophy at the University of Dundee. His last publications include: *The Dash – The Other Side of Absolute Knowing* (with Rebecca Comay, MIT Press, 2018); *Reading Marx* (with Agon Hamza and Slavoj Žižek, Polity Press, 2018), and *Gegen-Freiheit: Fatalismus und Komik* (Konstanz University Press, 2018).

Rocío Zambrana is Associate Professor of Philosophy at Emory. She is the author of *Colonial Debts: The Case of Puerto Rico* (under contract, Duke University Press) and *Hegel's Theory of Intelligibility* (The University of Chicago Press, 2015), in addition to articles, book chapters, and columns on various themes. Her current work examines critiques of capitalism and coloniality in multiple philosophical traditions, especially Marxism, Decolonial Thought, and Feminisms of the Américas (Latinx, Latin American, Caribbean). She considers the manifestations of coloniality in a colonial context by examining fiscally distressed Puerto Rico. Zambrana is also Co-Editor, with Bonnie Mann, Erin McKenna, and Camisha Russell, of *Hypatia: A Journal of Feminist Philosophy*, and columnist for *80grados* (San Juan, Puerto Rico).

Acknowledgments

All efforts have been made to trace copyright holders. In the event of errors or omissions, please notify the publisher in writing of any corrections that will need to be incorporated in future editions of this book.

Axel Honneth's "Hegel and Marx: A Reassessment after One Century," from *Feminism, Capitalism, and Critique: Essays in Honor of Nancy Fraser*, ed. Banu Bargu and Chiara Bottici, published 2017 by Palgrave Macmillan, is reproduced with permission of SNCSC.

Sven Ellmers's "Abstract Labor and Recognition" is a slightly modified translation of "Abstrakte Arbeit und Anerkennung," published in *Zeitschrift für Praktische Philosophie* 4, no. 1, 2017: 81–108, under a CC-BY 4.0 licence, https://www.praktische-philosophie.org/ellmers-2017.html.

1

From Marx to Hegel and Back

Toward a Helical Approach

Victoria Fareld and Hannes Kuch

1 Why Hegel and Marx—Again, Today?

In the wake of the global financial crisis, growing social inequalities, rising populism, and a resurrection of social movements, there is a wide-ranging revival of interest in Marx and Marxist thought.[1] For the task of critically understanding and contesting our social and political world, a rereading of Marx is indeed of vital importance. But to *which* Marx should we return? Which of all the Marxian guises should be explored anew? In light of the impact of Marxism on the history of the last century—in its emancipatory as well as totalitarian forms—a return to its source has to take the form of a self-critical reassessment that can actualize its potentials in new ways. Our suggestion in this book is to explore anew the *Hegelian Marx*. Hegel's social and political philosophy, with its focus on recognition, desire, alienation, social freedom, and its critique of liberalism, was not only crucial for Marx but has become one of the most productive sites for critical theories today.[2] Such an elaboration of Hegel's philosophy on Marx's thinking can provide us with new standards for critically rethinking society—and for refiguring the concept of critique. In an attempt to explore and revitalize the Hegelian foundations of Marx's thinking, we return to some key questions: Was Marx Hegel's most important and merciless critic? Did he misread essential aspects of Hegel's thought? At what points was Marx more Hegelian than he realized himself? In exploring the Hegelian foundations of Marx's thinking, we also have to ask ourselves: *which* Hegel? The suggested answer is, with a temporal inversion, the *Marxian Hegel*. How can we reread Hegel in ways that were opened up by Marx? What would a Hegelian critique of Marx look like today? What place does Hegel have in contemporary critical thinking?[3]

Most schools of Marxism regard Marx's inversion of Hegel's dialectics as a progressive development, leaving behind Hegel's idealism by transforming it into a materialist critique of political economy. Other Marxist approaches argue that the mature Marx completely broke with Hegel, or at least that Marxism should be expunged of any Hegelian traces. Instead of regarding Hegel as a metaphysical idealist, many strands of Hegelian Marxism have understood him as an empirically informed theorist of the social, political, and economic world, rendering his philosophy much more 'materialist'.[4] Our focus in this volume is to point out new dimensions of this 'materialist' side of Hegel's thinking. We propose a spiral-shaped—or 'helical'— movement 'from Marx to Hegel and back'. The word 'helical' refers to something that has the form of a helix. We use it here to grasp an interpretive movement that follows a spiral course. Similar to the 'hermeneutic spiral', the helix only seemingly moves in circles; it incessantly finds new paths, looking at the previous ones from a different perspective. Correspondingly, the helical approach proposed here offers a rethinking of the Hegel–Marx relation through a movement that oscillates between the two thinkers, providing new associations and interpretations, aiming at encompassing a Marxian rereading of Hegel as well as a rereading of Marx from a Hegelian perspective. The promise is that, in this way, Hegel and Marx can complement one another, filling the gaps that the other left open or reinforcing one another's insights.

There are a number of strong affinities between Hegel and Marx: their critique of abstract liberalism, their view of freedom as communal or social, their attentiveness to the concept of need, their interest in the rabble and the proletariat, and their reflections on universalism and species-being. There are also, however, strong differences and disputes: Hegel's idealism is often seen as opposed to Marx's materialism; the former's appraisal of the actual is set against the latter's merciless criticism of it. The same goes for Hegel's social institutionalism and belief in the state, clashing with Marx's critique of the 'state machinery' and his hope for unmediated communality. Hegel's affirmation of personal property conflicts with Marx's critique of the private ownership of means of production. And although both thinkers strongly criticize free markets, Hegel defends a certain kind of market whereas Marx's critique of market capitalism is fundamental. Both of them criticize 'abstract rights', but they diverge in their assessment of the proper role and scope of individual rights. A helical approach highlights the overlap in Hegel's and Marx's social and political philosophies, not, however, without addressing the tensions and substantial disputes between them directly and systematically. Its central aim is to unify the ethical content of Hegel's philosophy with the explanatory power of Marx's social and economic critique of the contemporary world.

The relation between Hegel and Marx is among the most interpreted in the history of philosophy and the tradition of critical thought, and for good reasons: Hegel attempts to bring the philosophy of his day to a conclusion; his system absorbs the best insights from Aristotle to Kant. At the same time, it provides a thoroughgoing critique of his philosophical predecessors, of Kant even more than of Aristotle. Hegel demonstrates that philosophy cannot remain purely philosophical; even when dealing with core philosophical issues, such as reason, knowledge, truth, freedom, and universality, philosophy has to go beyond itself—into the realm of social theory, broadly conceived. After Hegel, philosophy must get involved with questions of recognition and human sociality, social norms and institutions, or power and authority. It is precisely at this point that Marx draws on Hegel, moving the focus even closer to the question of the conditions and shapes of social life, by reworking, transforming, criticizing, inverting, and eventually exceeding Hegel's thought.

When analyzing the various ways of relating Hegel and Marx, it is important to keep apart several distinct levels of analysis. One important level concerns Marx's own *explicit assessment* of Hegel, whether positive or negative, as well as his deliberate *appropriation* of Hegelian ideas, arguments, and concepts.[5] 'Dialectics' and 'alienation' are examples that immediately spring to mind when focusing on Marx's appropriative use of Hegel, whereas his critique of the state in capitalist societies, which is largely directed at a Hegelian understanding of it, exemplifies his conscious detachment from Hegel. This issue becomes even more multifaceted when we take into account that there is not only one Hegel or one Marx; there are, rather, many versions of both thinkers. A second level of analysis refers to the *implicit* ways Marx related to Hegel. Marx often remained Hegelian without explicitly saying it and sometimes even without acknowledging it, or still more, all the while criticizing a caricature of Hegel. Conversely, Marx did leave Hegel behind in many ways, yet at times without bothering to balance accounts with his 'teacher' explicitly.[6] Both these affinities and differences between Hegel and Marx are situated on an implicit level, but they may turn out to be highly significant. A third level of investigation is the *history of Marxism* (and Hegelianism) and the various ways in which the Hegel–Marx relation has been interpreted in the historical trajectory of the different schools of (Hegelian) Marxism. Certainly, there is no single school of Marxism, not even of Hegelian Marxism, but only a wide (and often incompatible) historical variety of ways to relate Marx's thinking to Hegel, from Vladimir Lenin and Georg Lukács to Slavoj Žižek and Axel Honneth.[7] This list of names—radically incomplete as it is—merely serves to exemplify the broad diversity of traditions that might be taken into account when interpreting the relation of Hegel and Marx.

Thus, there are multiple possibilities to reconstruct the Hegel–Marx connection, with at least three levels of investigation, where each of these levels again opens up diverse ties and points of dissociation. This means, in turn, that to relate the two thinkers in a particular way crucially depends upon the underlying subject in question. In our book, such a systematic reconstruction takes its guiding aim from substantive questions of Critical Theory (or critical theories, in lower case) that go beyond purely historical issues of de facto influences. In other words, we are not primarily interested in Marx's own stated or tacit relation to Hegel, or only interested in how the Hegel–Marx connection has been construed in different schools of Marxism and Hegelianism. Our examination of Hegel's and Marx's interrelated thinking is an attempt to critically examine our own contemporary situation.

2 Progression, Disruption, Reversion: Mapping the Terrain

It is impossible to give an encompassing overview of the immensely vast and rich literature on the relation between Hegel and Marx. But in a rough sketch, three general ways to relate Hegel and Marx can be distinguished: 'progression', 'disruption', and 'reversion'. This section provides a broad outline of these approaches. In the following section, we argue for a shift in perspective by proposing a conceptual framework that considers a dynamic, two-way, helical movement of interpretations.

(i) *Progression*: This line of relating Hegel and Marx assumes a substantial development between the two thinkers where Marx in some way aims at a 'sublation' (*Aufhebung*) of Hegelian insights. The idea is that there is a significant progress from Hegel to Marx, where Marx is seen as a corrective to Hegelian philosophy or even as the one who fulfills Hegel's philosophy by overcoming it. Within this field of interpretation, we situate readers of Hegel and Marx who, in various ways, emphasize Marx's critical appropriation and further development of Hegelian ideas, concepts, and arguments. One strand of progressive readings of the Hegel–Marx relation focuses on the idea that Marx brings Hegel's philosophy to its fulfillment by transforming it in different ways—radicalizing it, materializing it, overcoming it. The view on Marx's relation to Hegel as one of progressive development was brought to the fore by Georg Lukács. To Lukács, Marx critically completes Hegel's philosophy, and Hegelian Marxism is a theory of human realization by means of the revolutionary transformation of society. In *History and Class Consciousness*, published in 1923, Lukács articulates a conception of political praxis by drawing on Hegel's view of society as a totality, although radically modified by Marx. Crucial to Lukács' interpretation is the claim that Marx uncovered the true content of Hegel's idea of a collective subject of history by releasing it from its idealist and metaphysical constraints and transforming it into a theory of the historical agency of the proletariat.[8] From Lukács' point of view, as elucidated in *The Young Hegel* (1948), Marx's rejection of Hegel's idealist metaphysics was thus neither a rupture with, nor a rejection of, Hegel's philosophy, but a critical realization and transformative completion of it.[9] Lukács maintains that in Marx's critical fulfillment of Hegel's thinking, history appears as a revolutionary process toward human self-realization, in which humanity eventually recognizes itself in the social world it produces. The variety of progressive approaches, despite their many internal differences, is held together by the view that Marx qualitatively developed a form of thinking that originated from Hegel.[10] This proximity between the two is nicely captured by Adorno's remark that, in Hegel's philosophy, we can already see "society's dawning critical consciousness of itself".[11]

Many topics can be placed within the progressive tradition: Apart from the key concepts of alienation and dialectics, a progressive line of development can be found in the influence of Hegel's logic on Marx's *Capital*, in the idea of immanent critique, and in the philosophies of history of Hegel and Marx. In order to illuminate how progressive approaches operate, we will spell out the two latter themes in more detail. Marx and the Left Hegelians, particularly in the Frankfurt School tradition of Critical Theory, inherited from Hegel the idea that critique operates by way of critical standards that are derived from the very object under investigation.[12] In this respect, Hegelian and Marxist approaches are fundamentally at odds with vast strands of contemporary political philosophy that operate more or less on a Kantian basis, by construing abstract normative principles detached from social reality without asking about the foothold these principles have in social life, or the social forces that might help to realize their normative demands. Almost all schools of Hegelian Marxism reject this kind of moral condemnation of capitalist society where seemingly transcendent moral ideals are held against a bad reality. In contrast, immanent critique is based on norms, which the social orders or institutions in question necessarily rely upon themselves.

The object of critique is judged by its own avowed standards and norms, by accepting the self-conception and claims that the object itself established, and then by detecting the internal contradictions and inner conflicts characteristic of that object with respect to its foundational standards and norms. Marx articulates this approach with the claim that "we do not confront the world in a doctrinaire way with a new principle: Here is the truth, kneel down before it! We develop new principles for the world out of the world's own principles."[13]

Immanent critique clearly has its sources in Hegel. In the *Phenomenology of Spirit*, Hegel argues that when investigating even the earliest, most incipient forms of knowledge, it would be misguided to judge them by an external standard of truth, for example, derived from the established forms of science. For the task is to reconstruct the validity of knowledge forms that lead to these sciences in the first place. Instead, it is possible to take the claims to truth of the immediate forms of knowledge at their own word, because they themselves already involve immanent norms of self-evaluation.[14] The Left Hegelian tradition adopted Hegel's implicit model of immanent critique, while leaving behind his idealist presumption that the practices and institutions under investigation are always already structured conceptually (by 'the concept'), so that they inherently contain justificatory standards for self-evaluation. We can easily understand this relation as a progressive one. Marx and his successors transformed Hegel's concept of immanent critique by transposing it to the domains of social theory and history of philosophy. In criticizing the contemporary world, immanent critique would hereafter become an essentially social critique, by taking into account its own historical emergence, social potentials, and further lines of development.[15]

The second exemplary topic is Hegel's and Marx's strong reliance on the philosophy of history. For both of them, recourse to the philosophy of history serves the purpose of showing that the moral ought does not remain "a mere 'ought'",[16] but that it is an already historically established social force. On a more fundamental level, Hegel and Marx have often been interpreted as already being aligned in assuming that there is progress in human history. History exhibits a pattern of development; it is more than a collection of contingent events or pure chaos. There is progress in the movement from the Greek *polis* to the modern constitutional state, as Hegel would argue, or in Marx's framework, in the movement from slave societies to modern capitalism.[17] Moreover, Hegel and Marx would agree that the fundamental reason why it is even possible to speak of progress in human history is the enlargement of human freedom.[18] The historical process is an arduous and contradictory movement through which humankind seeks to enlarge and deepen the preconditions for individual autonomy, both on the objective, institutional level and the subjective, psychic level. For Marx, too, freedom is the core value advanced in the process of human history, although his focus lies more strongly on the material conditions of human freedom. Marx describes the historical process as a growing liberation from the constraints imposed on us by our surrounding natural conditions, a liberation brought about by the transformative power of human labor.[19] A further affinity in their conceptions of history is that Hegel no less than Marx construes historical transformations as contradictory, crisis-driven processes.[20] Historical developments do not unfold in a linear way. When existing institutions and social orders erode, when they exhaust themselves, they create tensions and problems, which, crucially, do not necessarily have to be paralyzing or destructive. They themselves may contribute to the emergence of new institutions and orders, by becoming "pregnant"[21] with their successive social formations.

There are, of course, also many differences between Hegel's and Marx's philosophies of history. Marx, for example, is deeply critical of Hegel's claim that "*what is*, is reason", advocating instead for a "*ruthless criticism* of all that exists".[22] Marx knew about Hegel's distinction between mere existence and actuality, as when Hegel stresses that a "bad state is one which merely exists", but has "no genuine reality".[23] According to Hegel, for something to be actual, it must be rational. But Marx still contends that Hegel's metaphysical approach skews given social institutions toward appearing to be rational even if they are not; it tends to mystify social reality in a way that "twists the empirical fact into a metaphysical axiom".[24] This difference between Hegel and Marx is merely one among many.[25] But leaving these differences aside, there is a remarkable affinity in *how* Hegel and Marx conceive their respective goals of human history: Both construe them as inherently processual and open-ended. Think of Marx's idea of communism being the end of human *pre-history*, thus only the *beginning* of true history, that is, the opening of the process of conscious self-determination toward an indeterminate future.[26] In Hegel's case, too, recent interpretations put forward the openness of Hegel's philosophy of history.[27] What Hegel wants to underline is that the modern world attained a certain maturity that allows for a novel form of self-comprehension of spirit vis-à-vis its own history. This maturing of spirit, or self-conscious life, does not paralyze free activity; rather, it widens the space of free activity within an unpredetermined world.

(ii) *Disruption*: Whereas progressive approaches hold Hegel to be the condition of possibility for Marx and Marxism, disruptive approaches construct him as Marx's overaged father figure from whom Marx could not sufficiently emancipate himself.[28] The word 'disruption' refers to a break or rupture but also to a disturbance or an interruption in the normal course or unity. Accordingly, disruptive approaches focus on how Marx attempted to break with Hegel; or, they challenge a progressive understanding of the relation between them by suggesting that Marx's thoughts should be reconstructed without any reference to Hegel, who is seen as the greatest obstacle to the realization of Marxian philosophy; or, they offer a deconstructive reading in which Hegel and Marx are used against themselves, in order to set free their immanent potentiality.

Marx breaks with Hegel both explicitly, by way of a direct critique, and implicitly, by departing from Hegel substantially, without even reckoning with his arguments. We shall illustrate Marx's break with Hegel by reference to three topics: the relation of civil society and state; the issue of domination and exploitation; and the category of social struggles. As to the first case in point: Hegel is the first philosopher to capture conceptually the modern separation of civil society and state; that is, the division of the social order into a market economy and a political system. He not only conceptually grasps this separation, but also justifies it.[29] In his view, civil society opens up a social sphere that allows individuals to exercise their arbitrary choice in pursuing their private purposes. Marx, however, scorns Hegel's hope that the state in its universality sits enthroned over the scattering particularity of civil society.[30] The idea of the separation between civil society and the state—a separation which for Hegel is an achievement of modern society—is in Marx's account at the heart of the problem. Marx insists that the source of modern social pathologies lies precisely in the differentiation of social spheres, for it creates an unlivable "division of the human being" into *bourgeois* and *citoyen*.[31] As a result, the political sphere remains a detached and alienated form of the communal existence of the members of society.[32] As long as human beings shy away from taking conscious collective control over their most fundamental way of interacting with one another and nature, that is, their economic life, the political sphere, Marx insists, remains powerless.

Another important demarcation line between Hegel and Marx is the issue of domination and exploitation. Domination, particularly class domination, is at the center of Marx's social theory. It involves processes of subordination and allows for exploitation. In Hegel's thinking, there is no genuine theory of domination or exploitation, and he tends to draw, especially in the *Philosophy of Right*, a rather harmonious picture of an undisturbed coexistence of various estates.[33] It is true that Hegel already knew about many of the bifurcations of market society, but instead of making them the object of criticism he tended to bestow dialectical blessings on them—by construing them to be productive engines driving forward the transition to the higher social sphere of the state.[34] On a fundamental level, Hegel does not take into account the possibility that the consent to contracts does not always owe to the autonomous choices of the participants; but, in fact, 'consent' can be coerced, even if only indirectly, because of the lack of alternatives. In other words, Hegel is not interested in what Marx called the "silent compulsion of economic relations".[35] A further layer of domination conceptualized by Marx, but neglected by Hegel, is ideological domination. Ideologies are here conceived of as structured sets of beliefs, which originate in social practices and structures, and which, in turn, have practical effects in regard to them, most importantly by obfuscating or dissimulating the asymmetries at play and the conflicting interests at stake, as in the case of the formal equality of legal rights and the labor contract.[36] For Marx, these are important institutional vehicles of ideology, while Hegel sees both institutions much more optimistically as progressive expressions of objective spirit, that is, as an enduring embodiment of mutual recognition. In his more radical veins, Marx even suspects Hegel's philosophy itself to be ideological at its core.[37]

A disruptive approach takes Marx to be the philosopher who brought social struggles into social theory at all. Although social struggles in a broad sense are surely relevant for Hegel, Marx places his account of social struggles at a fundamental, categorical level, and he takes pains to inform his analysis with historical evidence and empirical findings. Hegel, in contrast, keeps an arm's length from overly revolutionary or radical political struggles. Although embracing the French Revolution, he did this—as was often noticed—without embracing the revolutionaries.[38] Marx, on the other hand, makes social struggles and real political movements the starting point of critical analysis. For the early Marx, critical theory is in fact nothing other than the "self-clarification … to be gained by the present time of its struggles and desires".[39] Marx then extends this focus back into history, with a deliberate eye on class struggles where social groups are opposed to one another in virtue of their antagonistic material interests.

The list of contested issues between Hegel and Marx could be extended by a number of further points of difference, for example, the status of the nuclear family, or the role of religion. But let us turn to how various schools of Marxism relate to Hegel in a disruptive way. There is a dividing line between those successors of Marx who formulate their criticism of Hegel *in Hegelian terms*, and those who break with Hegel completely. Adorno's dictum about "the whole" being "false"[40] is emblematic for the first approach. This claim epitomizes a radical departure from Hegel but only by building on Hegel himself, on Hegelian methods, concepts, and frameworks, in this case, Hegel's concept of totality, all the while drawing on substantial insights from Marx's social theory. This is Marx's inversion of Hegel expanded and radicalized. A similar move occurs in Adorno's disruptive reworking of the Hegelian dialectic into his concept of 'negative dialectic', articulated as a relentless critique of every form of affirmative identity thinking.[41] A related position characterizes important strands of anti-Hegelian twentieth-century philosophy, not least the French post-metaphysical thinkers as different as Michel Foucault, Emmanuel Levinas, and Jacques Derrida, whose philosophies are attempts to settle accounts with the Hegelian dialectic. Foucault's inaugural lecture at the Collège de France is emblematic in its claustrophobic depiction of a philosophy hopelessly caught in the dialectical web: "to make a real escape from Hegel", Foucault admits, "presupposes an exact appreciation of what it costs to detach ourselves from him … It presupposes a knowledge of what is still Hegelian in that which allows us to think against Hegel."[42] Similarly, Derrida's acknowledgment of the "absolute proximity" between Hegel's *Aufhebung* and his own key notion of *différance*, capturing a symptomatic intellectual love–hate relationship to Hegel, can be situated within this strand of interpretations.[43]

Other disruptive approaches, however, make the break with Hegel more definitive, by attempting to purge Marxism completely of any Hegelian residues. The most famous version of this anti-Hegelian move was promoted by Louis Althusser in France. In the 1960s, Althusser argued for an "epistemological break" in Marx's writings, supposedly separating the humanist ideology of the young Marx from the scientific writings of the mature Marx.[44] Before the break, which Althusser situated at around 1845, Marx is said to have been influenced by Ludwig Feuerbach, and, particularly in the *Economic and Philosophic Manuscripts*, by Hegel, whereas after the break, he developed his general theory of historical materialism and the critique of political economy outlined in *Capital*. The idea of an epistemological break, borrowed from Gaston Bachelard, helped Althusser carve out the role of "problematics", that is, theoretical frameworks within which knowledge production is enabled, but that impose unarticulated, unconscious obstacles to scientific activity.[45] Such obstacles are not overcome by incremental improvements, but by sudden cuts, by fundamental reorganizations of knowledge, after which the old forms of knowledge become discernible as ideology. The idea of a sharp, anti-Hegelian break in Marx's writing is, however, contested today.[46] Indeed there are shifts in Marx's work, and certainly the early Marx had been immersed in the circle of Young Hegelians.[47] But this does not mean that Hegelian themes and arguments had later vanished.[48]

Another radical anti-Hegelian strand of Marxism can be found in analytical philosophy in the Anglo-Saxon world, from analytical Marxists such as Gerald A.

Cohen, John Roemer, and Jon Elster.[49] Analytical Marxism became influential in the 1980s, with the main goal of reconstructing Marxian theory without presupposing any special, 'Hegelian', methodology. Analytical Marxists criticized, without reservation, Hegel's logic and the idea of a dialectical method or dialectical thinking.[50] Another criticism was directed against Marx's Hegel-inspired supposition of 'Capital' as a supra-individual, anonymous, yet intentional, actor, modeled on Hegel's notion of *Geist*.[51] Finally, analytical Marxism criticized Marx's Hegelian trust in an ultimately harmonious 'sublation' of conflicting values, norms, or interests, in contrast to the difficult work of balancing conflicting goals and finding trade-offs.[52] It is not without some irony, however, that in their later works, some analytical Marxists unintentionally veered off their anti-Hegelian path, ending up miles into the territory of their adversary—yet without being aware of it, probably owing to their disregard of the history of philosophy. This inadvertent affinity to Hegel is manifest in Cohen's and, more recently, Roemer's recourse to the notion of 'ethos', a category at the center of Hegel's theory of ethical life (*Sittlichkeit*).[53] Cohen mounts this proto-Hegelian category as a weapon in his critique of John Rawls, the latter-day Kantian, in quite a similar way as Hegel employed it when criticizing Kant's 'impotence of the mere ought'.

(iii) *Reversion*: These approaches aim to reverse the movement from Hegel to Marx, or at least they argue for a strong Hegelian framing or grounding of Marxian ideas. Whereas disruptive approaches hold Hegel to be the source of the problem, 'reverse' readings believe him to be the solution. The reversion of the path from Hegel to Marx is considered indispensable to fully realizing Marx's philosophy, without which the latter is thought to remain incomplete or inchoate. In a more critical vein, Hegel is even treated as a necessary corrective to his disciple. Progressive and reverse readings share scope, to some extent, but their similarities tend to hide a major difference, namely, the line of influence, or, who is being used as a corrective to whom.

One of the first philosophers who attempted to reverse the path from Hegel to Marx was Alexandre Kojève, whose lectures on the *Phenomenology of Spirit* in Paris in the 1930s had a profound impact on the French intellectual scene, from Jean-Paul Sartre to Georges Bataille to Jacques Lacan and many others.[54] Kojève's unconventional appropriation of Hegel is inspired by Marx (and Heidegger), as can be seen most notably in his semi-Marxist interpretation of the Hegelian dialectic of master and slave. In Kojève's philosophy of history, the slave turns out to be the actual master, the true subject of history, whereas the master ends up in "an existential impasse", in Kojève's well-known phrase.[55] This is because the master's superiority becomes unsustainable, since it is recognized only by someone who the master does not recognize, effectively invalidating the validation expressed by the slave. Moreover, it is the laboring slave who transforms both the world and himself in his activity to achieve mastery over nature, in contrast to the passive idleness of the master.

Kojève departs from Marx, however, in the centrality he ascribes to the notion of 'desire'. In Kojève's account, desire for that which one does not have characterizes human beings and their striving for freedom. Yet desire becomes fully human only when its void can no longer be filled with material objects, as it does in the human metabolism with nature, which humans share with animals. Instead, the negativity of desire must be directed at another negativity: "To be anthropogenic, then, Desire must be directed toward a nonbeing—that is, toward another *Desire*, another greedy emptiness, another *I*", he claims.[56] To desire as a human being thus means to desire to be desired; it means, in other words, to desire to be recognized, confirmed, loved. Kojève is the first philosopher who placed the concept of recognition center stage in the reading of Hegel, long before the rise of contemporary recognition theory. In addition, Kojève's famous claim of the 'end of history' can also be situated within a reverse reconstruction. With the implementation of equal recognition of all individuals and the blossoming of economic prosperity, resulting from the growth in productive forces unleashed by capitalism, history comes to an end, he asserts, alluding to Hegel's ending in the *Phenomenology*.[57]

Other important reverse readings can be found in the second and third generation of Critical Theory, namely, in the work of Jürgen Habermas and Axel Honneth. The main reason for their return to Hegel was their adherence to the Left Hegelian legacy, which Marx himself helped to create: the idea that emancipatory goals and interests should not simply and abstractly be posited in theory, but must be detected as historically established forces already operative in social reality.[58] For Marx, that force was the proletariat, but for the early Frankfurt School, this specific solution to the Left Hegelian program was a blind alley, especially after they witnessed parts of the working class exhibiting authoritarian tendencies and partly supporting the rise of fascist movements.[59] Habermas's and Honneth's response was to situate Marxian themes in a more Hegelian framework. In their view, such a framework would also be better suited to encompass other social movements besides the proletariat, such as the student movement, the feminist movement, and eco-activism. We will return to Honneth's notion of recognition later and, at this point, focus on Habermas's work.

Habermas developed his account by substituting Marxist categories with Hegelian ones, most explicitly in his seminal paper on "Labor and Interaction".[60] Here, Habermas blames Marx for reducing social action primarily to work while neglecting the social potential of communicative interaction.[61] Returning to the early Hegel, he finds conceptual remedies in the Jena philosophy of spirit, which is distinct from Hegel's later system. Whereas Hegel in his later philosophy construed spirit as constituted in an autonomous movement of self-reflection, according to Habermas, the early Hegel offers a much more open, intersubjective, and, one could even say, materialistic account of the formation of spirit: Language, work, and interaction figure as the very media of the formation of spirit itself.[62] Habermas insists that these dialectical media of spirit are heterogeneous; that is, they cannot be reduced to, or derived from, one another. At the same time, all three categories are interwoven, since, for example, labor is always already embedded in a web of cooperative norms. Habermas credits Marx for having reformulated Hegel's distinction of labor and interaction into the dialectic of productive forces and relations of production (even though Hegel's early manuscripts were not available to Marx). But in Habermas's view, Marx tends to dissolve this dialectic in favor of subsuming communicative interaction to work—for example, when Marx assumes that social progress is primarily driven by increases in the productive forces, which burst the 'fetters' of the outdated relations of production, eventually triggering higher, more progressive forms of social relations.[63] However, as Habermas emphasizes, there is no inherent guarantee that the contradiction between the productive forces and relations of production is resolved progressively.⁶⁴ If there is potential for social progress, then this has to be sought in the "learning processes"⁶⁵ enabled by communicative action, not only in mere advances in the technical manipulation of nature. Habermas's basic idea is that as soon as humans participate in the social practice of communication, they have to at least pretend to adhere to norms of propositional truth and moral rightness: "In these validity claims communication theory can locate a gentle but obstinate, a never silent although seldom redeemed claim to reason, a claim that must be recognized de facto whenever and wherever there is to be consensual action."⁶⁶ This is Habermas's version of the actual emancipatory force that is already operative in social life. Finally, Habermas claims that the reduction of communicative to instrumental action is mirrored in a certain positivistic tendency in historical materialism, which tends to assimilate social theory to the natural sciences, something that became manifest in the scientism of the Second International.⁶⁷ The problem here, for Habermas, is that this kind of social theory foils its own obvious aspirations to contribute to the emancipatory self-transformation of human beings. It disregards the fact that social theory must always both comprehend how a law-like social process operates *an sich* (in itself) as well as how it appears *für uns* (for us), as self-interpreting participants of social life, and how we come to reproduce it. Otherwise, social theory is in danger of thwarting, rather than furthering, the potential for critical self-reflection.⁶⁸

3 Toward a Helical Approach

In the present volume, we suggest that parts of the progressive, disruptive, and reverse readings can be subsumed under the interpretive spectrum that we call 'helical'. Within a helical framework, Hegel's social philosophy has the potential to counterbalance the more dogmatic or narrowly economistic parts of Marx's thinking, and Marx's critique can radicalize the more conservative parts of Hegelian philosophy. In this way, a reexploration of the Hegelian foundations of Marx's thinking is linked with a rereading of Hegel in ways that were opened up by Marx. This approach allows us to see the productive and dynamic transfers that take place in various attempts at relating Hegel and Marx today.

Our attention in this volume is directed at Hegel's and Marx's political and social philosophy. A helical approach is not confined to these parts of their thinking, but the present book is, and not for arbitrary reasons. Other topics would be easy to find, say, questions of methodology, such as the influence of Hegel's *Logic* on Marx's *Capital*.⁶⁹ We believe, however, that the suggested approach creates the most interesting outcomes if the broader goal is to understand and critically contest our contemporary world. Our aim is to show that issues such as the normative foundations of a critique of capitalism, the idea of recognition, and questions of property in the means of production are topics where Hegel and Marx might intersect. Surely, we do not claim that the conceptual framework put forward here is without historical precursors. Many philosophers of the Hegelian-Marxist tradition can already be understood in helical terms, or even be said to have established a bidirectional understanding of the Hegel–Marx connection without naming it as such.⁷⁰

Three modalities of a helical spectrum can be distinguished. In a 'corrective' modality, the aim is to revise parts of Hegel's or Marx's arguments by relying on arguments of the counterpart. In a 'confrontational' modality, the goal is to target highly contested issues between the two thinkers head-on, by bringing forth arguments from both sides in a vigorous exchange. In a 'constructive' modality, attention is paid to how Marx and Hegel might reinforce one another; how new readings of Marx informed by a Hegelian framework can be discovered, or readings of Hegel within a Marxian framework. Let us go through each of the three modalities step by step.

(i) In a corrective mode, the direction might go from Marx to Hegel, that is, we might use Marx to revise parts of Hegel's thought. One might, for example, try to explore how Marx's analysis of the autonomization tendencies of capitalism can be used to revise those parts of Hegel's affirmative thinking where he flirts with the idea of an invisible hand of the market, allegedly catering to an unintended convergence of private interests and the common interest.[71] It is true that Hegel at some points hints at the abstract, alienating power of the market: He vividly explains that, from the perspective of the individual, the highs and lows of the market appear as an "alien power over which he has no control", a power that is "scarcely knowable, invisible, and incalculable".[72] This anticipates the later Marx much more than it echoes Hegel's predecessor, Adam Smith. But Hegel does not have a categorical apparatus at hand to grasp what in Marx's thought figures as "abstract domination", in Moishe Postone's trenchant formulation.[73] In Marx's work, systemic processes under capitalism take on a life of their own, gaining dominating power over the actors in the market, not just over workers but also over capitalists, even though this dominating power is nothing but the hidden product of the joint action of the market participants themselves.[74] It is important to note that this idea of a domination of things—of commodities, of money—over persons, characterizing market societies according to Marx, is the unifying thread tying Marx's early notion of alienation to his later reflections on commodity fetishism.[75]

In order for the corrective modality to qualify as a helical approach, however, the movement should also go in the opposite direction, that is, from Hegel to Marx, with the aim of using Hegelian insights to revise parts of Marx's thought. One might, for instance, discuss Marxian issues by letting Hegel have a say on the proper understanding of (the role of) social institutions. Marx's picture of a postcapitalist society is above all characterized by the absence of institutions: the state, the market, money, legal rights, private property, stabilized forms of a division of labor, institutionalized norms of justice.[76] Instead, Marx conceptualized his vision of communist relations on the guiding ideal of non-institutionalized direct interactions between peers, one-on-one.[77] Within the history of Marxism, Cornelius Castoriadis's work probably still provides the most pressing and thorough criticism of this aversion to institutional mediation found in certain passages in Marx.[78] In contrast to Marx, Hegel is the thinker of social institutions par excellence. His whole system of 'objective spirit', standing in the middle between 'subjective spirit' and 'absolute spirit', deals almost entirely with social institutions, which can be described as stabilized, enduring configurations of social norms and roles, including a certain distribution of social power and 'vertical' relations between individuals and institutions. Although institutions in Hegel resist individual tinkering at whim, they are made by humans and thus alterable through a process of social change.[79] It is true enough that Hegel and Hegelian approaches often exhibit a deep-seated—and problematic—bias toward *given* institutions. But the basic idea behind Hegel's institutionalism is worth retrieving. If institutions are rational, they are not at all restrictions but enlargements of individual freedom, conceptualized by Hegel as "concrete freedom".[80] When institutions entail the proper recognitive relations both upward (from individuals to institution) and downward (from institution to individuals), they enable freedom, in the negative sense of releasing individuals from "the debilitating burden of constant reflection and negotiation of every norm"[81] of interaction, as well as in the positive sense of offering and promoting meaningful social goals, activities, and roles.[82]

Thus, in a corrective mode, a helical approach spells out the ways in which Hegelian insights might be employed to modify claims, concepts, and arguments put forward by Marx—and vice versa. In fact, only when acknowledging the need for bidirectional revisions may engagements with Hegel and Marx truly count as helical approaches.

(ii) The confrontational mode stages the frame of interconnectedness between Hegel and Marx in terms of essential lines of conflicts and clashes. This might be exemplified by the question of what kind of separation (if any) we could want between economic and political institutions. Hegel seems to insist on a relatively sharp demarcation line between the market and the state, which leaves room for the freedoms of arbitrary consumption and professional choice allowed for, and even encouraged, by the market, unimpeded by democratic authority.[83] This is connected to Hegel's acknowledgment of negative freedom and liberal rights as fundamental achievements of modern society. To be sure, Hegel knew too well of the structural tendency in liberal rights to foster social pathologies, for example, the fixation of legal subjects on being always on guard to defend their subjective rights.[84] Yet he still acknowledged the value of this dimension of freedom. Marx, on the other hand, seems to be inclined toward a gesture of wiping the slate clean, viewing liberal rights as "nothing but"[85] the rights of egoistic market actors, something that will become unnecessary and even obstructive in a communist society.[86] Hegel aimed to sublate the valuable dimensions of legal freedom, by preserving its merits while overcoming its deficiencies with the help of adequate institutions of ethical life. But this in turn requires an intricate interlocking of civil society and the state, prominently mediated by the corporations.[87] Consequently, recent interpretations of Hegel have come to acknowledge this idea of a demanding interlocking of the economic and the political sphere. Still, Hegel does not go all the way in subsuming private interests to the common interest (as delineated by democratic processes).

In direct contrast to this, Marx insists on subjugating our economic practices to the "common control" of all.[88] From a Marxist perspective, the Hegelian hope in external regulation (by what Hegel calls 'the police') is futile. Indeed, even the more recent renewed interest in extending democracy to the workplace does not go far enough, since it often stops short of confronting the privatized structures of capital ownership.[89] The reluctance to deal with questions of socializing ownership makes such proposals an easy target for Marxist critique. But even if this criticism from a Marxist perspective is correct, is a full-blown (council) democratic planning procedure, encompassing the whole economy including work contributions and consumer shares of all participants, really desirable? Assuming that a fully democratized economy would work as well as ideally intended—already a strong assumption—this could still entail, for example, democratically enacted bans on idiosyncratic consumer wishes of minority groups (e.g., sexual minorities), something which would be thoroughly illegitimate from a liberal perspective. It would also imply higher-level councils directly governing large parts of our work life, often against the personal will of the affected. The point here is to underline that all these questions from both a Hegelian and a Marxian camp are justified to some extent, but that the tensions they create cannot easily be reconciled or sublated. Instead, we should acknowledge the difficulties and ambivalences and continue the lively debate by inviting the strongest arguments from both sides to challenge one another. The gist of this mode of helical reading is thus to let the clashes remain and to stress the productive character of their irreconcilability.

(iii) The third mode is the 'constructive' one: Here, the question is to what extent Hegel and Marx can complement one another, strengthen one another, supplement the other where gaps are left open, or establish new readings inspired by one another.

Perhaps the greatest affinity between Hegel and Marx lies in their notion of freedom as something fundamentally achieved in and through social relations. Freedom, for both of them, is deeply social or communal.[90] Hegel conceptualizes freedom with his idea of 'being-with-oneself-in-another', and Marx makes freedom dependent on the realization of a particular form of association, "in which the free development of each is the condition for the free development of all".[91] Hegel and Marx's shared idea of social freedom puts them both in sharp opposition to the liberal idea of conceiving freedom primarily in terms of negative liberty, where others predominantly come into view as potential sources of interference with one's own scope of arbitrary choice. In other words, they both turn the liberal concept of the individual upside down, by showing that the individual is not free to begin with—not equipped with an original freedom always already threatened by the presence of others—but acquires its freedom precisely as a result of communal efforts. Retrieving Hegel's and Marx's notions of freedom thus makes it possible to engage critically with the liberal emphasis on freedom, remaining on the same normative and conceptual territory, and not by mounting concepts and values that seem to be antithetical to freedom from the outset (e.g., equality or justice).

The central claim in Axel Honneth's and Charles Taylor's theories of recognition is that social freedom for Hegel is achieved through mutual recognition.[92] This claim can also, perhaps more unexpectedly, be applied to Marx. Marx's use of the notion of recognition is certainly surprising, not only because it went unnoticed until roughly two decades ago (and has been ignored in some Marxist circles up until now).[93] It is all the more surprising as Honneth's theory of recognition can be seen as part of the effort to reverse the movement from Hegel to Marx: Honneth's argument in the *Struggle for Recognition* is that class struggles should be interpreted as moral strivings in the sense of being motivated by demands for recognition, as opposed to being mere material struggles for economic goods, where it would seem that the proletariat is simply out to grab as many material possessions as possible.[94] Instead, Honneth stresses that social conflicts are heavily determined by the normative expectations of what the actors implicitly or explicitly hold to deserve. From the perspective of contemporary recognition theories, the concept of recognition in Hegel is interpreted as an expressive social relation where the individuals reciprocally confirm their supportive or appreciative stance toward one another. Relations of recognition imply interdependency, for it is only through these intersubjective relations that individuals gain an adequate relation to themselves as subjects. By recognizing their dependency on one another in various institutional forms, individuals progressively make themselves free.[95]

Let us at this point return to Marx's own reflections on recognition. In recent years, it has become increasingly clear that the category of recognition in fact plays an important role in Marx's thought, notably in the "Comments on James Mill".[96] A helical approach to the concept of recognition moving from Hegel to Marx and back renders visible how Marx deepens our insight into the question of recognition. It also brings to the fore how Marx's idea of recognition enriches our understanding of what kind of community he had in mind when he wrote about a communist society. If my production is carried out in non-instrumental and human-centered ways, as envisioned by Marx, then I would "become recognised and felt by you yourself as a completion of your own essential nature and as a necessary part of yourself, and consequently would know myself to be confirmed both in your thought and your love".[97] By conceiving of humans as both productive and needy beings, Marx is able to spell out a particular kind of recognition to be realized in our economic cooperation. In the postcapitalist society Marx envisions, the patterns of production and consumption would be ways of affirming and endorsing one another as members of a community of communal beings, or, with Marx's own words, *Gemeinwesen*.[98]

Community is also a key notion for communitarian and deconstructive strands within a constructive mode of helical interpretations. In the 1980s, a critique of the individualism underpinning modern liberalism was gathered under the label 'Communitarianism'. Different as they were, many communitarians can be seen as part of the reversion paradigm: They didn't go back to Marx but to Hegel (and Aristotle) in order to criticize the individualist primacy of liberalism and its inability to deal with questions of community.[99] The communitarian interpretation of Hegel's social philosophy became itself, however, the target of critique, not only from a liberal stance but also from the perspective of a profoundly different conception of community that also drew its inspirations from Hegel's thought. Jean-Luc Nancy was one of several philosophers who, responsive to a European postwar political context, tried to articulate new forms of political thinking attentive to the socially embedded human being without ending up in a substantial particularism or a formal universalism. The question of how to handle the idea of community after the triumph of fascism and the failure of communism was at the heart of Nancy's philosophical project. By way of Derridean deconstruction, Heideggerian *Mitsein*, and Hegelian *Sittlichkeit* he suggested a non-metaphysical social ontology of 'being-with', articulated as an original and constitutive relationality. Positing the co-appearance of the 'I' and the 'we', as a 'being-together', not grounded in an assumption of identity as an original and immanent totality (whether individual or shared), the concept of 'being-with' radically questions the idea of self-identity at the core of fascist, Marxist, and liberal theories.[100]

In Nancy's work, Hegel appears as a philosopher of constant becoming rather than of totality and identity, a processual thinker for whom everything is in a process of becoming something else, without essence or foundation.[101] Nancy thus mobilizes Hegel to dissolve the oppositions and binary structure that underpin the standard versions of dialectical critique. Through his own dialectical concept of community and co-existence, the oppositions between self and other, individual and community, identity and difference implode from within.[102] Nancy's social ontology, however, is not a proposal of a one-way return from Marx to Hegel. What qualifies his work as helical, in the sense suggested above, is a particular way of making use of Hegel and Marx in order to address questions of social urgency. What Marx called communism, Nancy argues, was precisely an appeal to the common, not as something opposed or superior to, but rather as something co-appearing with, the individual: "Communism", Nancy emphasizes, "wants to say that being is *in* common. It wants to say that we are, insofar as we 'are,' in common."[103] And he adds, stressing the importance of making contemporary use of Marx's theory: "It is no longer a question of rereading Marx but of what Marx must now make us write."[104]

Nancy's call to put Hegel's and Marx's thinking to work is taken one step further by Slavoj Žižek in his multidirectional appropriation of both thinkers. "Philosophers have hitherto only interpreted Hegel", he asserts with a Marxian allusion, "but the point is also to change him."[105] In Žižek's critique of current capitalism and his attempt to work out a new idea of communism, Hegel appears as a materialistic, indeed even Marxian, figure.[106] Like Nancy's Hegel, the Hegel of Žižek is not a thinker of mutual recognition and progress. Žižek emphasizes the systematic failures, symptomatic tensions, and power of negativity at the heart of Hegel's philosophy, filtered through Freud and Lacan.[107] His work points to another important issue within the domain of helical approaches, that of symptomatic reading. Such a reading is elaborated by Frank Ruda and Rebecca Comay. Their work, situated at the intersection between philosophy, psychoanalysis, and politics, retrieves the radical potential of Hegel's thinking in idiosyncratic readings, with special attention to the ruptures and displacements in Hegel's system, arguing for the radical, open, and unfinished character of his thinking.[108] In *Hegel's Rabble*, Ruda focuses on the long-neglected concept of the rabble in Hegel's work and returns to Marx in order to argue for a rereading of Hegel, or, more accurately, for a reconsideration of the relation between the two. Ruda locates the origin of Marx's concept of the proletariat in Hegel's failure to adequately address the problem of the rabble within his philosophical system. In 1843, when Marx writes about "a class of civil society which is not a class of civil society",[109] he addresses the issue of the growing and self-generated poverty in modern capitalist society, Ruda argues, by going back to the Hegelian figure of the rabble, which remains unrecognizable within Hegel's own philosophical categories. The figure of the rabble is, in other words, a symptom of Hegel's failure to systematically address the problem of poverty produced by the very institutions of modern life that Hegel places at the heart of his political philosophy.[110]

In a certain sense, Ruda's work can be situated in a progressive tradition: Marx's success originates in Hegel's shortcomings. In emphasizing Hegel's discovery of, and difficulties in dealing with, the contradictory and self-subverting character of capitalist modernity, Ruda, however, presents something other than a linear development from Hegel to Marx. He comes to the conclusion that Hegel can be read anew with the help of Marx. And more importantly still, that Marx in a certain sense was more Hegelian than Hegel himself, in transforming Hegel's failure to the very place from which a radical transformation of philosophy could take place. Exposing the inner tensions and contradictions, the moments where Hegel's philosophy comes into conflict with its own presuppositions, Ruda's helical reworking of Hegel thus actualizes traits from progressive as well as disruptive readings.

By way of a conclusion, we can say that helical approaches bring together philosophers and theorists from different traditions and backgrounds in order to discover new potentials in the multiple and still unexplored connections between Hegel and Marx. From this perspective, the relation between Marx and Hegel remains a site of contestation, as do their respective philosophies—which Hegel, which Marx? As a reading strategy or interpretive tool, a helical approach urges us to rethink interpretive circularity. We may move in circles, repeating Hegel and Marx again and again, but does that culminate in a "*circle of circles*"?[111] One can understand this circle as a closed space, as Althusser once did, from which we have to escape.[112] One can understand it, as Hegel himself did, as a way of thinking that lacks an absolute beginning and endpoint.[113] Or even as the very image of absolute knowing, "the circle that returns into itself, the circle that presupposes its beginning and reaches it only at the end".[114] One can also understand it, as we do here, as a spiraling movement that breaks away from its own circularity in an ongoing generation of new relations and points of convergence; a repetition that is also a production.

4 Capitalism, Critique, Utopia: A Synopsis of the Chapters

The journey from Marx to Hegel and back that this volume initiates aims at deepening the understanding of the dynamic, intertwined movement between the two thinkers. The contributions suggest a number of crucial points that call for new ways to draw the Hegel–Marx connection, beyond the opposition that marks received interpretations. Obviously, a single book cannot offer a comprehensive study covering the whole range of the long and rich tradition of interpretations of their relation. But our book aims to provide in-depth analyses as well as more systematic examinations of key issues in the tradition of Hegelian Marxism. The book contains three parts: the first dedicated to fundamental questions of how to relate Hegel and Marx, and how to retrieve the Hegelian-Marxist legacy; the second part is devoted to systematic questions of social critique, particularly with regard to the critique of capitalism; and the third part focuses on conceptualizing alternatives to capitalism.

Axel Honneth opens up the first part with his text "Hegel and Marx: A Reassessment after One Century", in which he considers the extent to which Hegel and Marx can be read as mutually complementary. For this task, he turns to Hegel's and Marx's philosophies of history, where he finds a congruency in the view that modern society is the most advanced stage of a process that progressively expresses the claims of reason. A major difference is detected in the location of the realization of reason: In Honneth's reading, Hegel sees reason at work in how our norms and institutions of social life are shaped, whereas Marx locates it in our increasing powers in the mastery of nature. Honneth argues that this speaks in Hegel's favor. At the same time, he praises Marx's social theory to be better suited to tracing the unfreedom of wage laborers and the expansionary dynamic of the capitalist market. But for the task of integrating Marx's insights into Hegel's framework, Honneth claims it to be essential that the economic sphere is conceptualized as malleable by social norms. Still, he sees a need for revision on Hegel's part, too, as Hegel, in his theory of ethical life, did not really take into account the possibility that the norms characteristic of one social sphere might intrude into other spheres, undermining their intrinsic norms.

In the following contribution, "Hegel, Marx, and Presentism", Emmanuel Renault shows that Hegel and Marx share one fundamental assumption: that philosophy should essentially aim at a comprehension of the present. For both of them, this means, according to Renault, identifying the processes of the actualization of the rational in the contemporary world and detecting the barriers obstructing these processes. Hegel comes to this position, as Renault explains, by developing an ontology that puts forward a processual idea of actuality. With the help of this framework, it becomes clear that Hegel's diagnosis of the rationality of the actual does in no way mean that the process of actualization of rationality has come to an end. Moving on to Marx, Renault demonstrates the extent to which Marx built on Hegel's presentism—not only the young Hegelian Marx, but also the mature Marx in his critique of political economy. Here, Renault offers a 'presentist' interpretation of Marx's idea of 'tendential laws' of capitalism.

In Jacob Blumenfeld's chapter on "Property and Freedom in Kant, Hegel, and Marx", he argues that Kant's and Hegel's idealistic approach and Marx's materialistic account require one another. Following Kant and Hegel, Blumenfeld grounds the normative value of property in its capacity to allow us to freely express ourselves by having external things at our disposal according to our own will, free of domination by others. On Marx's materialist account, property is viewed more instrumentally, as a socially mediated means to fulfill historically determined needs. Blumenfeld underlines a crucial insight of Marx's historical materialism: Only in pre-capitalist modes of production did the direct producers have immediate access to their means of subsistence, while under capitalism, almost no one has. Thus, most are compelled to sell their labor power for survival. In Blumenfeld's diagnosis, this means, in turn, that capitalism, instead of securing universal independence through property, implies a generalized interference by others, enacted through the market. Given the constant possibility that the whims of the market might cause a sudden and unpredictable loss of value, no one has secure property.

In the chapter by Frank Ruda, "I, the Revolution, Speak. Lenin's Speculative (Hegelian) Style", Hegel appears, by way of Lenin, as the one who reconstitutes the revolutionary legacy of Marxism. Ruda argues that Lenin re-revolutionized Marxism by going from Marx back to Hegel. Starting from the assumption that words can become revolutionary deeds, Ruda calls our attention to Lenin's linguistic style. Ruda focuses on the seemingly trivial, a point, and tracks Lenin's punctuation as a speculative (indeed Hegelian) political practice. He then explores more generally how Lenin's language can be seen as a discursive form of revolutionary politics. Ruda thus challenges the traditional understanding of the legacy of the Hegelian-Marxist tradition by placing Lenin center stage as the first Marxist making the move to re-Hegelianize Marx, before Lukács, Marcuse, and Adorno.

In the second part of the book, the rethinking of the interrelation between Marx and Hegel suggested in Part One is extended to the question of social critique, in particular the critique of capitalism. In the chapter "Critique in Hegel and Marx", Rocío Zambrana examines the concept of immanent critique, understood as a mode of critique whose normative criteria are inherently taken from the object of critique itself, the socio-historical situation at hand. Her contribution reconsiders the Hegelian-Marxist conception of critique by turning to Adorno's elaboration of critique as 'negativist', grounded in an experience of suffering (being, with Adorno's words, 'the medium of justice'). With the help of Adorno, Zambrana returns to Hegel in order to move beyond Marx in articulating a post-Marxian contemporary concept of critique that is attentive to the intricate ways in which freedom and domination are entangled in human life.

Frederick Neuhouser explores in his chapter, "Hegel and Marx on 'Spiritual Life' as a Criterion for Social Critique", how both Hegel and Marx assessed social practices and institutions with the help of a standard of critique derived from Hegel's idea of 'spiritual life'. In the case of Marx, with his alleged anti-idealist materialism, this seems surprising, but Neuhouser shows that crucial parts of Marx's mature critique of capitalism are animated by nothing other than Hegel's idea of spirit. Neuhouser explains that Hegel's category of 'spirit' aims to grasp the unity of self-conscious freedom and 'life', where life activities are at the same time avenues for realizing freedom while articulations of freedom are always also embodied, material practices. Hegel's analysis of lord and bondsman is the first exemplary case that serves Neuhouser to illuminate the pathologies resulting from the act of 'splitting' the unity of spiritual life: spiritless toiling for the necessities of life on one side, meaningless luxury consumption, cut off from its ties to life activities, on the other. Neuhouser then moves on to reread Marx's *Capital*, in particular the difference between the circulation of capital and the circulation of commodities: In the seemingly self-moving process of expanding value, capital quite literally takes on a life of its own, but it is a life process devoid of self-conscious human freedom.

In recent years, it has become increasingly clear that recognition played an important role not only for the young, but also for the mature, Marx.[115] In his contribution on "Abstract Labor and Recognition", Sven Ellmers goes a step further by situating the category of recognition within the discourse of the so-called '*neue Marx-Lektüre*'; an attempt at a new reading of Marx originally developed by Hans-Georg Backhaus and Helmut Reichelt in the context of Adorno's teaching activity in Frankfurt in the 1960s, today advocated by Michael Heinrich.[116] Ellmers now bridges the gap between this new tradition of reading Marx and the philosophy of recognition. He argues that one of the foundational categories in Marx's *Capital*, 'abstract labor', has a social quality that until now has been overlooked. Abstract labor is not only social in the sense that it is the socially necessary labor time to fulfill social needs. It is also social in the sense that the differing values of different acts of labor are constituted by practices of recognition.

Federica Gregoratto's contribution, "Love Will Tear Us Apart: Marx and Hegel on the Materiality of Erotic Bonds", explores how a reactualized Hegelian-Marxist perspective on love can be used to critically examine our contemporary society. Indeed, on Gregoratto's account, the issue of love figures as an indirect, yet powerful, way to develop a critique of capitalism. She suggests that Hegel and Marx can be read together in order to articulate a critique of the modern idea of love as an autonomous social domain, separated from other spheres of social life. By turning to the works of the young Marx, in which human interdependency, vulnerability, and need for recognition are explicitly thematized in relation to capitalist distortions of human relations, Gregoratto argues for a critical understanding of erotic love relationships as materially mediated and determined by economic and political structures. She then turns to Hegel's conception of love in order to further explore the material dimension of love relationships; more precisely, the mediating role of private property, in order to emphasize its double function in love relations, being both a uniting and dividing force and harboring an oppressive as well as emancipatory potential.

The third and final part of the book explores how to think of a world beyond capitalism by bringing Marx and Hegel together. A critique, which aims at transforming social institutions in ways that enhance human flourishing, can hardly do without a utopian horizon against which the potentials of the present can be explored. To carve out the desirability and viability of "real utopias",[117] which embrace the tension between radical possibilities and present practices, sharpens the edge of the critique of capitalism. It adds a powerful tool of contesting the seeming inescapability of the capitalist order. All the chapters of this part of the book share the assumption that Hegel and Marx are more positively utopian than is often assumed. This may seem surprising, but the contributions show that the works of Hegel and Marx provide fruitful ideas of how to think of postcapitalist institutions.

In "Marx's 'Hegelian' Critique of Utopia", David Leopold analyzes Marx's reluctance to specify any design of a future socialist organization of society, known as his anti-utopianism. Leopold challenges the received understanding of this anti-utopianism by scrutinizing the various elements in Marx's critique and critically examining three of its key arguments: that the plans and blueprints of a socialist future, offered by the utopians, are necessarily undemocratic (a normative argument); impossible (an epistemological argument); and unnecessary (an empirical argument). Leopold argues that these Marxian objections to utopian proposals are less convincing than often assumed. He then goes on to track Marx's arguments back to Hegel's understanding of philosophy as a kind of backward teleology, a way of belatedly understanding the world as it has become, from a retrospective position. Reading Marx and Hegel together, Leopold thus points to a connection between the task that Hegel gives philosophy and Marx's unwillingness to work out more concrete plans for a socialist future.

In the following chapter, "Where Are We Developing the Requirements for a New Society?", Eva Bockenheimer uses Marx's appropriation of Hegel's dialectic in the former's critique of political economy to comprehend contemporary changes in wage labor. In line with Marx's understanding of capitalism as developing through internal contradictions, Bockenheimer suggests that we should look for the potentials for a postcapitalist society at the very heart of our current economic system. Accordingly, she tracks the dialectic of today's capitalism in the ongoing transformation of wage labor: In recent decades, wage labor not only became more and more entrepreneurial, but has also become increasingly organized in semi-autonomous team-units, which has led to a growing consciousness of an 'entrepreneurial we' among wage laborers. Capitalist firms take advantage of the latent energies set free by this new form of team cooperation, but, inadvertently, this contributes to fostering the emancipatory potential of a new productive force: Enabling workers to jointly and autonomously organize social cooperation as a whole both realizes *and* points beyond a capitalist understanding of labor power, production, and profit.

In "Social Freedom beyond Capitalism: Three Alternatives", Hannes Kuch examines prominent alternatives to capitalism discussed in contemporary critical thought, by reconstructing these debates within the normative framework of Hegel's and Marx's notion of social freedom. He argues that, contrary to many of the established interpretations of Hegel and Marx, it is both possible and promising to discuss alternatives to capitalism with reference to these two philosophers. Three economic systems are discussed: (i) *commons economies*, where people make productive contributions to satisfy the needs of others voluntarily and freely; (ii) *democratic planning*, with a special focus on attempts to institutionalize planning procedures without the need for overly centralized institutions; (iii) and *market socialism*, where goods are bought and sold in markets, but where these goods are produced in enterprises that are collectively owned. Kuch concludes that, from the viewpoint of social freedom, market socialism is in a certain respect only the third best alternative. But still, it embodies a real alternative to capitalism. Moreover, he underlines that market socialism, without buying into the disadvantages of the other two models, is able to integrate their merits to some degree—both the horizontalism of commons economies and the practice of collective autonomy characteristic of democratic planning.

In the final chapter, "Honneth's Democratic *Sittlichkeit* and Market Socialism", Michael Nance picks up on the question of the sense in which a neo-Hegelian notion of social freedom might provide arguments in support of market socialist proposals. Nance suggests a double movement: The first one, 'from Marx to Hegel', acknowledges the indispensability of some forms of markets and highlights the appeal of a Hegel-inspired ethics; the second one, 'from Hegel back to Marx', demonstrates the importance of social ownership in productive resources. Nance proceeds from the observation that the institution of the market vacillates between promoting a negative idea of freedom (the untrammeled pursuit of self-interest) and a social one (freedom as uncoerced cooperation in the reciprocal realization of material needs and wishes). Nance's main argument is that the issue of private or social control of capital is crucial in tilting the balance in one direction or the other. Hence, the major virtue of market socialist institutions, with collectively owned enterprises, would be to clearly express the social purpose of market institutions to all participants, thus advancing and stabilizing a social-freedom interpretation of the market.

The collection of essays covers a wide array of strands of the Hegel–Marx relation. The main body of contributions demonstrates how essential aspects of this relation can be understood in a helical way. The perspectives are diverse, sometimes even conflicting; some contributions tend toward a progressive reading, others lean toward a reverse one, and still others even to a disruptive reading. But the chapters, taken together, constitute a variety of distinct, yet related, perspectives that contribute to more than a richer understanding of the Hegel–Marx connection; they offer a unified set of contemporary actualizations of the critical potential of this connection.[118]

Notes

1 Among the growing literature on Marx in recent years we find David Harvey's *Marx, Capital, and the Madness of Economic Reason* (Oxford: Oxford University Press, 2017); Michael Heinrich, *An Introduction to the Three Volumes of Karl Marx's* Capital, trans. Alex Locascio (New York: Monthly Review Press, 2012); Terry Eagleton, *Why Marx Was Right* (New Haven, CT: Yale University Press, 2011); Fredric Jameson, *Representing* Capital: *A Reading of Volume One* (New York: Verso, 2013); Sven-Eric Liedman, *A World to Win: The Life and Works of Karl Marx*, trans. Jeffrey N. Skinner (New York: Verso, 2018); Harry Harootunian, *Marx after Marx: History and Time in the Expansion of Capitalism* (New York: Columbia University Press, 2015); John Bellamy Foster, *Marx's Ecology: Materialism and Nature* (New York: Monthly Review Press, 2000); *Marxism and Feminism*, ed. Shahrzad Mojab (London: Zed Books, 2015); Lise Vogel, *Marxism and the Oppression of Women: Toward a Unitary Theory*, rev. ed (Chicago: Haymarket, 2014); *Marx for Today*, ed. Marcelo Musto (New York: Routledge, 2013); Slavoj Žižek, Frank Ruda and Agon Hamza, *Reading Marx* (Cambridge: Polity, 2018); Nancy Fraser and Rahel Jaeggi, *Capitalism: A Conversation in Critical Theory*, ed. Brian Milstein (Cambridge: Polity, 2018); *Reassessing Marx's Social and Political Philosophy*, ed. Jan Kandiyali (London: Routledge, 2018).
2 See, for instance, *Hegel and Resistance: History, Politics and Dialectics*, ed. Bart Zantvoort and Rebecca Comay (London: Bloomsbury, 2017); Axel Honneth, *Freedom's Right: The Social Foundations of Democratic Life*, trans. Joseph Ganahl (Cambridge: Polity, 2014); Rahel Jaeggi, *Alienation*, trans. Frederick Neuhouser and Alan E. Smith, ed. Frederick Neuhouser (New York: Columbia University Press, 2014); Christoph Menke, *Reflections of Equality*, trans. Howard Rouse and Andrei Denejkine (Stanford, CA: Stanford University Press, 2006); Axel Honneth and Nancy Fraser, *Redistribution or Recognition? A Political-Philosophical Exchange* (New York: Verso, 2003).
3 Some telling examples of the growing literature on Hegel in recent years: Axel Honneth, *The Pathologies of Individual Freedom: Hegel's Social Theory* (Princeton, NJ: Princeton University Press, 2010); Frank Ruda, *Hegel's Rabble: An Investigation into Hegel's Philosophy of Right* (London: Continuum, 2011); Slavoj Žižek, *Less Than Nothing: Hegel and the Shadow of Dialectical Materialism* (New York: Verso, 2012); Rahel Jaeggi, *Critique of Forms of Life*, trans. Ciaran Cronin (Cambridge, MA: Harvard University Press, 2018); Rocío Zambrana, *Hegel's Theory of Intelligibility* (Chicago: University of Chicago Press, 2015); Karin de Boer, *On Hegel: The Sway of the Negative* (Basingstoke: Palgrave Macmillan, 2010); Fredric Jameson, *The Hegel Variations* (New York: Verso, 2010); Frederick Neuhouser, *Foundations of Hegel's Social Theory: Actualizing Freedom* (Cambridge, MA: Harvard University Press, 2000).
4 For a variety of recent materialist interpretations, see for example, Žižek, *Less Than Nothing*; Adrian Johnston, *A New German Idealism: Hegel, Žižek, and Dialectical*

Materialism (New York: Columbia University Press, 2018); Tony Smith, *Dialectical Social Theory and Its Critics* (Albany: State University of New York Press, 1993); Neuhouser, *Foundations of Hegel's Social Theory*; Terry Pinkard, *Hegel's Naturalism: Mind, Nature, and the Final Ends of Life* (Oxford: Oxford University Press, 2013); Domenico Losurdo, *Hegel and the Freedom of Moderns* (Durham: Duke University Press, 2014).

5   On Marx's assessment and appropriation of Hegel's philosophy, see Norman Levine, *Marx's Discourse with Hegel* (Basingstoke: Palgrave Macmillan, 2012); *The Hegel–Marx Connection*, ed. Tony Burns and Ian Fraser (Basingstoke: Macmillan, 2000); Zhang Shuangli, "Marx and Hegel," in *The Oxford Handbook of Hegel*, ed. Dean Moyar (New York: Oxford University Press, 2017), 647–69; Andrew Chitty, "Hegel and Marx," in *A Companion to Hegel. Blackwell Companions to Philosophy*, ed. Michael Baur and Stephen Houlgate (Malden, MA: Blackwell, 2011), 477–500.

6   Marx declared himself to be a "pupil" of that the "mighty thinker" Hegel; see *Capital I*, Afterword to the 2nd edn, *Marx & Engels Collected Works*, Vol. 1–50 (London: Lawrence & Wishart, 1975–2004), Vol. 35: 19 (hereafter MECW).

7   For an excellent overview focusing on the variety of Hegelian Marxisms, see *The Hegel–Marx Connection*, ed. Burns and Fraser. See also *Hegelian Marxism: The Uses of Hegel's Philosophy in Marxist Theory from Georg Lukács to Slavoj Žižek*, ed. Anders Bartonek and Anders Burman (Huddinge: Södertörn University, 2018). The early Frankfurt School usually counts as the emblematic protagonist of Hegelian Marxism: Georg Lukács, *History and Class Consciousness: Studies in Marxist Dialectics*, trans. Rodney Livingstone (Cambridge, MA: MIT Press, 1971 [1923]); Herbert Marcuse, *Reason and Revolution: Hegel and the Rise of Social Theory* (London: Oxford University Press, 1941); Theodor W. Adorno, *Hegel: Three Studies*, trans. Shierry Weber Nicholsen (Cambridge, MA: MIT Press, 1993 [1963]). Among Italian and French philosophers we have Antonio Labriola, *Socialism and Philosophy*, trans. Ernest Untermann (St. Louis: Telos Press, 1980 [1898]), *Essays on the Materialistic Conception of History*, trans. Charles H. Kerr (New York: Cosimo Books, 2005 [1903]); Alexandre Kojève, *Introduction to the Reading of Hegel: Lectures on the Phenomenology of Spirit*, trans. James H. Nichols, Jr., ed., Allan Bloom (New York: Basic Books, 1969 [1958]); Jean Hyppolite, *Studies on Marx and Hegel*, trans. John O'Neill (New York: Harper and Row, 1969 [1955]). Some telling contemporary examples are Slavoj Žižek, *The Most Sublime Hysteric: Hegel with Lacan*, trans. Thomas Scott-Railton (Cambridge: Polity, 2014), *Tarrying with the Negative: Kant, Hegel, and the Critique of Ideology* (Durham, NC: Duke University Press, 1993); Jean-Luc Nancy, *The Speculative Remark*, trans. Céline Surprenant (Stanford, CA: Stanford University Press, 2001), *Hegel: The Restlessness of the Negative*, trans. Jason Smith and Steven Miller (Minneapolis: University of Minnesota Press, 2002); Jürgen Habermas, "Toward a Reconstruction of Historical Materialism," in *Communication and Evolution of Society*, trans. Thomas McCarthy (Boston: Beacon, 1979), 130–77; Axel Honneth, "Moral Consciousness and Class Domination: Some Problems in the Analysis of Hidden Morality," *Praxis International* 2, no. 1 (1982): 12–24.

8   Lukács, "Reification and the Consciousness of the Proletariat," in *History and Class Consciousness*.

9   Lukács, *The Young Hegel*, trans. Rodney Livingstone (London: Merlin, 1975 [1938]).

10   See, for instance, Marcuse, *Reason and Revolution*; Erich Fromm, *Marx's Concept of Man* (New York: Frederick Ungar, 1961); Ernst Bloch, *The Principle of Hope*, Vol. 3,

trans. Neville Plaice, Stephen Plaice and Paul Knight (Cambridge, MA: MIT Press, 1986 [1954]); Karl Korsch, *Marxism and Philosophy*, trans. Fred Halliday (New York: Verso, 2013 [1923]); Hyppolite, *Studies on Marx and Hegel*; Vladimir Lenin, "Abstract of Hegel's Science of Logic" [1929], in Lenin, *Collected Works*, Vol. 38 (Moscow: Progress, 1963).

11 Adorno, *Hegel: Three Studies*, 75.

12 Andrew Buchwalter, "Hegel, Marx, and the Concept of Immanent Critique," *Journal of the History of Philosophy* 29, no. 2 (1991): 253–79; Rahel Jaeggi, "Rethinking Ideology," in *New Waves in Political Philosophy*, ed. Boudewijn Paul de Bruin and Christopher F. Zurn (New York: Palgrave Macmillan, 2009), 63–86; Titus Stahl, "What Is Immanent Critique?," *SSRN Working Papers* (2013), http://ssrn.com/abstract=2357957 (accessed January 16, 2019); Karin de Boer, "Hegel's Conception of Immanent Critique: Its Sources, Extent, and Limit," in *Conceptions of Critique in Modern and Contemporary Philosophy*, ed. Ruth Sonderegger and Karin de Boer (New York: Palgrave Macmillan, 2012).

13 Karl Marx, "Letters from *Deutsch-Französische Jahrbücher*," Marx to Ruge, September 1843, MECW 3: 144.

14 Georg Wilhelm Friedrich Hegel, *Phenomenology of Spirit*, trans. A.V. Miller (Oxford: Oxford University Press, 1977 [1807]), §84, 54: "Consequently, we do not need to import criteria, or to make use of our own bright ideas and thoughts during the course of the inquiry; it is precisely when we leave these aside that we succeed in contemplating the matter in hand as it is *in and for itself*."

15 Max Horkheimer, for instance, provides a typical example of relating immanent critique and the history of philosophy when stating that the "viewpoints" which critical theory "derives from historical analysis as the goals of human activity, especially the idea of a reasonable organization of society that will meet the needs of the whole community, are immanent in human work but are not correctly grasped by individuals or by the common mind." Max Horkheimer, "Traditional and Critical Theory" (1937), in *Critical Theory: Selected Essays*, trans. Matthew J. O'Connell and others (New York: Continuum, 1972), 213.

16 Hegel, *Elements of the Philosophy of Right*, ed. Stephen Houlgate, trans. T.M. Knox (New York: Oxford University Press, 2008 [1820]), §57R, 70.

17 Hegel, *Lectures on the Philosophy of World History*, Vol. 1: *Manuscripts of the Introduction and the Lectures of 1822–3*, edited and translated by Robert F. Brown and Peter C. Hodgson (Oxford: Clarendon, 2011), 205–10; for Marx, see, for example, his assessment of the French revolution: "*Political* emancipation is, of course, a big step forward. True, it is not the final form of human emancipation in general, but it is the final form of human emancipation *within* the hitherto existing world order" (Marx, "On the Jewish Question," MECW 3: 155). See also the chapter on the working day in *Capital*, where Marx discusses legislation on child labor and the length of the working day, which he clearly saw as legal gains, signifying a progress in history brought about by social struggles; Marx, *Capital I*, MECW 35: ch. 10. For critical reflections on the idea of progress and its role in Critical Theory, see Amy Allen, *The End of Progress: Decolonizing the Normative Foundations of Critical Theory* (New York: Columbia University Press, 2017).

18 "World history is the progress of the consciousness of freedom" (Hegel, *Philosophy of World History*, 88).

19 See, for example, Marx, *Capital I*, 187: "Labour is … a process in which both man and Nature participate, and in which man of his own accord starts, regulates, and

controls the material re-actions between himself and Nature. He opposes himself to Nature as one of her own forces, setting in motion arms and legs, head and hands, the natural forces of his body, in order to appropriate Nature's productions in a form adapted to his own wants. By thus acting on the external world and changing it, he at the same time changes his own nature. He develops his slumbering powers and compels them to act in obedience to his sway." See also George G. Brenkert, *Marx's Ethics of Freedom* (New York: Routledge, 1983), 98–102.

20 See Rahel Jaeggi, "Crisis, Contradiction, and the Task of a Critical Theory," in *Feminism, Capitalism, and Critique: Essays in Honor of Nancy Fraser*, ed. Banu Bargu and Chiara Bottici (New York: Palgrave Macmillan, 2017), 209–24.

21 Marx, "The Civil War in France," MECW 22: 335.

22 Hegel, *Philosophy of Right*, 15; Marx to Ruge, September 1843, 142.

23 Hegel, *Philosophy of Right*, §270A, 253.

24 Marx, *Critique of Hegel's 'Philosophy of Right'* (Cambridge: Cambridge University Press, 1977 [1844]), 25.

25 One major difference concerns the driving force of historical progress: Marx imputes Hegel to treat 'the Idea' as "the demiurgos of the real world" (Marx *Capital I*, Afterword to the 2nd edn, 19), where the Idea figures as a supra-individual and antecedent agent of history. It is true that Hegel claims that "reason governs the world" (Hegel, *Philosophy of World History*, 79). But, anticipating approaches that attempt to reverse the path from Hegel to Marx, we might argue that the historical process can be said to embody rationality only in retrospect, by way of a reconstructive recollection of the diverse struggles for freedom to be found in human history. And here, spirit is not something prefabricated that merely awaits its realization; rather, it only emanates from the cumulative actions of those beings whose inner principle is itself 'spiritual'—that is, human beings who are defined by their free will, the "precise place and point of origin" of the "realm of spirit" (Hegel, *Philosophy of Right*, §4, 26). Thus, in Hegel, the driving force of historical progress can be located in 'spiritual' demands for more encompassing forms of freedom, while Marx gives much more weight to material interests.

26 Marx, *A Contribution to the Critique of Political Economy*, "Preface," MECW 29: 264. Similarly, Marx and Engels describe communism not as a "state of affairs" but as a "real movement" (Marx and Engels, *The German Ideology*, MECW 5: 49). See also Howard Williams, "The End of History in Hegel and Marx," in *The Hegel–Marx Connection*.

27 See, for example, Terry Pinkard, *Does History Make Sense? Hegel on the Historical Shapes of Justice* (Cambridge, MA: Harvard University Press, 2017); Eric Michael Dale, *Hegel, the End of History, and the Future* (Cambridge: Cambridge University Press, 2014); Catherine Malabou, *The Future of Hegel: Plasticity, Temporality, Dialectic*, trans. Lisabeth During (New York: Routledge, 2005).

28 Roberto Finelli even diagnoses a failed attempt on Marx's part to kill his 'father'; see Roberto Finelli, *A Failed Parricide: Hegel and the Young Marx* (Leiden: Brill, 2015).

29 "[T]he creation of civil society is the achievement of the modern world which has for the first time given all determinations of the Idea their due" (Hegel, *Philosophy of Right*, §182A, 181). See also Manfred Riedel, *Between Tradition and Revolution: The Hegelian Transformation of Political Philosophy* (Cambridge: Cambridge University Press, 2010 [1969]), ch. 6.

30 Marx, "On the Jewish Question."

31 Ibid., 155.

32 Communal life in the sphere of the state appears as "the heaven of its universality in opposition to the earthly existence of its actuality" (Marx, *Critique of Hegel's 'Philosophy of Right'*, 31–2). In other words, the political sphere, although realizing the universal potential of the human 'species-being', figures as something "otherworldly" (*als ein Jenseitiges*); it remains unreal and ineffective, by being restricted to a confined sphere, separated from and even opposed to the other social spheres (Marx, *Critique of Hegel's 'Philosophy of Right'*, 31; translation amended).
33 Hegel, *Philosophy of Right*, §§201–7.
34 Schnädelbach, for example, holds that Hegel's idea of the dialectical movement from 'identity' to 'non-identity' to the 'identity of identity and non-identity' almost compels him to construe civil society as a sphere that represents the "loss of ethical life" (Hegel, *Philosophy of Right*, §181, 180). See Schnädelbach, *Hegels Praktische Philosophie* (Frankfurt: Suhrkamp, 2000), 139–40. A similar reading was recently put forward by Andrew Buchwalter, "The Ethicality in Civil Society: Bifurcation, Bildung and Hegel's Supersession of the Aporias of Social Modernity," in *Hegel's Elements of the Philosophy of Right: A Critical Guide*, ed. David James (New York: Cambridge University Press, 2017). On this account, it is only the negation of ethicality in civil society, dissolving the ethical immediacy of the sphere of the family, that makes possible the mediated ethical status of the sphere of the state. This brings along the danger of ennobling the contradictions of civil society as painful, but productive—and even ethical—driving forces of progress.
35 Marx, *Capital I*, 726 (translation amended). See, however, Nicholas Mowad, "The Purest Inequality: Hegel's Critique of the Labor Contract and Capitalism," in *Hegel and Capitalism*, ed. Andrew Buchwalter (Albany: SUNY Press, 2015), for a more Marx-inspired reading of Hegel, particularly the *Phenomenology of Spirit*.
36 See Marx's derision of "Freedom, Equality, Property and Bentham" ruling the sphere of market; *Capital I*, 186. For recent—more helical—approaches, see Jaeggi, "Rethinking Ideology," and Karen Ng, "Ideology Critique from Hegel and Marx to Critical Theory," *Constellations* 22, no. 3 (2015): 393–404.
37 For example: "There can therefore no longer be any question about an act of accommodation on Hegel's part *vis-à-vis* religion, the state, etc., since this lie is the lie of his principle" (Marx, *Economic and Philosophic Manuscripts*, MECW 3: 339). See also Shuangli, "Marx and Hegel."
38 See Rebecca Comay, *Mourning Sickness: Hegel and the French Revolution* (Stanford, CA: Stanford University Press, 2011), 5: "Hegel loves the French Revolution so much he needs to purge it of the revolutionaries."
39 See Marx to Ruge, September 1843, 145.
40 Theodor W. Adorno, *Minima Moralia: Reflections on a Damaged Life*, trans. E.F.N. Jephcott (London: Verso, 2005 [1951]), 50. Although it is, as Simon Jarvis rightly points out, just as one-sided to describe Adorno's thinking from the principle "the whole is the false" as it is to let "the whole is the true" be emblematic for Hegel's philosophy; see Simon Jarvis, "The 'unhappy consciousness' and conscious unhappiness: On Adorno's critique of Hegel and the idea of an Hegelian critique of Adorno," in *Hegel's Phenomenology of Spirit: A Reappraisal*, ed. G. K. Browning (Dordrecht: Kluwer, 1997), 58.
41 Theodor W. Adorno, *Negative Dialectics*, trans. E.B. Ashton (London: Bloomsbury, 1981 [1966]). See also Adorno, *Hegel: Three Studies*.
42 Michel Foucault, "The Discourse on Language," in *The Archeology of Knowledge*, trans. A.M. Sheridan Smith (New York: Pantheon, 1972 [1969]), 235.

43 Jacques Derrida, *Positions*, trans. Alan Bass (Chicago: Chicago University Press, 1981 [1972]), 44. See also Derrida, "From Restricted to General Economy: A Hegelianism without Reserve," in Derrida, *Writing and Difference*, trans. Alan Bass (New York: Routledge, 2001 [1967]), 317–50. For an illuminating overview of the "resistance to Hegel" within modern philosophy, see Bart Zantvoort, "Introduction," in *Hegel and Resistance: History, Politics and Dialectic*, ed. Rebecca Comay and Bart Zantvoort (London: Bloomsbury, 2018), 1–11.

44 Louis Althusser, *For Marx*, trans. Ben Brewster (New York: Verso, 2005 [1965]), 33–5.

45 Ibid., particularly "'On the Young Marx,'" 49–86. Marx himself already hinted at this epistemological position (in his criticism of the Young Hegelians): "Not only in their answers but in their very questions there was a mystification" (*The German Ideology*, MECW 5: 28).

46 See, for instance, Urs Lindner, "Repenser la 'coupure épistémologique'. Lire Marx avec et contre Althusser," *Actuel Marx* 49, no. 1 (2011): 121–39.

47 Recent studies on Marx and the Young Hegelians include *The New Hegelians: Politics and Philosophy in the Hegelian School*, ed. Douglas Moggach (Cambridge: Cambridge University Press, 2006); David Leopold, *The Young Karl Marx: German Philosophy, Modern Politics, and Human Flourishing* (Cambridge: Cambridge University Press, 2007); Emmanuel Renault, "The Early Marx and Hegel: The Young Hegelian Mediation," in *Reassessing Marx*, 43–59. The shared goal of the Young Hegelians was to realize Hegel's philosophy, which, according to them, achieved reconciliation only in the heights of absolute knowledge. In contrast to this, they aimed at criticizing the existing social reality, with the purpose of making reconciliation a practical achievement.

48 In any case, Althusser always had to acknowledge that Marx's idea of history as a "process without a subject" is a Hegelian inheritance; see Louis Althusser, "Lenin before Hegel," in *Lenin and Philosophy and Other Essays*, trans. Ben Brewster (New York: Monthly Review Press, 2001 [1968]), 81.

49 Gerald A. Cohen, *Karl Marx's Theory of History: A Defence* (Princeton, NJ: Princeton University Press, 1978); John E. Roemer, *A General Theory of Exploitation and Class* (Cambridge, MA: Harvard University Press, 1982); Jon Elster, *Making Sense of Marx* (Cambridge: Cambridge University Press, 1985). See also the contributions in *Analytical Marxism*, ed. John E. Roemer (Cambridge: Cambridge University Press, 1986).

50 See, for example, Elster, *Making Sense of Marx*, 37–8: "Hegel, in *The Science of Logic*, derived the various ontological categories from each other according to certain deductive principles which have resisted analysis to this day. The connection is neither that of causes to effect, nor that of axiom to theorem, nor finally that of given fact to its condition of possibility. The 'self-determination of the concept' appears to be nothing more than a loose *ex post* pattern imposed by Hegel on various phenomena that he found important."

51 Ibid., 3–7, 514.

52 Ibid., 88–92.

53 Gerald A. Cohen, *Rescuing Justice and Equality* (Cambridge, MA: Harvard University Press, 2008); John E. Roemer, "Socialism Revised," *Philosophy & Public Affairs* 45, no. 3 (2017): 261–315. For the affinity between Cohen and German Idealism, see Julius Sensat, "Classical German Philosophy and Cohen's Critique of Rawls," *European Journal of Philosophy* 11, no. 3 (2003): 314–53.

54 Vincent Descombes, *Modern French Philosophy*, trans. L. Scott-Fox and J.M. Harding (Cambridge: Cambridge University Press, 1981) and Judith Butler, *Subjects of Desire: Hegelian Reflections in Twentieth-Century France* (New York: Columbia University Press, 1987) provide excellent reconstructions of the history of Kojève's influence.
55 Alexandre Kojève, *Introduction to the Reading of Hegel* (Ithaca, NY: Cornell University Press, 1980 [1947]), 19.
56 Ibid., 40 (translation amended).
57 In comparison to the self-congratulatory triumphalism exhibited in Francis Fukuyama's best seller, *The End of History and the Last Man* (New York: Free Press), published in 1992, Kojève's end-of-history claim was much more ambivalent, since the fulfillment of desire is at the same time the "death of man" (Kojève, *Introduction*, 245), in virtue of the fact that, according to Kojève, human beings are characterized by a negativity that would be overcome at the end of history (see ibid., particularly the long footnote 6, ranging from 158 to 162).
58 This idea is best captured in Axel Honneth's "The Social Dynamics of Disrespect: On the Location of Critical Theory Today," *Constellations* 1, no. 1 (1994): 255–69.
59 Cf. Erich Fromm, *The Working Class in Weimar Germany: A Psychological and Sociological Study* (Cambridge, MA: Harvard, 1984). This study is based on an extensive survey among blue- and white-collar workers during the years 1929–1931, although its results remained unpublished until 1980. The research was conducted at the Institute for Social Research, Goethe-University Frankfurt.
60 Jürgen Habermas, "Labor and Interaction: Remarks on Hegel's Jena *Philosophy of Mind*" (1967), in *Theory and Practice*, trans. John Viertel (Boston: Beacon Press, 1973), 142–69. See also Tony Flood, "Jürgen Habermas's Critique of Marxism," *Science and Society* 41, no. 4 (1977): 448–64, and Bob Cannon, *Rethinking the Normative Content of Critical Theory: Marx, Habermas and Beyond* (London: Palgrave Macmillan, 2001).
61 Habermas, "Labor and Interaction," 168–9.
62 In the first of the Jena outlines of his philosophy of spirit, Hegel devotes the first three chapters to "Speech," "The Tool," and "Possession and the Family"; Hegel, *First Philosophy of Spirit*, in *Hegel's System of Ethical Life and First Philosophy of Spirit*, ed. and transl. by H.S. Harris and T.M. Knox (Albany: State University of New York Press, 1979 [1802–4]), 218–34. Habermas claims: "[I]t is not the spirit in the absolute movement of reflecting on itself which manifests itself in, among other things, language, labor and moral relationships, but rather, it is the dialectical interconnections between linguistic symbolization, labor, and interaction which determine the concept of spirit." Habermas, "Labor and Interaction," 143.
63 See, for example, Marx, *The Poverty of Philosophy*, MECW 6: 166: "Social relations are closely bound up with productive forces. In acquiring new productive forces men change their mode of production; and in changing their mode of production, in changing the way of earning their living, they change all their social relations. The hand-mill gives you society with the feudal Lord; the steam-mill, society with the industrial capitalist." For a systematic defense, see Cohen, *Karl Marx's Theory of History*.
64 "[T]o set free the technical forces of production … is not identical with the development of norms which could fulfill the dialectic of moral relationships in an interaction free of domination, on the basis of a reciprocity allowed to have its full and noncoercive scope" (Habermas, "Labor and Interaction," 169).

65 Habermas, "Toward a Reconstruction," 163.
66 Habermas, "Historical Materialism and the Development of Normative Structures," in *Communication and Evolution*, 95–129, at p. 97.
67 So, when Marx talks about "the evolution of the economic formation of society … as a process of natural history," this tendency is obvious enough (*Capital I*, Preface to 1st edn, 10). To be sure, it is sometimes argued that such statements are *critical* claims about capitalism's tendency to unfold in the manner of natural processes, that is, beyond the reach and control of human intervention; see, for example, Moishe Postone, *Time, Labor, and Social Domination: A Reinterpretation of Marx's Critical Theory* (Cambridge: Cambridge University Press, 1993), 227–41. But there are also passages in Marx where he clearly welcomes this allegedly nature-like evolution of the social, for example, when he asserts that "capitalist production begets, with the inexorability of a law of Nature, its own negation" (Marx, *Capital I*, 751).
68 On this point in particular, see Habermas, *Knowledge and Human Interests* (Boston: Beacon, 1972); for further reflections see Flood's "Jürgen Habermas's Critique of Marxism."
69 Important recent studies include Ali Shamsavari, *Dialectics and Social Theory: The Logic of Capital* (Braunton: Merlin, 1991); Tony Smith, *The Logic of Marx's Capital: Replies to Hegelian Criticisms* (Albany: SUNY Press, 1990); Christopher J. Arthur, *The New Dialectic and Marx's Capital* (Leiden: Brill, 2004); *Marx's 'Capital' and Hegel's 'Logic': A Reexamination*, ed. Fred Moseley and Tony Smith (Leiden: Brill, 2014). On Hegel's logic in the *Grundrisse*, see Hiroshi Uchida, *Marx's Grundrisse and Hegel's Logic* (London: Routledge, 1988). An early influential study is Helmut Reichelt, *Zur logischen Struktur des Kapitalbegriffs bei Karl Marx* (Freiburg: Ça ira, 2001 [1968]).
70 See, for example, George Lichtheim, *From Marx to Hegel and Other Essays* (London: Orbach & Chambers, 1971); Marek Siemek, *Von Marx zu Hegel. Zum sozialpolitischen Selbstverständnis der Moderne* (Würzburg: Königshausen & Neumann, 2002).
71 See, for example, Hegel's basic idea that in civil society, "subjective self-seeking turns into a contribution to the satisfaction of the needs of everyone else" (Hegel, *Philosophy of Right*, §199). On the relation of Hegel and Adam Smith, see Lisa Herzog, *Inventing the Market: Smith, Hegel and Political Theory* (Oxford: Oxford University Press, 2013). On the 'invisible hand' motif in particular, see John B. Davis, "Smith's Invisible Hand and Hegel's Cunning of Reason," *International Journal of Social Economics* 16, no. (1989): 50–66.
72 Hegel, *System of Ethical Life*, in: *Hegel's System of Ethical Life and First Philosophy of Spirit*, 167. The early System outlines by Hegel just cited were unavailable to Marx. Norman Levine offers a detailed account of Hegel's works that Marx did not know or that were published after Marx's death; see Levine, *Marx's Discourse with Hegel*. On Hegel's early critique of the market, see Ivan Boldyrev, "The Beast and the Universal: Hegel's Critique of Political Economy," *Crisis and Critique* 4, no. 1 (2017): 84–91.
73 Postone, *Time, Labor, and Social Domination*, 29–33.
74 See Michael Quante, "Handlung, System der Bedürfnisse und Marktkritik bei Hegel und Marx," *Deutsches Jahrbuch Philosophie* 7 (2016): 153–75.
75 See Marx's 1844 formulation: "What was the domination of person over person is now the general domination of the *thing* over the *person*, of the product over the producer" (Marx, "Comments on James Mill's *Éléments D'économie Politique*," MECW

3: 270). The definition of commodity fetishism in *Capital* is strikingly close: In a commodity-producing society "social action takes the form of the action of objects, which rule the producers instead of being ruled by them" (Marx, *Capital I*, 85). This continuity in Marx's work is elucidated more thoroughly in Sean Sayer, *Marx and Alienation: Essays on Hegelian Themes* (Basingstoke: Palgrave Macmillan, 2011).

76 To sustain this claim, we cite for each concept important texts of Marx (and Engels) as well as systematic Marxist defenses. On the absence of the state, see Engels on the 'dying out' (or 'withering away') of the state (Engels, *Anti-Dühring*, MECW 25: 268) and Miguel Abensour, *Democracy against the State: Marx and the Machiavellian Movement* (London: Polity Press, 2011). On the absence of market relations and money see Marx, "Critique of the Gotha Programme," MECW 24: 85–6, and Peter Hudis, *Marx's Concept of the Alternative to Capitalism* (Leiden: Brill, 2012). On the absence of legal rights, see Marx's talk of rights being "nothing but" the rights of egoistic men of bourgeois society (Marx, "On the Jewish Question," 162) as well as Lukács, with his claim that the "ultimate objective of communism is the construction of a society in which freedom of morality will take the place of legal compulsion in the regulation of all behaviour" (Lukács, "The Role of Morality in Communist Production," in *Tactics and Politics. Political Writings, 1919-1929*, trans. Michael McColgan, London: NLB, 1972, 48). On the absence of private property, see "Comments on James Mill" (218–28) and Andrew Chitty, "Recognition and Property in Hegel and the Early Marx," *Ethical Theory and Moral Practice* 16, no. 4 (2013): 685–97. On the absence of a stabilized form of a division of labor, see the remarks on hunting, fishing, cattle rearing, and philosophizing (in the *German Ideology*, 47) and James Furner, "Marx's Sketch of Communist Society in *The German Ideology* and the Problems of Occupational Confinement and Occupational Identity," *Philosophy and Social Criticism* 37, no. 2 (2011): 189–215. On the absence of institutionalized norms of justice, see Brudney's interpretation of Marx's needs-abilities principle from the "Critique of the Gotha Programme" as being descriptive and non-normative in Daniel Brudney, "Community and Completion," in *Reclaiming the History of Ethics: Essays for John Rawls*, ed. Andrews Reath, Barbara Herman, Christine M. Korsgaard, and John Rawls (Cambridge: Cambridge University Press, 1997).

77 Quante recently argued in detail that Marx conceptualized social relations in a communist society "on the model of an immediate and completely non-instrumental relation between two individuals" and "the exclusion of any indirect mediation"; Michael Quante, "Recognition as the Social Grammar of Species Being in Marx," in *Recognition and Social Ontology*, ed. Heikki Ikäheimo and Arto Laitinen (Leiden: Brill, 2011), 239–67, at p. 265. One might object that this tendency is confined to the early Marx. But even the late Marx relies on his early anthropology, and he does so precisely at the point where he introduces and defends the principle 'From each according to his abilities, to each according to his needs', which is at the core of the second stage of communism, by claiming that, by then, labor will have become "not only a means of life but life's prime want" (Marx, "Critique of the Gotha Programme," 86).

78 See Cornelius Castoriadis, *The Imaginary Institution of Society*, trans. Kathleen Blamey (Cambridge: Polity, 1997 [1975]), 110–4.

79 Rahel Jaeggi, "Was ist eine (gute) Institution?," in *Sozialphilosophie und Kritik*, ed. Rainer Forst, Martin Hartmann, Rahel Jaeggi, and Martin Saar (Frankfurt: Suhrkamp, 2009); available in English online: "What Is a (Good) Institution?,"

	https://www.philosophie.hu-berlin.de/de/lehrbereiche/jaeggi/mitarbeiter/jaeggi_rahel/RJWhat%20is%20a%20-good-%20institution.pdf (accessed January 16, 2019).
80	Hegel, *Philosophy of Right*, §260.
81	Heikki Ikäheimo, "From the Old Hegel to the Young Marx and Back: Two Sketches of an Evaluative Ontology of the Human Life-Form," in *Reassessing Marx*, 97.
82	Hegel sees the three social spheres of ethical life—the family, economic cooperation, and the state—as different realms to realize freedom as "the living good" (Hegel, *Philosophy of Right*, §142). Each realm provides an institutional framework to realize meaningful goals by participating in a shared life with others, with mutually attuned patterns of recognition. See also Joshua Goldstein, *Hegel's Idea of the Good Life* (Dordrecht: Springer, 2006).
83	Accordingly, recent neo-Hegelian approaches assume that the relation between the functionally differentiated spheres of modern society should be such that they are enabled "to follow their own independent norms"; Axel Honneth, *The Idea of Socialism: Towards a Renewal* (Cambridge: Polity, 2017), 91–2.
84	On the pathologies of legal freedom, see Honneth, *The Pathologies of Individual Freedom*, and *Freedom's Right*, ch. 4.3.
85	Marx, "On the Jewish Question," 162. For critical reflections on Marx's 'clean-slate' attitude, see Frederick Neuhouser, "Marx and Hegel on the Value of 'Bourgeois' Ideals," in *Reassessing Marx*; Hans-Christoph Schmidt am Busch's contribution in the same volume ("How Do Rights Affect Our Freedom?"); Jay Bernstein, "Right, Revolution and Community: Marx's 'On the Jewish question'," in *Socialism and the Limits of Liberalism*, ed. Peter Osborne (London: Verso, 1991).
86	See, for example, Allen E. Buchanan, *Marx and Justice: The Radical Critique of Liberalism* (Totowa, NJ: Rowman & Littlefield, 1982).
87	A typical interpretation is Shlomo Avineri's assumption of a "universal egoism" that allegedly governs civil society, as opposed to the "universal altruism" characterizing relations within the sphere of the state, Shlomo Avineri, *Hegel's Theory of the Modern State* (London: Cambridge University Press, 1972), 132. For more recent positions that underline the interweaving of civil society and the state, see Frederick Neuhouser, "Marx (und Hegel) zur Philosophie der Freiheit," in *Nach Marx*, ed. Rahel Jaeggi and Daniel Loick (Frankfurt: Suhrkamp, 2013), 25–47; and Sven Ellmers, *Freiheit und Wirtschaft: Theorie der bürgerlichen Gesellschaft nach Hegel* (Bielefeld: Transcript, 2015). Rahel Jaeggi's notion of adequate 'relations of fit' is particularly apt; see Jaeggi, "'Resistance to the Perpetual Danger of Relapse': Moral Progress and Social Change," in *From Alienation to Forms of Life*, ed. Amy Allen and Eduardo Mendieta (University Park: Pennsylvania University Press, 2018).
88	Marx, *Capital III*, MECW 37: 807.
89	There is an explosion of interest in workplace democracy of late, but most recent authors shy away from the idea of socializing ownership itself. See, for example, the otherwise excellent studies by Elizabeth Anderson, *Private Government: How Employers Rule Our Lives (and Why We Don't Talk about It)* (Princeton, NJ: Princeton University Press, 2017) and Isabelle Ferreras, *Firms as Political Entities: Saving Democracy through Economic Bicameralism* (Cambridge: Cambridge University Press, 2017).
90	For an exposition of this idea of freedom see Neuhouser, *Foundations of Hegel's Social Theory*; Honneth, *Freedom's Right*; and Andreas Arndt, "Hegel, Marx and Freedom," *Revista Opinião Filosófica* 7, no. 1 (2016): 206–21.

91 Hegel, *Philosophy of Right*, §7A, 33; Marx and Engels, *Manifesto of the Communist Party*, 506. See also Allen Wood, *The Free Development of Each: Studies on Freedom, Right, and Ethics in Classical German Philosophy* (Oxford: Oxford University Press, 2014).
92 Axel Honneth, *Struggle for Recognition: The Moral Grammar of Social Conflicts*, trans. Joel Anderson (Cambridge: Polity, 1995); Charles Taylor, "The Politics of Recognition," in *Multiculturalism: Examining the Politics of Recognition*, ed. Amy Gutmann (Princeton, NJ: Princeton University Press, 1994).
93 Marx, "Comments on James Mill." There are several detailed and highly illuminating interpretations of Marx's "Comments" in contemporary Marx scholarship. See particularly Daniel Brudney, *Marx's Attempt to Leave Philosophy* (Cambridge, MA: Harvard University Press, 1998), 169–91; Chitty, "Recognition and Property"; Quante, "Recognition as the Social Grammar."
94 Honneth calls this a "utilitarian" understanding of social conflicts; see Honneth, *Struggle for Recognition*, 145–52.
95 Honneth, *Struggle for Recognition*; see also Fraser and Honneth, *Redistribution or Recognition?*; Taylor, "The Politics of Recognition"; Robert Williams, *Hegel's Ethics of Recognition* (Berkeley: University of California Press, 1997).
96 Marx, "Comments on James Mill."
97 Ibid., 228.
98 Ibid., 217.
99 Charles Taylor, *Hegel and Modern Society* (Cambridge: Cambridge University Press, 1979); Alasdair MacIntyre, *After Virtue: A Study in Moral Theory* (Indiana: University of Notre Dame Press, 1981).
100 Jean-Luc Nancy, *The Inoperative Community*, trans. Peter Connor (Minneapolis: University of Minnesota Press, 1991), xxxvii.
101 See his *Hegel: The Restlessness of the Negative*, 6 (*Geist* as "absolutely restless" is a quote from Hegel's *Encyclopedia of Science*).
102 See Jean-Luc Nancy, *Being Singular Plural*, trans. Robert D. Richardson and Anne E. O'Byrne (Stanford, CA: Stanford University Press, 2000).
103 Jean-Luc Nancy, "La Comparution/The Compearance: From the Existence of 'Communism' to the Community of 'Existence,'" *Political Theory* 20, no. 3 (1992): 378. See also Nancy, "Communism, the Word," in *The Idea of Communism*, ed. Costas Douzinas and Slavoj Žižek (New York: Verso, 2010), 145–53.
104 Nancy, "La Comparution/The Compearance," 378.
105 Slavoj Žižek, *The Plague of Fantasies* (New York: Verso, 2008), 122.
106 Slavoj Žižek, "How to Begin from the Beginning," in *The Idea of Communism*, ed. Costas Douzinas and Slavoj Žižek (New York: Verso, 2010), 209–26; Žižek, "The Politics of Alienation and Separation: From Hegel to Marx.... and Back," *Crisis and Critique* 4, no. 1 (2017): 447–79.
107 See, for instance, the chapter on Hegel in his *The Ticklish Subject* (New York: Verso, 1999), 70–123.
108 See Rebecca Comay and Frank Ruda, *The Dash: The Other Side of Absolute Knowing* (Cambridge, MA: MIT Press, 2018). See also Comay's *Mourning Sickness* and *Hegel and Resistance*. Other influential works that address the openness and restless character of Hegel's philosophy are Malabou, *The Future of Hegel*; de Boer, *On Hegel*; Jameson, *The Hegel Variations*; Zambrana, *Hegel's Theory of Intelligibility*.
109 Marx, "Contribution to Critique of Hegel's Philosophy of Law. Introduction," MECW 3: 186.

110 Ruda, *Hegel's Rabble*.
111 Hegel, *Hegel's Science of Logic*, trans. A.V. Miller (Amherst, NY: Humanity Books, 1998 [1816]), 842. See also Andrew Cole, "How to Think a Figure; or, Hegel's Circles," *Representations* 140, no. 1 (2017): 44–66; Ludwig Feuerbach, *Principles of the Philosophy of the Future*, trans. Manfred Vogel (Indianapolis: Hackett, 1986 [1843]), 65. On the circularity of reading Hegel see Werner Hamacher, *Pleroma: Reading in Hegel*, trans. N. Walker and S. Jarvis (Stanford, CA: Stanford University Press, 1998).
112 Louis Althusser, "From Capital to Marx's Philosophy," in *Reading Capital: The Complete Edition*, trans. B. Brewster and D. Fernbach (New York: Verso, 2016 [1965]), 54.
113 Hegel, *Philosophy of Right*, §2, 18.
114 Hegel, *Phenomenology of Spirit*, §802, 488.
115 Andrew Chitty, "Recognition and Social Relations of Production," *Historical Materialism* 2, no. 1 (1998): 57–97; Emmanuel Renault, "Three Marxian Approaches to Recognition," in *Ethical Theory and Moral Practice* 16 (2013): 699–711; Michael Quante, "Recognition in Capital," in *Ethical Theory and Moral Practice* 16 (2013): 713–27.
116 For an overview, see Riccardo Bellofiore and Tommaso Redolfi Riva, "The *Neue Marx-Lektüre*: Putting the Critique of Political Economy Back into the Critique of Society," *Radical Philosophy* 189 (2015): 24–36, and Werner Bonefeld, *Critical Theory and the Critique of Political Economy: On Subversion and Negative Reason* (London, New York: Bloomsbury, 2014). Few works are translated into English; important exceptions are Hans-Georg Backhaus, "On the Dialectics of the Value-Form," *Thesis Eleven* 1 (1980): 99–120; Helmut Reichelt, "Marx's Critique of Economic Categories," *Historical Materialism* 4 (2007): 3–52; and Heinrich, *Introduction to the Three Volumes*.
117 Erik Olin Wright, *Envisioning Real Utopias* (New York: Verso, 2010).
118 We would like to thank Jacob Blumenfeld, Sven-Eric Liedman, Daniel Hoffman-Schwartz, and Just Serrano Zamora for instructive comments and helpful remarks on earlier versions of this article. We are also grateful for the collaboration with Anders Bartonek and Anders Burman from the "Hegelian Marxism" research project (CBEES, Södertörn University, Stockholm) and their efforts in co-organizing the conference "From Marx to Hegel and Back to the Future," Stockholm, February 2016, with us. Finally, we would like to thank the Swedish Research Council and the German Research Foundation (DFG) for their generous support.

Part One

Reassessing the Legacy of Hegel and Marx

2

Hegel and Marx

A Reassessment after One Century

Axel Honneth

Opinions about the relationship between Hegel and Marx have been subject to significant variation from the very beginning. Since the end of the nineteenth century, every era seems to have had its own idea about the relation between them. Right after Marx's death, during the early development of social democracy, the prevailing judgment was that there were few points of contact between the two thinkers. What was acknowledged was the important influence of Feuerbach on Marx's thinking, as well as the relevance of Kant. But the significance of Hegel's philosophy went unnoticed.[1] This changed significantly when the discovery of the "Paris manuscripts" shed new light on the young Marx, leading scholars to pursue the traces of Hegel's thought in Marx's work all the way to his mature critique of political economy. It was soon recognized that the structure of the latter was deeply informed by Hegel's dialectical method.[2] After the Second World War, when interest in Marx's work was initially centered on themes such as alienation and reification, other connections between their respective theories began to be drawn. Now, a central issue was the influence on Marx of Hegel's idea of a necessary self-alienation of spirit into its other.[3] These Hegelian-Marxist interpretations were decisively opposed by Althusser, who launched the thesis that there was an 'epistemological break' between Marx's early writings and his later ones, marking a complete emancipation of his mature economic works from the influence of Hegel. Today, the prevailing view is again the opposite. One might even say that the two thinkers are now more closely associated and read in a more cross-fertilizing way than ever before. Not only is Hegel's work regarded as a source of philosophical inspiration for Marx, as it was in Lukács's time, but it is also recognized as a treasure trove of insights in social theory that can be used to supplement and improve on Marx's doctrines.

This new evaluation of the relationship between Hegel and Marx was prompted by a number of barely noticeable interpretive shifts over the course of the past several decades. For instance, Charles Taylor's path-breaking studies have made it seem much more natural to us to view Hegel not simply as a system builder seeking to comprehend the world in its totality, but also as an empirically informed social theorist.⁴ His *Philosophy of Right* is viewed today as an attempt to diagnose the dynamics and crises of modern societies, containing the seeds of a sociological analysis that anticipated central insights of this not-yet existing discipline. Further scholarship has made it much clearer to us how Hegel's notion of 'objective spirit' conceptualizes the integration of societies as the result of acts of mutual recognition.⁵ This, too, has brought the sociological dimension of his theory into much sharper relief compared with past readings.

At the same time, interpretation of Marx's theory has been subject to similar shifts. Max Weber and Josef Schumpeter had already taken the sober approach of viewing Marx's work simply as a competitor to their own efforts to explain capitalist societies. This trend has continued since and has even increased as actual circumstances have presented increasingly less of a reason to think of Marx's theory as a revolutionary replacement of philosophy as such and an alternative to merely explanatory approaches to understanding modernity. By now, we have become accustomed to detaching Marx's diagnosis of capitalism from its political and practical context and to treating it as what it has always been, at least in part: a determined attempt to theorize the dynamics and crises of modern societies. As a consequence of these various interpretive shifts, we no longer assume that the relationship between the two authors is marked by any sharp break or discontinuity. Instead, we tend to view them as offering competing analyses of modern society, so that it makes sense to ask what one might have learned from the other.

My goal is to compare the theories of these two authors from this still somewhat unaccustomed perspective. My starting point will be the assumptions about the philosophy of history that served as a frame of reference for both Hegel's and Marx's diagnoses of modern society. In a second step, I then turn to the advantages of Hegel's social theory vis-à-vis that of Marx. My third step consists in reversing the perspective and considering the merits of Marx's analysis of capitalism. This will finally bring me to question under what conditions and in what way the two approaches might be brought to fruitfully complement each other.

A Shared Vision of History

Looking back to the works of Hegel and Marx from a contemporary perspective, one soon notices that their social analyses rely to a surprising degree on shared premises concerning the philosophy of history. Today, these theoretical commonalities allow us to treat the two thinkers from a comparative perspective. To be sure, many other nineteenth-century social theorists shared Hegel's and Marx's aim of uncovering the moving forces and dynamic laws of modern society. Henri Saint-Simon and Alexis de Tocqueville in France and John Stuart Mill in England can stand in for an entire spectrum of views. But even abstracting from the significant differences among these three authors, Hegel and Marx are further set apart from them by the fact that both relied on a philosophy of history to grasp the social challenges of their time. Despite the differences between them, they share the peculiar assumption that modern society is the most recent stage of a developmental process in which reason manifests itself in the external world.

It is a familiar fact that Hegel's interpretation of modern society rests on a philosophy of history that postulates a process in which spirit realizes itself. He faults both Kant and Fichte for failing to properly understand the nature of reason. Although both acknowledge that reason is the basis of all reality, they fail to see that reason is not simply a human faculty, but rather an all-comprehending entity that gradually unfolds over time until it has fully realized its own potential.[6] This ontological assumption allows Hegel to interpret the whole of human history as one particular stage in the process of spirit's self-realization. After first realizing itself in nature through its own spontaneous activity, spirit then returns back into itself and gradually lets the social world be shaped by its determinations, amounting to a "progress of the consciousness of freedom".[7] Today this framework, which appears to postulate an objective teleology of increasing freedom underlying all human history, appears quite alien to us.[8] Yet without it, Hegel's interpretation of modern society is not properly intelligible. To him, modern institutions and practices are above all embodiments of the most advanced stage within the world-historical process of an increasing consciousness of liberty, a stage marked by the realization of all the preconditions for a truly self-determined life on the part of each individual. Modern society, which Hegel views as the outcome of a drawn-out and conflict-ridden developmental process, is for him an institutional realization of freedom.[9]

Even though Marx does not subscribe to this result of Hegel's philosophy of history, he derives from it an essential element of his own interpretation of the specific structure of modern society. Born almost half a century after Hegel, Marx is no longer a philosophical idealist willing to countenance the thought that all reality is the realization of a self-determining spirit. Right at the beginning of his intellectual development, he was profoundly influenced by Feuerbach's naturalism, and the idea that all that exists is a product of the process of reason's unfolding was entirely remote to him.[10] For Marx, we as human beings are first of all surrounded by nature, and we must relate to nature in productive ways to maintain ourselves. We are capable of doing this because we have the ability to use tools, which sets us apart from all other living beings. Where Marx is at his best, he conceives of the special status of human beings as consisting in a capacity to cooperate with each other by mutually relating to one another's intentions and thus establishing an entirely new, irreducibly social class of mental operations.[11] Supplemented by recent empirical findings, this basic idea points the way to theories such as that of Tomasello, who claims the establishment of cooperative labor enabled us humans to develop basic forms of morality and multi-perspectival thinking.[12]

Despite this distance between Marx and Hegel, Marx's account of the process by which humans modify nature through their labor, based on their capacity for cooperation, closely mirrors Hegel's account of the self-development of spirit. Marx argues that once we have learned to use tools cooperatively by mutually taking up each other's perspectives, nature comes to be gradually shaped by us and comes to reflect our own rational determinations, resulting in a cumulative expansion of the realm of our freedom.[13] What Marx says here about the essential spiritual powers of man, meaning our species' capacity for cooperation, is structurally similar to the features of spirit as characterized by Hegel. Although 'reason' means two different things to them—a human capacity for Marx, a property of an all-encompassing spirit for Hegel—both think of reason as something that comes to be fully developed only by realizing itself in something external to it. The difference between the two thinkers is that Marx's naturalistic assumptions lead him to date the beginning of the process of reason's self-unfolding to a point that in Hegel's view is already the result of reason's realization in nature itself. But like Marx, Hegel views the history of human society as a process in which natural constraints are gradually diminished through the work of spiritual energy, with a corresponding increase of freedom in our social practices. These parallels show that Marx always remained Hegel's disciple regarding the central assumption that the development of society over time constitutes a "progress of the consciousness of freedom". Enabled by practices of cooperation, we give objective reality to our own spirit by laboring on the natural world surrounding us, and, in so doing, we come to be at home in that world in a way that opens up ever-increasing opportunities for shaping social norms and institutions.

Marx's adoption of Hegel's central assumptions regarding the philosophy of history explains why he, too, is forced to describe modern society as the most advanced stage in the historical evolution of social structures. Numerous passages in Marx's work show that he conceives of human history up to the present as a process of overcoming natural constraints and fetters, which comes to a preliminary conclusion in the comparatively free practices of contemporary bourgeois society.[14]

Yet, there are some differences between Marx's and Hegel's respective assessments of the balance of gains and losses as far as the freedom of modern societies is concerned. These differences are an indication that they do, after all, have somewhat different conceptions of the history of civilization, understood as a process of the self-alienation of spirit. Whereas Marx thinks of this process as consisting first and foremost in mankind's increasing domination over nature, as its emancipation from the constraints of both external and internal nature, Hegel's conception gives greater weight to the progressive transformation of the ways in which human beings relate to each other. For Hegel, the overcoming of natural limitations always has an impact on socially practiced moral norms, whereas Marx identifies such an overcoming more narrowly with an expansion of human productive forces—conceived broadly as encompassing the means to control both our environment and our own motivational potential. This fundamental difference shows that, despite their shared commitment to the self-alienation model of spirit, Hegel and Marx take quite divergent views regarding the substance and character of the process of alienation. With regard to both the content of reason and the mechanism through which reason is realized in history, there is so little consensus between them that they inevitably arrive at rather different assessments of the accomplishments of modern societies. Attending more closely to these differences between Hegel and Marx regarding the character of historical progress will make it easier to appreciate the advantages of Hegel's social theory vis-à-vis that of Marx.

Both Hegel and Marx seem to proceed on the assumption that human history is a process in which our freedom is gradually realized. In Hegel's view, this is so because spirit, having realized itself in nature and then returned into itself, seeks to embody in the world of social institutions its own determinations, which consist in its self-realization free from external constraints. Spirit must therefore manifest itself in human history and society in such a way that it gradually produces the institutional preconditions required for a free communal life of all the members of a society. As we have seen, what remains of this idealist conception in Marx is the thought that spirit or reason can realize itself only by alienating itself into something external to it. But in line with his naturalist assumptions, Marx's version of this thought focuses on the process of man's engagement with nature. This gives rise to his lifelong commitment to the idea that we as human beings are capable of making freedom an historical reality just to the extent to which we rely on our cooperative potential to turn nature into a reflection of our rational aims and thereby into a place that will accommodate those aims.

Whatever differences we may discover between Hegel and Marx will be, in my view, a consequence of the fact that they locate the social realization of reason in different spheres. Hegel locates this process in the relationship between spirit and our social institutions, because spirit has antecedently exerted itself on the natural world. Marx, by contrast, locates this process in the relationship between human reason and our natural surroundings, because he is unable to countenance a prior spiritualization of nature unmediated by social practices. This divergence can also be expressed as follows: Marx describes social progress in terms of a developmental pattern that Hegel introduced to capture the prior process of spirit's realization in nature. The result of this skewed adaptation of the Hegelian schema is perhaps best described as a neglect of the ways in which the activity of reason shapes the normative order of our institutionally regulated social life. Even though his theoretical starting point—that is, the fact of human cooperation—would have allowed Marx to attend to the phylogenetic sources of social norms, his reconstruction of our species history remains limited to the ways in which our rational capacities lead to an expansion of our dominance over nature. The realization of reason thus comes to be wholly identified by him with our increased freedom vis-à-vis the natural world. The corresponding neglect of the ways in which freedom is increased in what Habermas called the "internal framework of our social interactions" (*Binnenverhältnis unserer sozialen Interaktionen*) entails a number of disadvantages of Marx's theory compared with the implications that Hegel's philosophy has for social theory.[15]

The Advantages of Hegel's Social Theory

The first advantage of Hegel's social theory is that his concept of 'society' allows him to consider a much broader spectrum of institutional forms than can Marx, given the latter's more limited focus on the manipulation of nature. It is clear that when Hegel seeks to comprehend society as 'objective spirit', this must include for him all those social forms in which human beings learn to satisfy their merely 'natural' needs. Spirit can attain objectivity and come to be at home within a social formation only to the extent that it gives rise to the institutions that allow human beings to reproduce across generations. When Hegel speaks of what we now call 'societies',[16] he therefore has in mind a totality of social practices that are calibrated with each other by way of cultural and normative commonalities but that also, and importantly, must be capable of satisfying our most basic needs. Setting aside Hegel's idealist assumptions, the concept of 'objective spirit' anticipates in a surprising way the basic insight of classical sociology: that is, the observation that societies are normatively integrated units in which a variety of stable, institutionalized, and interconnected practices serve a range of functions essential to social reproduction. By contrast, Marx's narrower focus on humanity's relation to nature leads him to adopt a more restricted conception of society. The unfortunate term 'relations of production', often used by him synonymously with 'society', creates the impression that all of a society's institutions are ultimately aimed at the productive appropriation of nature. But neither political rule nor familial reproduction, to name just these two arenas of social activity, can be adequately understood in their normative structure by reference to economic purposes alone.

The drawbacks of Marx's terminological choices compared with Hegel's become more fully apparent when we consider the studies of Karl Polanyi, which show that only few pre-capitalist societies knew anything like a distinctive and separate sphere of economic reproduction.[17] If we are to believe Polanyi and other economic historians,[18] economic relations of labor and exchange used to be so thoroughly embedded into other social functions that they were neither experienced as self-standing activities nor normatively regulated as such. It is then quite misleading to follow Marx in conceiving of all societies as 'relations of production', as institutional manifestations of various particular forms of mastery over nature. Hegel's approach is much more persuasive here: The concept of 'objective spirit' merely captures the fact that the various spheres of social activity, including those devoted to the performance of vital functions, are in the first place manifestations of general norms and thus of something 'spiritual', whereas the specific content of those norms and the relations between the various functional spheres depend on the progression of human history. The idealist surplus of this conception, which consists in the idea that such norms are the products of a self-determining entity called 'spirit', can be removed without too much difficulty given more recent philosophical developments. We can follow John Searle and other social theorists in thinking of the 'spiritual' generation of norms as a cognitive activity performed by mutually cooperating subjects. What is then left of 'idealism' is just the claim that societies depend on a certain intersubjective consensus among their members concerning the normative regulation of each of the various functional spheres.[19]

Things are no different regarding a further point of comparison between Hegel and Marx: namely, the question of how to think about the social mechanism by which the progressive realization of freedom is brought about over the course of human history. Here, too, the German idealist seems to be better positioned than his materialist successor. As we have seen, both thinkers proceed from the assumption that this process should be regarded as a consequence of the gradual externalization or alienation of spiritual processes, that is, the interaction of spirit with something other than itself. In Hegel's theory, for systematic reasons, this 'other' encompasses all the institutions that are required for the reproduction of a society. For Marx, on the other hand, spirit's 'other' is external and internal nature, both of which we can gradually master thanks to our cooperative abilities, and in which we can, in this way, come to be at home.

If we now ask how each of the two philosophers proposes to explain the dynamic driving this process of reason's self-realization, we can see that Hegel's explanatory strategy has some distinct advantages. Even though he thinks of the realization of reason as a process effected by reason itself, and in that sense as an automatic development, he also needs to offer at least a broadly plausible account of how this kind of progress in human history can be understood as a worldly, social occurrence. Here he relies on the instructive idea that an historical form of life comes to an end when it no longer offers sufficient normative space for the realization of those claims on the part of individuals that have been able to arise on the basis of the ethical structure of this form of life.[20] Thus, for Hegel, each social formation contains the seeds of its own transformation, because it inevitably leads some groups of people to develop moral hopes and expectations that cannot be properly realized within the established institutional framework. It is true that this 'moral' explanation is sociologically unsatisfactory, as it leaves us largely in the dark about the way in which these structurally unsatisfiable claims are supposed to arise in the context of social conflicts. Only in a few places does Hegel let on that he conceives of this kind of conflict as a struggle for recognition, in which desires for the social realization of new and previously unknown freedoms clash with an established social order that immanently gives rise to these very desires. But this brief sketch suffices to show how fertile Hegel's endeavor is to find an everyday social complement to the self-propelled process of spirit's self-realization in objective institutions. Enriched by sociological hypotheses, Hegel's basic approach can be developed into the fruitful idea that what drives the historical process of freedom's realization is the occurrence of struggles for the social inclusion of previously excluded groups.[21]

By comparison, Marx's account of the social mechanism said to be responsible for the gradual extension of our freedom looks much less convincing. As many have observed,[22] his explanatory proposals generally rely on a technological determinism that tends to obscure, rather than illuminate, the connection he asserts between an increased mastery over nature and an increase in freedom. The point of departure for this explanatory model is again the thesis that our capacity for cooperation enables us increasingly to appropriate both external and internal nature. But when it comes to explaining the driving force of progress in the realization of freedom, Marx attends only to the latter dimension, our relation to the natural world around us. Marx's term for the extent of our dominion over this aspect of nature at any given time is 'productive force', which refers to the totality of technological means and methods that a society has at its disposal to exploit existing natural resources for its own purposes. In a second step, Marx thinks that our ability to constantly improve and increase our capacity for cooperation entails an historical process whereby a society's productive forces are constantly increased. He believes that the further history progresses, the greater becomes societies' technical capacity for the productive appropriation of the natural world. The decisive step in Marx's explanation is the third one. He asserts that the institutional structures of all societies—all that he attempts to subsume under the term 'relations of production'—are characterized by a certain inertia and rigidity, so that any boost in productive forces brings with it a lagging adjustment of those institutional structures to the new technologies and modes of production. The essence of Marx's explanation is thus that endogenous progress in the technological capacities for manipulating the natural world regularly and necessarily brings in its wake a normative improvement in the modes of social interaction.[23]

What remains especially unclear about this model is why we should believe that the development of productive forces will at each stage lead institutionalized social orders to realize a greater degree of freedom. Although it may be true in some trivial sense that technological advances increase our elbowroom vis-à-vis natural constraints, it is quite dubious to infer from this an automatic increase in social freedom. Often the contrary will be the case, and improved technologies will endanger the continued existence of previously attained liberties. Marx's proposed explanation of the gradual realization of freedom is far too optimistic regarding the normative potential inherent in the development of productive forces. Unlike Hegel, he believes that technological progress as such is capable of liberating institutionalized social orders from social domination and inherited dependencies.

As though he had a sense of this weakness, Marx supplemented his first explanatory approach by a second one, developed at least in broad outline.[24] On this second proposal, the moving force behind the social realization of freedom is not simply the endogenous growth of our technological abilities, but rather the struggles of oppressed social classes for the realization of their needs and interests. It becomes apparent in the *Communist Manifesto* in particular that this alternative model is not entirely independent of the first one because Marx ties the interests of the various classes struggling for predominance to the opportunities for influence afforded by a given stage in the development of productive forces.[25] Just as the bourgeoisie is said to have begun fighting for social domination at the very moment in history when its increased control over the means of production allowed it to do so, the proletariat will also be in a position to come to power once the new factory system has created the necessary economic preconditions. It is easily seen that this second explanation of social progress, which focuses on the transformative power of class struggle, still fails to accord an independent role to the historically changing ensemble of social practices. Instead, Marx claims that progress in the realization of freedom ultimately results from a series of struggles of oppressed groups fighting for the social predominance of their respective economic interests—as though we were entitled to assume that all premodern societies had already established and been centered around something like a distinctive sphere of economic production. Thus, Marx's second explanatory proposal, too, does not measure up to Hegel's approach of postulating a social equivalent to the self-realization of spirit in social institutions. Instead of leaving open exactly what kind of social inclusion and recognition are at issue in any given social group's struggle, Marx simply assumes the primacy of economic interests in a way unsupported by historical evidence. This reinforces the earlier observation that Marx was unwise to reduce the large range of forms of social organization to the unitary category of 'relations of production'.

A third drawback of Marx's economic reductionism comes into focus when we compare his analysis of the achievements of modern societies with Hegel's. As we saw above, both thinkers proceed on the assumption that the modern social order is the most advanced stage of the world-historical process of reason's self-realization, because the modern set of social institutions has considerably extended the space of individual liberties. Like Hegel, Marx holds that the overcoming of feudal and aristocratic social orders amounted to a liberation from the fetters of inherited dependencies and forms of subjection, so that persons now enjoy much more extensive opportunities for individual self-determination.[26] But when it comes to the further theoretical task of offering a more detailed account of those newly created liberties, we find substantial differences between the two thinkers, which I already briefly mentioned at the outset. Hegel's view was that the 'rationality' of the modern social order consists in the fact that it offers its members a whole spectrum of social roles that will allow them to realize their individuality under the conditions of mutual recognition, and in that sense freely. For Hegel, this includes all the central institutions of the new social order: the family, founded on mutual sympathy, the market, and the state. Taken together, these three spheres of activity were regarded by Hegel as amounting to a modern form of 'ethical life', a term he employed to indicate that individual freedom is realized in the shared exercise of established practices rather than in private acts of choice.[27] Yet despite asserting the primacy of communicative freedom over personal or private freedom, Hegel never went so far as to doubt the normative significance of modern structures of right. On the contrary, throughout his work he continued to regard the then only recently established principle of free and equal liberties as a central achievement of modern societies, because these liberties require the state to protect each individual's opportunity to check and consolidate his or her ethical decisions without the intervention of others.

This is an issue on which Marx is quite unsure how to position himself. For one, Marx harbors substantial doubts concerning Hegel's entire doctrine of ethical life, since he suspects it of glossing over the defects of actually existing social structures. I say more on this below. But in addition to this, Marx doubts that modern liberal rights should really be accorded the normative significance that his predecessor attributed to them. If we recall how Marx pictures the historical process whereby freedom is realized in the world, we are led to a quite different assessment of the achievements of modern societies. What is distinctive of this new social structure is an extension of freedom not in the interpersonal domain, but rather with respect to the relation between the human species and its natural environment. Marx believes that the liberties gained in this way, which are embodied in vastly increased productive capacities, are not yet adequately reflected in the capitalist relations of production. Our increased ability to control natural processes and to harness them for our own purposes calls for a different type of social freedom than the one established within the present institutional order. As Marx sees it, owing to social inertia, these present arrangements reflect a purely private and egoistical conception of freedom. The massively improved technologies and methods of production create the possibility—and indeed the historical need—to replace this narrow, market-based conception of freedom by a broader, cooperative conception. In the present day, the only social relations of production adequate to the state of modern productive forces would be ones that subject the organization of labor and the distribution of goods to the shared will of freely cooperating producers. But however engaging and forward-looking this socialist vision may be, it leads Marx to completely overlook the democratic potential of modern liberal rights. The protection of individual self-determination afforded by such rights appeared to him to be too focused on private interests and therefore to be of a piece with the competitive economic system of capitalism. Hence, he regarded them not as normative achievements of a new social order but as remnants of a declining one.[28]

On this point too, then, Hegel's strengths outweigh those of Marx. It is true that Hegel, like Marx, has deep reservations about the liberal tendency to equate individual freedom with the liberty to pursue one's own private interests without restraint. Like his materialist successor, Hegel does not yet recognize the enormous contribution these liberal rights were to make in advancing democratic political decision making on the part of equal citizens. Nevertheless, Hegel viewed the novel principle of according all members of a society an equal right to individual self-determination as an irreversible achievement of modern societies. Unlike Marx, he was convinced that any other, more communicative or ethical form of freedom would continue to require as its normative basis a protected right on the part of individuals to develop and pursue their own particular aims.[29]

Marx's Insights and Their Possible Place in Hegel's Social Theory

What I have been saying so far might make it appear as though Hegel's social theory was in every respect superior to Marx's historical materialism. With regard to an adequately complex conception of society, to the identification of the moving force behind the realization of freedom, and to the diagnosis of the normative achievements of modernity, Hegel offers explanations that are better or at any rate more fruitful for our purposes today. Yet, this initial comparison is misleading to the extent that it is exclusively focused on the conceptual resources for a social theory supplemented by a philosophy of history. Once we direct our attention away from these foundational issues and toward the empirical content of the two rival theories, things begin to look somewhat different and the advantages of Marx's social analysis come to light. In this final section, I present this other side of the balance sheet in broad outline. In doing so, it is important to bear in mind that Marx had the benefit of an additional fifty years' time to observe the actual development of modern societies. Whereas Hegel devised his social theory at the outset of capitalist industrialization, Marx was writing at the apex of that development, placing him in an advantageous epistemic position regarding the destructive potential of the modern economic order. It is likely that the advantages of his social theory vis-à-vis Hegel's are partly owed to this surplus of historical experience, but also in part to the greater depth of his analysis of power and domination.

As we have seen, Hegel assumed that the world-historical process of a "progress of the consciousness of freedom" had reached at least a preliminary conclusion in the social structure of modern ethical life. He took himself to be entitled to this judgment because in his view the three spheres of modern society—the family based on reciprocal affection, the capitalist market, and the modern constitutional state—provided the institutional preconditions that would allow the members of this society to realize their particularity through free cooperation with others, based on the legal protection of their individual freedom of choice.[30] It is just this image of modern society that

Marx is unwilling and unable to accept. Based on his research on political economy, he assumes against Hegel that the second element of this tripartite structure, the capitalist market, contains destructive forces that undermine both the freedom of the individual and the normative autonomy of the two other spheres. To be sure, Hegel also had been skeptical of the market system (i.e., of what he called 'civil society'). In his *Philosophy of Right*, he therefore recommended that the threat of market excesses be held in check by regulative and cooperative institutions.[31] But the Marxian notion that the existence of a sphere that allows for the free exchange of economic goods and services might undermine the entire web of ethical practice remained alien to Hegel. Yet, this was just what Marx's critique of political economy was intended to demonstrate and to illustrate, and his efforts yielded a number of insights with which we can substantially enrich Hegel's social theory.

In developing this critical project, all the comparative disadvantages of Marx's theory discussed so far paradoxically work in his favor. The conceptual reduction of society to a set of 'relations of production' allows him to focus exclusively on the economic sphere and to study its development in abstraction from political or institutional influences. Here, Marx attends to several important phenomena that had been only dimly foreseen in Hegel's *Philosophy of Right*, if at all. Thus he argues that the employment contract, one of the normative foundations of the new economic order, does not fulfill its promise of realizing individual freedom of choice because those who depend on wage payments are forced to agree to the contract's terms given their lack of alternative options for making a living.[32] Moreover, according to Marx, their productive labor generates a surplus value for which they are not compensated, so that they are subject to structural and unjustifiable exploitation.[33] The entrepreneur reaping the resulting profits is for his part continually forced to reinvest his gains with the aim of generating further profit, requiring him to tap ever-new markets for his products. This gives the capitalist market an expansionary dynamic, leading to a gradual subjection of all areas of life under the principle of marketability, which Marx calls 'real subsumption',[34] and resulting also in a further expansion of the capitalist's power, to the point where government turns into class domination and the rule of law yields to 'class justice'. These four elements of Marx's analysis of capitalism are complemented by an explanation of why it is so difficult for those involved in this economic system to understand its harmful mechanisms. The explanation, in his view, lies in the existence of legitimizing, concealing, and obfuscating interpretations that he calls 'ideologies'. One of his aims is to show that practices of economic exchange necessarily give rise to such ideologies.[35]

Not all of these basic assumptions of Marx's analysis of capitalism have survived the critical scrutiny to which his theory was soon subjected. Some claims have needed refinement in the light of objections from economists and other social scientists and some claims have had to be abandoned altogether. For instance, there is probably hardly anyone today who still subscribes to Marx's labor theory of economic value, which forms the background of his thesis about the structural exploitation of wage laborers. Similarly contested are his assumptions concerning the cognitive effects of ideologies said to emerge in some way from the economic practices themselves. But the two central elements of Marx's analysis of capitalism—his thesis about the unfreedom of wage laborers and his thesis about the expansionary dynamic inherent in the competitive market—have turned out to be resilient in the face of later developments and hardly open to doubt. Especially after witnessing the so-called neoliberal breakdown of economic barriers over the past several decades, we can safely assume today that there is a pressure inherent in our economic system that tends to undermine individual freedom of choice both for wage laborers and in other areas of life. But this sober observation should prompt us to turn to Hegel's social theory once again.

We have seen that, despite its philosophical merits, the engagement of Hegel's social theory with contemporary society did not take sufficient account of the perilous dynamic of capitalist economic systems. Therefore, the question now is how the aspects of capitalism identified by Marx might be incorporated into the framework of Hegel's social theory without completely destroying its inner architectonic. In conclusion, I would like to offer some conjectures about how this problem might be addressed.

Every attempt to reconcile the two theories in the way just hinted at—that is, by retaining a mitigated version of the German idealist's social theory and supplementing it with the results of his materialist disciple's analysis of capitalism—faces a number of serious obstacles. The greatest challenge is certainly the fact that Marx presented his analysis of capitalism in a way that seems to shield it from any attempt at adapting it for other purposes. The internal structure and the expansive dynamic of the modern economic system are depicted, under the influence of Hegel yet in an idiosyncratic fashion, as though they were being caused by the automatic activity of 'capital', forming a closed cycle immune to external influences. Whichever interpretation of this methodology one chooses, whether one regards it as modeled on Hegel's *Logic* or rather on his *Phenomenology*,[36] it is not straightforwardly compatible with Hegel's sketch of a social theory. For Hegel, after all, social structures are shaped most basically not by 'capital', but rather by an 'objective spirit' consisting of shared social norms.

To integrate the results of Marx's analysis of capitalism into the framework of Hegel's social theory, we need first and foremost to break through Marx's apocryphal mode of presentation. We must abandon the idea that 'capital', like Hegel's 'spirit', proceeds autonomously and pervades all areas of society with its inner dynamic. Instead, we should adopt a much more open conception of the capitalist economic sphere that gives due place to the influence of changing social norms.[37] Only through such a reorientation of political economy can we do justice to the historical fact that the opportunity to pursue the profit principle varies with institutional and cultural circumstances, being much greater today, for instance, than forty or fifty years ago.[38]

A consequence of this first modification is that the capitalist economy comes to be seen as partly dependent on the content of the institutional rules that Hegel designated by the term 'objective spirit'. A second modification that is needed to fuse Marx's analysis of capitalism with a social theory inspired by Hegel concerns not its explanatory content but its sociological framing. We have already seen that Marx's notion of 'relations of production' depicts all social spheres as directly or indirectly concerned with the goal of mastery over nature. In the context of his analysis of capitalism, this gives rise to the problem that he lacks the conceptual resources to identify just what norms are being violated when the dynamic capitalist principle of marketization comes to permeate other spheres of social life.[39] Another way of describing this deficit would be by saying that Marx lacks an understanding of the functional complexity of societies, which requires that different spheres of activity be subject to different sets of norms that allow those activities to fulfill their various specific functions. He is therefore unable to explain why we should find it in any way dangerous or problematic when the capitalist principles of profitability and marketization come to inform and eventually to dominate other areas of social reproduction not previously governed by economic concerns. Thus on this point, too, Marx's analysis of capitalism needs certain revisions if it is to become a fruitful element of a Hegelian social theory. What is needed is an awareness that, within modern societies, the capitalist market is only one sphere of social activity among others and that each of these spheres serves particular functions requiring that its activities be governed by their own specific set of norms.

What I have just said indicates that Hegel's social theory, for its part, does not meet all the requirements that it would need to fulfill to fruitfully incorporate the important insights of Marx's analysis of capitalism. If Marx lacks an understanding of the functional complexity of modern societies, Hegel fails to recognize that there can be deep normative tensions between the various functionally specialized social spheres.[40] Hegel's doctrine of ethical life admits the possibility that failures on the part of the state or deficits of rationality on the part of its members may cause the norms governing any particular sphere to dry up, as it were. But he does not allow for the possibility that one of these different sets of norms might intrude into other social spheres and undermine or incapacitate the norms proper to them. We could say that Hegel took the process of social differentiation to be an irreversible given, something that could not possibly be changed by future developments. Whatever other internal threats a modern, rationally ordered society might face, the functional separation among the family, the market, and the state is taken for granted as a permanent feature of the new social order of modern societies. Yet this assumption deprives Hegel's theory of the conceptual means to analyze the kinds of processes that Marx sought to describe under the aspect of a 'subsumption' of all spheres of life under relations of capital. Hegel never allowed for the possibility that the capitalist mindset might come to intrude into the non-economic spheres of life. In this respect, then, his theory stands in need of fundamental revision. The functional differentiation of modern societies should not be regarded as a permanent empirical given but merely as a normative goal that may be more or less fully realized in a society's institutions at any given time, depending on the social struggles present at that moment.

This is not the only element of Hegel's social theory that needs to be systematically revised if his theory is to serve today as a conceptual framework for Marx's analysis of capitalism. A further revision concerns Hegel's reliance on the idea that the notion of contract supplies the economic system of the market with a legal foundation that ensures its general rationality and legitimacy, since the obligations of contracting parties are voluntarily undertaken. What is wrong with this picture is not the idea that contract is a legitimate basis of the new economic order in that it grants to each individual the freedom to determine how to employ his or her economic resources and services, in contrast with previous economic systems resting on personal ties and dependencies. This normative virtue of contract-based economic orders is one that

Adam Smith articulated quite clearly in *The Wealth of Nations*, so that Hegel was able simply to follow him on this point.[41] The problematic aspect of Hegel's view lies rather in the fact that he simply transposes the features of contracts between commercial parties onto the relationship between entrepreneurs and wage laborers. His naïve disregard for the influence of duress and coercion testifies to his more general tendency to neglect the phenomena of power and domination. Hegel's doctrine of ethical life seems to be completely unaware of the possibility that individuals' consent to existing, 'ethical' obligations may be owed, not to rational considerations, but instead to a lack of alternatives, to threats of force, or to subtle persuasion. Yet these are just the kinds of factors that Marx aimed to place at the center of his account of capitalism when he depicted the apparent voluntariness of the employment contract as a mere illusion, given that those dependent on wages had no choice but to consent or face indigence. Hegel's faith that the ethical structure of modern societies had given institutional reality to the idea of freedom led him to completely overlook the kinds of social mechanisms that continue even today to contribute to the coercion and oppression of particular groups of people. He went astray in dating the conclusion of the historical struggle for inclusion and recognition to the beginning of modernity and in depicting social relations after this point only in the optimistic terms of voluntary and uncoerced cooperation.

Correcting this serious deficit of Hegel's social theory would require more than simply supplementing his model of modern ethical life with the notions of force and coercion. Rather, it would require that we use Hegel's own categories to demonstrate for each of the social spheres which mechanisms inherent to it enable some subset of its participants to dominate others: for instance, how the norms of love and mutual affection may be used by men to oppress women, or the norms of loyalty to country be used to mobilize consent, by way of a 'naturalization' and rigidification of the associated duties. Only when this has been accomplished—that is, only once it has been shown that the different institutional forms of mutual recognition can give rise to specific kinds of exclusion and coercion[42]—can the results of Marx's analysis of capitalism be properly incorporated into Hegel's social theory. For only then can the deprivations of freedom generated by the market and targeted by Marx's critique of political economy be integrated into a more comprehensive picture of modern societies, one that extends its focus to other forms of oppression as well.

The various revisions I have outlined still take us only halfway toward the goal of establishing a cross-fertilizing relationship between Hegel's and Marx's approaches to social theory. So far, I have not mentioned what is surely the greatest challenge facing such a conciliation of views: namely, to revise Hegel's concept of spirit in such a way that it would come to be at least somewhat closer to Marx's theoretical starting point, that is to say, the cooperation among socially embedded individuals. My call for revisions on both sides notwithstanding, the question remains how one might go about reconciling materialism and idealism, the image of man placed in nature and the appeal to a self-determining spirit. But for the purposes of this contribution, I hope to have shown that Marx's analysis of capitalism could only benefit from being embedded within a social theory derived from Hegel. The valuable insights contained in the younger philosopher's theory could be better and more accurately articulated if they were transposed into the framework developed by his older predecessor.[43]

Notes

1. Clear evidence of this is found in the debate about the extent of Kant's influence on Marx, which goes back to the late nineteenth century; see *Marxismus und Ethik*, ed. Hans Jörg Sandkühler and Rafael de la Vega (Frankfurt: Suhrkamp, 1970).
2. One example is Herbert Marcuse, "New Sources on the Foundation of Historical Materialism" (1932), in *Heideggerian Marxism*, ed. Richard Wolin and John Abromeit (Lincoln and London: University of Nebraska Press, 2005), 86–121.
3. A useful overview is offered by Jürgen Habermas, "Literaturbericht zur philosophischen Debatte um Marx und den Marxismus," in *Theorie und Praxis. Sozialphilosophische Studien*, 2nd edn (Frankfurt: Suhrkamp, 1971), 387–463, esp. 402–13.
4. Cf. especially Charles Taylor, *Hegel and Modern Society* (Cambridge: Cambridge University Press, 1979).
5. Honneth, *The Struggle for Recognition: The Moral Grammar of Social Conflicts* (Cambridge: Polity, 1995); Michael Quante, *Spirit's Actuality* (Münster: Mentis, 2018), 171–86.
6. For a concise but very accurate summary, see Dina Emundts and Rolf-Peter Horstmann, *Georg Wilhelm Friedrich Hegel. Eine Einführung* (Stuttgart: Reclam, 2002), 32–7.
7. Georg Wilhelm Friedrich Hegel, *Lectures on the Philosophy of World History*, Vol. 1: *Manuscripts of the Introduction and the Lectures of 1822-3*, ed. and trans. by Robert F. Brown and Peter C. Hodgson (Cambridge: Cambridge University Press, 2011), 88; Joseph McCarney, *Hegel on History* (London: Routledge, 2000), ch. 8.
8. There is an ongoing debate about whether Hegel's philosophy of history is in fact best read as asserting that world history exhibits an 'objective' teleology ensuring the realization of freedom; Hegel, *Elements of the Philosophy of Right*, ed. Stephen Houlgate, trans. T.M. Knox (New York: Oxford University Press, 2008). Many of the relevant passages also admit of a more Kantian interpretation to the effect that such a teleology is found in human history only when the latter is regarded from the perspective of a philosophical outlook committed to reason. This becomes especially clear in Hegel, *Philosophy of Mind*, trans. W. Wallace and A.V. Miller, rev. and ed. Michael Inwood (Oxford: Oxford University Press, 2007), §§ 548–9.
9. On Hegel's ambitions in this book, see Honneth, *The Pathologies of Individual Freedom: Hegel's Social Theory* (Princeton: Princeton University Press, 2010), and "The Realm of Actualized Freedom: Hegel's Notion of 'Philosophy of Right'," in *The I in the We: Studies in the Theory of Recognition* (Cambridge: Polity Press, 2012), 19–31.
10. Karl Löwith, *From Hegel to Nietzsche. The Revolution in Nineteenth-Century Thought* (New York: Holt, Rinehart and Winston, 1964), 65–121; Daniel Brudney, *Marx's Attempt to Leave Philosophy* (Cambridge, MA: Harvard University Press, 1998), 6–12.
11. Cf. especially Marx, "Comments on James Mill's *Éléments D'économie Politique*," *Marx & Engels Collected Works* (MECW), Vol. 3 (London: Lawrence & Wishart, 1975), esp. 227, and Marx, *Economic and Philosophic Manuscripts*, MECW 3, esp. 270–82. More generally on this topic, see Brudney, *Marx's Attempt*, ch. 5.
12. Michael Tomasello, *A Natural History of Human Morality* (Cambridge, MA: Harvard University Press, 2016), ch. 3.
13. See Marx's famous dictum that "the history of industry" is "the open book of man's essential powers" (Marx, *Economic and Philosophic Manuscripts*, 302).
14. See the reference to the "most revolutionary part" the "bourgeoisie" played in history; Marx and Engels, *Manifesto of the Communist Party*, MECW 6: 486.

15　Habermas, "Labor and Interaction," in *Theory and Practice*, trans. John Viertel (Boston: Beacon, 1973), 142–69.
16　Hegel's own use of the term 'society' (*Gesellschaft*) is limited to the 'system of needs' (*System der Bedürfnisse*), to which he also refers as 'bourgeois society' (*bürgerliche Gesellschaft*) in his *Philosophy of Right*. What he has in mind by these latter terms, following Adam Smith, is the historically recent structure of a capitalist market society; cf. Franz Rosenzweig, *Hegel und der Staat*, ed. Frank Lachmann (Berlin: Suhrkamp, 2010 [1920]), 391–401, and Paul Vogel, *Hegels Gesellschaftsbegriff und seine geschichtliche Fortbildung durch Lorenz Stein, Marx, Engels und Lassalle* (Berlin: Heise, 1925). In the present context, when I speak of Hegel's concept of society I have in mind what Hegel calls 'objective spirit' (concretely represented in particular 'national spirits'), that is to say, the most general unit to which processes of social differentiation can be attributed.
17　Karl Polanyi, *Ökonomie und Gesellschaft* (Frankfurt: Suhrkamp, 1979), part 2, and *The Great Transformation: The Political and Economic Origins of Our Time*, 2nd edn (Boston: Beacon, 2001), esp. ch. 4–5.
18　Marcel Mauss, *The Gift: Forms and Functions of Exchange in Archaic Societies* (London: Norton, 1969).
19　See John Searle, *The Construction of Social Reality* (New York: Free Press, 1995). An interesting comparison, along with a critique of Searle from a Hegelian perspective, is offered by Sebastian Ostritsch, "Hegel and Searle on the Necessity of Social Reality," *Rivista di Estetica* 57 (2014): 205–18.
20　The model for this explanation is Hegel's interpretation of Sophocles's Antigone in his *Phenomenology of Spirit*, trans. A.V. Miller (Oxford: Oxford University Press, 1977). On the interpretation proposed here, see more generally Arvi Särkelä, "Ein Drama in drei Akten. Der Kampf um öffentliche Anerkennung nach Dewey und Hegel," *Deutsche Zeitschrift für Philosophie* 61 (2013): 681–96.
21　Following Hegel, an explanation of this sort was offered by John Dewey, *Lectures in China, 1919–1920* (Honolulu: University of Hawaii Press, 1973), 64–71.
22　Among others, cf. Cornelius Castoriadis, *The Imaginary Institution of Society*, trans. by Kathleen Blamey (Cambridge: Polity, 1997 [1975]), ch. I.2.
23　See, especially, Marx, *A Contribution to the Critique of Political Economy*, MECW 29, "Preface," 262–4.
24　On the tension between these two interpretative models, cf. Castoriadis, *The Imaginary Institution*, 29–32.
25　Marx and Engels, *Manifesto*.
26　See Frederick Neuhouser, "Marx (und Hegel) zur Philosophie der Freiheit," in *Nach Marx. Philosophie, Kritik, Praxis*, ed. Rahel Jaeggi and Daniel Loick (Berlin: Suhrkamp, 2013), 25–47, esp. 39–40.
27　Neuhouser, *Foundations of Hegel's Social Theory. Actualizing Freedom* (Cambridge, MA: Harvard University Press, 2000).
28　Cf. Marx, "On the Jewish Question," MECW 3. For more detailed commentary, see Honneth, *The Idea of Socialism* (Cambridge: Polity Press, 2017), 34–7.
29　Neuhouser, "Marx (und Hegel) zur Philosophie der Freiheit."
30　At the same time, Hegel faces great difficulties in establishing that the state, too, is a sphere of intersubjectivity that is enabling of freedom. These difficulties have been treated, with impressive precision, by Michael Theunissen, "The Repressed Intersubjectivity in Hegel's Philosophy of Right," in *Hegel and Legal Theory*, ed. D. Cornell, M. Rosenfeld, and D. Carlson (London: Routledge, 1991), 3–63.

31 Hans-Christoph Schmidt am Busch, 'Anerkennung' als Prinzip der Kritischen Theorie (Berlin: de Gruyter, 2011), part III.
32 Marx, *Capital I*, MECW 35: 177–86.
33 Ibid., 51–6.
34 Ibid., 509–19.
35 Ibid., 81–94.
36 See Helmut Reichelt, *Zur logischen Struktur des Kapitalbegriffs bei Karl Marx* (Frankfurt: Suhrkamp, 1973); Volkam Çidam, *Die Phänomenologie des Widergeistes. Eine anerkennungstheoretische Deutung von Marx' normativer Kritik im Kapital* (Baden-Baden: Nomos, 2012).
37 I have put forward a proposal of this kind in Honneth, "Die Moral im 'Kapital,'" in *Nach Marx*, 350–63.
38 See, for instance, Wolfgang Streeck, *Buying Time: The Delayed Crisis of Democratic Capitalism*, 2nd edn (London: Verso, 2017); David Kotz, *The Rise and Fall of Neoliberal Capitalism* (Cambridge, MA: Harvard University Press, 2015).
39 Habermas, "Literaturbericht zur philosophischen Debatte," and *The Theory of Communicative Action*, Vol. 2: *Lifeworld and System: A Critique of Functionalist Reason*, trans. Thomas McCarthy (Boston: Beacon 1985), ch. VIII, 2.
40 On these difficulties regarding the foundational concepts of the traditional theory of social differentiation, see Uwe Schimank and Ute Volkmann, "Economizing and Marketization in a Functionally Differentiated Capitalist Society: A Theoretical Conceptualization," in *The Marketization of Society: Economizing the Non-Economic*, ed. Uwe Schimank and Ute Volkmann (Bremen: Forschungsverbund 'Welfare Societies', 2012), 37–63.
41 Lisa Herzog, *Inventing the Market: Smith, Hegel and Political Theory* (Oxford: Oxford University Press, 2013).
42 Some initial suggestions can be found in Honneth, "Recognition as Ideology: The Connection between Morality and Power," in *The I in the We*, 75–97.
43 My thanks to Juliane Rebentisch and Ferdinand Sutterlüty for helpful comments and suggestions. Text translated from German by Felix Koch.

3

Hegel, Marx, and Presentism

Emmanuel Renault

Presentism is far from being an easily defined philosophical notion. It is not a category that belongs to the vocabulary of the philosophical tradition and it is subject to various contemporary uses. On the one hand, this notion can be used to articulate a historical diagnosis. It then denotes the fact that our contemporary experience of history would be characterized by some kind of tyranny of the present, correlated with a vanishing of the past and future as dimensions of our experience of history.[1] On the other hand, it can be used in a series of philosophical debates: firstly, in ontological debates, to denote a variety of actualism;[2] secondly, in epistemological debates concerning the relations between knowledge of the past and present;[3] and thirdly, in theory of action, where it denotes the contention that action is to be explained by interactions with the actual environment rather than by causal antecedents or by the representation of goals to be reached in the future.[4] As a comprehensive philosophical notion, presentism can also refer to Mead and Dewey's defense of a 'philosophy of the present' that consisted of assuming a primacy of the present from practical, ontological, and epistemological points of view.[5] Dewey and Mead supported a presentist theory of action, in the sense mentioned above. They also supported an ontological and epistemological version of pragmatism, since they pointed out that these actual interactions are the locus of reality and that knowledge is a tool intended to solve actual practical problems. Even if Dewey and Mead's presentism was part of the Hegelian "deposit in their thinking",[6] it would make no sense to define Hegel's own presentism from a pragmatist point of view in order to disclose the Hegelian origins of Marx's presentism. It would neither make sense to presuppose that Hegel's or Marx's presentism is just as explicit and consistent as Dewey's or Mead's presentism. Hegel's presentism consists of a set of converging ontological, epistemological, and political orientations of his writings rather than a general principle, and in Marx, it is mostly the political and epistemological presentism that deserves consideration.

In what follows, rather than taking the point of view of contemporary debates and contemporary uses of the notion of presentism, I analyze the functions given by Hegel to his own references to the present, and I contend that his philosophy can be labelled 'presentist' in two respects: firstly, because it depicts the present as the most legitimate philosophical object; secondly, because the concepts and methods he uses to focus on the present also give some kind of primacy to the present. I also contend that not only the Young Hegelian Marx but also the mature Marx draws on this Hegelian presentism to elaborate his own views. My purpose is twofold: to shed light on certain dimensions of the Hegel–Marx relation that have been ignored by the numerous debates on this relation; and to recall that series of concepts or methodological traits of contemporary critical theory, such as historical diagnosis, immanent critique, or interconnection of social critique with knowledge of the contemporary situation, were originally rooted in Hegel's and Marx's presentism, and should still be thought of in presentist terms.

On the Relation between Hegel and Marx

It could seem highly paradoxical to analyze Hegel's presentism rather than his concepts of dialectics and alienation, if the purpose is to shed light on the Hegel–Marx relation. But this paradox is also the symptom of the fact that, until recently, debates concerning the relation between Hegel and Marx have deeply suffered from unconscious, retrospective bias. The main contributors to these debates have assumed a Marxian perspective on Hegel while pretending to elaborate Hegelian readings of Marx. To put it provocatively, they have elaborated Marxian readings of Hegel in order to show that Marx was a true Hegelian, just as Thomists have elaborated Thomist readings of Aristotle in order to show that Thomas Aquinas was a true Aristotelian. It is not less paradoxical that even those who wanted to depict Marx as a non-Hegelian nevertheless presupposed a traditional Marxist image of Hegel.

Let's consider the concepts of dialectics and alienation as an illustration. They are usually depicted as the two main Hegelian concepts that Marx would have taken on from Hegel and that would constitute the Hegelian core of his thought. For an author such as Lukács, there is no doubt that this hypothesis is relevant,[7] whereas for Althusser, for instance, the concept of alienation no longer plays any decisive role in the mature Marx, while the concept of dialectics is understood in a non-Hegelian sense.[8] Nevertheless, both Lukács and Althusser agree on the fact that dialectics and alienation are the two major concepts in addressing the Hegel–Marx relation. Neither of them takes into account the fact that the concept of alienation is not central in Hegel's writings. It plays a substantial role only in the *Phenomenology of Spirit*—more precisely, section B of chapter VI (as *Entfremdung*) and chapter VIII (as *Entäusserung*)—and it is not even the same concept of alienation that is then at play. How, then, could a unified concept of alienation define a Hegelian deposit in Marx's writings? It is worth noting that in his most Hegelian period, that of his *Dissertation* (1841) and the articles in the *Rheinische Zeitung* (1842–1843), Marx makes no decisive use of this concept. It is only later, in the *Parisian Manuscripts*, when he starts to distance himself radically from Hegel, adopting a Feuerbachian perspective, that this concept becomes central. But then, in 1844, it is not so much on Hegel than on Feuerbach and Hess that Marx draws when he elaborates his own reflections on alienation. He indeed reads Hegel's *Phenomenology* as a philosophy of alienation, but this reading clearly consists of a reconstruction of Hegel from a Feuerbachian and Hessian point of view. The purpose of this reading is not to disclose the true Hegel, but to decide in what respect the Hegelian presuppositions of the Young Hegelians are compatible with the criticism of Hegel elaborated by Feuerbach. What is also at stake is to decide in which respect B. Bauer's concept of alienation is compatible with Hess and Feuerbach's concepts of alienation. Indeed, Marx is more responsible than Bauer, Feuerbach and Hess for the promotion of the notion of alienation as one of the main concepts of the philosophical tradition and of critical history. But this also means that it is Marx himself, and not Hegel, who is responsible for the fact that it has become conventional to read Hegel through the lens of a theory of alienation.[9]

Similar considerations apply to the concept of dialectics. In the Marxist debate concerning the Hegel–Marx connection, it is usually not taken into account that "dialectics" occupies a lower rank than "speculation" in Hegel's own definition of these notions in the Logic of the *Encyclopedia* (§81–2). Nor it is taken into account that the concept of dialectics was not considered central to Hegel's thought in the first phases of the development of the Hegelian school. Interestingly, this concept was never used in the Young Hegelian period of Marx. The only occurrences come up in the *Parisian Manuscripts*, but then, 'dialectics' is understood in a non-Hegelian and often pejorative sense.[10] Moreover, in the first phases of the development of the mature Marxian thought, 'dialectics' does not play a greater role. There are no traces of some kind of appropriation of a Hegelian concept of dialectics in *The German Ideology, The Poverty of Philosophy* and *The Communist Manifesto*. It is only after having reread Hegel's *Science of Logic*, while preparing the *Grundrisse*, that Marx will give a theoretical function to this concept. The famous reference, in *Capital*'s postface, to the necessity of a transformation of Hegel's dialectics into a materialist dialectics, should certainly be taken seriously, and there is no doubt that it has strongly contributed to the perception of 'dialectics' as one of the major concepts in Hegel's thought. But here again, just as with alienation, retrospective readings should not be confused with genetic analysis.[11]

Avoiding such confusion does not mean rejecting the idea that Marx has drawn on Hegel to elaborate his own views. Rather, it implies that the genuinely Hegelian elements of his thought are to be found elsewhere than in the retrospective reconstruction of this Marxist Hegel who would have been a dialectical philosopher of alienation. Where, then, should they be located? The best way to locate these elements is probably the genetic method that reconstructs Marx's evolution from the beginning of his intellectual career. The most appropriate method for deciding whether an element of Marx's thought comes from Hegel is to analyze his Young Hegelian period, the period when he was elaborating his own ideas within a Hegelian framework. As already noted, the *Parisian Manuscripts* are a turning point in this respect, since what is at stake in 1844 is not so much to make use of a Hegelian framework rather than to subject the Hegelian presuppositions of the Young Hegelian movement to a critical examination. Even if it has been disputed in Marxist readings of Marx, there is no doubt that before 1844, Marx was a Young Hegelian and, more precisely, one of the leaders of the Young Hegelian movement.[12] Now, there are many important insights from Marx's Young Hegelian period that will persist after this period and could therefore be considered as genuinely Hegelian elements in the thought of the mature Marx. I have contended elsewhere that the definition of theory as critique is one of them.[13] For the Young Hegelians, Hegel's philosophy is not so much dialectical than critical: It matters because it gives a critical form to the theoretical activity. This critical dimension of Hegel's philosophy broadly corresponds to what Marxist discussion has depicted as the dialectical dimension of Hegel's philosophy, namely, the role given to contradictions in thought and in actuality, but it also refers to Hegel's conception of the critical relation of speculation to understanding, a critical relation that also remains a methodological model for the relation of the critique of political economy to classical political economy. Disclosing this Hegelian origin of the Marxian concept of the critique of political economy enables a recasting of the debate about the Hegelian dimensions of Marx's *Capital*. It also sheds a new light on the legacy of the Hegel–Marx connection in the tradition of the Frankfurt school, and notably on the fact that, for the early Horkheimer as well as for the late Adorno, Marx's critique of political economy remained a methodological model for their critical theory of society.[14]

In what follows, I focus on another Hegelian element that has exerted a long-lasting influence on Marx's thought as well as on the historical development of a variety of Hegelianisms and Marxisms. It consists of Hegel's presentism. In Marxist discussions about the Hegel–Marx connection, as well as in Hegel scholarship, Hegel's presentism is usually underestimated. Hegel's philosophy of history is usually conceived of either as a theory reducing the present to a product of the past, or to a theory reducing historical development to some kind of logical, or supra-temporal, development. Both of these images come from Marx himself, who was influenced by other Young Hegelians, partly by Cieszkowski's interpretation of Hegel's philosophy of history as centered on the past (and by others, such as Hess, who have been influenced by Ciezkowski's *Prolegomena to a Historiosophy*, dated 1838), and by Feuerbach's interpretation of Hegel as an absolutist philosopher.[15] In the *Parisian Manuscripts* and *The German Ideology*, Marx read Hegel's theory of history as both conservative and idealist: conservative because the contemporary social order would have been defined by Hegel as the final result of past efforts made by the *Weltgeist* in order to actualize its essence, namely, freedom; idealist because history would have been considered by him mainly as some sort of logical process of the actualization of ideas. Rather than being a presentist philosopher (giving primacy to the present), Hegel appears as a thinker of the primacy of the past (the past producing the present) and a logical absolutist (the historical present being reduced to an eternal present). This reading of Hegel is not only wrong; it also thwarts a correct understanding of Marx's own presentism, a presentism inherited from Hegel.

Hegel's Primacy of the Present

The fact that Hegel has afforded some kind of primacy to the present as a philosophical object is well known. As Hegel famously put it in the Preface to the *Elements of the Philosophy of Right*:

> To comprehend what is, this is the task of philosophy, because *what is*, is reason. As far as the individual is concerned, each individual is a *child of his time*; thus philosophy, too, is *its own time comprehended in thoughts*. It is just as foolish to imagine that any philosophy can transcend its contemporary world as that an individual can overleap his own time or leap over Rhodes.[16]

Here, the primacy of the present concerns the present as the most legitimate object of philosophical discourse. This legitimacy is epistemological, since it concerns the relationship of philosophical knowledge to its objects. This epistemological presentism has a descriptive and a normative sense. From a descriptive point of view, it is simply a fact that nobody can jump over his own time, since one is always thinking his own time even when one tries to know the past or to imagine the future. The problem is, then, that one is usually unaware that one thinks the present when one tries to know the past or to imagine the future, so that one's thought suffers either from a reflective deficit or from some kind of thematic inconsistency (if it is assumed that the knowledge of the past or future is independent of the present situation).

Hegel's epistemological presentism also has a normative meaning, since the value of a philosophical discourse depends on its capacity to make sense of the rationality of the present. It is the very meaning of the passage in the Preface to the *Elements of the Philosophy of Right* when Hegel states that this book "shall be nothing other than an attempt to *comprehend and portray the state as an inherently rational entity*. As a philosophical composition, it must distance itself as far as possible from the obligation to construct a state *as it ought to be*."[17] In fact, according to Hegel's philosophy of world history, such as it is summarized at the end of the *Elements of the Philosophy of Right*, the historical present is characterized by the reconciliation of the rational and the actual. In this respect, the purpose of this book makes explicit the historical presupposition of its very method and it is precisely this historical presupposition that is articulated in advance, in the previous quote. It is worth noting that Hegel introduces not only the *Elements of the Philosophy of Right* but each part of his system with references to recent developments in world history and the history of ideas. The Preface of the *Phenomenology of Spirit* analyzes the philosophical situation of the post-revolutionary period. In the *Encyclopedia*, the "Preliminary Concept" of the *Science of Logic* refers to contemporary debates between empiricism, Kantianism, and immediate knowledge, and in the introduction to the *Philosophy of Spirit*, recent developments in the study of animal magnetism are mentioned.[18] For Hegel, the present does not consist only of the most legitimate philosophical object; it also defines the main challenges that the philosopher should take over and therefore offers a means of philosophical justification. Hegel's presentism becomes provocative with respect to the definition of philosophical discourse as having eternal validity, when he contends that a philosophical project can be justified by the fact that it is *an der Zeit*. A philosopher must be in tune with his own time and try to satisfy the needs of this time. So the justification of the project of a transformation of philosophy into science, in the words of the Preface the *Phenomenology of Spirit*:

> To demonstrate that it is now time for philosophy to be elevated into science [*dass die Erhebung der Philosophie zur Wissenschaft an der Zeit ist*] would therefore

be the only true justification of any attempt that has this as its aim, because it would demonstrate the necessity of that aim, and, at the same time, it would be the realization of the aim itself.[19]

The traditional way of mitigating Hegel's presentism is to balance this epistemological presentism with an ontological absolutism. The objection can be phrased as follows: Isn't the historical present defined as an 'eternal present'? Indeed, the idea of an 'eternal present' seems incompatible with a genuinely presentist philosophical orientation. But if one carefully reads the passages mentioning the 'eternal present', one easily realizes that this latter notion does not so much denote the present than the past.[20] Hegel's point is that if a knowledge of the past is possible, it is because something in the past keeps on making sense in the present; in other words, because it is not only in the past but has also acquired some kind of eternity. In this respect, the notion of 'eternal present' defines a presentist position in the epistemological debates about knowledge of the past. This knowledge is a knowledge of the present, not only a knowledge made possible by present traces of the past (archives, vestiges of the past, etc.), not only a knowledge underpinned by present interests and a knowledge conditioned by present prejudices, but also a knowledge of what remains nowadays understandable of the past. Indeed, Hegel's approach to the present consists of reconstructing it from the point of view of a theory of history. His philosophy of history intends to produce a knowledge of the present as produced by past processes. But the knowledge of these processes is made possible by the presence of the past, and it is conceived of as a means for the contemporary *Zeitgeist* to become aware of itself. In a word: The knowledge of the present via the past remains a knowledge of the present.

I have just contended that the notion of 'eternal present' is epistemological rather than ontological. But it could also be argued, more generally, that Hegel's ontology is incompatible with a presentist orientation. The famous definition of essence (*Wesen*) as "what has been" (*was gewesen ist*),[21] at the beginning of the 'Doctrine of Essence', seems to support this argument. I would argue, however, that Hegel's thinking also gives primacy to the present from an ontological point of view. Given that Hegel points out that his "objective logic" as a whole replaces "ontology",[22] it is tempting to consider that the last developments of the 'Doctrine of Essence', rather than its initial definition of essence, articulate Hegel's own ontological position.[23] Now, with the concept of *Wirklichkeit*, translated as 'actuality', Hegel clearly tries to overcome the contrast between 'possibilitist' ontologies (equating essence with possibility, as in Leibniz) and actualist ontologies (equating being with actuality, as in Aristotle). More precisely, Hegel tries to overcome this contrast from the point of view of a processual definition of actuality. Hegel's point is that a possibility has reality only when engaged in a process of actualization and that the reality of actuality is nothing else than this process of actualization. Now, if it is legitimate to consider, as in contemporary debates, that as an ontological category, the notion of 'presentism' denotes a variety of actualism, one consisting of contending that the only actual being is the present being, then, Hegel undoubtedly supports a version of ontological presentism. In fact, the *Encyclopedia* makes it clear that only the present, and not also the past and future as distinct from the present, exists (§202). Indeed, the idea of a process of actualization seems to imply a temporal extension of actuality in the past, where a process began, and in the future, where it will end. Therefore, it is tempting to conclude that a processual definition of actuality is incompatible with any presentism. But, according to Hegel, one should not think of the present as a '*finite* present', exclusive of the past and future. Instead, one should think of the present as a 'present', integrating a past and a future (§202R). In other words, the only present that exists is the actual present defined by some ongoing processes of actualization.

In Hegel, the definition of the present as the philosophical object *par excellence* is then consistent with the epistemological and ontological presuppositions of the method used to analyze this present. Hegel's approach to normativity provides another illustration of this thematic and methodological presentism. Hegel points out that it is from the point of view of the processes of rationalization that underpin the present, that normative issues have to be articulated: In the *Elements of the Philosophy of Right*, the constitutional state is a state in the making that defines the true challenge of the contemporary time—and the fact that the rational state is not yet achieved should suffice to show that for Hegel, History has not yet ended! In the Preface to the *Elements*, Hegel also highlights the fact that normative discourses lose their function and legitimacy if they cannot contribute to contemporary processes of rationalization of the world: "If reflection, feeling, or whatever form the subjective consciousness may assume, regards the *present* as *vain*, and looks beyond it in a spirit of superior knowledge, it finds itself in a vain position; and since it has actuality only in the present, it is itself mere vanity."[24] On the one hand, the contrast between the *is* and the *ought*, between the present state of affairs and the ideals that define what the future should be, makes it impossible to achieve the unity of the theory (that deals with the past and the present) and the praxis (that works toward a better future). On the other hand, these contrasts make it impossible to elaborate a theory of the processes of actualization of the rational, and to think of theory as being able to play a role in such a process. Now, philosophy of history is precisely the Hegelian concept that defines the ways in which this unity of theory and practice should be thought of. Its task is to identify the processes of actualization of the rational that are currently ongoing, as well as the obstacles with which these processes are confronted: intellectual obstacles such as an abstract conception of normativity, or a reactionary conception of normativity reducing it to tradition, as well as practical obstacles such as those rooted in the contradictions of civil society.

Nowadays, the idea of philosophy of history is generally conceived of as some kind of metaphysical discourse with a merely theoretical purpose. According to this pejorative image, philosophy of history would only be interested in the laws of history. It would only try to subsume the empirical variety of past events to a set of universal principles. But the truth is that from Vico to Hegel, that is, at the time when the knowledge of history was taking the form of philosophies of history, philosophers of history have thought of their models of historical evolution as a means to orient the practical endeavors of their contemporaries.[25] In Vico already, the notion of 'diagnostic art' is used to denote the practical dimension of the philosophy of history.[26] Philosophy of history appeared then as a science of history as well as a form of political philosophy that is an alternative to natural law and contract theories. While these types of normative discourses on society defined the *ought* from an abstract and non-historicized point of view, philosophy of history defined the *ought* from the point of view of a historical diagnosis disclosing the historical tasks of the present. This contrast between two types of political philosophy, which anticipated contemporary distinctions made between normative political philosophy and social philosophy,[27] becomes fully explicit in Hegel. The Preface to the *Elements of the Philosophy of Right* highlights that political philosophy should not define the *ought* from the point of view of an abstract theory such as a theory of natural law, but through a theory of the specificities of the present as a period of reconciliation of the rational with the actual. The function of Hegel's philosophy of history is not to reduce the present to a product of the past, but instead to locate the present in the overall development of world history in order to identify the historical tasks of the present. In other words, the practical function of Hegel's philosophy of history is to produce a theory of the *ought* in the form of a historical diagnosis of the present, or, more precisely, in the form of the actual dynamics of actualization of the rational, notably the emergence of a type of constitutional state that is described as a rational state.[28]

The Early Marx and the Struggle against the Philosophy of the Future

There is no doubt that the early Marx is a sort of Hegelian, a Young Hegelian, and that his Hegelianism manifests itself notably in some kind of presentism, a Hegelian presentism. Like Hegel, Marx deals with the *ought* from the point of view of a theory of history that is intended to spell out the historical tasks of the present situation. The texts published in the *Deutsch–Französische Jahrbücher* provide the purest illustration of this presentism. In the "Contribution to the Critique of Hegel's Philosophy of Law. Introduction", Marx highlights that philosophy cannot fulfill its practical function except as a tool that could be useful to the historical dynamic that specifies the present situation. What is at stake for Marx is to identify the "immediate *task of philosophy* which is at the service of history".[29] Like Hegel, he refers to history as a process of gradual actualization of the rational[30] in order to distinguish the practical tasks of the present situation. And just as Hegel was contending that since the French Revolution and the foundation of a constitution upon rational principles, the present is defined by the fact that the rational is no longer located in an ideal world external to the actual world,[31] so too Marx writes that "the *task of history*, therefore, once the *world beyond the truth* has disappeared, is to establish the *truth of this world*".[32] Like Hegel, Marx also defines philosophy as a theory of the present, and he grounds social critique on historical diagnoses of the present situation. He refers to a normative definition of the present as the highest stage of the actualization of the rational, and instead of simply identifying the present with the exiting situation, he identifies it with the process triggered by actual social and political contradictions.

Marx's normative conception of the present manifests itself when he states that Germany remains "*below the level of history*" because of the permanence of certain feudal institutions and its incapacity to satisfy the requisites of a constitutional state. Therefore, Germany is not a legitimate object of philosophical criticism, but only of radical denunciation:

War on the German conditions! By all means! They are *below the level of history, beneath any criticism,* but they are still an object of criticism like the criminal who is below the level of humanity but still an object for the *executioner*. In the struggle against those conditions criticism is no passion of the head, it is the head of passion. It is not a lancet, it is a weapon. Its object is its *enemy,* which it wants not to refute but to *exterminate*. For the spirit of those conditions is refuted. In themselves they are not objects *worthy of thought,* but *phenomena* which are as despicable as they are despised. Criticism does not need to make things clear to itself as regards this subject-matter, for it has already dealt with it. Criticism appears no longer as an *end in itself,* but only as a *means*. Its essential sentiment is *indignation,* its essential activity is *denunciation*.[33]

Here, Hegel's presentism expresses itself in the ways in which Marx refers to anachronism, a term often used in this text, in order to define the illegitimate objects of philosophical criticism. According to Marx, B. Bauer instantiates a kind of philosophical approach focusing on such illegitimate objects. In fact, he elaborated a philosophical criticism of the German religious state, which consisted in a disclosure of the contradiction between state and religion. For Marx, the problem with such criticism is that its subject matter is anachronistic, in the sense that the religious state already belongs to the past. Such a theory thinks of itself as unmasking the contradictions of the contemporary situation when it, in truth, only deals with the contradictions of the past:

If one wanted to proceed from the *status quo* itself in Germany, even in the only appropriate way, i.e., negatively, the result would still be an *anachronism*. Even the negation of our political present is a reality already covered with dust in the historical lumber-room of modern nations. If I negate powdered pigtails, I am still left with unpowdered pigtails. If I negate the German state of affairs in 1843, then, according to the French computation of time, I am hardly in the year 1789, and still less in the focus of the present.[34]

Paradoxically, it is this Marxian conception of philosophical criticism, as a theory of the tasks of the present, that explains why the criticism of the contemporary social and political order has to take the form of a critique of Hegel's Philosophy of Right. Some Young Hegelians, like Ruge, believed that Hegel's Philosophy of Right was a theory of a situation that already belonged to the past, because of Hegel's effort to bridge the gap between certain feudal institutions (such as the 'corporation' and the monarchic character of the state) and modern constitutional state.[35] On the contrary, in Marx's opinion, this very contradiction between past and present elements of Hegel's Philosophy of Right makes it relevant for the contemporary situation, as it discloses the fact that the rational principles of political emancipation are fully compatible with the persisting irrationality of forms of social life that are similar to those of the feudal situation. In this sense, "German *philosophy of law and state* [Hegel's Philosophy of Right] is the only German history which is *al pari* with the official modern reality."[36]

Hence, Marx is not only articulating his arguments in a Hegelian presentist framework; he also contends that Hegel's philosophy remains relevant for the present times. Feuerbach and Ruge identified Hegel's philosophy with a philosophy of the past, and they argued that the practical tasks of the present situation call for a philosophy of the future. In contrast, in a letter to Ruge, dated September 1843 and published in the *Deutsch–Französische Jahrbücher*, Marx denounces, from a Hegelian point of view, the separation between the future and the present as a new version of the abstract *ought* and as a source of theoretical and practical sterility. In an implicit reference to religion as an expression of a series of hopes to be actualized, Marx writes:

> Hence, our motto must be: reform of consciousness not through dogmas, but by analysing the mystical consciousness that is unintelligible to itself, whether it manifests itself in a religious or a political form. It will then become evident that the world has long dreamed of possessing something of which it has only to be conscious in order to possess it in reality. It will become evident that it is not a question of drawing a great mental dividing line between past and future, but of *realising* the thoughts of the past. Lastly, it will become evident that mankind is not beginning a *new* work, but is consciously carrying into effect its old work.[37]

The whole argumentation of this letter is that philosophers should not think of themselves as leaping outside of their time, but rather, as participating in the conflicts of their time and attempting to make explicit the prejudices and desires of their contemporaries. Criticizing the traditional definition of philosophy as *philosophia perennis*, Marx calls for a 'secularization' or 'mundanization' of the philosophical activity in the form of a theoretical activity consisting of a critical examination of the beliefs of the contemporary world, and of participation in the practical struggles of the contemporaries.

> Hitherto philosophers have had the solution of all riddles lying in their writing-desks, and the stupid, exoteric world had only to open its mouth for the roast pigeons of absolute knowledge to fly into it. Now philosophy has become mundane, and the most striking proof of this is that philosophical consciousness itself has been drawn into the torment of the struggle, not only externally but also internally.[38]
>
> Hence, nothing prevents us from making criticism of politics, participation in politics, and therefore *real* struggles, the starting point of our criticism, and from identifying our criticism with them. In that case we do not confront the world in a doctrinaire way with a new principle: Here is the truth, kneel down before it! We develop new principles for the world out of the world's own principles.[39]

These quotes illustrate the ways in which Marx rephrases some of the arguments of the Preface to the *Elements of the Philosophy of Right*. These quotes also show that, as in Hegel, presentism is associated with immanent critique. The normative conception of the present is made possible by the fact that it embodies the principles of its own critique. Hence, the major difference between Hegel and Marx is to be found neither in the type of presentism supported by Marx, nor in the conception of the present as being still structured by contradictions between the rational and the actual. It consists of the ways in which theory should contribute to the process of the actualization of the rational. In Hegel, this contribution was thought of as a theory of the rational state, that is, as a theory of the rational promises of the contemporary situation. In Marx, this contribution was thought of as a *"ruthless criticism of all that exists"*,[40] as a criticism of all the factors that create obstacles to rational promises of the present world. In other words, the difference between Hegel and Marx, at that time, consisted less in philosophical or methodological principles than in historical diagnoses. Marx's "ruthless criticism" is grounded upon a historical diagnosis concerning a blockage of the historical process of actualization of the real, especially in Germany.

The Mature Marx and the History of the Present

The conviction that political issues have to be tackled from the point of view of a theory of history characterizes the early as well as the mature Marx. Nevertheless, since *The German Ideology*, Marx's theory of history is based on a criticism of the very idea of a philosophy of history, and especially of Hegel's version of it. Does this rupture with Hegel also imply a rupture with his presentism? The answer is, clearly, no. The mature Marx still believes, just like the early Marx, that theory should become a theoretical means that could be useful for human attempts to cope with contemporary social and political problems. In order for this to happen, theory can no longer think of the present as a process of actualization of the rational, but it must still focus on contemporary tendencies and contradictions that structure the context of practical attempts to make the world better.

The presentist orientation of the writings of the mature Marx expresses itself in a historiographical as well as in a political and epistemological primacy of the present. On the one hand, Marx should be considered as a historian of the present, as demonstrated through *The 18th Brumaire*, *The Class Struggles in France* and *The Civil War in France*.[41] As we will see, *Capital* also contributes to a history of the present. On the other hand, Marx's famous definition of communism illustrates a political presentism: "Communism is for us not a *state of affairs* which is to be established, an *ideal* to which reality [will] have to adjust itself. We call communism the *actual* movement which abolishes the present state of things."[42] This presentism also expresses itself when Marx criticizes the French revolutionaries of 1848 for seeking their political models in the past (in the French Revolution), rather than elaborating the specific demands of their times:

> The social revolution of the nineteenth century cannot take its poetry from the past but only from the future. It cannot begin with itself before it has stripped away all superstition about the past. The former revolutions required recollections of past world history in order to smother their own content. The revolution of the nineteenth century must let the dead bury their dead in order to arrive at its own content. There the phrase went beyond the content—here the content goes beyond the phrase.[43]

Moreover, an epistemological presentism manifests itself when Marx contends that all political programs have to be modified in the light of historical evolutions. For instance, Marx himself revised some of the propositions of the *Communist Manifesto* after the Paris Commune.[44] In what follows, I will try to show that some kind of epistemological primacy of the present is also at play in the very logical structure of *Capital* and in the way it focuses on the actual transformations of the capitalist mode of production.

It is well known that the materialist conception of history seems to elaborate two distinct, if not contradicting, conceptions of history: one that conceives of history as an economic process, the other as a political process. At first sight, in *Capital*, only the first model plays a decisive role, and Marx's masterpiece is often criticized for this very reason. It seems to propose too economistic an interpretation of history, and therefore, it seems to lie in contradiction to the conception of history as the history of class struggles sketched in the *Communist Manifesto*, as well as to the political project of a self-emancipation of the proletariat put forward in the "Inaugural Address of the International Working Men's Association".[45] But, as I will show, on closer reading, it appears that Marx has neither thought of the 'natural laws of the capitalist production'[46] as analogous to natural laws, nor analyzed the historical evolutions of capitalism from a merely economic point of view.

A first point to note is that Marx has explicitly criticized classical political economy for having searched for its methodological model in Newtonian mechanics. Two reasons make the laws of capitalist production distinct from the laws of motion or gravitation. Marx points out, firstly, that the laws studied by political economy are historical and not natural laws; secondly, that these laws are not deterministic in the same sense as mechanical laws. In *Capital*, the laws of evolution of capitalist societies are conceived of as 'tendential' laws. They are deterministic, insofar as they describe a tendency that necessarily operates. But they are non-deterministic, insofar as the ways in which these tendencies operate depend on 'counteracting factors'. For instance, Marx mentions a series of counteracting factors of the law of the tendential fall in the rate of profit: a higher degree of exploitation, reduction in wages, increasing unemployment, international trade, and so on. All of these counteracting factors, he maintains, can tentatively slow down or even stop the fall in the profit rate.[47]

The idea of 'tendential' law entails a highly original concept of law, from an epistemological point of view, as well as from the perspectives of social ontology and theory of history. From an epistemological point of view, its function is to explain social evolution. Far from simply describing an empirical regularity, the tendential law explains social evolution by making explicit the economic dynamics that are at work in this evolution. The concept of tendential law elaborates an original theoretical model in which some forces, on the one hand, have an explanatory power, since they are necessarily at work, but on the other hand, always act in conjunction with a plurality of other factors, some of which counteract the effects produced by these forces. From an ontological point of view, the concept of tendential law is dependent on a vision of the social not only as a set of structures and relations, but also as a set of processes that are not only an actualization of the properties of permanent structures and relations, but also continuous transformations of the structures and relations. In other words, the ontological assumptions of Marx's theory of tendential law belong to a processual ontology according to which there is a primacy of processes over structures and relations.[48] This ontology is clearly inspired by Hegel's theory of 'actuality', and in this respect, by his ontological presentism.

From the point of view of the theory of history, the concept of tendential law entails a vision of social evolution being not only subjected to the development of permanent principles, but also being characterized by the emergence of the new.[49] In other words, far from leading to a reduction of the present to a result of past processes, tendential laws can capture the present in its irreducibility to the past. And instead of assuming a homogeneity of development that would make history susceptible to being described by the traditional concept of law, the conception of tendential law makes it possible to account for a diversity of heterogeneous factors at play in historical developments.

It is worth recalling that Marx's conception of capitalism is incompatible with a conception of capitalism as a set of permanent social structures or as an essence of capitalism gradually actualizing itself in its purest form. Indeed, there is a tendency in contemporary critical theory to speak of contemporary capitalism as 'pure' or 'absolute' capitalism. But far from paving the way for such essentialist conceptions of capitalism, Marx supports a historical conception of capitalism as constantly attempting to find new solutions to its structural contradictions. This is manifest in the Preface to *Capital*: "the present society is not a solid crystal, but an organism capable of change, and constantly engaged in a process of change."[50] Marx tried to identify the contemporary forms of these changes in *Capital*, for instance, when he described the emergence of shareholder firms and cooperatives.[51]

Now, it is precisely with regard to some of the tendencies and mutations of his time that Marx thought of the possibility of revolutionary action in *Capital*. Among the immanent laws of capitalist production that are studied in *Capital*, some are presented as 'antagonistic'. This is the case with what Marx presents in chapter 25 as the fundamental law of capitalist production: The law of the production of relative overpopulation (or structural unemployment), and the subsequent effects of impoverishment. The term 'antagonism' is then used to describe the fact that the law of capitalist accumulation defines a contradiction that is not economic, or functional, but sociopolitical. The law of the centralization of capital, formulated in this same chapter 25 of volume I, and that of the tendency of the rate of profit to fall formulated in the third section of volume III, describe only economic or functional contradictions. They describe the mechanisms by which the development of capitalism destroys its own presuppositions, namely, private ownership of the means of production and the production of surplus value. On the contrary, the law of relative overpopulation that describes the production of structural unemployment relates to a process that contributes to the reproduction by capitalism of its own conditions. In other words, it describes a functional necessity rather than a functional contradiction. The existence of a relative overpopulation, or of a reserve army of unemployed, makes it possible to exert a pressure on the wage that makes it possible to counteract the decline in the rate of profit. In this respect, it responds to a functional need. Nevertheless, it also defines a contradiction, a contradiction of a social and political nature. It keeps the working class in a misery that transforms it into an antagonistic social class and thus creates the conditions for a political struggle against the capitalist mode of production. Marx writes in chapter 25:

> In proportion as capital accumulates, the situation of the worker, be his payment high or low, must grow worse ... Accumulation of wealth at one pole is, therefore, at the same time accumulation of misery, the torment of labour, slavery, ignorance, brutalization and moral degradation at the opposite pole, i.e. on the side of the class that produces its own product as capital. The antagonistic character of capitalist accumulation has been enunciated in various forms by political economists.[52]

In this excerpt, the notion of antagonism expresses social antagonism, a 'class antagonism' to use a formula that occurs several times in *Capital*, and it is worth noting that in the conclusion to *Capital* book one, it is precisely this type of antagonism that will explain the transition from capitalism to communism:

> Along with the constant decrease in the number of capitalist magnates, ... the mass of misery, oppression, slavery and degradation and exploitation grows; but with this there is also growth of revolt of the working class, a class constantly increasing in numbers, and trained, united and organized by the very mechanism of the capitalist process of production. The monopoly of capital becomes a fetter upon the mode of production which has flourished alongside and under it. The centralization of the means of production and the socialization of labour reach an integument. This integument is burst asunder. The knell of capitalist private property sounds. The expropriators are expropriated.[53]

On the one hand, this passage highlights that certain immanent tendencies of capitalist production are preparing the transition from capitalism to the communist mode of production: The centralization of capital and the socialization of labor are paving the way for communism. On the other hand, this passage connects the idea of an immanent economic evolution of capitalism toward communism, due to its tendential—functional laws, to the idea of a political action of the proletariat made possible by tendential—antagonist laws. This interconnection is expressed in the double sense given to the idea of expropriation of expropriators, which refers to both an immanent law (that of the centralization of capital) and a political act: The expropriators will be expropriated by the revolutionary action of the working class. Finally, this text emphasizes the twofold origin of the revolutionary struggles of the proletariat: on the one hand, motivation (the 'growth of revolt'), and on the other hand, the social processes that allow the feelings of revolt to be shared and organized; the working class is "trained, united, and organized by the very mechanism of the capitalist production process", notably by the constitution of large-scale industry and the formation of trade unions. All of this relates to the latest developments of the workers' movement history. All of this relates to an epistemological and political presentism.

Conclusion

In depicting Hegel and Marx as presentists, my purpose was to contribute to recasting the debates concerning the Hegel–Marx connection. I argued that one of the fruitful approaches would be to take seriously Hegel's and Marx's presentism rather than focusing solely on alienation and dialectical method. Marx appears as a more interesting philosopher when he is conceived of as one who takes on the Hegelian task of thinking his own time and re-actualizing his own thinking in tune with historical evolution, than when he is depicted as the one who discovered the eternal laws of history or the essence of the capitalist mode of production. Hegel also appears in a more interesting light when it becomes evident that his presentism has not only triggered a process of numerous attempts to re-actualize his own thought (in the Hegelian school of the 1830s and in the Young Hegelian movement of the early 1840s, but also in British Idealism, in the early Dewey and Mead, as well as in critical theory, until Honneth's *Freedom's Right*). Hegel has also taught us to take seriously the primacy of the present from ontological, practical and epistemological points of view, as in Marx, Dewey, and Mead, and also in critical theory. For critical theory, being loyal to Hegel and Marx's presentism should not mean only trying to re-actualize Hegel, Marx, Adorno, or other theorists of its tradition, but also trying to ground the critical models upon historical diagnosis rather than abstract theories of justice and democracy, and to interconnect theory with the emancipatory practices of our times. For critical theory, being loyal to Hegel and Marx's presentism could also mean addressing political issues from the point of view of immanent critique rather than through a theory of the *ought*. The normativist turn in critical theory and the growing tendency to disconnect social critique and knowledge of the present are not consistent with the implications of Hegel and Marx's presentism. Hence, a final reason why their presentisms should be taken seriously: They provide a corrective to some of the most problematic contemporary trends in critical theory.

Notes

1 François Hartog, *Regimes of Historicity: Presentism and Experiences of Time* (New York: Columbia University Press, 2003).
2 Arthur Prior, "Changes in Events and Changes in Things," and "Quasi-propositions and Quasi-individuals," in *Papers on Time and Tense* (London: Oxford University Press, 1968), 7–20, 213–22; John Bigelow, "Presentism and Properties," in *Philosophical Perspectives X, Metaphysics*, ed. James E. Tomberlin (Cambridge: Blackwell Publishers, 1996), 35–52; Ned Markosian, "A Defense of Presentism," *Oxford Studies in Metaphysics* 1, no. 3 (2004): 47–82.
3 William H. Dray, "Some Varieties of Presentism," in *On History and Philosophies of History* (Leiden: Brill, 1989), 164–91.
4 Hans Joas, *The Creativity of Action* (Chicago: University of Chicago Press, 1996).
5 See notably John Dewey, *Human Nature and Conduct. An Introduction to Social Psychology* (New York: The Modern Library, 1930), 189–209, 215–26, 238–45, 281–90, *Logic. The Theory of Inquiry* (New York: Henry Holt and Company, 1939) 230–9; George H. Mead, *The Philosophy of the Present* (LaSalle: Open Court, 1932).
6 As I have suggested elsewhere, see Emmanuel Renault, "Dewey's Relations to Hegel," *Contemporary Pragmatism* 13, no. 3 (2016): 219–41.
7 Georg Lukács, *The Young Hegel* (London: Merlin Press, 1975).
8 Louis Althusser, *For Marx* (London: Verso, 2005).

9   On these different points, see the contributions of Jean-Michel Buée, Jean-Christophe Angaut and David Wittmann, in *Lire les Manuscrits de 1844*, ed. Emmanuel Renault (Paris: PUF, 2008).
10 Karl Marx, *Economic and Philosophic Manuscripts of 1844*, in *Marx & Engels Collected Works*, Vol. 3 (London: Lawrence & Wishart, 1975–2005), 327: "Feuerbach both in his 'Thesen' in the *Anekdota* and, in detail, in the *Philosophie der Zukunft* has in principle overthrown the old dialectic and philosophy." Marx makes a very vague use of the term dialectic in the *Manuscripts*, speaking of the "Hegelian dialectic" and sometimes also of the "Feuerbachian dialectic" (ibid., 328). Sometimes, the notion seems to have a clear pejorative meaning, for instance, when Marx talks about Hegel as elaborating a "divine dialectic" (ibid., 345).
11 I have developed this point in *Marx et la philosophie* (Paris: PUF, 2014), "Dialectique," 40–60.
12 For a reading of Marx as a Young Hegelian, see Emmanuel Renault, "The Early Marx and Hegel: The Young Hegelian Mediation," in *Reassessing Marx's Social and Political Philosophy*, ed. Jan Kandiyali (New York: Routledge, 2018).
13 Emmanuel Renault, *Marx et l'idée de critique* (Paris: PUF, 1995) and *Marx et la philosophie*, "Critique," 25–39.
14 This is notably apparent in Theodor W. Adorno's introduction to *The Positivist Dispute in German Sociology* (New York: Harper Torchbook, 1976). On *Capital* as a methodological model for critical theory, see Emmanuel Renault, "Le *Capital* comme modèle pour la théorie critique," in *Que reste-t-il de Marx?*, ed. Catherine Colliot-Thélène (Rennes: PUR, 2017), 45–58.
15 See, for instance, Ludwig Feuerbach, *Principles of a Philosophy of the Future* (Indianapolis: Hackett Publishing Company, 1986).
16 Georg W.F. Hegel, *Elements of the Philosophy of Right* (Cambridge: Cambridge University Press, 1991), 21–2.
17 Ibid., 21.
18 The connection of the prefaces and introductions to the present is also apparent in the introduction to the *Naturphilosophie* (the name itself is a reference to contemporary debates) and of many of the lectures. I have studied the relation to the present in these various prefaces and introductions to published texts or unpublished lectures, in the first three chapters of my *Connaître ce qui est. Enquête sur le présentisme hégélien* (Paris: Vrin, 2015).
19 Terry Pinkard's translation: §5, https://fr.scribd.com/document/49157331/Phenomenology-of-Spirit-Entire-Text-of-T-Pinkard-Translation (accessed September 12, 2019).
20 See for instance: "In our understanding of world history, we are concerned with history primarily as a record of the past. But we are just as fully concerned with the present. Whatever is true exists eternally in and for itself—not yesterday or tomorrow, but entirely in the present, 'now' in the sense of an absolute present. Within the Idea, even that which appears to be past is never lost." Hegel, *Lectures on the Philosophy of World History* (Cambridge: Cambridge University Press, 1975), 150.
21 Hegel, *The Science of Logic* (Cambridge: Cambridge University Press, 2010), 337: "The German language has kept 'essence' (*Wesen*) in the past participle (*gewesen*) of the verb 'to be' (*sein*), for essence is past—but timelessly past—being." See also Hegel, *Encyclopedia of the Philosophical Sciences in Basic Outline. Part I: Science of Logic* (Cambridge: Cambridge University Press, 2010), §112R, 174.
22 Hegel, *The Science of Logic*, 42.

23 Hegel, *Encyclopedia of the Philosophical Sciences*, §§142–58.
24 Hegel, *Philosophy of Right*, 20.
25 See Renault, *Connaître ce qui est*, 31–55, 233–63.
26 See Pierre Girard, *Giambattista Vico. Rationalité et politique. Une lecture de la Scienza Nuova* (Paris: PUPS, 2008), 327–38.
27 See Axel Honneth, "Pathologies of the Social: The Past and Present of Social Philosophy," in *Handbook of Critical Theory*, ed. David M. Rasmussen (Oxford: Blackwell, 1996), 369–98; Franck Fischbach, *Manifeste pour une philosophie sociale* (Paris: La Découverte, 2009); Robin Celikates and Rahel Jaeggi, *Sozialphilosophie. Eine Einführung* (München: C.H. Beck, 2017).
28 See Manfred Riedel, "Hegel und Marx. Die Neubestimmung des Verhältniss von Theorie und Praxis," *System und Geschichte. Studien zum historischen Standort von Hegels Philosophie* (Frankfurt: Suhrkamp, 1973), 11–5.
29 Marx, "Contribution to the Critique of Hegel's Philosophy of Law. Introduction," MECW 3, 176.
30 Ibid., 143: "Reason has always existed, but not always in a reasonable form. The critic can therefore start out from any form of theoretical and practical consciousness and from the forms *peculiar* to existing reality develop the true reality as its obligation and its final goal."
31 Hegel, *Philosophy of Right*, §360, 380: "In the hard struggle between these two realms—whose difference has now reached the stage of absolute opposition, despite the fact that both are rooted in a single unity and Idea—the spiritual realm brings the existence of its heaven down to earth in this world to the ordinary secularity of actuality and representational thought. The secular realm, on the other hand, develops itself to the level of thought and to the principle of rational being and knowing, i.e. to the rationality of right and law. As a result, their opposition has faded away in itself and become an insubstantial shape."
32 Marx, "Contribution to the Critique," 176.
33 Ibid., 177.
34 Ibid., 176.
35 Arnold Ruge, "Die Hegelsche Rechtsphilosophie und die Politik unserer Zeit" (1842), in *Die Hegelsche Linke. Dokumente zu Philosophie und Politik im deutschen Vormärz*, eds. Heinz and Ingrid Pepperle (Leipzig: Reclam, 1985), 443–71.
36 Marx, "Contribution to the Critique," 180.
37 Ibid., 144.
38 Ibid., 142.
39 Ibid., 144.
40 Ibid., 142.
41 See Jean Hyppolite, "La compréhension de l'histoire vécue chez Marx," *Figures de la pensée philosophique* (Paris: PUF, 1971), 353–9.
42 Karl Marx, Friedrich Engels, *The German Ideology*, MECW 5: 49.
43 Marx, *The Eighteenth Brumaire of Louis Bonaparte*, MECW 11: 154.
44 As highlighted, in the Preface to the 1872 German edition.
45 Marx, "Inaugural Address of the International Working Men's Association," MECW 20: 5–13.
46 Marx, *Capital I* (London: Penguin, 1990), 91.
47 Marx, *Capital III* (London: Penguin, 1990), 339–48.
48 On this primacy, see Emmanuel Renault, "Critical Theory and Processual Social Ontology," *Journal of Social Ontology* 2, no. 1 (2016).

49 Adorno has insisted on these dimensions of Marx's concept of "Tendenz" that makes it irreducible to a simple 'trend'; see his lectures *Philosophische Elemente einer Theorie der Gesellschaft* (Frankfurt: Suhrkamp, 2008), 37–40.
50 Marx, *Capital I*, 93.
51 Marx, *Capital III*, 572: "Capitalist joint-stock companies as much as cooperative factories should be viewed as transition forms from the capitalist mode of production to the associated one, simply that in the one case the opposition is abolished in a negative way, and in the other in a positive way."
52 Marx, *Capital I*, 799.
53 Ibid., 929.

4

Property and Freedom in Kant, Hegel, and Marx

Jacob Blumenfeld

In this chapter, I criticize some common approaches to conceptualizing *property*, and I propose instead a more normatively attuned, historically situated framework for thinking about what it means to call something *mine*. Whereas many legal theorists are busy constructing elaborate doctrines for justifying the absolute supremacy of property rights (and, consequently, normalizing the status quo distribution of wealth), I am more interested in understanding the social bonds, normative expectations, and material constraints produced in property relations. I do this with the help of Kant, Hegel, and Marx, each of whom placed property in relation to the development and denial of human freedom. But first, I discuss my shirt.

My Shirt

This shirt is mine. I bought it at H&M one day with money that I earned by working at a bar. The money was given to me because that is what the job contract stated, that I would receive money in return for working. And I did. The money I earned came from the customers, who themselves could have acquired it from their jobs, families, friends, loans, or whatever. My boss took some money for herself and some for the bar, to buy the required goods a bar needs, drinks and glasses, and so on, and to pay the bar's rent, and maybe to invest the profit somewhere. Part of that money went to me, which I put into food, I mean, I gave it to someone working behind a counter who let me take food out of the store once I gave them money, and part of the money went to rent, that is, an online transfer to a bank account to someone I have never met, and part of it went to buy this shirt, or, went to a company that already bought the shirt from the producer and then sold it to me at a higher cost to cover the wages and overhead and earn a profit for their store. The shirt was made from fabrics and dyes whose origins are undoubtedly international, with the final labor of sewing it together perhaps the result of a machine and some horrendously cheap labor, that is, the hands of people who were paid low wages by others who owned the building, materials, and right to the product of labor. In the end, this shirt, which I bought with the money I earned from working at the bar, is mine, and I have the right to do whatever I want with it. That is, I can wear it, tear it, paint it, rip it, cut it, burn it, sew it, give it away, throw it away, donate it, decorate it, and destroy it. What I do with it is my decision.

There are some limits to what I can do with it. I cannot strangle someone with this shirt, or better, I can strangle someone with it, but then I am subject to the legal ramifications of committing a criminally wrong deed, which includes arrest, trial, conviction, and, most probably, jail-time. The shirt is still mine when I do it even though what I did with it is wrong. The court may take the shirt away from me as evidence, but perhaps I can get it back later. Yet this prohibition not to harm another with my property is not actually a limit internal to the idea of property, but rather a general moral constraint on social action as such in a civil community.[1] Not harming one another is a constraint on all sorts of social relations, and the property relation is just one of these. So, given the general background constraints on action in general, there is nothing limiting my particular dominion over this shirt. I am free, unconstrained, comfortable, at home with myself and others in my shirt. It is mine.

How did this web of social and material relations, crystallized in the shirt I'm wearing, end up at my disposal? What grants authority to me to do whatever I please with this object, to have a realm of freedom in which I can utilize this shirt for any purpose? What, in the last instance, makes this shirt truly mine? It is neither its substance nor origin, use nor qualities, form nor function. Since all things mine are different in those senses, we cannot use any one of those criteria to explain what is, in fact, mine. Any appeal to facts will not help here, for we cannot find the fact of 'mineness' attached to my shirt. Sometimes, we do find a sign that says, 'Stay off! This is mine!' But unfortunately, such a sign is not ubiquitous. And even if it were, what would convince us to believe it? How can we trust the sign? Would we need not another sign, pointing to the first sign and saying that this sign does in fact belong to the owner, and that it is supposed to be exactly where it is? But why should we believe that second sign? Maybe very clever thieves put those signs up in order to deflect any suspicion away from them, so that they could claim something that was not theirs.

But let us just say that the signs were real, and accurate. They willfully expressed the belief of an alleged owner over something they thought was theirs. Well, what if we came across something that was claimed by two different owners, something that had contradicting signs. Both said 'Mine!' How would we decide on the rightful owners? Do we ask them questions to define the thing at hand? To see who knows the thing better? Do we get references? Documents? Stories? If we have stepped outside the boundaries of physical identification, then we have already left behind the realm of empirical facts, and have entered something else, the realm of social, political, legal, and ethical reason. But what are the criteria within the space of reasons that can definitively prove why something is mine, and not yours? Again, this does not seem to be a natural scientific question, with clearly demarcated procedures for testing hypotheses that provide falsifiable results and allow for certain amounts of prediction. This is a normative question, a question of *right*.

Normatively speaking then, there are two standard *reasons* that justify why something is mine and not yours: Either I rightfully *acquired* something that was previously unowned, however one determines the procedure of rightful acquisition, or, the ownership of something was rightfully *transferred* to me, however one determines the process of rightful transfer.[2] With these two principles in place, the mess of property relations can be legitimately and legally solved. What is mine and what is yours is ideally fixed in principle. All that is left to do is create a set of institutions for managing this in reality: a police for enforcing property boundaries, courts to impartially judge the cases of wrongful violation, governments to determine the laws according to which the courts can make legal decisions, lawyers to prosecute or defend those who bring claims forward about property violations, and a system of justice to devise ways to punish those at fault or compensate those who are wronged. This is all technical work, best left to experts and administrators. The task of the philosopher interested in this field is then to provide rigorous arguments, clear distinctions and functional categories that can help lawyers, judges, police, civil servants, and governments better adjudicate over property claims. By doing this, the philosopher contributes to the general good, to justice and to freedom.

But that is not the task of a critical theory of property, and that is not what I intend to do. For that way of approaching the problem of *mineness* takes for granted the object which needs to be explained: property itself. The question is not how to best determine what is mine and yours, but what it means to structure the world in terms of mine and yours in general. This initial formulation of the problem is still too abstract because it is unclear *what* is doing the structuring here, but let us leave that to one side for now. What is important is that the strange quality of something being 'mine' is not illuminated by deriving principles to justify how certain things can become mine or yours. Although this is a common strategy, it just buries the problem deeper. Starting with a diversity of cases that have something in common, the fact of mineness, and building up a theory to explain what binds the experiences together has created a vast literature on bundles of rights, taxonomies of claims, categories of contracts, theories of desert, and principles of utility.[3] Yet property is not a concept that can be understood just by looking at how the word is used in various contexts, because the various contexts themselves are contentious.[4] If we want to go deeper than just reaffirming what appears, then another strategy will be needed.

Bundles of Property Theory

The fact of property does not give us the right to property. But what would it mean for something to 'give us' a right to property? Property *already is* a right, and some even claim that all rights are just forms of property, individual possessions we carry around with us wherever we go. If this is correct, then trying to ground a right *to* property is like searching for an original right to rights, an original possession of possessions. This circular game has led many philosophers to posit a state of nature in which the entire earth was either originally possessed in common by all or possessed by no one, and then introduce a factor (e.g., scarcity, conflict, greed, labor) which upsets the balance, bringing private property into the world as such.[5]

When philosophers begin to look beneath the positive laws of legal ownership, property rights, and forms of possession, and to ask the more fundamental question of what the function and meaning of property is *as such*, we tend to get the following kinds of answers:

- property is a natural right that protects the valuable interests of individuals
- property is the just desert of labor
- property is a social convention that promotes benefits and welfare for the advantage of all
- property is a set of rules for determining the allocation of material resources in a situation of scarcity

Along with these natural rights, libertarian, utilitarian, and economic kinds of answers, usually a reference to the 'market' is made, a reference that further confuses the problem. Markets are sometimes taken to be the necessary condition for property rights, and the free market especially is taken to be the final rational form for the realization of property as such. However, although markets are intrinsically tied up with property, as a form in which property can be distributed, property is not intrinsically bound to markets. Property comes into being in these various accounts for a host of interesting but implausible reasons: It is in human nature to divide the world into mine and yours; it is a result of greed; it is an efficient way of distributing land; it is necessary for everyone to avoid violence.

All of these theories have been debated, refined, and perfected by the acolytes who subscribe to them.[6] The reason why they are so unhelpful in getting to the core of the problem is that they are lacking on two fronts: normatively and historically. On the one side, these theories fail to explain the value of property in itself, always reducing it to a good *for* some other interest or need. In this sense, property is only instrumentally valuable, never justified as such. If other contingent circumstances change—for example, natural, political, or economic conditions—then the form of property might just disappear as a relic of history. In this sense then, property itself is neither explained nor justified, but rather only accounted for as a side effect of other, more fundamental phenomena.

On the other side, these accounts naturalize the emergence of property when it is precisely its unnaturalness and historical specificity that needs to be explained. Whereas many theories of property try to explain just how normal it is that we own things according to complex set of rules that change over time but are somehow still considered sacred, a critical theory of property should emphasize its uniqueness as a social institution, its distinctiveness within the manifold of life's activities and human relations. Not only that, but the limits of property, the conflicts and antagonisms within it, should also be brought into focus here, and not just as irrational, contingent affairs, but as crucial elements of this complex phenomenon.

Taking these factors into account will allow us to answer the following two questions. First, what is the normative status of property, and second, what is its historical role? To grasp the normative status of property would require showing how property is indispensable for the development of our own self-conception as modern free individuals. To understand the historical role of property would be to make sense of the determinate function that different property relations play in materially constituting our relations to ourselves, each other, and our world, irrespective of our reflections on it.

By keeping in mind both ways of understanding property, a more unified picture of its place in our modern world can emerge, one which allows us to broach the more general worries that hang in the background: What does it mean to *own* something at all? What does it do to us, and what does it do to the world? There is a legacy of philosophical investigations that has taken these kinds of systematic questions seriously: the strange line that cuts across German idealism and materialism extending from Kant through Fichte and Hegel to Marx and the young Hegelians. These thinkers grappled with the emergence of modernity on a philosophical level, directly confronting the challenge of explaining the new kinds of subjects, values, institutions, and social relations that were emerging in the post-revolutionary world. Despite their different judgments, they all shared an understanding of private property as a modern right bound up with the historical emergence of the bourgeois state and a new normative order centered around individual freedom. The fact of private property was a historical challenge to the old regimes of feudal ownership and absolute monarchies, and this called for rethinking the fundamental categories of social life. In their different versions, private property either expresses, conditions, secures, limits, or deforms the freedom of modern individuals. In their various narratives, private property enters the world as a rational duty, civil contract, positive law, individual act, or economic relation.

Here, I am interested in two different argumentative strategies for understanding what makes something *mine* in this world. First are those normative, ideal arguments which start with a general theory of freedom, and then claim that securing or realizing said freedom requires the existence of a particular social relation, that is, private property. These arguments consider the historical development of modern societies toward private property rights as *progress toward freedom*, although such progress is never completely fulfilled. Second are those materialist, non-ideal arguments that start with a descriptive account of modern society, and then show how different forms of property emerge in accordance with changes in the economic and social relations that bind society together. On the first reading, a kind of free will is initially posited, and depending on one's interpretation of what constitutes the specific *freedom* of this will, certain social and material conditions will be required to make such freedom actual, effective, universal, and secure. Kant's deduction of intelligible possession in the *Doctrine of Right* is the paradigm case for this strategy.[7] On the second reading, a kind of social property relation is initially posited, and depending on one's interpretation of what constitutes the specific *constraints* of this relation, certain freedoms and wills emerge to make it actual, effective, universal and secure. Marx's analysis of social forms of property relations in *The German Ideology* and the *Grundrisse* are the classic examples here. Between these readings stands Hegel with one foot in both, for in the *Philosophy of Right*, he infers the necessity of private property as an indispensable element for the development of free personality, while at the same time locating the conditions of possibility for private property within a historically specific social form of modern ethical life.

Although these approaches appear to be contradictory, they can in fact be complimentary. The form of freedom that emerges through the transformation of social property relations can be exactly that kind which a rational theory of freedom claims is secured only through a certain form of property. The question I will be pursuing is whether or not this is in fact the case, whether or not the freedoms we need and the freedoms we get converge in our modern relation to property. In fact, what I hope to show is how both approaches, while insufficient on their own terms, require each other; what is lacking in one is made up for in the other. The idealist account of property helps us grasp the normative consequences of conceiving individuals to be irreducibly free. This analysis, however, is not necessarily connected to the world in which we live. Since rights to property crystallize a particular way of organizing the material reproduction of society, they require a materialist explanation as well. But materialist theories ignore the normative dimension of property as a form of recognition, freedom, and right. Hence, such theories cannot really critique or evaluate property other than in functional terms. They do, however, help us to grasp the tectonic shifts that human beings go through when property relations change.

Now this is all still very abstract, and it does not say much about any particular cases, rules, relations, or rights that make up the content of a determinate property system, especially a system of private property. The point so far is just to pose the more general question of what it means to even conceptualize property, and then to figure out the ways in which our conceptions of it have determinate consequences for our understanding of freedom, our world and ourselves. As I hope to show, the consequences will be stark. I will claim, following Marx, that given a certain understanding of the modern form of property relations under which we live, *either* we have to reject Kant and Hegel's normative conception of property as a condition of individual freedom *or* we have to reject the modern form of property relations itself in market society. The first path leads us to abandon the project of realizing the forms of freedom that Kant and Hegel defend as necessary for human flourishing, resigning us to accept the unfreedom of modern property relations, while the second path holds open the possibility of attaining that ideal of freedom after all. To get there, I will now turn to the theories of property and freedom in Kant, Hegel, and Marx.

Kant

For Kant, external freedom means the formal capacity for rational beings to act purposively in the world in relation to others.[8] This entails the ability to formulate ends and choose means to pursue those ends, independently of coercion. The basic normative requirement for the existence of external freedom is the distinction between *mine and yours*. Without this distinction, such freedom cannot even get off the ground, for how could I act purposively, that is, how could I choose the means for accomplishing my purposes if I am not allowed to determine when and how to use objects of my choice as means at all? Being able to determine when and how to use certain objects for my purposes is just another way of saying that something is *mine* and *not yours*.

According to Kant, what makes something 'mine' is that my possession, use, and claiming of it can rightfully coexist with the freedom of everyone else, that is, it does not interfere with the freedom of others to act and choose objects for their own purposes. But, pushing further, this cannot be the reason for *why* these specific things are mine, but rather only the effect of them already being mine. It is the effect of a certain social arrangement *that* something is mine, that my use of it does not interfere with your use of things, and vice versa. So, we are back to the beginning: We need to know why *these* things are mine at all, not what does it mean for them to be mine or how can I properly act within the normative boundaries of 'mineness' and 'yourness'. For Kant, these things are mine because, at some point, I acquired them in conformity with the universal principle of right and the postulate of practical reason. That is, since there is no *a priori* law of reason preventing the exclusive use of external things for my own ends, I am authorized to take possession, use, and dispose of things, as long as my taking possession does not conflict with another's claim on the object, and my use of the object does not interfere with the external freedom of everyone else.[9]

To call something mine is not, for Kant, a relation between the object and myself. Rather it is an interpersonal relation between you and me that says, *do not interfere!* Non-interference from others in using my object is the content of claiming something as mine; in fact, Kant's *Doctrine of Right* begins only with the possibility that someone else *can* wrong me by interfering with my use of something. In other words, without the possibility of wrong, Kant's theory of right is empty. The system of rules and duties that guarantees each person's independence from another is called Right [*Recht*], and the particular duties that can be coercively enforced in accordance with this system are called rights. Property—as the right to intelligible possession of objects of choice, the right to use what is mine, and the right to forcibly exclude others from interfering with it—is the foundational right in the system of Right. Without the right to possess, own, and distinguish between mine and yours, according to Kant, individuals are denied the possibility of using their innate freedom in the external world.[10]

Hegel

For Hegel, property is the minimal condition for individuals to know themselves as free.[11] To claim something as one's own is to express one's will in the objective world, a will that needs to recognize itself as capable of freely disposing over the constraints of nature. To say that the will 'needs' to recognize itself in this way, and furthermore that it 'needs' to be recognized by others in this way, means that such recognition is required for it to be considered as *free*. To be free here means to be a free *person* and not just a bundle of natural characteristics, genetic data, or animal instincts. A person can 'negate' its given characteristics by acting in the world such that its own self-determined purposes become essential for it.[12] This ability is not a natural fact but a normative achievement, and owning property is the thinnest layer of proving this achievement to oneself and others. In possessing something, one sees the efficacy of one's own will in bringing about changes in the circumstances of the world. This action, as expressed in the uses one makes of one's property, individualizes the will, and separates oneself out as a distinctly rational being in the world of things.

Taking possession, using, and alienating objects as property are the primary ways in which this abstract freedom of the will is exercised. Yet the world consists not only of things, but other wills. Normative relations between persons as free wills begins with the mutual recognition of one another's property, for only through property is each person's freedom made *objective* to one another. To recognize one another's property in contracts is another key moment in the ethical development of individuals, for such recognition produces a common will that can transcend individual interests and legitimatize political authority. If freedom consists in recognizing one's own efficacy as an agent over nature, and in being recognized as an agent in just that way, then property relations are the pure realm of freedom on this earth.[13]

But that is not all freedom consists in. As the elementary form of expression for individual agency and the first medium of mutual recognition between persons, property is a necessary, but insufficient, condition for individual and social freedom to be realized. Rights to property provide rules for the exercise of individual freedom of choice, but such rules do not provide the normative resources for determining what to pursue. The content of freedom itself must be freely determined and not a given; this content emerges for Hegel from morally grounded social institutions. Beyond rights to property then, freedom requires a system of interlocking institutions—for example, family, civil society, and the state—which Hegel collectively names *Sittlichkeit*, or ethical life. The institutions of ethical life mediate the individual will, moral values, and social roles in a self-reflective, but holistically satisfying, manner. The sphere of civil society and the laws of the state constitute the background conditions within which individuals can rightfully and freely interact as private persons with rights to property. To be free is to be more than a private person; it includes one's duties, roles, choices, values, and entire form of life. But without property, that is, without having an external sphere upon which my will can impose itself and create new purposes, I do not even recognize myself as free. One can have property without being fully free, but no one can ever be fully free without owning property.[14]

Hegel regards property not instrumentally, as a means, but rationally, as an end in itself. To see property only as a means to an end is to reduce it to an economic standpoint of particular needs and wants; to see property as an end is to treat it normatively from the standpoint of universal freedom and right. "If emphasis is placed on my needs", Hegel states, "then the possession of property appears as a means to their satisfaction, but the true position is that, from the standpoint of freedom, property is the first existence of freedom and so is in itself a substantial end."[15] Having possessions does, of course, satisfy needs, but that is *incidental* to its essence. From the normative standpoint, to own property is to carve out a space of freedom in the world upon which the individual will can act according to its own reasons. "The rationale of property", Hegel claims, "is to be found not in the satisfaction of needs but in the supersession of the pure subjectivity of personality. In his property a person exists for the first time as reason."[16] In owning property, the individual relates to itself as self-determining. It separates itself from its immediate drives and reflects on itself through the object it possesses as its own.

When Hegel locates the bearer of abstract right in the *person*, he makes it clear that the content of right "is not a matter of particular interests, of my advantage or my welfare, any more than of the particular motive behind my volition, of insight and intention."[17] Right concerns *freedom*, abstract right deals with freedom of the person, and freedom of the person manifests itself objectively in the freedom to own property. This objective freedom, however, is buttressed by a subjective, particular aspect, albeit one not rational. "The particular aspect of the matter, the fact that I make something my own as a result of my natural need, impulse, and caprice, is the particular interest satisfied by possession."[18] This "subjective" aspect is, properly speaking, called *possession*, but "the true and rightful factor in possession", where "I as free will am an object to myself in what I possess and thereby also for the first time am an actual will" is called *property*.[19] Since the rational, formal element of property is separable from the subjective, material element of possession, the question of what, why, or how much I own is irrelevant here.[20]

In other words, the realm of freedom over which abstract right presides, the domain of the property-owning person, begins in the contingent desires and needs motivating someone to possess things. These 'external circumstances' are not the basis of freedom; rather, they are just triggers for the possible transformation of 'mere possession' into property. The rational aspect of property is the recognition of one's own individual freedom in the power over the thing—not anyone's freedom but *my* freedom. Only one form of property has this power of reflecting the *uniqueness* of my will to others and myself: private property. In the *Zusatz* to §46, Hegel makes this clear: "Since property is the means whereby I give my will existence, property must also have the character of being 'this' or 'mine'. This is the important doctrine of the necessity of private property."[21] The irreducible *mineness* of freedom becomes concrete when I have the absolute power to dispose of things around me, when all things become private property for me. In external property, I see my internal agency reflected back to me in material form. In the property of others, I see their freedom as well. To make contracts with others concerning my property, that is, for us to alienate our property to each other in exchange, is the highest form of freedom that abstract right can recognize. For there, the freedom of one is achieved only through the freedom of another. Freedom, as the condition of being at home in another, finds its first refuge in commerce.

So far, I have tried to show how Kant and Hegel explain the essence of property by taking it to be fundamentally a rational form in which individual freedom is either secured or expressed in the world. Although the kinds of freedom differ in their accounts—Kant's external freedom of choice does not exactly align with Hegel's personal freedom of the will—they both make it exceptionally clear that they are not concerned with anything like the 'material' causes for the existence of property, such as the particular needs, desires, or welfare of individuals or groups to possess certain things for sustenance, luxury, pleasure, or any purpose whatsoever. To see property that way is not to treat it *rationally*, as an end in itself, but instrumentally, or economically, dependent on contingencies of nature and whim. Property is not a fact of nature or a convenience of society, but a normative accomplishment in the development of freedom.

Marx

Against this stands Marx. Submerged in the filth of material life, Marx begins from exactly the opposite of freedom: need, raw need.[22] Here, property is not anything like a coercive right based on the demands which practical reason places on all rational beings who share the earth together to live in equal freedom. Nor is it anything like the mode by which the free will stamps its uniqueness on external things for the purpose of demonstrating its own minimal freedom, and in so doing, demands that others recognize its freedom as well. Marx takes property to be fundamentally a form of fulfilling historically determined material needs, not a norm for regulating free, individual action. But unlike Kant and Hegel, these needs are not individual, natural, or contingent—the main complaints waged against them—rather they are social, artificial, and necessary. The first premise of history that Marx lays out in *The German Ideology* is the production of means to satisfy the material needs of life; the second premise is that the satisfaction of the first need by the production of means leads to the creation of new needs.[23] The way these needs are created and fulfilled is not simply natural but is a socially specific mode of appropriation and distribution of nature. To categorize the different forms in which such appropriation takes place in history is to conceptualize relations of *property*. In this account, property, emerging from material conditions of life, is an economic *means* for satisfying needs, not a juridical *end* based on norms of the free will.

By refusing to naturalize or individualize the content of such needs, Marx evades Kant and Hegel's criticisms of treating property as simply a means. Property is still conceived as universal and necessary, for it is a universal and necessary condition of all life that material needs be satisfied in some way.[24] But the ways in which such needs are born and met is socially constrained, historically dependent, and contingently accomplished. To think of property this way is to think of it less as an individual relation to a thing mediated by others, and more as *rules for reproduction* of society as a whole.[25]

Such rules for reproduction have normative consequences and, for Marx, such consequences are most important when they concern the freedom of the individual. Contrary to many interpreters, Marx's lifelong obsession with the question of private property and capital is motivated by the desire to understand how it is possible for individuals to be truly free, and to recognize themselves in their freedom as well. Freedom for Marx encapsulates both the independence that Kant's legal subject finds in a condition of right and the satisfaction that Hegel's recognition-desiring agent discovers in social roles, but it also includes more: Freedom for Marx also entails the socially achieved capacity to freely dispose over one's own *time*. The conditions of possibility for this freedom are inextricably tied to the development of capitalist private property; the actuality of this freedom, however, is ultimately bound to its abolition.[26]

Private Property, Freedom, and Capitalism

Kant grounds property in the individual's innate right to freedom.[27] Rights to property enable individuals to freely pursue their own ends among other such individuals without interfering with their freedom; this right is conditioned by the fact that human beings share space together on a limited planet and must find ways to coexist together in harmony.[28] Hegel takes property to be the expression of the individual will in things by means of one's activity or labor over it. Any form of property that does not reflect the freedom of the individual will is distorted, partial, and, in Hegel's terms, untrue. For Marx, Kant is right to see property as a kind of rule for living together, and Hegel is right to see property as an expression of individuality. For contemporary readers, Kant and Hegel are usually taken as preemptively defending the institution of private property against Marx's communist alternative.[29] But is this really the case? In my reading, Marx does not present an alternative to Kant or Hegel's normative visions of property, but rather questions the very idea that private property can fulfil these ideals of freedom in a modern capitalist world.

To put it together, I am making two claims. First, private property *is* a rule for living together, but this rule is in no way rational, free, or desirable. For in modern market societies, it is a rule imposed on the wills of all not for the purpose of protecting freedom, but for coercing individuals to work for others to meet their basic needs. And second, private property *is* an expression of the individual will, but one that is in no way rational, free, or desirable. For in modern market societies, the individual will appears detached from the social relations that gives it content, and thus, it becomes distorted beyond recognition.

What was just written depends on an argument about what modern market societies are, and why private property within them is *different* than the forms of private property that Kant, Hegel, and most other commentators describe. As previously said, for Marx, all societies have forms of property that regulate their metabolism with nature and their own internal reproduction. Each kind of property is not simply a technique for distributing resources, but a form of membership within a community. As Marx argues in the *Grundrisse*, different property relations mark different ways in which individuals relate to a social totality which they collectively compose. In describing the individuals of pre-capitalist social relations, Marx calls them all *proprietors*. A proprietor relates to his natural conditions as his *own,* "mediated by his natural membership of a community."[30] To bring the point home, Marx directly compares this to the use of language: "With regard to the individual, for instance, it is evident that he himself relates to his language as *his own* only as the natural member of a human community. Language as the product of an individual is an absurdity. But this is equally true of property."[31] On these terms, property is a form of social mediation specified by the particular ways in which the individual relates to his own conditions of life, or rather, his own freedom.

Private property, on this reading, is *not* the distinguishing feature of modern society. It is rather a still too general category of property that exists across many epochs. In fact, Marx describes the advance of feudalism exactly in the forms of *individual private property* that come to predominate. He is not talking about modern legal rights but about the underlying economic form. For Marx, and a certain brand of Marxists that follow him here, pre-capitalist forms of property share a single trait: Direct producers have immediate access to their means of subsistence; or, everyone who directly produces the necessities of life also controls the means for reproducing themselves.[32] Individual private property in this sense means the right to permanently access and use one's own means of reproduction, a condition which both peasants (in relation to their land) and artisans (in relation to their tools) shared in the pre-capitalist world.[33] To have this right of access to land and tools means having the ability to control one's conditions of reproduction. Now this is not the same as ownership in the form of modern property rights, for it does not grant one the legal right to sell something, but only to access and live off it. Yet, Marx still calls this 'individual private property' because individuals are not separated from it, but rather have immediate 'private' access to it. Seen from a contemporary perspective, this form of property can be said to provide a buffer of independence from the abstract domination of the market, for one's life is not dependent on the contingencies of market prices, but rather on one's own land and labor. When one controls one's own conditions of reproduction—tools, land, etc.—then domination occurs through *extra-economic coercion*: political force and violent oppression. The class of those who do *not* directly produce their own means of existence—the class of nobles, lords, and so on—can only exist by means of appropriating the surplus from the direct producers, that is, the peasants and farmers, artisans and serfs. For this surplus appropriation to function, a whole world of social norms and material structures is required: noble privilege and divine birthright, fortified castles and massive armies, ubiquitous enemies, and incessant taxes. The 'class of exploiters' lives off a portion of the property of the direct producers, a portion that is usually taken by force as a tax.[34]

Both Kant and Hegel vehemently opposed the idea that someone could own the 'value' of land, but not the land itself. In this sense, their accounts of private property were resolutely anti-feudalist, placing land and its value in the hands of those who work it; but this does not mean that their theories were henceforth *capitalist*. This is where all the confusion lies. For Marx, the transition from a feudal world—in which individuals *de facto* own their means of reproduction but must give up portions of their surplus at the will of a master or lord—to a capitalist world is not simply one in which people now fully own their property without the interference of other individuals (an ideal condition that Kant seeks to defend in his account). The modern form of private property that divides history into a pre-capitalist and capitalist epoch is one defined by *separation* of individuals from their means of reproduction. Capitalism does not make everyone into universal property-owners; on the contrary, it tries to make everyone essentially *property-less*.

This is the stunning inversion that Marx wracks his head on. Whereas the ideologists of the modern era defend capitalism as the true Elysium of private property and freedom, the fact is that this is the first era in which the fundamental norm is to be without property and forced into work for survival. The specific form of social mediation between individuals and their community, and between individuals and their own reproduction is the *market*, or, as Hegel calls it, *civil society*. But the modern market is not the result of free individuals bringing a portion of their surplus product to exchange for the goods of another; it is not an 'opportunity' to take up at one's will, but a form of compulsion over our lives.[35] The market is the presupposition of even having private property at all, the basic starting point which structures the way in which individuals relate to each other and themselves. When the basic elements of life are determined through market mechanisms of competition, then a new form of property has entered the world, the form of *absolute* private property, or *capitalist* private property.[36]

Capitalist private property is a social form whose rules for reproduction are *market-dependent:* To meet the social needs of material life, all appropriation and distribution of nature must be subjected to market constraints. Consequently, "this distinct system of market-dependence means that the requirements of competition and profit-maximisation are the fundamental rules of life."[37] These rules require constant innovation in the methods of production, a ceaseless drive to improve the productivity of labor, the impulse to specialize both the kind of product and type of labor, and the imperative to expand the market of sale.[38] For these are the only mechanisms by which one can produce and sell at a profitable rate of return. Because satisfying all of one's basic needs are mediated by how such needs are produced and alienated competitively, these rules for reproduction are not merely individual choices, but structural imperatives for survival. These rules mean that everyone *must* produce and/or acquire private property through the market for their own sustenance. But this presumes that one has already lost direct access to the 'individual private property' that Marx describes as the norm of pre-capitalist existence. This dissolution of individual private property by those who directly produce is one of the great preconditions of capitalism, a precondition that is simultaneous with the transformation of property relations into relations of market-dependency. Near the end of *Capital*, Marx describes this process in normatively soaked language:

> The expropriation of the direct producers was accomplished by means of the most merciless barbarism, and under the stimulus of the most infamous, the most sordid, the most petty and the most odious of passions. Private property which is personally earned, i.e., which is based, as it were, on the fusing together of the isolated, independent working individual with the conditions of his labour, is supplanted by capitalist private property, which rests on the exploitation of alien, but formally free labour.[39]

The fact that individuals are now formally 'free' to sell their capacity to labor on the market to meet their needs causes all sorts of confusion concerning the nature of freedom, property, labor, and the market. Formally speaking, it appears as if separate individuals meet on the market and engage in contracts as equals to exchange their private property, contracts that are coercively binding and authorized by the rule of law. Kant's principle of right appears to be fulfilled, for the independence of each actor is secured against interference since each one engages in consensual, contractual relations. Hegel's standard of abstract freedom also appears validated, for individuals must first place their will into an object; that is, they must labor, for them to have any private property with which to exchange. In terms of the content of the exchange, however, it is anything but free or equal. What one exchanges on the market (labor for wages), what one produces (commodities for capitalists), and how one does it (in competition with other firms) fundamentally constrain the possibility of individual freedom in both Kant and Hegel's sense.[40] This brings us back to the problem of abstracting from the *matter* of property to look purely at its form. Formally, the conditions of right are satisfied, while materially they are denied. The freedom to use objects of choice for pursuing one's ends without the interference of others, the right to property in Kant, is now possible only by making oneself constantly dependent on the choices of others, choices which are not even *their* own, but constrained by others, and others, *ad infinitum*. The hope of universal independence has become the reality of generalized interference. The power to determine the fate of external things so as to make one's freedom objective to oneself and others, the right to property in Hegel, is now the power to be determined by external things, making one's alienation objective to oneself and others. The appropriation of freedom has become the expropriation of life.[41]

Conclusion

Where does this leave us? Are property relations rules for maintaining the total economic reproduction of society, or are they norms for ensuring individual coexistence according to autonomy and non-interference? Are property relations a set of natural constraints on social survival or do they express the individual liberation from natural constraints of scarcity? Is property a right of coercive protection against others or a realm for the development of individual, free personality? Is the market a presupposition for the emergence of property relations or is it the outcome of the interaction of individual proprietors? Is it possible to have it both ways? And what about my shirt? Are we any closer to understanding why it is mine? Perhaps by going back to my shirt, we can illuminate some of the questions floating around.

For Kant, this shirt is mine because I am authorized by reason to acquire things as my property in order to pursue my ends independently of the interference of others. This authorization is grounded in my one innate right, the inalienable right to freedom, but my owning and using of this shirt must not conflict with the freedom of anyone else. It is my rational duty to own things so as to preserve the formal structure of freedom between individuals who share space together. When realizing this concept of ownership is made untenable due to contingent social conditions, then there is a duty to change those conditions so as to make a world of property the norm. This shirt I own, and all the myriad property relations that mediated its acquisition, serve this one ultimate purpose: to allow me to be me through doing whatever it is I choose to do with it. As an object, this shirt is nothing, and I am merely a body that it covers. As property, this shirt is mine, and I am the soul which gives it life.

For Hegel, this shirt is mine because in owning it, my will is reflected back to me as free from any natural constraints, and free to determine itself as it may. This shirt shows others and myself that I am irreducibly unique; for only I have the power and authority to do whatever it is that I want with it. In so doing, I bind myself to my property, forming my freedom through it, though never being subject to it. Recognizing that this shirt is mine binds others to me in the mutual constitution of our freedom as equal persons. More than that, I am bound to all the people whose free activity brought this shirt to me in a web of respect that provides the basic foundation for modern ethical life.

For Marx, this shirt is not the source of my freedom, but the crystallized result of all the coercion that led to my acquiring it. What makes it mine is that I happened to have enough money to exchange for its value, an exchange determined by the market-dependent choices of others. I acquired this money by adapting my life to the rule for reproduction for how to acquire means to pursue one's end in this society: by selling my time to work for others, work that I found only because of the market-determined requirements of others; these means for which I labored sufficed only due to the market-dependent needs of my employers; their 'needs' do not have anything to do with their individual motives, but are the needs of maintaining a competitive business. All the elements that went into bringing the shirt to me, and all the elements that brought me to the shirt, were filtered at every point by a form of property that grants dominance to market-imperatives which regulate the lives of all. Succumbing to the market is my only possibility for staying alive, and owning this shirt is nothing but the minimal recognition that my existence is not yet worthless. To call this freedom is an assault on all those who fought in the word's name.

When presented with Marx's account of modern property relations, reactions usually follow the same path as the five stages of grieving: first denial, then anger, bargaining, depression, and, finally, acceptance. What is so shocking about Marx's explanation of capitalist property relations is how banal it is today. Of course we live in a capitalist society where all needs are subordinated to market requirements; of course we live in a world where no one has any guarantee to own property unless they work on the market in return for a wage; of course we live on a planet structured by the telos of productivity, competition, and growth above all. Any businessman can confirm Marx now. What is harder to grasp is what this means for individual freedom.

If we take Marx's analysis seriously, then either Kant and Hegel are right about property, but we need a non-capitalist world to realize it, or they are wrong, and property has nothing to do with freedom at all. The easy option would be to go for the latter, arguing that property systems are just amoral, economic schemes for the distribution of scarce resources, and that freedom is something completely different. But, if we take concrete freedom to mean, on the one hand, the capacity to pursue one's ends free of domination, and, on the other hand, the ability to express oneself by disposing over individual things according to one's will, then the form of capitalist private property that mediates both individual action and social membership in market-dependent societies is incompatible with the essence of freedom.

In the *Doctrine of Right*, Kant states that if you cannot live together with others in a state of nature without harming others, then you have the duty to leave that state and enter a civil condition, a condition of law and justice where the property of each can be secured.[42] This is not a social contract argument based on self-interest, avoiding violence, or maximizing efficiency; it is a demand of practical reason itself. Only when property is secured, enforced, and authorized by the will of all in accordance with the principle of right, does individual freedom reign. Furthermore, Hegel's entire philosophy of spirit, including his *Philosophy of Right*, can in fact be read as one long story about leaving the state of nature behind and finding ourselves at home with each other instead.

What is the state of nature? A situation where no one has secure property, where anything can be taken away at any moment due to the wills of others. But is this not the state of capitalism, where anyone's property can be immediately rendered valueless depending on the contingent choices of others, as reflected in the market?[43] Where no one has any secure property but his or her own laboring body? Even one's own laboring body can be rendered useless and disposable when the market conditions are not right, and then there is nothing left to do but beg, steal, and plunder. If this is the state of capitalism, then according to Kant and Hegel, we have a duty to leave it.[44]

Notes

1. On not including this prohibition within the concept of property, see Jeremy Waldron, *The Right to Private Property* (Oxford: Clarendon, 1988), 32–3.
2. Classically, these are Nozick's entitlement principles of acquisition and transfer. See Robert Nozick, *Anarchy, State, and Utopia* (New York: Basic, 1974).
3. For the classic bundle, see Anthony M. Honoré, "Ownership," in *Oxford Essays in Jurisprudence*, ed. A.G. Guest (Oxford: Oxford University Press, 1961), 107–47. On a pluralist account that tries to incorporate all these principles into one theory, see Stephen Munzer, *A Theory of Property* (Cambridge: Cambridge University Press, 1990). Most accounts reduce property to one or two principles, usually gleaned from Locke or Bentham.
4. See Waldron (*The Right to Private Property*, 51–2) on property as an "essentially contested concept." To get around this, Waldron separates the *concept* of property (its essence) from its many contested *conceptions* (its practical realizations). Although this is helpful in seeing the diversity of forms of property that can exist, it is not helpful in understanding why property exists.
5. Variations on this theme appear in Grotius, Hobbes, Locke, Rousseau, and Kant.
6. For a good overview, see Peter Garnsey, *Thinking about Property: From Antiquity to the Age of Revolution* (Cambridge: Cambridge University Press, 2007).
7. See sections §1–9 of Kant's *Doctrine of Right*, collected in: Immanuel Kant, *Practical Philosophy*, ed. Mary J. Gregor (Cambridge: Cambridge University Press, 1996).
8. The focus here is on Kant's *Doctrine of Right*. For helpful guides, see Arthur Ripstein, *Force and Freedom* (Cambridge: Harvard University Press, 2009); Robert Pippin, "Mine and Thine: The Kantian State," in *The Cambridge Companion to Kant and Modern Philosophy*, ed. Paul Guyer (Cambridge: Cambridge University Press 2006), 416–46; Wolfgang Kersting, "Politics, Freedom and Order," in *The Cambridge Companion to Kant*, ed. Paul Guyer, 342–66; Katrin Flikschuh, *Kant and Modern Political Philosophy* (Cambridge: Cambridge University Press, 2004); Mary Gregor, "Kant's theory of property," *The Review of Metaphysics* 41, no. 4 (1988): 757–87; B. Sharon Byrd and Joachim Hruschka, *Kant's Doctrine of Right: A Commentary* (Cambridge: Cambridge University Press, 2010).
9. See the Postulate of Practical Reason and the Permissive Law in Kant's *Doctrine of Right*, 6:246–247.
10. The core of the *Doctrine of Right*, from §1 to 18, concerns how legal possession can be (rationally) possible and (normatively) justified. The second half of the *Doctrine of Right* argues that coercive rights to property can only be permanently authorized in a civil condition based on public right. Until then, all claims of possessions are only *provisionally rightful*.
11. My focus here is only on property as an "abstract right" in Hegel's *Philosophy of Right*. See Georg Wilhelm Friedrich Hegel, *Elements of the Philosophy of Right*, ed. Wood (Cambridge: Cambridge University Press, 1991). For helpful texts on Hegel's theory of property, see Joachim Ritter, "Person and Property in Hegel's Philosophy of Right

(§§34–81)," in *Hegel on Ethics and Politics*, ed. Robert B. Pippin and Ottfried Höffe (Cambridge: Cambridge University Press, 2004), 101–23; Alan Patten, *Hegel's Idea of Freedom* (Oxford: Oxford University Press, 1999), ch. 5; Margaret Jane Radin, "Property and Personhood," *Stanford Law Review* 34, no. 5 (1982): 957–1015; Paul Thomas, "Property's Properties: From Hegel to Locke," *Representations* 84, no. 1 (2003): 30–43; Peter G. Stillman, "Property, Freedom, and Individuality in Hegel's and Marx's Political Thought," in *Nomos XXII: Property*, ed. J. Roland Pennock (New York: New York University Press, 1980), 130–67.

12 On Hegel's theory of the freedom of the will, see the introduction to the *Philosophy of Right*, §1–33, and on the concept of the person and personality, see the beginning of the section on "Abstract Right," §34–40. It should be noted that Hegel's claim that the efficacy of the will can be objectively recognized in property overlaps greatly with Fichte's theory of property. See Johann Gottlieb Fichte *Foundations of Natural Right*, ed. Frederick Neuhouser (Cambridge: Cambridge University Press, 2000).

13 See Hegel, *Philosophy of Right*, §44–77.

14 The rabble [*Pöbel*] is Hegel's name for the figure of the propertyless will. See §244–7 in the *Philosophy of Right*. For more on this, see Frank Ruda, *Hegel's Rabble: An Investigation into Hegel's Philosophy of Right* (London: Continuum, 2011), and my review, Jacob Blumenfeld, "Hegel's Rabble by Frank Ruda," *Bulletin of the Hegel Society of Great Britain* 34, no. 2 (2013): 280–5.

15 Hegel, *Philosophy of Right*, §45R.

16 Ibid., §41A.

17 Ibid., §37.

18 Ibid., §45.

19 Ibid.

20 See §49 of the *Philosophy of Right*, where Hegel drives the point home once more: "In relation to external things, the rational aspect is that I possess property, but the particular aspect comprises subjective aims, needs, arbitrariness, abilities, external circumstances, and so forth (see §45). On these mere possession as such depends, but this particular aspect has in this sphere of abstract personality not yet been posited as identical with freedom. What and how much I possess, therefore, is a matter of indifference so far as rights are concerned."

21 Ibid., §46A.

22 One could also add Nietzsche and Freud to this line of thinking.

23 Karl Marx and Friedrich Engels, *The German Ideology* (Amherst, NY: Prometheus, 1998), 47–8.

24 It is tempting to interpret Marx's object as empirical *possession* and not legal *property*. But Marx treats the juridical category of property as emerging from the economic practices of possession, labor, and exchange, and *not* from some independent institutional authority.

25 My reading of property relations in Marx is indebted to Robert Brenner and Ellen Meiksins Wood. See Robert Brenner, "Social Basis of Economic Development," in *Analytical Marxism*, ed. John Roemer (Cambridge: Cambridge University Press, 1986), 23–53, and Ellen Meiksins Wood, *The Origin of Capitalism: A Longer View* (London: Verso, 2002).

26 On freedom as the ownership of time in Marx, see Jacob Blumenfeld, "The Abolition of Time in Hegel's 'Absolute Knowing' (and its Relevance for Marx)," *Idealistic Studies* 43, no. 1 (2013): 111–9.

27 Kant, *Doctrine of Right*: "There is only one innate right," 6:231.

28 Ripstein and Flikschuh take Kant's thinking of space and the shape of the earth very seriously as the material precondition for the normative theory of right.
29 Concerning Kant, see Kersting, "Politics, Freedom and Order." For Hegel, see Patten, *Hegel's Idea of Freedom*.
30 Karl Marx, "Outlines of the Critique of Political Economy," in *Marx & Engels Collected Works* (MECW), Vol. 28 (New York: Lawrence & Wishart, 2010), 414.
31 Marx continues: "Language itself is just as much the product of a community as in another respect it is the being of the community, its articulate being, as it were." (Ibid.)
32 In Brenner's terms: "The direct producers held direct (i.e. non-market) access to their full means of subsistence, that is the tools and land needed to maintain themselves" (Brenner, "Social Basis of Economic Development," 27).
33 See Karl Marx, *Capital I* (London: Penguin Classics, 1990), 927.
34 See Brenner "Social Basis of Economic Development," and Wood, *Origins of Capitalism*.
35 See the *Ellen Meiksins Wood Reader*, ed. Larry Patriquin (Leiden: Brill, 2012), 39–40, where Wood demystifies the conventional view of the market as being an 'opportunity' instead of being a form of compulsion.
36 Marx calls this capitalist private property; Ellen Meiksins Wood calls it absolute private property.
37 Ibid., 37.
38 "The specific precondition of capitalism is a transformation of social-property relations that generates capitalist 'laws of motion': the *imperatives* of competition and profit-maximisation, a *compulsion* to reinvest surpluses, and a systematic and relentless *need* to improve labour-productivity and develop the forces of production." (Ibid., 43)
39 Karl Marx, *Capital I*, 928.
40 "The relation of exchange between capitalist and workers becomes a mere semblance belonging only to the process of circulation, it becomes a mere form, which is alien to the content of the transaction itself, and merely mystifies it. The constant sale and purchase of labour-power is the form; the content is the constant appropriation by the capitalist, without equivalent, of a portion of the labour of others which has already been objectified, and his repeated exchange of this labour for a greater quantity of the living labour of others." (Ibid., 729)
41 The very last line of Marx's *Capital* reiterates this point: "The capitalist mode of production and accumulation, and therefore capitalist private property as well, have for their fundamental condition the annihilation of that private property which rests on the labour of the individual himself; in other words, the expropriation of the worker." (Ibid., 940)
42 See the third Ulpian formula in Kant's *Doctrine of Right*, 6:237, as well as paragraphs 41–2, the Transition from Private Right to Public Right. On this demand, see Pippin, "Mine and Thine."
43 Even Hegel remarks on the "remnants of the state of nature" in civil society. See *Philosophy of Right*, §200R.
44 Thanks to Matt Congdon, John Clegg, and the members of Rahel Jaeggi's *Sozialphilosophie* Colloquium at Humboldt-Universität zu Berlin for helpful comments.

5

I, the Revolution, Speak

Lenin's Speculative (Hegelian) Style

Frank Ruda

1. Volumes have been filled with varying answers on how to understand the move, if it is one—and be it an inversion or a progression, a turn away or an excavation of some unrevealed core, a revolution in thought, a reform, or just a repetition in disguise, perhaps with a difference—from Hegel to Marx. Formulas have been coined, repeated, modified, explained, revoked, dispatched, revived. Has the time now come—after the failures of traditional forms of Marxism—to repeat the same procedure, only in reverse? Does a resuscitation of Hegel need to be undertaken when Marx(ism) seems to have become a historical fossil, once dangerous but now banished to state museums of history? In any case, it is obvious that the move from Marx back to Hegel can also take a variety of forms and may entail a panorama of varying motivations: from conservative ones, attempting to replace the emphasis on practical emancipation with a revitalized right-wing Hegelian defense of moribund institutions or any state whatsoever, to emancipatory ones seeking to add to Marx all those moments where Hegel actually seemed to be more radical than Marx himself. And even within the emancipatory family of thinkers making the move from Marx back to Hegel, there is an entire and complex set of different paths to explore. To recall only some of the most influential German thinkers of the last century who can be considered members of this family, say Adorno, Bloch, Lukács, or Marcuse, is enough to see its variety. In the following, I want to examine a thinker who might not usually be the first to come to mind when one thinks about moving back from Marx to Hegel, but who was in fact the first to make this very move as a Marxist: Lenin.

2. Between 1914 and 1915, Lenin read Hegel. Closely. The politically shattering experience of 1914[1] led Lenin to exile to Switzerland and this is where he turned to the one philosopher who never explicitly wanted to change the world, but solely to comprehend it. He turned to one of the very few philosophers for whom the eleventh thesis on Feuerbach actually sounds true.[2] In exile, Lenin turned to a philosopher who (thought in such way as if he always already had) exiled himself in advance from any practical intervention in the world. Exile squared (exile[2]), a kind of meta-exile. This

is not an overemphasis, because when Lenin was theoretically working through the disappointing practical experiences of 1914, he did not turn to Hegel's more 'practical' writings (e.g., the *Philosophy of Right* or the *Realphilosophie*), but to the one book whose aspiration could not have been more out of sync with a dedicated revolutionary, since it is in this book, namely, in his *Science of Logic*,[3] that Hegel contends to depict God's thought before the creation of the world. When there seemed to be no (practical-revolutionary) way out of and in the world as it was, the way out (of the world) seemed to be the only way out. Hegel was this way out.[4]

3. When the political situation turned out to be catastrophic, "Lenin was ... the only one to articulate the Truth of the catastrophe ... via a detour of a close reading of Hegel".[5] So, Hegel allowed Lenin to articulate the truth of the catastrophe. This truth was, *inter alia*, that all avowed Marxists were Marxists only by name. And it took Hegel to see how this was possible and even worse, to see that because the Marxists never understood Hegel, they also did not understand Marx.[6] So, the move from Marx to Hegel is crucial, since without it, there is no Marx(ism) properly understood. But with this, there is a lot more at stake in Lenin's reading of Hegel: If exiling oneself to Hegel[7] could be considered a part not only of a rescue mission of the Marxism of which Lenin was a contemporary, but also of a potential strategy for revolutionizing what needs to be revolutionized (socio-democratic Marxism) in order for there to be a thought of revolution (and thus Marxism) at all, the conceptual tools that Hegel provided Lenin with can hardly be overestimated. Lenin went from Marx to Hegel in order to (re)constitute Marx.

4. We can enter into the details by referring to an aspect of the *Science of Logic* that Lenin does not explicitly comment on. But this point is nonetheless not entirely contingent. It is a relevant starting point because it has a crucial immanent relation to the totality of Hegel's elaborations, namely, to the speculative means of (re)presenting dialectics itself. Hegel calls these means speculative words. After having established in the *Phenomenology of Spirit* the proper representation that allows for the speculative movement of philosophy—a form that he refers to as speculative proposition—Hegel refers to speculative words in the *Logic*. He notes: "It can delight thought to come across such words, and to discover in naive form, already in the lexicon as one word of opposite meanings, that union of opposites which is the result of speculation but to the understanding is nonsensical."[8] Some words are not only condensations of a multiplicity of even contradictory meanings; they are also embodiments, material manifestations, manifest traces of the speculative nature of spirit itself. And they are thus not understood by ordinary thinking. It is from such words that a thought can commence, and it is in such words—*Aufhebung* being certainly the most famous one—that a speculative spirit (sometimes) speaks.[9] Philosophy, ideally, speaks in speculative sentences and words.

5. Why is this peculiar dimension of language that was rarely systematically examined, even in the context of Hegel's philosophy, relevant for the following observations? Answer: because one might thereby be able to investigate the effects that Lenin's return to Hegel had on Lenin's own discourse. This can be done by addressing *the* Leninist question par excellence, the question of organization. Yet, this does not mean to focus on what Lenin may have learned from Hegel about the constitution of

the party or about the dictatorship of the proletariat (or of the bourgeoisie—which exists when the former does not). Rather, my question will be a different one, namely: How does the revolution speak? Why? Because the revolution took place after Lenin had read Hegel. So, this is my hypothesis: One may detect in Lenin's discourse a peculiar Hegelian effect. In other words, the question that will stand at the forefront of what follows is: Is there, and can there be, a revolutionary symbolic form or a revolutionary use of language? Like speculative sentences and words, only in and for politics?

6. To answer this question, one would have to analyze the singular consistency of concrete revolutionary discourses. Yet the subsequent reflections will only be able to point in the direction in which such an analysis would have to be developed. The idea behind this investigation, to allude to the famous prosopopoeia coined by Lacan—"I, truth, speak"[10]—is the following: If Lenin's position was continually linked not only to thinking from the standpoint of the proletariat but also to that of "the actuality of the revolution",[11] his discourse is linked to an implicit "I, Revolution, speak." Trotsky noted that Lenin's texts and speeches often "contained the pronoun 'I'"[12] and that they always resembled a kind of conversation.[13] One can thus assume that one reads a kind of revolutionary soliloquy with which Lenin attempts to express the inner voice[14] of the revolution; the inner voice of the subject of the revolution. How does this voice speak? This question I take to point in the direction of what one may call Lenin's speculative style.

7. My starting point is a series of rather parenthetical observations. Yuri Tynjanov once noted that Lenin's polemical-rhetorical methods contained a "revolution in the field of the style of speeches and writing".[15] And Victor Shklovsky characterized such a revolution as being part and parcel of the "language of revolution".[16] Because as much as the dictatorship of the proletariat was an institution of a new kind, the kind of language Lenin used appeared to be a "language of a new kind".[17] All this seems to indicate that Daniel Bensaïd was right to point out that every emancipatory politics "has its own language, grammar, and syntax"[18]—but it also points to the fact that one may detect in Lenin's discourse, and similar to Marx's famous comment about the Paris Commune, "the political form at last discovered",[19] something like the linguistic or discursive form of the revolution at last discovered. This is fundamentally consistent with Lenin's repeated invective "to show [or voice, F.R.] things as they actually are",[20] or with his insistence to articulate what he referred to as "truth" against all obscuration, for example when he claims in 1917 that "the crux of the political situation at this moment is to be able to make the masses see the truth".[21] Lenin's discourse speaks a language supposed to make people see truth; a political vision and language of truth. Yet, as Lenin learned from Hegel, truth necessitates its own form of discursive (re) presentation. And it is important to immediately remark that truth here does not simply mean objective truth. Rather, it is a truth that does not exist outside of its articulation; no truth without the subjective engagement of bringing it out and forth. So, it is an engaged, a subjective—not subjectivist—truth; a one-sided "proletarian truth".[22] But how does such truth become visible? How does it speak?

8. Already in his notebook on Hegel's *Logic*, Lenin excerpted a passage in which Hegel deals with "pure truth" and where the average materialist thinker is surprised to read (in Lenin's transcription of Hegel's words) that: "this formal element must

therefore be thought of as being in itself much richer in determinations and content, and as having infinitely more influence upon the concrete than it is generally held to have."[23] The influence on the concrete hinges on the form, on the formal element (of the discourse). Hence, Lenin must have learned from Hegel that any politics of truth must have a specific discursive form.

9. Famously, long before Lenin but not as long before Hegel, Kant noticed a specific link between the revolution and the symbolic. In the second section of his *Conflict of Faculties*, where Kant elucidates the conceptual exigencies that need to be fulfilled to avoid the merely abstract positing of a constant progress of mankind toward the better, he claims that one needs a "prediction".[24] But predictions are essentially problematic, simply because there can always be more than one. And some are not emphasizing the progress toward the better but rather toward the worse. Kant inferred that there was no empirical way to resolve this conflict, which is why "[t]here must be some experience in the human race which, as an event, points to the disposition and capacity of the human race to be the cause of its own advance toward the better".[25] There must be an event that provides us with the concrete experience that humanity itself determines its own development, and how could this not be toward the better? Even though this may not "happen in my life and I [may not] have the experience of it",[26] such an event, "undetermined with regard to time", that is, undetermined with regard to its concrete historical context, must be considered as a "historical sign", that is, as a "*signum rememorativum, demonstrativum, prognostikon*".[27] Some events in the course of human history are more than mere objective occurrences. They are signs that "point to" the better. They have the character of signs punctuating history, signs that mankind sends to itself, receives and interprets to better (or at all) understand its historical mission. They are historical points, points in history, punctuations in and of history from which one can project a vector toward the better: One should never forget (*signum rememorativum*) that mankind's future (*signum prognostikon*) tends toward the better and that this has been proven (*signum demonstrativum*). The sign-character of these events thus depends on being inscribed in the framework of mankind's history that provides them with their very own readability. Those events are signs, yet the meanings of those signs are already determined. They all mean the same: progress. And thus they all point in the same direction.

10. Alain Badiou has quite harshly criticized this Kantian conception. Yet, his criticism is not primarily a criticism of Kant's determination of the historical sign; rather, it is related to Kant's prominent definition of the enthusiasm that he attributes to the observers of events with such sign-character, more precisely of the French Revolution. In his *Critique of Judgment*, Kant defines enthusiasm as "a straining of our forces by ideas that impart to the mind a momentum",[28] and as sublime, that is, as a moment in which "the senses no longer see anything before them, while yet the unmistakable and indelible idea of morality remains".[29] Enthusiasm is an interpenetration of idea and affect. As such, it is "comparable to madness"[30] because our imagination works rampantly within it. In the latter *Conflict of Faculties*, Kant recalls this definition when he talks about the spectators of the French Revolution and attributes to them "a wishful participation that borders closely on enthusiasm".[31] It is precisely this definition of enthusiasm as wishful participation, as enjoyment of the wish to participate, which

becomes the target of Badiou's harsh critique, since the wish to participate does not amount to actual participation. So, enthusiasm is experienced only by those who do not act, and only at a distance to the actual events.

11. If one rearticulates this claim and links it to Kant's theory of the historical sign, this very sign proves peculiarly detached from the very practice of which it is supposed to be the sign. This does not simply bring forth the problem that the historical sign loses the particularity and singularity of the event of which it is supposed to be a sign (as it always means the same, namely, progress). The problem is rather that Kant articulates his theory in the face of the events of 1789—events that, as Hegel will later insist, manifest the historical moment in which there was a (finally violent) liberation of the very concept of freedom itself. In other words, Kant wants to argue that to conceive of progress in history one must conceive of progress in a history of free, collective self-determination. But when he actually refers to an event of free, collective self-determination he pacifies the radicality of it—not only because it has an already pre-assigned meaning, but also because this meaning only emerges from the perspective of the spectator, hence externally. Thus, and this is Badiou's critical point, we don't end up with self-determination but with heteronomous determination. Kant eliminates from 1789 precisely what he attributes to it because of the way in which he attributes to it.

12. Badiou's quite harsh conclusion from this analysis runs as follows: If one wants to understand what happened in and with the French Revolution, Kant does not help. He writes: "It is through Saint-Just and Robespierre that you enter into this singular truth unleashed by the French Revolution, and on the basis of which you form a knowledge, and not through Kant or François Furet."[32] The only way not to misjudge it (by applying some external standard, such as the progress of human freedom, i.e., as Kant does, or by judging and evaluating a historical event only by its final outcomes, as Furet does) is to judge the revolution from an immanent perspective. This means that one must take the perspective of an active participant, not a passive observer, evaluating the revolution by means of the very standards it is in the process of establishing.

13. This can be translated into the following: Kant's take on the revolution as historical sign is important, but it has to be elaborated in a different manner. If there is something like the dimension of the historical sign in political practice, that is, if there is any internal link between political practice and the symbolic, it can be grasped only by assuming the subjective position of the very agent of these practices; only by analyzing the singular sign-use of the participants of these practices and not by reference to a transhistorical framework (the *one* history of progress). One thereby gives an immanent account of the very specific usages of signs, words, propositions, war-cries, watchwords, slogans, and so on. One can thereby account for the constitution of historical signs as much as for their singularly historical dimension. It is only from an immanent perspective, and never from an external one, that the functioning of sign-practice becomes intelligible, of practices that one may call subjective (not subjectivist). What is at stake is thus the purely subjective constitution and significance of historical signs. Only in this way can one think how the revolution speaks.

14. The danger arising here has been paradigmatically formulated in the famous Wittgensteinean argument about the impossibility of a private language. This

argument was already formulated by Marx in the *Grundrisse*, even though this is often forgotten.[33] The coordinates of this argument are well known: All language exists before the individual. And it does not exist in the abstract but is adapted and determined by historically varying social-collective practices. An individual can speak a language only by becoming a member of a language community that represents a historical, specific adaptation of a particular language. A private language cannot exist simply because language is per se a social phenomenon, and a language that only I understand thus ontologically loses the status of being a language. Yet, there are moments in the lives of human beings where they seem to do the impossible: They seem to create their own language and at the same time separate it, cut it off, and liberate it not only from its objective references, but even from the dimension of meaning and thereby from its potential comprehensibility by others. The language practice of love is a good example here. It may appear—to non-participating onlookers—(often) as meaningless, devoid of sense, repetitive, childish and infantile, peculiarly self-contained and self-enclosed, perhaps even self-immunizing. This is because it is indifferent not only to the world and to others, but also to the standard communicative ways of language usage. Language no longer serves as a tool for objective meaning, knowledge production, and communication but, rather, as a subjective truth-articulation. Peculiarly indifferent to communication, this practice may appear to be a language not of 'l'art pour l'art' but of 'l'amour pour l'amour', as it were, or even of 'le langue de l'amour pour le langue de l'amour'.[34] People in love make a different use of language, as if they misuse or even abuse it, since they subtract its seemingly constitutive relation to meaning and communication with others. It is as if such language use turns one's own language into a foreign language, a language estrangement.[35] But this is not simply a private language; it is at least minimally collective as it involves two people. And such a language practice can potentially be the practice of whosoever (falls in love). There seems to be a universality that pertains to a language that stands as an exception to the ordinary laws of language.

15. So, if historical events have a symbolic dimension, which cannot be grasped in a transcendental manner but only immanently, what kind of sign is the historical sign? I believe Lenin's answer to this question was: It is a point. He constantly emphasizes the turning points, the pivot points, the reversal points, the points of decision, the *punctum saliens* of a particular historical situation in which he intervenes. In 1905 for example—I single out just a few of the numerous cases—he states that "a turning-point in Russia's history has been reached";[36] in 1917, he emphasis that not only "the world war" but "as well the Russian Revolution has reached a turning-point",[37] and even publishes a text under this very name.[38] For Lenin, the question is always to get to a point, to get the point, to demonstrate it, to treat it properly and to not not get it. The point is for Lenin the crucial orientation mark of political practice. It is as if Lenin modified the famous eleventh thesis into: Philosophers have only interpreted the world; the point is to get the point and to treat it. His discourse continually runs off to the points that are essential; where a decision cannot not be taken. These are the points in which a whole situation in its complexity is condensed; they are what I want to call—with reference to Paul Celan—its *fugue*.[39] It is by finding and treating its fugue that a situation can be transformed.

16. Lenin's discourse traces these fugues and reduces the respective situation to them; he condenses it by abbreviating and creating a fugue that always takes the form of 'x or non-x'. Lenin may have learned this lesson from Hegel, who writes in his *Philosophy of History*:

> A history ... must indeed foreshorten its pictures by abstractions, must epitomize, abbreviate; and this includes not merely the omission of events and deeds, but whatever is involved in the fact that Thought is, after all, the most trenchant epitomist. A battle, a great victory, a siege, no longer maintains its original proportions, but is condensed into its simple determinations.[40]

Lenin constantly abbreviates, epitomizes, omits, and condenses into (and to reach) the form of the point. His discourse is one of pointed condensation and condensing punctuation.

17. These points have in Lenin always a doubly spatial and temporal dimension. They are turning-points and points in time at and in which one has to decide, and of whose treatment the continuation and further existence of the emancipatory movement and the revolutionary party hinges. In a letter to the central committee from 1917, entitled "Marxism and Insurrection", Lenin defends the thesis that as a Marxist one must treat insurrection as an art. This means for him that "[i]nsurrection must rely upon that *turning-point* in the history of the growing revolution where the activity of the advanced ranks is at its height", that is, where there is a "*revolutionary upsurge of the people*".[41] To treat insurrection as an art (always) means to locate it at a historical turning-point; at a fugue. Otherwise, in short, one falls into Blanquism; into the idealist belief that a small group of intellectuals alone will change the world. But to root insurrection properly in the situation, one also needs the right point in time, "*the right moment to start the insurrection*".[42] Even though one must tirelessly analyze the situation, objectively, there will never be the right moment—all localization and timing implies a subjective assessment of the situation and hence a risk, a bet on political timing or rhythm in which one wagers that now is either the time to act and one must not reflect or to exile and reorganize oneself. Such punctuation is essentially speculative—in all possible senses of the term. But for emancipatory politics (in Lenin), one needs the punctuations of time and space. If one can find the right fugues—this is Lenin's version of Hegel's positing of one's own presuppositions—or is able to force them, it is important to also find a condensed representation of them. As Lenin states: "The briefer and more trenchant the declaration, the better."[43] The question of properly combining the timing and the localization of the fugue is what Lenin calls the crux, key point, or crucial point of the revolution.[44]

18. The key point is the vector that allows for a proper connection of temporal and spatial fugues; it not only begins with a concrete analysis of concrete situations, emancipatory politics furthermore begins thereby and point by point to unfold a space and time of its own.[45] This issue of connecting points also—at a pragmatic as well as theoretical level—explains Lenin's interest in certain media and institutions (such as the telephone and the post office): "We must ... occupy the telegraph and the telephone exchange at once, move our insurrection headquarters to the central

telephone exchange and connect it by telephone with all the factories, all the regiments, all the points of armed fighting."[46] If there is a historical, a speculative-historical sign[47] in Lenin, it is the point. His discourse is one of points, pointed, punctuating, punctuated.

19. What does it mean to get, to hit, to make a point in political practice? It always implies to take a standpoint, "exclusively ... the standpoint of the proletariat".[48] But it is important that this standpoint does not always preexist the act of taking a position. Sometimes it must be generated in the very act of positioning oneself. It also means to speak pointedly, that is, from a one-sided, partial perspective so that one punctuates the situation by condensing it in a single fugue. The famous concrete analysis of concrete situations is never an objective analysis of objective situations; it is always pointed and pointing analysis, from one point toward another. From the fugues to a building. Lenin, almost in a Kleistian manner, gradually unfolds a clear and distinct line in the process of detecting the points. There is no line before the points and there are no points before one starts consistently connecting them. Perhaps this is why he liked Napoleon's saying, "On s'engage et puis on voit." But this also means, as Žižek has remarked, that he "has to cut out [his] path ... struggle, looking for the proper language to express it."[49] This is to say that finding and articulating the fugues and connecting the dots means to create what Trotsky called a "picture in perspective of the whole".[50] The points at stake here are points of a Hegelian concrete universality. From articulating them thus arises a claim to universality that cannot not be contested. The truth of such a punctuating politics of truth is an engaged, practical, subjective, and subjectivizing truth. But if truth could speak, how would it?

20. It is instructive to pause for a moment and raise the question of whether this means that for Lenin there is—according to the famous claim of Althusser that there is class struggle in theory and philosophy, notably between idealism and materialism—class struggle in language. This question is a real question for at least two reasons: The first is that Hegel's emphasis on the speculative mode of the presentation of philosophy indicates that there are not only two different ways of presenting but also two ways of reading philosophy: speculatively and non-speculatively. This leads to similar paradoxes to the just depicted (only with a speculative mind will we be able to read a speculative text). The second but no less pressing reason is that in 1950, Stalin published a text with the title "Marxism and the Problem of Linguistics"[51] in which he harshly refutes this very idea. He states that language is not a part of what traditional Marxism called the superstructure and therefore cannot be changed by transformations of the economic base (by means of revolution, for example). There can be new words and expressions, but the "basic word stock" and the "grammatical system of the language" remain stable. Language is for Stalin not created by a class but from society as a whole and there is therefore, in spite of class struggle, always sociality in language even of those who are otherwise enemies: "However sharp the class struggle may be, it cannot lead to the disintegration of society." Even antagonistic classes speak one language. Language is a neutral medium of communication and has thus never a class character, but therefore also no history in the strong sense of the term. It is rather an ideal synchronic social medium that may allow for variation but for no profound transformations.[52] Lenin's conception and use of language is profoundly anti-Stalinist;

Stalin's theory of language is anti-Leninist. For Lenin, language is no neutral medium of communication; rather, there are context-bound, different uses of language.

21. Is there thus, for Lenin, class struggle in language (and might this be a consequence of his reading of Hegel)? To begin answering this question, one can recall an anecdote from Trotsky. It took place at the first all-Russian congress of the central committee:

> For his second speech, too, Lenin chose fearfully simple words from the letter of a certain peasant: 'We must grab the bourgeoisie more firmly so that they will burst in all their seams, then the war would come to an end; but if we do not grab the bourgeoisie thus, it will be nasty for us.' And this simple naive quotation is the whole program?[53]

The program and its points are—at least in this case—not decreed autocratically but rather originate in the masses, who Lenin literally takes at their word. The same obviously holds for the slogan 'All power to the soviets', which Lenin saw at a protest after the publication of the Milyukov note[54] and turned into a principle. One is here clearly not dealing with a new language, but with a specific usage of signifiers and watchwords that already circulated among the proletarian and peasant masses.[55] Lenin thus takes an immanent perspective to these very masses and speaks their tongue. This is to say that Lenin's discourse is ready to be punctuated and irritated by such signifiers; it does not generate them but allows itself to be oriented by them. This is a discourse neither of political elites, nor of the state, but is, rather, a people's language.

22. Lenin's discourse structurally takes a remark from the *Science of Logic* seriously, where Hegel deals with how to begin with his very project and answers: "setting aside every reflection", one has "simply to take up, *what is there before us*".[56] It follows this point faithfully, taking upon itself and incorporating what is there before it. And Lenin perceives what is there as if with a Freudian, evenly suspended attention, suspending all prejudice regarding what may or may not count as a valid political opinion. Lenin's discourse is one that lets itself be determined—taking the lead from the people, as Hegel in the *Phenomenology* takes the lead from the thing that is to be thought itself. But, clearly, Lenin considered himself to be part of the avant-garde, yet, the avant-garde in this understanding is structurally a repetition of the immediate conceived as a result. Lenin's avant-garde discourse thus does not assume that where there was it (or id, the people), there shall become I (the leader of the political subject). Rather, he follows the idea that the ego and the id shall become indistinguishable, without abolishing either. It is precisely the repetition and taking up of signifiers that are already there and that originated elsewhere—"new prophetic words".[57] A creative repetition. The discourse of the revolution is thus itself punctuated by the very points it tries to detect. Accordingly, Lenin does not want to tell the truth, but he wants himself to be told the truth; he tries to let (the) truth (of the situation, i.e., the proletariat) itself speak. *Moi, la vérité, je parle.*

23. Lenin takes up what is in front of him because what is before him already entails a punctuation of the situation. But to see this one needs a particular, an immanent, partisan gaze. These points are there but they do not yet (symbolically)

exist. Revolutionary language articulates them, lends them existence, and thus needs a certain "porosity", a "dispersive flexibility",[58] maybe even a plasticity[59] of its own, so that they hammer through it.

24. Lenin's usage of language is a profane use. Recall that *State and Revolution* begins by depicting the following scenario:

> What is now happening to Marx's theory has, in the course of history, happened repeatedly to the theories of revolutionary thinkers and leaders of oppressed classes fighting for emancipation ... After their death, attempts are made to convert them into harmless icons, to canonise them, so to say, and to hallow their names ... while at the same time robbing the revolutionary theory of its substance, blunting its revolutionary edge and vulgarising it. Today, the bourgeoisie and the opportunists within the labour movement concur in this doctoring of Marxism. They omit, obscure, or distort the revolutionary side of this theory, its revolutionary soul.[60]

Such doctoring of Marxism effectuates disorientation on crucial points of orientation, such as on 'Marx' when he is turned into a harmless idol. Lenin's politics of truth is thus always in danger of being transformed into obdurate knowledge. And this is an essential dimension of class struggle; the loss of the speculative or true revolutionary edge. Marx can be studied, venerated, but his ideas then no longer have any relation to the present. This happens when one does not epitomize but abstracts, since what is holy is abstracted and "removed from the free use and commerce of men".[61] Marx is turned into Saint Marx and his doctrine is thereby removed from any practical use. Practically, this has led to the effect that "all social-chauvinists are now 'Marxists'"[62] because they transformed Marx's thought into a transhistorical doctrine and so made it abstract. Social chauvinists are people who declare themselves to be socialist—and claim to be working for change—but are not—and practically do everything they can to prevent change. Abstraction thus not only leads to revisionism but even to a profound disorientation and confusion about the signifiers that one uses to orient oneself. All those new 'Marxists'—and this could not be any more actual today—love to quote and refer to Marx, have always already understood him, but are also well habituated to the idea that revolution is impossible. This is what Lenin calls distraction.[63] This holds not only for 'Marx' but also for 'social democracy', 'freedom', 'equality', and any potentially emancipatory signifier imaginable. It can be turned into what Lenin calls a "phrase", a linguistic opium for the masses, and the very transformation of orientation-signifiers into phrases is used by the "*watchdogs of capitalism*".[64] Lenin's discourse seeks to regain traction.

25. Lenin's profane discourse is addressed against any sacralizing, distracting, transhistoricizing use of signifiers. It opposes phrases. But it also indicates that there is no substance in any signifier that would protect it from any such privative usage. There is always the possibility of being appropriated by the "dominant ideology of the word".[65] The entire question is: What is a signifier able to do in this or that situation? This is a central element of emancipatory tactics. This is class struggle not in, but of, language. Language is a battlefield (in Lenin).

26. Lenin's methods of class struggle are manifold. I want to single out three of the most frequent ones:

I. He replaces disorienting signifiers with new ones; he, for example, gets rid of the signifier social democracy as a name for and thus as having determining influence on the party.⁶⁶ First, Lenin tried to distinguish two ways in which to subjectivize the signifier 'social democracy', yet he noticed that from a certain moment on, this distinction could no longer be really politically represented in the world. Social democracy becomes the self-description of those who are neither social nor democrats and therefore the proper demarcation between the social chauvinist and the real Marxists must no longer amount to a struggle about the signifier social democracy but must be symbolized by a new signifier, that of the communist party. This procedure is necessary because "the customary ways of thinking under capitalism have given everyone … the tendency always to want to explain the new completely in terms of the old"⁶⁷ and thereby seek to absorb the potential newness of any new politics. There is a systemic tendency to reify language, as in an unconscious filiation of Lenin, which later thinkers such as Debord and Agamben will analyze. Yet, the problem with this procedure of renaming is that it very quickly exhausts its effects and can flip over into disorientation. It is thus only strategically useful when it allows for thinking and doing something new and productively detaching oneself from something old—yet as a technique, it can easily become too habitualized. Lenin's punchline here is again a Hegelian one. Hegel had determined the concept of duty in such a way that it named the appropriateness of one's actions to the exigencies of the objective circumstances (and is thus minimally reflexive). For Lenin, it is the duty of a revolutionary to generate the appropriate symbolizations for the specific exigencies of a revolutionary situation; it is a duty to find an appropriate symbolization of the real.

II. The prohibition of using certain words. Lenin states time and again from 1918 onward that certain words lose all meaning and practical intensity when they are overused: words such as 'commune' or 'dictatorship'. "Dictatorship, however, is a big word and big words should not be thrown around carelessly."⁶⁸ Otherwise, the intensity-inhibiting effect of habit kicks in, a form of "mechanical usage of the word."⁶⁹ If, as someone once remarked, all true revolutionaries are figures without habit, this must also hold for their language practice. One should not get used to that which one cannot get used to. Because the dictatorship of the proletariat is something that one cannot imagine before it has been established, one has to prohibit what is anyhow impossible.

III. Lenin also exposes and debunks discourses by means of placing an emphasis through punctuation. In his writings, in the discussion of adversarial positions, he repeatedly uses periphrasis, parentheses in which he provides the quotations that he uses as specific emphasis. Sometimes this is done solely by adding an exclamation mark. It is as if one reads an analyst of the concrete discourse of a concrete enemy, like an analyst in a psychoanalytical session interrupting the analysand by an "aha" so that he directs the attention to certain signifiers or exposes the emptiness of others. This is a technique to debunk reifications of terms or whole sentences.

27. But Lenin's discourse has another element as its founding block: the slogan. The word "slogan," "lozung" in Russian, etymologically comes from the word "Los" (lot),

the object or slip by means of which a contingent decision is precipitated. The lot not only decides fate, but also the share, for example of an inheritance, that one gets. To cast lots thus also means to speak the truth and to address the future from the present point in time. To cast lots means to inscribe the future into the present. This is a maneuver consigned to chance, but it tries to see the present with the eyes of the future. The "lozung" is moreover the resolution that is taken after a period of deliberation and that "must proceed *not* from what is possible but from what is real"[70] in a particular situation. It is not about revolutionary possibilities, but about the constitution of a new reality, about the reality of the slogan. In short, the slogan is the symbolic form of the fugue, of the forced point. "Death or freedom for the whole Russian people!"; "Death or freedom"; "All power to the soviets!", etc.

28. Jean-Jacques Lecercle has recalled the relevance of the slogan in Lenin. He emphasizes that slogans I. identify a specific point in time; II. name a specific task; III. incorporate this task itself because part of the task is always to identify the task; and IV. are thus an expression of a concrete analysis of concrete situations.[71] Slogans are a kind of historically specific categorical imperative. They are historically specific because Lenin, for example, constantly emphasizes that the slogan 'revolution' is too indeterminate and that one always needs situation-specificity; they are categorical imperatives because the slogan symbolizes a point of orientation starting from which one can unfold a measure with regard to one's own actions. Slogans are the very form of the inner voice of the revolution—because in them the revolution assures and reassures itself of its own continuation. Slogans are not performative enunciations, but they determine the constitution of collective practice. Slogans are afformative: They do not rely on a given form, but they are also not negations of form.[72] They are the form of a practice whose form is not preformed before it forms the practice. Lenin has accordingly stated that negative slogans are less mobilizing than positive ones. Slogans present a form that is at the same time specific,[73] that is, determinate enough, and specifically indeterminate enough so that all possible desires can be attracted by it and, by this attraction, collectivized. They make determinacy and indeterminacy indistinguishable. The slogan collectivizes singular perspectives and creates a commonality of singularities, a concrete-universal-singular-collective fugue. Slogans articulate fugues.

29. Slogans force a choice. Either one follows them or one does not. There is no indifference in front of a slogan, or, rather, any indifference is itself a choice. This is why they are mobilizing. They force a decision and trigger an awakening from political slumber. They are the speculative words of politics. Slogans are particles of a subjectivizing, subjectivized language of emancipation since for it, one sometimes has to speak in tongues.

Notes

1   All European social-democratic parties, except for the Russian social-democratic party, proved themselves nationalist and voted for the military, that is, war credits.
2   Unlike other philosophers (just think of Plato, Aristotle, Hobbes, Hume, Fichte, and Kant), Hegel did not have a political agenda in mind, in the sense of an ideal state,

a theory of political progress through history, and so on. I owe this observation to Mladen Dolar.

3   The result of which is an extensive conspectus of annotations, excerpts, and comments. Cf. Vladimir Lenin, "Conspectus of Hegel's *The Science of Logic*," in *Collected Works*, Vol. 38 (Moscow: Progress Publishers, 1961), 85–237.

4   One may even see in Lenin's reaction to the disaster of 1914 itself a very Hegelian move, comparable to when Hegel states that "[p]hilosophy first commences when a race [*ein Volk*] for the most part has left its concrete life, when separation and change of class have begun, and the people approach toward their fall … Philosophy is the reconciliation following upon the destruction of that real world which thought has begun." Georg Wilhelm Friedrich Hegel, *Lectures on the History of Philosophy: Greek Philosophy to Plato* (Lincoln: University of Nebraska Press, 1995), 52.

5   Slavoj Žižek, *Lenin 2017: Remembering, Repeating, and Working Through* (London: Verso, 2017), xv.

6   Althusser argued that this means that Lenin even knew Hegel before he actually ever read him, cf. Louis Althusser, "Lenin before Hegel (April 1969)," in *Lenin and Philosophy and Other Essays* (New York, London: Monthly Review Press, 1971), 107–26.

7   Walter Benjamin remarked that in Moscow there was a children's theater called 'Lenin' and that people visiting used to state that they were 'going into Lenin'— thereby suggesting that 'Lenin' is something one can inhabit. Maybe Lenin moved for some time into Hegel. I owe this remark to Lars Bullmann.

8   Georg Wilhelm Friedrich Hegel, *The Science of Logic* (Cambridge: Cambridge University Press, 2010), 12.

9   For a longer examination of this in Hegel, cf. Rebecca Comay and Frank Ruda, *The Dash—The Other Side of Absolute Knowing* (Cambridge, MA: MIT Press, 2018).

10 Jacques Lacan, "Science and Truth," in *Écrits. The First Complete Edition in English* (New York: W.W. Norton & Company, 2002), 340.

11 Georg Lukács, *Lenin: A Study of the Unity of His Thought* (London: Verso, 2009), 9ff.

12 Leon Trotsky, *Lenin*. Available online: https://www.marxists.org/archive/trotsky/1925/lenin/01a.htm (accessed January 5, 2019).

13 Ibid.

14 Mladen Dolar has clearly done more work on this than anyone else. And Eva Ruda-Heubach has demonstrated the imminent importance of the voice for Beckett and the novel.

15 Yuri Tynjanov, "Das Wörterbuch des Polemiker Lenin," in *Sprache und Stil Lenins* (Hamburg: Hanser, 1970), 92. All translations from sources that do not exist in English are my own, F.R.

16 Viktor Shklovsky, "Lenin als Dekanonisator," in *Sprache und Stil Lenins*, 32.

17 Fritz Mierau, "Sprache Lenins—Sprache der Literatur," in *Sprache und Stil Lenins*, 22.

18 Daniel Bensaïd, "Leap! Leaps! Leaps!," in *Lenin Reloaded: Toward a Politics of Truth*, ed. Sebastian Budgen, Stathis Kouvelakis, and Slavoj Žižek (Durham: Duke University Press, 2007), 153.

19 Karl Marx, *The Civil War in France*, in *Marx & Engels Collected Works* (London: Lawrence & Wishart, 1986), Vol. 22, 334.

20 Cf. Lenin, "Bourgeois and Socialist Pacifism," in *Collected Works*, Vol. 23 (Moscow: Progress Publishers, 1974), 179.

21 Lenin, "The Petrograd City Conference of the R.S.D.L.P (Bolsheviks)," in *Collected Works*, Vol. 24 (Moscow: Progress Publishers, 1974), 145.

22 Lenin, "Soviet Power and the Status of Women," in *Collected Works*, Vol. 30 (Moscow: Progress Publishers, 1974), 122.
23 Lenin, "Conspectus of Hegel's *The Science of Logic*," 174.
24 Immanuel Kant, *The Conflict of Faculties* (New York: Abaris Books, 1979), 153.
25 Ibid., 151.
26 Ibid.
27 Ibid.
28 Immanuel Kant, *Critique of Judgment* (Indianapolis: Hackett Publishing, 1987), 132.
29 Ibid., 135.
30 Ibid., 136.
31 Kant, *Conflict*, 153.
32 Alain Badiou, *Metapolitics* (London, New York: Verso, 2005), 23.
33 He states therein: "[a]s regards the individual, it is clear e.g. that he relates even to language itself as his own only as the natural member of a human community. Language as the product of an individual is an impossibility … Language itself is the product of a community." Karl Marx, *Grundrisse* (Harmondsworth: Penguin/New Left Review, 1973), 490.
34 I here modify the title of a famous book: cf. Jean-Claude Milner, *L'amour de le langue* (Paris: Seuil, 1978).
35 One may simply recall the 'pet names' people give each other that clearly do not have an objective or descriptive character. If one calls one's loved one 'sweetie', 'baby', 'honey bee', or even more creative names, these are obviously descriptively wrong, or only in some rare and illegal cases are they not. They indicate a renaming that seems to go along with what one may call a becoming-minoritarian of language.
36 Lenin, "Revolutionary Days," in *Collected Works*, Vol. 8 (Moscow: Progress Publishers, 1977), 103.
37 Lenin, "The Revolution, The Offensive, and Our Party," in *Collected Works*, Vol. 25 (Moscow: Progress Publishers, 1974), 113.
38 Cf. Lenin, "The Turning-Point," in ibid., 82–84.
39 Lenin speaks, *inter alia*, of the turning-point (*povorotny*), the point in time (*vremya*), the key-point/crux (*sut*), and the *punctum saliens* (*tochtka pryzhka*).
40 Hegel, *The Philosophy of History* (Ontario: Kitchener, 2001), 19. Translation modified, F.R.
41 Lenin, "Marxism and Insurrection," in *Collected Works*, Vol. 26 (Moscow: Progress Publishers, 1977), 22.
42 Ibid., 27.
43 Ibid., 26.
44 Ibid., 24. In the English translation, this is rendered as "chief reason".
45 This is what also accounts for Lenin's repeated attempts to re-periodize what happened thus far in the revolutionary process.
46 Lenin, "Marxism and Insurrection," 27.
47 For the term "speculative sign," cf. again: Comay and Ruda, *The Dash*.
48 Lukács, *Lenin*, 53.
49 Žižek, *Lenin 2017*, xxv.
50 Trotsky, *Lenin*.
51 Joseph Stalin, *Marxism and the Problem of Linguistics*. Available online: https://www.marxists.org/reference/archive/stalin/works/1950/jun/20.htm (accessed January 5, 2019). All Stalin quotes are from this text.

52 This is why Jean-Jacques Lecercle has—in a polemical way—pointed out that Stalin's philosophy of language is in fact comparable to that of Jürgen Habermas. Cf. Jean-Jacques Lecercle, *A Marxist Philosophy of Language* (Chicago: Haymarket Books, 2005), 45–104.
53 Trotsky, *Lenin*.
54 A note that was supposed to assure the Western powers that there would be no separate peace between Russia and Germany.
55 Where do such slogans then come from? Lenin answers that there is no way to answer this question. It is the drive of the masses or workers: "Their revolutionary instinct at once prompted the St. Petersburg workers to adopt the right slogan—energetic continuation of the struggle, and utilisation of the newly-won positions for a continued onslaught and the actual destruction of the autocracy." Lenin, "The First Victory of the Revolution," in *Collected Works*, Vol. 9 (Moscow: Progress Publishers, 1977), 432.
56 Hegel, *Science of Logic*, 47.
57 Trotsky, *Lenin*.
58 Badiou, *Metapolitics*, 74.
59 Catherine Malabou, *The Future of Hegel: Plasticity, Temporality and Dialectic* (London: Routledge, 2004).
60 Lenin, *The State and Revolution. The Marxist Theory of the State and the Tasks of the Proletariat in the Revolution* (Moscow: Progress Publishers, 1974), 390.
61 Giorgio Agamben, *Profanations* (New York: Zone Books, 2007), 73.
62 Lenin, *The State and Revolution*, 390.
63 Cf. for example: Lenin, "From a Publicist's Diary," in *Collected Works*, Vol. 25 (Moscow: Progress Publishers, 1977), 54. Lenin's epitome of distraction is Fabius Cunctator.
64 Lenin, "Imperialism and the Split in Socialism," in *Collected Works*, Vol. 23 (Moscow: Progress Publishers, 1974), 110.
65 Boris Kasanski, "Lenins Sprache," in *Sprache und Stil Lenins*, 124.
66 On this cf. Lenin, "The Tasks of the Proletariat in Our Revolution," in *Collected Works*, Vol. 24 (Moscow: Progress Publishers, 1974), 84ff.
67 Lukacs, *Lenin*, 73f.
68 Lenin, "The Immediate Task of the Soviet Government," in *Collected Works*, Vol. 27 (Moscow: Progress Publishers, 1974), 265.
69 Shklovsky, "Lenin als Dekanonisator," 42.
70 Lenin, "Letters on Tactics," in *Collected Works*, Vol. 24 (Moscow: Progress Publishers, 1974), 46.
71 Lecercle, *A Marxist Philosophy of Language*, 50ff.
72 Werner Hamacher, "Affirmative, Strike," in *Walter Benjamin's Philosophy: Destruction and Experience*, ed. Andrew Benjamin and Peter Osborne (London: Routledge, 1994), 155–82.
73 Much more specific than the Kantian categorical imperative.

Part Two

Capitalism and Critique

6

Critique in Hegel and Marx

Rocío Zambrana

In his Contribution to the Critique of Hegel's *Philosophy of Right*, published in the *Deutsche-Französische Jahrbucher* in 1844, Marx defined the proletariat as the formation of a class with "radical chains".[1] For Marx, this particular class, which is no class of civil society, represents the "loss of humanity".[2] It "can only redeem itself by a total redemption of humanity".[3] The proletariat's suffering is "universal", in other words, since it is rooted in the very structure of capitalist modernity.[4] Accordingly, emancipation requires dismantling the economic, political, and social structures distinctive of capitalist modernity.

Within Frankfurt School critical theory, the dialectic of universal and particular at play in these famous lines has often been regarded as the political heir of the Hegelian conception of immanent critique. Drawing from Hegel's 1807 *Phenomenology of Spirit*, immanent critique is said to be a form of critique that takes its bearings from social reality while at the same time aiming to transform that very reality for the better. A particular experience sheds light on structural conditions—conceptual, institutional, historical—that produce and sustain it. Addressing forms of suffering distinctive of this experience thus requires dismantling such structural indeed universal conditions. In this chapter, I reexamine the received left-Hegelian, Marxist conception of critique as immanent critique. I do so by positioning immanent critique squarely in line with what is sometimes called a 'negativist' critique.

A negativist critique draws from Adorno's appropriation of Hegel and Marx, and underscores injustice—"suffering" (*Leiden*), to use Adorno's term—as the "medium of justice".[5] Adorno's critical theory can perhaps be summed up by the subtitle of his 1951 *Minima Moralia*: "Reflections on a Damaged Life".[6] It represents an inversion of Hegel's emphasis on articulating the structure and strictures of a rational life, and it develops Marx's insistence on the false character of capitalism as an economic, political, and social form of life.[7] Yet it also represents an inversion of the conception of critique we find in Hegel and Marx. A negativist critique relies on the experience of suffering, which guides any articulation of normative concepts such as a 'rational life' or 'human emancipation'. It is this inversion that I explore, since it provides a key to reexamining Hegel and Marx's conceptions of critique.

In what follows, I treat Adorno's negativist critique as a heuristic device for assessing Hegel and Marx's notions of critique. Adorno's inversion will allow me to assess a common assumption underlying conceptions of immanent critique, namely, that it seeks to develop normative criteria for critique from its object of study yet exempt from the object's fate. Adorno's inversion, I suggest, makes possible specifying a Hegelian conception of critique post-Marx that centers Hegel's notion of negativity thereby rendering contradiction as inversion and determinate negation as ambivalent mediation. This is a conception of critique that, rather than being guided by normative criteria that can be distilled from the socio-historical phenomenon at hand, is attuned to, following Adorno, the "undiminished persistence of suffering" that remains in a world "which could be paradise here and now—[yet] can become hell itself tomorrow".[8] It is a form of ongoing critique that remains vigilant of the inversion of any normative criteria immanent to social reality.

My argument will proceed in four steps. First, I clarify the notion of a negativist critique by considering some features of Adorno's writings, especially *Minima Moralia*. Second, I examine the notion of immanent critique in Hegel, focusing on the *Phenomenology of Spirit*. In this context, I evaluate three variations of Hegelian immanent critique, clarifying some systematic issues that frame Marx's as well as the critical-theoretic reception of Hegel. Third, I examine two versions of critique within Marx's corpus that have been central to Adorno's negativist conception of critique. Fourth, I sketch a Hegelian conception of critique post-Marx that reactualizes the insights of immanent criticism.

Negativist Critique

In 1985 Nancy Fraser suggested that in 1843 Marx provided the best definition of a critical theory. "[T]he work of our time", Marx wrote, "[is] to clarify to itself ... the meaning of its own struggle and its own desires."[9] Fraser argues that this is the best definition of critical theory, given its distinctively political character.[10] Critique remains critical if it is oriented by the potential for social transformation embedded in the struggles of the present. This political commitment, however, sets a theoretical agenda for critical theory, and it is this aspect of critique with which I will be concerned. Critical theory remains critical when it reflects on its own assumptions in light of the struggles of the age, when it transforms its own assumptions in light of the strictures of those struggles. The theoretical task, then, is to work out a conception of critique that inscribes within itself the idea that critique takes its bearings from social reality while at the same time aiming to transform that very reality for the better. The theoretical task thus requires working out what is known as the dialectic of immanence and transcendence.[11]

Axel Honneth has argued that the dialectic of immanence and transcendence is the legacy of left-Hegelianism.[12] Critical Theory can be treated as a distinctive tradition insofar as it has sought, albeit in different ways, to work out this dialectic. The Frankfurt School is a distinctive form of critical social theory insofar as it seeks to "inform us about the pretheoretical resource (*vorwissenschaftliche Instanz*) in which its own critical viewpoint is anchored extratheoretically as an empirical interest or moral experience".[13] Critical theory thus prioritizes, in Honneth's terms, the "social dynamics of disrespect".[14] Experiences of suffering or harm disclose that the normative core of conceptions of justice is constituted by expectations of respect.[15] In Honneth's own work, this represents the legacy of Hegelian recognition, but it articulates aspects of the negativist strategy that was already distinctive of Adorno's work.[16]

To suffer, in Adorno's corpus, is tied to the loss of the capacity for the "realization of human potentials", as Jaeggi puts it quoting *Minima Moralia*.[17] Such a loss follows from social deformations rooted in a particular form of life, specifically late capitalism.[18] But such a loss is always indexed to the body and, particularly, to somatic processes.[19] Such a loss is tied to our mimetic capacities, rather than a conception of rational willing.[20] The crucial point, for our purposes, is the connection between suffering and truth. In the Introduction to *Negative Dialectics*, we famously read that "the need to lend a voice to suffering is a condition of all truth".[21] Suffering, according to Adorno, is "objectivity that weighs upon the subject".[22] Subjective experience is an expression of objective conditions. By indexing suffering to the body, as Jay Bernstein explains, Adorno is suggesting bodily suffering as the "paradigm of social suffering" and abhorrence to suffering as the "practical ground for norms and practices".[23]

A negativist critique develops the connection between the experience of suffering and truth. Because late capitalism structures subjectively and objectively conceptions of rationality or the good life, as Adorno following Lukács maintains, experiences of suffering are the only candidates for gaining any critical traction. A negativist critique isn't 'negative' because it dwells on suffering, but rather because it takes negative experiences as guides for articulating the truth of a given form of life. As Rahel Jaeggi succinctly puts it, "the question of the good life can only be posed indirectly, as a question of how life is damaged".[24] *Minima Moralia*, for example, traces varieties of "coldness" as the "*Stimmung* of identity thinking in its exploded bourgeois form", to borrow Bernstein's nice formulation.[25] It reflects on the conditions that make it impossible to live a life "rightly", to be ethical within fundamentally unethical institutions.[26] It examines habits, practices, and institutions, presenting the logic of equivalence that structures them into varieties of coldness.[27] Such presentation neither relies on nor provides a picture of the good life. Rather, it provides an analysis of what prevents this life from so being.[28]

There is an important difference between the Honnethian formulation of immanent critique and Adornian negativism. In Honneth's work, experiences of disrespect are pretheoretical resources in the sense that quotidian experiences of suffering are prepolitical. They have not been publicly articulated, for example, in legal terms. The public articulation of those experiences makes possible and, when successful, represents an expansion of the varieties of right that comprise a democratic form of life.[29] Indeed, according to Honneth, they make possible an account of the social foundations of democratic life.[30] A rationally reconstructed concept of recognition not only makes possible an analysis of the normative force of experiences of disrespect. It also makes possible an account of right and the expansion of right. Recognition allows us to assess the ways in which freedom is or isn't actualized.

Adorno's negativist form of criticism does not trade on a normatively reconstructed category for critique, such as Honnethian recognition. Rather, critique proceeds by tracking experiences of suffering as rooted in the specificities of a form of life. Neither does Adorno offer a master concept that might allow us to sketch the foundations of democratic life. He provides an analysis of the structures of impossibility distinctive of 'actuality', to use a good Hegelian term. The object of critique not only remains the modes of suffering distinctive to a given form of life, but also the normative commitments implicated in these forms of suffering. This is perhaps best explored under the rubric of a dialectic of enlightenment, developed with Max Horkheimer in 1944, which examined the entanglement of freedom and domination distinctive of Western culture.[31] *Minima Moralia*'s exploration of coldness continues this project of tracing the entanglement of freedom and domination to Western rationality itself.

To be sure, increasingly we find in Adorno's writings images of transcendence and a significant place for the notions of "redemption" and "utopia".[32] However, Adorno's deployment of these notions is consistent with his denial of a defined picture of the good life. It functions against cynicism, since it holds onto the *possibility* of that which does not agree with actuality.[33] Negativist criticism, then, is far from pessimistic. It is a mode of critique that takes its bearings from social reality while at the same time aiming to transform that very reality for the better. Yet it is invested in a presentation of the forms of suffering that express the truth of that reality. It insists on articulating the ways in which normative commitments that structure that reality are implicated in those forms of suffering. It tracks not how these commitments are distorted by contingent conditions. Rather, it tracks how suffering is an effect of the work of those commitments. Negativist criticism finds critical traction from rather than against the impurity of its standpoint and criteria.

Immanent Critique in Hegel

Although Hegel's concept of experience (*Erfahrung*) in the *Phenomenology* is the *locus classicus* for the Hegelian conception of immanent critique, it is false to assume that we find agreement about what exactly constitutes Hegelian immanent criticism. I will examine three ways of understanding immanent critique in the *Phenomenology*, which will in turn help me further explore some systematic issues left implicit in my discussion of Adorno.[34]

In the context of laying out the "method" or "general pattern"[35] of the education of consciousness in the Introduction to the *Phenomenology*, Hegel writes: "[c] onsciousness in itself provides its own standard, and the investigation will thereby be a comparison of itself with itself ... Therefore, in what consciousness declares within itself to be the in itself, that is, to be the true, we have the standard which consciousness itself erects to measure its knowledge."[36] The *Phenomenology* advances by examining claims that natural consciousness makes *on their own terms*, without appealing to an external standard (*Maßstab*) of judgment. Because consciousness makes a distinction between its knowledge and its object, it has a standard within itself. Such standard allows it to compare its knowledge with its object.[37]

The comparison that consciousness performs with itself reveals failure when "neither corresponds with the other", as Hegel puts it.[38] Consciousness must therefore "alter its knowledge in order to make it adequate with the object".[39] A change of knowledge, however, entails a change of object as well as a change of standard.[40] The revision implied is threefold, since it is a revision of the very distinction that natural consciousness instituted in the first place. "This dialectical movement", Hegel famously writes, "is what consciousness practices on itself as well as on its knowledge and its object, and, insofar as, to consciousness, the new, true object arises out of this movement, this dialectical movement is what is genuinely called experience."[41]

Hegel's concept of experience serves as the model for immanent critique. Critique aims to pass judgment on a given matter.[42] It is a form of evaluation by discriminating between competing, indeed opposing options—for example, freedom versus domination. To rely on standards of judgment that are external to the matter at hand, Hegel argues, would only distort the matter itself.[43] External standards imply a conception of cognition as instrument or medium. The former delivers an object according to our form of knowing, the latter renders the object inaccessible to us. Stressing Hegel's account of the comparison that natural consciousness performs, then, the first variation on critique defends the view that critique must draw resources from its object. And this implies that critique must take stock of the fact that the form of knowing is implicated in the object. Critique works through failures that entail a change in how we conceive of the object as well as the form of criticism.

Hegel's powerful insight, however, is that embedded in any claim are distinctions that establish something as an object, as a form of knowing, and indeed as a subject. But to say that there is a distinction at work is to say that there are normative commitments already framing what appears as the object, the knowledge, and their relation.[44] The distinction bespeaks a relation between subject and object. That relation is normatively laden. Now, by normative I do not mean moral or political, though I do mean *sittlich*. A distinction is the product of an institution. It is the product of a positing (*Setzung*), but also one that is embedded in a social-historical context. Hence, any such positing is part of a history, indeed has a history. Failure entails revision, as per Hegel's concept of experience, but such revision need not be straightforwardly morally or politically grounded. It can be a matter of historical change. Of course, historical change has irreducible moral and political valence, yet the point is that such a transformation can't be captured by conceptions of what ought to be done that are not immanent to the matter at hand (as per Hegel's famous critique of Kant).

A second variation on critique reads the texts that I have quoted in stronger terms.[45] This variation stresses the Hegelian notions of contradiction and determinate negation. For Hegel, contradictions are objective, rather than logical. Although Hegel's emphasis on contradiction certainly helps us grasp the dynamic character of reality, Hegel's point is not to assert dynamism or fluidity for its own sake.[46] It is rather to stress that contradictions disclose the truth of any given matter at hand, suggesting concretely their own overcoming. Contradictions, then, take different form given a specific institutional arrangement, form of self-understanding, or concept. In Hegel's work, normative expectations revert to their opposite, the unfolding of an action undermines its very actualization, incompatible expectations generate a clash between subjects, institutions, concepts. Contradictions, then, refer to the normative structure of a given institution, self-understanding, or concept. Contradictions, accordingly, express a failure between a self-conception and truth.[47]

Contradictions are not obstacles, for Hegel. They are occasions for development and indeed enrichment. From the dialectical movement that Hegel describes under the rubric of experience a "new, *true* object arises".[48] The overcoming of a contradiction improves on the object, since the mode of address and the revision are tailored to the contradiction at hand. But it also improves on the form of knowing, making possible further claims that incorporate the truth that was revealed. For this reason, Hegelian transitions are necessary. As Hegel puts it, "when the result is grasped as determinate negation, that is, when it is grasped as it is in truth, then at that point a new form has immediately arisen, and in that negation the transition has been made by virtue of which the progression through the complete series of shapes comes about on its own accord".[49]

On this variation, immanent critique refers to a process of revision whereby standards for critique are enriched through the unfolding of a given contradiction. The justifiability of any form of knowing, conception of the object, criterion refers to the way in which the contradiction is addressed. For readers of Hegel like Robert Brandom or Rahel Jaeggi, the necessity at hand is not causal. It is the "practical-rational necessity" of the contradiction and its mode of address.[50] What is enriched, then, are the normative commitments that are at work within the distinction-relation of subject and object. There is a retrospective and a prospective component here as well. Normative commitments are refined in the process of overcoming shortcomings, offering a newly improved standard by which to know the new object and by which to assess the new form of knowing.

This second variation deepens the claim that Hegel's contribution to immanent critique lies in the comparison that consciousness performs on itself. Immanent critique not only draws its resources from the object, but also ameliorates the normative commitment that failed to adequately articulate truth. The normative commitments that are always already structuring the distinction-relation of subject and object are substantive criteria in which the immanent critique is invested, such as the Hegelian conception of freedom. Enrichment, then, means a better conception and better institutional arrangements, since they better actualize freedom. Enrichment is the enrichment of a rational form of life. Honneth's version of immanent critique draws from this variation.

A third variation on Hegel's notion of experience does justice to elements of Hegel's own texts that are tamed in the two variations that I have discussed. This third variation stresses negativity as the central Hegelian category, rewriting Hegelian immanent critique in a negativist key. In the Introduction to the *Phenomenology*, Hegel argues that the progress toward the "goal" of knowledge is "unrelenting".[51] He adds that "satisfaction is not to be found at any prior station on the way".[52] The failures that natural consciousness faces are not experienced as mere invitations to revise and indeed enrich its claims. Natural consciousness suffers crises, since what falls into contradiction are orienting world-views. Experience entails, as Hegel puts it, "the loss of its own self".[53] For this reason, Hegel famously describes the experience of consciousness not as a path of doubt, but a path of despair (*Verzweiflung*).⁵⁴ Rather than revision, natural consciousness can thus be said to undergo a form of "conversion", as Ludwig Siep and Robert Pippin have suggested.⁵⁵

Attention to this frame helps specify the centrality of negativity, more specifically, of *self-negation*.⁵⁶ Actualization, according to Hegel, is a process of self-negation. Negation, for Hegel, is always negation of something—whether a logical category, a philosophical position, a historically specific identity or institution. Negation yields an alternative determination. It is never mere negativity, sheer destruction. It is an exclusion that sets or posits boundaries and hence a relation of something and its now established other. It is because negativity establishes new boundaries that it can be understood as a process of actualization—a process whereby a norm, practice, institution "becomes other" thereby "returning-to-self", as Hegel puts it in the Preface to the *Phenomenology*.⁵⁷

This means that any thing or identity is such because it has boundaries (*Grenze*), and maintains itself—determines itself—by asserting its boundaries. A boundary, however, is something that marks a limit (*Schranke*). Marking a limit, Hegel emphasizes, is coextensively transgressing it. A boundary marks what some thing is on the basis of what it is not, and hence establishes its opposite as intrinsic to it. Because any identity is both itself and its other, any concrete identity, any individual, is subject to a logic of ambivalence. If understood as exempt from ambivalence, any given identity is but reified—an abstract, one-sided determination.⁵⁸

Natural consciousness, Hegel writes, "suffers this violence *at its own hands* and brings to ruin its own restricted satisfaction".⁵⁹ As a type of existential breakdown, as the collapse of orientating modes of understanding and self-understanding, experience offers a different model for immanent critique. Self-negation is indexed to the object, and hence the tensions, inversions, clashes, and contradictions that natural consciousness falls into require transformation of the form of knowing as well as the standard. The overcoming of such crises is the feat of *Geist* "tarrying with the negative" and recollected in what Hegel calls "absolute knowing".⁶⁰ Absolute knowing recollects all such failures by presenting them in a "gallery of pictures".⁶¹ The narrative that it constructs thematizes patterns of self-undermining, such as the versions of sovereign subjectivity that throughout the book we see revert to dependence, violence, and so on. On this version, then, immanent critique tracks *varieties of self-negation*. It tracks the disparate ways in which norms, practices, institutions *undermine themselves*. It is guided by the pathos of the specificity of a given breakdown, rather than the logos of a conception of a rational form of life that remains unscathed. Immanent critique is therefore necessarily a form of ongoing critique, since it tracks the heterogeneous ways in which normative commitments undermine themselves and presents them as a pattern, as rooted in the very structure of a form of life.

Immanent Critique in Marx

In Marx's corpus, we find critiques of religion, politics, and political economy. We also find variations on how Marx pursues these criticisms, given the way in which he conceives of the relation between theory and practice at given times within his career.[62] Given this complexity, I will restrict my analysis to variations of critique found in the 1844 Economic and Philosophical Manuscripts and *Capital*.[63] These are not only influential texts for a negativist conception of critique, but are also closest in their philosophical structure.

In the third of the 1844 *Economic and Philosophical Manuscripts*, Marx famously criticized Hegel's speculative philosophy, while praising the power of Hegelian negativity. As the "moving and generating principle", Marx writes, negativity allows Hegel to conceive of the "self-creation of man as a process".[64] Hegel is thereby able to specify the essence of labor, yet because he does so as a matter of consciousness rather than real, active human being—indeed, as a "species-being" (*Gattungswesen*)—Hegel undermines his own conception of negativity.[65] For Marx,

> whenever real, corporeal *man*, man with his feet firmly on the solid ground, man exhaling and inhaling all the forces of nature, *posits* his real, objective *essential powers* as alien objects by his externalization [*Entäußerung*], it is not the *act of positing* which is the subject in this process: it is the subjectivity of *objective* essential powers, whose action, therefore, must also be something objective.[66]

Marx seeks to invert Hegel's dialectics in order to understand actualization as a process not of the subjectivity of things, but rather the objectivity of material conditions.[67] It is not the rationality of matters themselves that dialectics can present. It is the material relations of the reproduction of the species as a species that a 'dialectics of negativity' is able to present.

These notes are consistent with the description of communism, provided in earlier notes within the third manuscript, as a "naturalism that is a humanism and a humanism that is a naturalism".[68] Most importantly, they are consistent with the famous discussion of alienated labor (*die Entfremdete Arbeit*) found in the first manuscript. And it is the first manuscript where we find the first variation of immanent critique in Marx that I would like to discuss. The notion of *Gattungswesen*, species being, has been understood as the central normative category in Marx's early humanism. It makes possible Marx's elaboration of key critical concepts, such as alienation (*Entfremdung*).[69] This first variation follows the structure of the second Hegelian variation I have discussed, since it relies on a stable normative criterion that guides critique.

Marx famously argues that, under capitalist conditions, labor is alienated. He distinguishes between objectification (*Vergegenständlichung*) and alienation (*Entfremdung*). Objectification elaborates the thought that as corporeal, living creatures, human beings necessarily have a metabolic relation with nature. Hence, productive activity is essential to what it is to be human. Alienation, in contrast, tracks the ways in which the aims of capitalism—profit, accumulation—distort the human's relation to (1) the product of labor, (2) productive activity itself, (3) nature, (4) and other human beings. The product of labor appears as autonomous, in fact as a lord over the producer. Productive activity, which is the source of realization, is turned against the human through wage labor and dehumanizing working conditions. Nature appears as something to exploit. The life of the species is turned into a means for individual life. Capitalism, in short, distorts the fact that human beings produce as a species and for the species.

Although the role of Marx's naturalism in his discussion of alienated labor is undeniable, we should not lose sight of the fact that, first, he begins his notes situating his analysis otherwise. He does so by appealing to "the premises of political economy"[70] and hence as a critical engagement with the central concepts of the economic theory of his time. And indeed, the main argument of the text, if we can speak of one, is to challenge the view that private property is the source of alienated labor. For Marx, private property is the *result* of alienated labor.[71] Second, he situates his analysis within what he calls "an actual economic fact", namely, that "the worker becomes all the poorer the more wealth he produces"; that "the worker becomes an ever cheaper commodity the more commodities he creates"; and that "the *devaluation* of the world of men is in direct proportion to the *increasing value* of the world of things".[72] One could equally argue, then, that Marx's normative concepts are developed *out of* the concrete conditions he was seeking to address. This order of normativity, however, is proper to Marx's later writings.

Marx's naturalism helps explain why the text with which I began is a model for immanent critique, in addition to being an articulation of the political valence of the proletariat. Marx described the proletariat as a class whose sufferings are universal, since they are rooted in the very structure of capitalism. Emancipation of this particular class is universal emancipation, since it requires dismantling the structures of alienated labor. Emancipation, as Marx writes in the 1844 manuscripts, returns the human to "his real social life", where "the enjoyment of others has become our own appropriation".[73] It emancipates "human senses and attributes". "[S]ocial organs" sustain the "direct association with others", which "becomes a way of expressing my own life". In a word, emancipation is universal because it returns the human to "human life activity", one that is not guided by the aims of capital.[74] Immanent critique, then, relies on a humanism that is a naturalism to articulate normative criteria for critique. In these texts, immanent critique naturalizes the Hegelian commitment to the rational organization of life.

We find a second variation on critique in the first chapter of *Capital*, in the section on the Fetishism of the Commodity.[75] Like the 1844 manuscripts, *Capital* is situated as a critical engagement with the categories of political economy. Like the analysis of the manuscripts, these categories cannot explain the phenomenon that they purport to explain. For example, political economy posits the unity of labor and property, yet the capitalist mode of production is predicated on the radical separation of the property of labor power from the ownership of means of production.[76] Yet *Capital* is not a mere category analysis. Marx is not merely invested in *comparing* economic categories and economic phenomena, form of knowing and its object. For Marx, political economy is an important entry point for a substantive critique of capitalism because its categories are consequent.

Seyla Benhabib has argued that Marx pursues at least two additional types of criticism in *Capital*—what she calls "normative" and "defetishizing".[77] While normative critique assesses the fate of bourgeois ideals, defetishizing critique seeks to reveal the historical nature of the forms of sociality that comprise actuality.[78] The power of Marx's analysis in the famous section on the Fetishism of the Commodity Form, in my view, is that it does both at once. It pursues a form of normative critique yet in a negativist key by pursuing a form of defetishizing critique. Marx's notion of immanent critique in these pages, then, "bypasses the need for dogmatic normative grounds", to borrow Nick Nesbitt's nice formulation.[79] It critically tracks the distortions and inversions distinctive of capitalism by characterizing them as modes of self-undermining.

In chapter 6 of *Capital*, while discussing the buying and selling of labor power, Marx argues that "the sphere of sale and purchase of labor" is the "Eden of the innate rights of man": "[f]reedom, equality, property and Bentham".[80] Both the buyer and the seller of labor power can do so because they are 'free'. Their interaction bespeaks of equality, since "they exchange equivalent for equivalent". Each disposes only what is his own. And they interact on the basis of each "looking to himself" and himself alone. An argument reminiscent of the 1844 *On the Jewish Question*, the claim here is that capitalism distorts these bourgeois ideals, which is to say, the central normative commitments of European modernity. Because they are imbued with the ends of accumulation and profit, they undermine their social, moral, and political meaning and effects.

One of the ways in which Marx accounts for this distortion in *Capital* is by accounting for the fetishism of the commodity form. As Benhabib nicely puts it, "the exchange of commodities in the capitalist market place actualizes the norms of equality, freedom, and property".[81] Marx's analysis of the commodity develops the distinction between use-value and exchange-value. The common measure that makes possible exchanging incommensurable products is provided by labor time.[82] The commodity is, as a result, a "very strange thing", indeed "abounding in metaphysical subtleties and theological niceties".[83] A commodity is a mysterious thing, Marx argues, because "in it the social character of men's labor appears to them as an objective character stamped upon the product of that labor".[84] The producers' relation to their labor, Marx maintains, is presented as a "social relation existing not between themselves, but between the products of their labor".[85]

That these passages inherit features of Marx's discussion of alienated labor has been well documented. And it is clear that in both chapters 1 and 6 of volume 1 of *Capital*, Marx is tracking the lack of transparency of social relations and normative ideals. The crucial point for our purposes is that the fetish character of the commodity represents a pervasive *inversion*. However, this inversion should *not* be understood as an illusion. The discussion ought not be reduced to an account of ideological unmasking.[86] In good Hegelian form, the fetish character of the commodity is a manifestation of the essence of capitalism.[87] It is the expression of capitalism as a form of life. Indeed, when Marx writes that "a definite social relation between men ... assumes, in their eyes, the fantastic form of a relation between things", he is tracking the essence of capitalism in its very manifestation.[88] Crucial here, then, is what the fetishism manifests and hence exposes. Relations between things are *social* relations because they organize social, economic, and political life. Relations between humans are thing-like, since they are rooted in a fundamental relation of power. The aims of capitalism instrumentalize sociality, turning interaction into a means for individual life.

This second variation on critique rewrites Marx' conception of immanent critique in a negativist key. Immanent critique here begins from a concrete economic relation. It specifies that relation's essence by tracking its central distortions and inversions. It does not refer to or elaborate normative criteria or a picture of the good, rational life as exempt from capitalist resignification. Indeed, it finds critical traction by exposing the work of normative distortions and social inversions. It seeks to track the ways in which this form of life undermines itself, and the ways in which that undermining causes forms of suffering—exploitation, alienation, but also expropriation.[89] Notwithstanding some of Marx's claims about the overcoming of capitalism in some of his political writings,[90] it is clear from *Capital* that Marx is tracking a "persistent conflict" distinctive of capitalism.[91] Indeed, when he writes, in volume 3 of *Capital*, that "the real barrier of capitalist production is capital itself", he is assessing a form of negativity indexed to empirical conditions.[92] It is therefore an ongoing critique, since it draws its resources from a historically specific phenomenon and must change with its object.

Critique Reconsidered

I have discussed variations of critique in Hegel and Marx, aiming to position Hegelian-Marxist immanent critique squarely in line with negativist critique. As we have seen, drawing from Hegel and Marx, immanent critique takes its bearings from social reality while aiming to transform that very reality for the better. It is commonly assumed, however, that immanent critique entails normative grounding, since it entails not only finding but also developing criteria for critique from social reality. Such criteria—right, freedom, equality, justice—draws normative force from being exempt from the fate of the reality in question. Hegelian contradiction and determinate negation, along these lines, provides a progressive enrichment of a conception of a rational life that makes possible the actualization of freedom. Marx's dialectic of species being and alienation, also along these lines, provides an account of human emancipation as the restoration of human life activity.

While these are powerful conceptions of critique, I have argued that we find an alternative in Hegel and Marx that remains attuned to the ways in which critical standards are entangled with and hence implicated in ongoing forms of suffering. Negativist critique, I have suggested, aims to gain critical traction from social reality without developing normative criteria seen to be exempt from that very reality. It seeks to disclose the truth of a given form of life by tracking its history and effects. It seeks, moreover, to track the meaning and effects of normative concepts implied in any critical exposition, since it maintains that these are features of the reality in question. Hegel and Marx developed powerful versions of critique in a negativist key, ones that suggest that we might recover the Hegelian-Marxist tradition of dialectical criticism anew.

Recovering negativist aspects of Hegel's and Marx's texts delivers a Hegelian conception of critique post-Marx. This notion of critique centers Hegel's notion of negativity thereby rendering contradiction as *inversion* and determinate negation as *ambivalent mediation*. Contradiction here is more precisely understood as self-negation, and is sensitive to the varieties of self-undermining of specific norms, institutions, or concepts. It seeks to track the *thwarting* of the goal at work within given norms, institutions, and concepts. This thwarting complicates any conception of progress, enrichment, indeed historical learning. A negativist critique thus also seeks to track the ambivalent mediation of forms of negation. It thematizes the ways in which freedom and domination are entangled in any conception of a rational life, or any conception of human activity. Critique here tracks, in other words, the coextensive positive and negative meaning and effects of any critical, emancipatory practice. Following Adorno, then, we might hope that, so understood, critique can do justice to the undiminished persistence of suffering by remaining vigilant of the inversion and distortions of critique itself.

Notes

1. Karl Marx, *Contribution to the Critique of Hegel's 'Philosophy of Right': Introduction*, in *The Marx-Engels Reader*, ed. Robert C. Tucker, 2nd edn (New York: W.W. Norton & Co., 1978), 64.
2. Ibid.
3. Ibid.
4. Ibid.
5. Jay M. Bernstein, "Suffering Injustice: Misrecognition as Moral Injury in Critical Theory," *International Journal of Philosophical Studies* 13, no. 3 (2005): 303. Cf. Fabian Freyenhagen, *Adorno's Practical Philosophy* (Cambridge: Cambridge University Press, 2013).
6. Theodor W. Adorno, *Minima Moralia*, trans. E.F.N. Jephcott (London: Verso, 2005) tracks the impossibility of living a life rightly at an ethical register.
7. "The whole is the false," as Adorno famously put it in Adorno, *Minima Moralia*, 50.
8. See Theodor W. Adorno, "Why Still Philosophy?," in *Critical Models and Interventions* (New York: Columbia University Press, 1998) and Bernstein "Suffering Injustice," 304.
9. Marx, "For a Ruthless Criticism of Everything Existing," in *The Marx-Engels Reader*, 15.
10. Fraser argues that a theory is critical when it "frames its research program and its conceptual framework with an eye to the aims and activities of those oppositional social movements with which it has a partisan though not uncritical identification". See Nancy Fraser, "What's Critical about Critical Theory: The Case of Habermas and Gender," *New German Critique* 35 (1985): 98.
11. Important contributions to this topic include Max Horkheimer's "Traditional and Critical Theory," in *Critical Theory: Selected Essays* (New York: Continuum, 1975); Axel Honneth, *Disrespect: The Normative Foundations of Critical Theory* (London: Polity Press, 2007) and *Pathologies of Reason: On the Legacy of Critical Theory*, trans. James Ingram (New York: Columbia University Press, 2009); Seyla Benhabib, *Critique, Norm, and Utopia* (New York: Columbia University Press, 1986); Reymond Guess, *The Idea of Critical Theory* (Cambridge: Cambridge University Press, 1981); Maeve Cooke, *Re-Presenting the Good Society* (Cambridge, MA: MIT Press, 2006); and Rahel Jaeggi, *Kritik von Lebensformen* (Frankfurt: Suhrkamp, 2014).

12 See Axel Honneth, "Social Dynamics of Disrespect," in Honneth, *Disrespect*, 63–4.
13 Ibid., 64.
14 Ibid.
15 Ibid., 71.
16 Honneth calls Adorno's critical theory "negativist" in this context, but by this he means "pessimist" (ibid.). He is following Habermas in seeing Adorno as a pessimist, and in understanding critique as primarily normative critique. See Jürgen Habermas *Philosophical Discourse of Modernity*, trans. Frederick G. Lawrence (Cambridge, MA: MIT Press, 1990), chap. 5.
17 Rahel Jaeggi, "'No Individual Can Resist': *Minima Moralia* as a Critique of Forms of Life," *Constellations* 12, no. 1 (2005): 73.
18 Axel Honneth, "A Physiognomy of the Capitalist Form of Life: A Sketch of Adorno's Social Theory," *Constellations* 12, no. 2 (2005): 60.
19 See e.g. Theodor W. Adorno, *Negative Dialectics*, trans. E.B. Ashton (London: Bloomsbury, 1981), esp. "Suffering Physical," 202ff.
20 For example, in *Minima Moralia* he writes that "the human is indissolubly linked with imitation: a human being only becomes human at all by imitating other human beings" (Adorno, *Minima Moralia*, 154).
21 Adorno, *Negative Dialectics*, 17–8.
22 Ibid., 18.
23 This is Bernstein's suggestion. He writes: "by speaking of suffering … Adorno placed the body at the forefront of moral experience. For him bodily suffering is the paradigm of social suffering; and bodily experiences of abhorrence, revulsion, and disgust at the suffering (bodily or otherwise) of others, together with compassion for suffering others, form the practical ground for ethical norms and practices" (Bernstein, "*Suffering Injustice*," 304–5).
24 Jaeggi, "'No Individual Can Resist,'" 72.
25 See Jay M. Bernstein, *Adorno: Disenchantment and Ethics* (Cambridge: Cambridge University Press, 2011), 402.
26 Adorno, *Minima Moralia*, §18.
27 He examines from love, marriage, and dwelling to high art and philosophy.
28 Jaeggi, "'No Individual Can Resist,'" 75. She writes: "We cannot say how a liberated society would live, but we can analyze objectively what prevents it from doing so."
29 There are important differences between early and mature Honneth. Compare *The Struggle for Recognition: The Moral Grammar of Social Conflict*, trans. Joel Anderson (Cambridge, MA: MIT Press, 1996) and *Freedom's Right*, trans. Joseph Ganahl (New York: Columbia University Press, 2014).
30 See Honneth, *Freedom's Right*.
31 For a full account of this point, see my "Normative Ambivalence and the Future of Critical Theory: Adorno & Horkheimer, Castro-Gómez, Quijano on Rationality, Modernity, Totality," in *Critical Theory and the Challenge of Praxis*, ed. Stefano Giachetti Ludovisi (London: Ashgate, 2015).
32 In *Minima Moralia*, for example, he writes that "the only philosophy which can be responsibly practiced in the face of despair is the attempt to contemplate all things as they would represent themselves from the standpoint of redemption" (Adorno, *Minima Moralia*, §153).
33 See Iain MacDonald's "Adorno's Modal Utopianism: Possibility and Actuality in Adorno and Hegel", https://umontreal.academia.edu/IainMacdonald, accessed

September 12, 2019. See also Gordon Finlayson, "Hegel, Adorno and the Origins of Immanent Criticism," *British Journal for the History of Philosophy* 22, no. 6/2 (2014).

34 It is important to note that Hegel himself never characterized the method of the *Phenomenology* as 'immanent critique', though we have reasons to believe that the term is first used in relation to Hegel after his death. See Finlayson, "Hegel, Adorno and the Origins Immanent Criticism".
35 G.W.F. Hegel, *Phenomenology of Spirit*, trans. Terry Pinkard, https://de.scribd.com/document/49157331/Phenomenology-of-Spirit-Entire-Text-of-T-Pinkard-Translation (accessed September 12, 2019).
36 Hegel, *Phenomenology of Spirit*, §§81, 84.
37 See Stephen Houlgate, *A Reader's Guide to Hegel's* Phenomenology of Spirit (London: Bloombury, 2013).
38 Hegel, *Phenomenology of Spirit*, §85.
39 Ibid.
40 Ibid.
41 Ibid., §86.
42 Note that *Krinein* means to cut, rift, separate, discriminate but also to decide, and cf. the Kantian conception of critique as self-knowledge.
43 See Hegel, *Phenomenology of Spirit*, §§73–4.
44 Ibid., §82: "Consciousness distinguishes something from itself and at the same time it relates itself to it."
45 Those that gloss immanent critique as comparison include Ritter (see Finlayson), Titus Stahl, "What Is Immanent Critique?" https://www.academia.edu/5462936/What_is_Immanent_Critique_Working_Paper (accessed September 12, 2019), and Steven B. Smith, *Hegel's Critique of Liberalism: Rights in Context* (Chicago: The University of Chicago Press, 1989).
46 In the *Science of Logic*, Hegel famously argues that "everything is contradiction". For this point, see my *Hegel's Theory of Intelligibility* (Chicago: The University of Chicago Press, 2015).
47 Self-conception here equals form of knowing.
48 Hegel, *Phenomenology of Spirit*, §86.
49 Ibid., §79.
50 See Jaeggi, *Kritik von Lebensformen*.
51 Hegel, *Phenomenology of Spirit*, §80.
52 Ibid., §80: "where the concept corresponds to the object and the object to the concept".
53 Ibid., §§56, 78.
54 Ibid., §78.
55 See Robert Pippin, "The 'Logic of Experience' as 'Absolute Knowledge' in Hegel's *Phenomenology of Spirit*," in *Hegel's* Phenomenology of Spirit: *A Critical Guide*, ed. Dean Moyar and Michael Quante (Cambridge: Cambridge University Press, 2010).
56 See part 1 of my *Hegel's Theory of Intelligibility*; see also Pippin, "The 'Logic of Experience'."
57 See, e.g., Hegel, *Phenomenology of Spirit*, §65.
58 See my *Hegel's Theory of Intelligibility*.
59 Hegel, *Phenomenology of Spirit*, §80; emphasis mine.
60 See Pippin, "The 'Logic of Experience'."
61 Hegel, *Phenomenology of Spirit*, §808.
62 In 1980, George Markus cogently argued that there are at least four "types or forms of critical theory" in Marx's corpus: (1) in the 1844 *Economic and Philosophical*

Manuscripts; (2) in the writings of 1846–7; (3) in the *Grundrisse*; and finally (4) in *Capital*. See George Markus, "Four Forms of Critical Theory—Some Theses on Marx's Development," *Thesis Eleven* (1980).
63 Throughout Marx's 1843–4 writings we find variations on critique, central to all is the critique of religion as a model of demystification. See Robin Celikates, "Karl Marx: Critique as Emancipatory Practice," *Conceptions of Critique in Modern and Contemporary Philosophy*, ed. Karin De Boer (London: Palgrave Macmillan, 2012), esp. 109ff.
64 Karl Marx, "Economic and Philosophical Manuscripts of 1844," in *The Marx-Engels Reader*, 112.
65 Ibid.
66 Ibid., 115.
67 See also ibid., 116, where he argues for "man" as a "suffering being".
68 Ibid., 84.
69 See, for example, Karen Ng, "Ideology Critique from Hegel and Marx to Critical Theory," *Constellations* 22, no. 3 (2015).
70 Marx, "Economic and Philosophical Manuscripts," 70. See also ibid.: "We have accepted its language and its laws. We presupposed private property, the separation of labor, capital and land, and of wages, profit of capital and rent of land—likewise division of labor, competition, the concept of exchange value, etc."
71 Ibid., 79: "Private property is the product, the result, the necessary consequence, of alienated labor, of the external relation of the worker to nature and to himself."
72 Ibid., 71.
73 Ibid., 86–9.
74 Ibid.: "to a human relation to the world".
75 This famous section was fundamental for Lukács's concept of reification, which became influential for Adorno's views on late capitalism. Keeping in mind Lukács's insistence on the concept of totality is helpful, as Marx's critique of capitalism remains a critique of a form of life, rather than a merely critique of economic relations.
76 This is a paraphrase from Seyla Benhabib, "The Marxian Method of Critique: Normative Presuppositions," *Praxis international* 4, no. 3 (1984): 286.
77 See ibid.
78 Benhabib explains: "With the method of defetishizing critique Marx analyzes the historicity of theoretical and everyday forms of consciousness, as well as of social formations, from the standpoint of a future actuality" (ibid.).
79 See Nick Nesbitt, *Caribbean Critique* (Liverpool: Liverpool University Press, 2013), 5.
80 Marx, *Capital I*, in *The Marx-Engels Reader*, 343.
81 Benhabib, "Marxian Critique," 287.
82 See Marx, *Capital I*, 229, 230, 232.
83 Ibid., 319.
84 Ibid., 320.
85 Ibid.
86 The exposition gains critical traction precisely by examining a phenomenon that might seem illusory, in need of unmasking, but which in reality is the expression of a reality that is itself topsy-turvy, upside down: relations between things order relations between people. Although it is certainly the case that the issue here for Marx is 'stripping off the mystical veil' that this inversion requires, the inversion itself expresses the *reality* of capitalism.

87 See Markus, "Four Forms of Critical Theory." See also Nicole Peperelli, "Fetish and Reification: On Being, versus Appearing to Be, an Objective Social Relation" (ms.).
88 Marx, *Capital I*, 321.
89 Another crucial aspect is captured under the rubric of primitive accumulation. Recent insightful accounts of the relation between the exploitation and expropriation include: Nancy Fraser, "Behind Marx's Hidden Abode," *New Left Review* 86 (2014) and "Expropriation and Exploitation in Racialized Capitalism," *Critical Historical Studies* (2016).
90 Michael Heinrich explains that Marx saw the revolutionary movements of 1848–9 as a consequence of the economic crisis of 1847–8, and he generalized this result, expecting the next revolution to come with the next crisis. See Michael Heinrich, *An Introduction to the Three Volumes of Karl Marx's Capital*, trans. Alexander Locascio (New York: Monthly Review Press, 2004), 175.
91 See ibid. Marx then speaks of a "persistent conflict" between the unrestricted development of the forces of production and the restricted capitalist aim—but there is no mention of a "collapse" of any sort.
92 Quoted in ibid., 176.

7

Hegel and Marx on 'Spiritual Life' as a Criterion for Social Critique

Frederick Neuhouser

In this chapter I explore the thought that Marx's critique of capitalism can be re-animated by thinking about how the normative foundations of his critique are appropriations of the standards that Hegel employs in his account of rational social life (*Sittlichkeit*). There are various respects in which Hegel and Marx share fundamental normative commitments, but the specific commitment I address here concerns what I will call 'the demands of spiritual life'. To some it will no doubt seem strange to make any conception of spirit central to a reconstruction of Marx's normative perspective. For, as everyone knows, Hegel was an idealist and Marx a materialist, and—so it would seem—their positions must be polar opposites. Fortunately, the relationship between Hegel and Marx is more interesting than this simple opposition suggests. Apart from the fact that the precise meaning of these philosophical labels is far from clear, there is more materialism in Hegel's idealism, and more idealism in Marx's materialism, than standard accounts of their positions suppose. Nowhere is the convergence of their positions more consequential than in their treatment of the fundamental concept of Hegel's philosophy: spirit (*Geist*). That Hegel's (Aristotelian) conception of spirit contains a substantial materialistic element can be seen in his definition of spirit as 'sublated life' (*aufgehobenes Leben*). Life, for both Hegel and Marx, I will argue, remains a constitutive element of spirit, and any way of being in the world that negates life without preserving it is both spiritless and dead. One way of formulating Hegel's position that makes clearer its proximity to materialism is to say that spiritual being is characterized by a range of ways in which free subjects relate self-consciously to *life*, including to their own nature as living beings. In the domain of social philosophy, for Hegel, spirituality is at work wherever humans engage in the project of reconciling their natural, biological neediness with their supreme spiritual aspiration, freedom. This implies that the form of social life appropriate to our nature as spiritual beings is one in which every essential life activity we engage in is also a site of freedom and where every expression of freedom is at the same time a material practice, addressed to our needs as living beings.

When Hegel's conception of spirit is articulated in this way, it is not difficult to find it in Marx's thought, too. It is at work, for example, in "On the Jewish Question", where Marx writes that "human emancipation will be complete only when the real, individual human being ... , in his empirical life, in his individual labor, in his individual relations, has known and organized his 'own forces' as social forces"[1] (where knowing and organizing our own forces is part of what free, or self-determined, agency consists in). Marx's concept of alienation is no less indebted to this Hegelian ideal, insofar as *un*alienated labor is activity that both satisfies our material needs and fulfills our aspiration to be self-determining in all our activity. And the same ideal informs Marx's later work, too. Consider the well-known passage in *Capital* that characterizes free activity in conformity with a Hegelian conception of spirit: "Freedom [in the sphere of material production] can consist only in socialized human beings—associated producers—rationally regulating their material exchange with nature, bringing it under their collective control, instead of being dominated by it as by a blind power, and achieving this ... under the conditions most appropriate to ... their human nature."[2] What unites all three of these positions is a vision of what free activity in general consists in (knowing and organizing one's own forces or activities), as well as two further points, namely: that the type of free activity characteristic of humans is *material*—responsive to needs we have qua living beings—and intrinsically social, or cooperative. In other words, two fundamental features of the human condition—our material neediness and our dependence on others in satisfying our needs—means that, for us, freedom— the self-conscious control of our life activity—will require collectively knowing and organizing our own forces as the cooperative activities they (in some sense) already are.

Sometimes Marx seems to lose sight of Hegel's materialist conception of spiritual activity, replacing—or perhaps supplementing—it with a less attractive 'idealist' model.[3] In fact, this occurs in the very passage I just cited, when Marx goes on to say that "the true realm of freedom" begins only beyond the sphere of "material production", that is, only where human activity ceases entirely to be motivated by natural need and, so, is no longer undertaken for the sake of the 'external ends'— maintaining and reproducing life—that are imposed on us by nature.[4] In my view, this quasi-Kantian ideal of freedom—activity that is completely undetermined by natural ends—represents an abandonment of the more earthbound conception of spirit that informs Hegel's social philosophy. Even if there might be human activities completely unrelated to natural need, why consider them higher expressions of freedom than what can be had in our everyday activities of labor and family life, as long as these are organized in conformity with "the conditions most appropriate to ... [our] human nature", including our aspiration to be self-determining?

Hegel

1 The Nature of Free Spiritual Activity

That a rational (or good) social order enables us to give expression to these two sides of our nature—our membership in both the realm of freedom and the realm of necessity—within the very same activities is precisely what Hegel takes himself to show in the *Philosophy of Right*, when demonstrating that the modern nuclear family, the market economy ('civil society'), and the constitutional monarchical state are rational institutions.[5] It is clear enough how the family and civil society serve the material reproduction of society: The self-preservation of individuals is facilitated by economic cooperation in producing the goods needed to sustain life, and the reproduction of the species is served by sexual cooperation as structured within the family. For spiritual beings like us, however, there is always more at stake in raising children and producing goods than merely reproducing life: As spiritual activities they at the same time promote (or express) freedom, broadly conceived, and in doing so they unite the ends of life with the ideal of freedom. One thing this means is that these forms of social participation serve vital functions, but because they are activities of spiritual beings, capable of free agency, they are also carried out with a consciousness on the part of social members of the ends their own activities serve, and in this respect they differ from the life-maintaining behaviors of merely living (animal) beings. Spiritual activities not only have a point; they are also self-conscious in the sense that they have a point *for* the very beings that engage in them (even if it is also possible for agents to have mistaken or merely partial understandings of what they do and why).

Moreover, because these agents are spiritual beings, the point (or ends) of their activities cannot be reduced to the mere reproduction of life. As spiritual activities, they are also ways in which social members realize, and take themselves to realize, freedom. Hegel's account of how, and in what forms, freedom can be realized in social activity is too complex to articulate fully here,[6] but two aspects of that account are especially important: First, when individuals see the point of their social activities and embrace them as good, those activities—participation in the family and civil society, for example—count as deep and satisfying expressions of free, or self-determined, agency, for they are ways in which individuals successfully live in accordance with their own understanding of what is good and important in human life. Under these conditions, individuals can affirm the social world and their activities within it as meaningful and good; their social world is a 'home' for them (rather than a hostile or indifferent environment), and they themselves are its authors, insofar as it is they who continually re-create their social 'home' through their own activity. Freedom, from this perspective, consists in (collectively) creating a social world that, because it is regarded as good, can be affirmed as such by its own creators.

The second aspect of Hegel's account of free social activity derives from the consideration that, since such activity is essentially cooperative, the conceptions of the good realized in social life must be shared with others. Raising a family and laboring to satisfy material needs are not projects in which I realize my own idiosyncratic conception of the good but rather ways in which we realize together a shared understanding of what makes human life meaningful. Because in this domain I can act freely only by incorporating myself into a larger 'we'—into a community with shared values and norms—there is an important intersubjective element in the freedom realized in social life. In fulfilling the various roles that social members occupy in rational institutions, each affirms the contributions of his or her fellow members and recognizes them as beings of value, united in a common project of realizing the human good. Part of what it is to be a successful mother or father, or a competent producer of goods, is to have one's activity in those roles affirmed, or recognized, by other social members, and this in turn is a condition of affirming oneself in a satisfying way. As Freud was to emphasize later, finding affirmation in both love and work is—in the modern world, at least—essential to satisfaction, and achieving recognition through one's own self-determined activity is a further way in which freedom can be taken to be realized in social participation.

The spiritual nature of social life is also a prominent theme in Hegel's *Phenomenology of Spirit*, as can be seen by examining the most primitive model of human society he considers there, the relation between bondsman and lord.[7] The easiest point to see here is that the activities of bondsman and lord serve the vital ends of both: The lord commands, the bondsman labors, and together these two complementary activities produce the goods necessary for sustaining life. But these same activities also have a significance in relation to freedom. The lord's commanding and the bondsman's obedience are grounded in and expressive of a shared conception of what freedom is; of the superior value it has in relation to mere life; and of who among them possesses normative authority based on having proved himself to be free (above mere life) in the struggle unto death. The resulting asymmetric relation between bondsman and lord is a consequence of the fact that the former 'gives in' at the decisive moment of the struggle unto death and chooses his own life over freedom, but his doing so does not signal an abandonment of the basic normative position he held before the struggle. That the bondsman continues to subscribe to the higher normative authority of freedom is revealed by the fact that for both him and the lord, prestige and authority—in short, recognition—attach to the individual who has given expression in his deeds to the superior value of freedom in relation to mere life.

The interaction between bondsman and lord is spiritual, then, because it imbues jointly undertaken activities of life with significance in relation to freedom. Moreover, it is social in the sense Hegel has in mind when he characterizes the structure of their relation as an "*I* that's a *we*",[8] where this expresses the thought that no individual member of a social world can be what he is or do what he does (within that social nexus) without being integrated in various ways into the collective life of a *we*. One illustration of this *I-we* structure is that neither of the life-related activities of bondsman and lord is complete without the activity of the other, and neither makes sense on its own without being brought into relation with the more 'universal' end of social reproduction. But the *I-we* structure of social life also has spiritual dimensions, which is to say, a significance in relation to freedom. In the best human societies, *I*'s are not simply absorbed into the *we* without remainder; rather, individuals in such societies retain a degree of independence from the *we* they compose, and each aspires to be, and to be recognized as, both free and valuable in his own right. This shared aspiration implies that each *I* requires the recognition of others in order to find complete satisfaction of its own ends. At the same time, a spiritual *we* is present—a normatively oriented recognitive community—because those *I*'s are united by a shared conception of what is of ultimate value, where this shared commitment determines the relations of normative authority, including the hierarchy of recognition, among social members.

Finally, Hegel's understanding of the spiritual aspects of the bondsman–lord relation is materialistic in a way that Marx would endorse: The shared values, the relations of recognition, the norms of freedom that make this communal life spiritual do not exist merely in the minds of social members; instead, they are real only insofar as they are expressed in material activity, in this case, the labor of the bondsman (and the commanding of that labor by the lord). Labor in this society is not merely a means for reproducing life; it is also an activity in which the values, the freedom, and the recognitive relations of its members are expressed. Although a society made up of bondsmen and lords represents an unsatisfying way in which humans attempt to unify their immersion in life with their understanding that they are free, all human societies, according to Hegel, are engaged in some version of this project and exhibit the same basic structural components as the bondsman–lord relation.

2 Spiritual Failings of Bondsman and Lord

One of the points of Hegel's analysis of bondsman and lord is that there are better and worse—more and less spiritually satisfying—ways of arranging social relations. The bondsman–lord relation is ultimately unsatisfying (for both its participants), but the important question is why. Hegel never suggests that its deficiency has to do with an inability to reproduce the material conditions of life; the problem, instead, resides at the level of spiritual satisfaction. One could locate the problematic character of the bondsman–lord relation in any number of its features: Neither party finds recognition that is genuinely satisfying; their relation is, in fact, one of domination rather than freedom; and the bondsman, in both his self-understanding and his way of life, is alienated from his true essence (as free). None of these claims is wrong, but a more comprehensive description of the deficiency is that the social order to which bondsman and lord belong fails to bring together freedom and the ends of life in a satisfying way. As I have suggested, this means that the various ways in which social members participate in life are not, at the same time, expressions of their freedom and that the activities they regard as expressions of freedom are not, at the same time, ways of participating in life.

One indication of this failure can be seen in the fact that the bondsman's labor is unfree in the straightforward sense that someone other than himself—the lord—directs his activity and does so in a way that serves the lord's ends rather than those of the laborer himself. A second indication of social failure is that, rather than successfully uniting freedom and life, a society of bondsmen and lords responds to its spiritual task with a strategy of 'splitting'. Life itself gets split into two, insofar as production and consumption fall to different, mutually antagonistic social classes. This has the result that consumption takes place in ignorance of the activity and of the agents that make it possible, while production is carried out not in order to satisfy spiritual aims but only because obeying the lord, and providing for him, are prerequisites of staying alive. This division within the activities of life implies a spiritual division as well: Society divides into two groups, one of which is absorbed in life but unfree, while the other, as far removed from life as possible, enjoys, precisely for that reason, a kind of freedom. The problem is not only that some are free while others are not but also that both freedom and life remain empty and unsatisfying. Labor for the necessities of life becomes a site of domination and self-denial rather than of freedom, and its counterpart, enjoyment, devolves into luxury consumption that fails to satisfy. Those who labor do so merely in order to survive, while those who consume have a spiritual end in view (expressing their freedom) but are moved by a distorted vision of what that freedom consists in (complete independence from the ties of life).

When Hegel's analysis of bondsman and lord is understood in this way, it is easy to see where many of the resources for Marx's critique of alienated labor in capitalism come from. (Marx expresses precisely Hegel's idea when he describes alienated labor as a condition in which "the worker no longer feels himself to be freely active in any but his animal functions, ... and in his human functions no longer feels himself to be anything but an animal."[9]) But there is a key feature of Hegel's view—a strand of idealism—that is generally regarded as distinguishing Hegel's understanding of the bondsman–lord relation from Marx's account of alienation. According to this interpretation, Hegel holds that the spiritual failings of bondsman and lord can ultimately be traced back to inadequate self-conceptions—more precisely, to conceptions of how a free being must relate to life that either disavow our connectedness to life or misconstrue the threat it poses to being free. What unites bondsman and lord is an overly exalted conception of the freedom we should aspire to. Both take freedom to consist in what eventually shows itself to be a one-sided relation to life in which a human being asserts his freedom by acting as though he had no essential relation to life, thereby demonstrating his 'superior' status in relation to the merely living.

That bondsman and lord subscribe to the same stark conception of freedom explains why the result of the struggle unto death is so asymmetric: If freedom requires absolute independence from everything 'other', then avowing one's ties to life, as the future bondsman does, is incompatible with being free. The unequal relation between bondsman and lord is an expression of this shared all-or-nothing view of freedom, conjoined with the fact that, facing the prospect of death, one subject affirms the value of his life while the other persists in valuing only absolute independence. Thus, the one-sided recognitive relation between bondsman and lord is grounded in a certain conception of freedom and in the different relations to life that (in the struggle unto death) each has taken up in the world. Since patterns of recognition manifest themselves in material practices, bondsman and lord take up relations to life within society that are just as one-sided as the relations of recognition they express. As I have noted, in the economic sphere the two moments of the reproduction of material life—production and consumption—are torn apart, each falling to one of the relation's opposing poles: The bondsman labors while the lord enjoys, and in doing so each at the same time relates to the other in the mode of recognition. For the bondsman, labor is at once a relating to life; a relating to self (an expression of his own attitude to freedom and life); and a relating to another subject (through relations of recognition that define conditions of authority and subjection). This is merely to say that his servile labor is spiritual activity since it is a way, however unsatisfying, of negotiating the opposition between freedom and life.

3 Summary

Before turning to how Marx appropriates Hegel's conception of spiritual activity, it may be useful to summarize what I have said thus far about that conception. According to Hegel, the hallmark of spirituality is the aspiration to unify freedom and life, where this means that there is no essential life activity that is not also a site of freedom and no expression of freedom that is not at the same time a material practice. Moreover, Hegel has told us something about what our material activities must look like if they are to be sites of freedom rather than alienation: First, we must be aware of the 'point' of what we do and regard it (and the world we produce through it) as good; second, we ourselves, and not some alien 'other', must direct and organize our material activities; third, since human material activities are nearly always cooperative undertakings, we must incorporate ourselves into a community—a 'we'—that is defined by shared understandings of what is important in human life, and where the activity of each 'I' makes sense only in the context of what 'we' do together; finally, we must find our material activities sources of self-affirmation, which itself depends on being recognized by others as valued cooperators.

Marx

1 The Circulation of Capital

In addressing what Marx's normative perspective takes over from Hegel's, I focus on one specific passage in *Capital* in order to show how, without being named as such, Hegel's conception of spirit—and of its central task as uniting freedom and life—underlies Marx's critique of capitalism. Taking its cue from this conception of spirit, the basic thrust of the critique expressed in this passage is that in capitalism activities directed at satisfying the ends of life (labor) are necessarily unfree. This amounts to the claim that what is in truth human activity (and therefore ought to be an expression of freedom) appears in capitalism instead as the behavior of merely living beings, devoid of free agency. Another way of formulating Marx's point is to say that freedom and life will not be satisfactorily united until our laboring activities are collectively known, organized, and affirmed by ourselves, at which point our alienated forces will be activities appropriate to a genuinely spiritual mode of life.

The passage of *Capital* I focus on initially seems simple and normatively innocent, but, when elaborated further, it reveals a rich critique of capitalist production as predicated on a type of alienated activity (labor) that necessarily fails to integrate life and freedom. The passage at issue is Marx's attempt to define capital by articulating what he calls the general formula for its circulation. According to Marx, the key to grasping what capital is lies in distinguishing 'money that is capital' from 'money that is merely money'. When money functions merely as money—as a medium of exchange—its form of circulation can be represented by the simple formula C—M—C, which designates a series of exchanges in which the owner of a commodity that she does not wish to consume herself sells that commodity (converts it into money) with the aim of purchasing a different commodity that she does wish to consume. The point of such a transaction is obvious and depends on the different use values of the commodities exchanged: The first is not desired by the person who sells it, whereas the second is.

The formula for the circulation of capital appears at first to be just the reverse of this, M—C—M, where the owner of money buys a commodity for the purpose of reconverting it later into money. Since money "is simply the ... form of commodities in which their particular use values vanish",[10] no appeal to the use values of the commodities involved can make sense of this set of exchanges. Converting money into commodities with the aim of converting them back into money again makes sense only if there is a quantitative difference between beginning and end, that is, only if the second M is larger than the first. Hence M—C—M reveals itself to be, in truth, M—C—M', where M' is greater than M and where the difference between the two is surplus value, the ultimate aim of capital's circulation.

Marx's point that capital can be distinguished from mere money only by specifying their forms of circulation is equivalent to the claim that it is their functions that distinguish them: Mere money functions as a medium of exchange, whereas capital's function is to create surplus value. In both cases the functions Marx ascribes to these processes depend on the conscious aims of the individuals who participate in them. Since both processes rely on the voluntary actions of the individuals involved, their functions cannot be specified without referring to the subjective aims of those individuals. At the same time, whatever problem Marx claims to find in the circulation of capital does not consist in its failure to achieve the specific subjective aim—the accumulation of surplus value—that (for the capitalist) motivates it. His claim, rather, is that when the totality of social conditions that makes M—C—M' possible is revealed, other systematic failures of free agency come into view. One is that there are subjective aims of other necessary participants in the creation of surplus value (laborers) that are satisfied only accidentally, if at all, in the process. But further failures of free agency emerge as well, failures that cannot be described simply in terms of agents' failure to realize their subjective aims: When the circulation of capital is regarded not as the project of a few individuals but as the basis of a society-wide system of production, that process necessarily produces consequences that are *unintended*, and often *unknown*, by its participants; that elude the *control* of the agents who produce them; and that cannot be *affirmed* by those agents collectively. In all these respects the conditions under which the circulation of capital takes place guarantee that the labor that makes that process possible will fail in the spiritual task of uniting life with freedom.

Now, if we extend these two formulas beyond a single cycle of exchange, we discover more differences between the species of circulation they represent. Since the subjective aim behind C—M—C is to consume a specific use value, its second phase—where money functions as a medium of exchange to purchase the desired commodity—brings the cycle to completion in the sense that the end for the sake of which it was undertaken has been achieved. As new needs and desires arise, as they inevitably do in living beings, this process will be repeated, but repetition takes the form of a new cycle formally indistinguishable from the first. Thus, C—M—C reveals itself to be, in truth: C—M—C; C—M—C; C—M—C; and so on, where the renewal of the cycle is governed by something external to it: the rhythm of human needs and desires as they arise in the domain of life. Since what is aimed at in the circulation of capital is an abstract quantity shorn of all specific qualities, it has no such natural stopping point rooted in life's needs. Renewal takes place instead as a *continuation* of the first cycle, where the original M increases even more (to M") and where, because purely quantitative aims can always be improved on through further quantitative increases, no logical resting point is in sight. M—C—M' reveals itself to be, in truth: M—C—M'–C—M"—C—M'" … , and so on, ad infinitum.

2 The Relation between Capital and Life

We should ask now whether Marx means for this formula for the circulation of capital itself to constitute a critique of capitalism. It is not immediately clear that he does, and yet there is something unsettling about a social process that exhibits the logic of what Hegel calls 'bad' infinity, and Marx reinforces this impression when he characterizes the circulation of capital as "the never resting augmentation of value".[11] Just as unsettling is the biological language he uses when characterizing what he calls capital's "life-cycle".[12] When money functions as capital, Marx says, "value presents itself as a self-moving process".[13] "The movement in which [capital] adds surplus value is its own movement, a movement of self-expanding value. [It] acquires the occult quality of being able to add value to itself … It brings forth living offspring, or at least lays golden eggs."[14]

It is clear here that Marx means to describe capital's movement with the same language Hegel uses to characterize life and that his intention in doing so is to portray the circulation of capital as analogous to the vital processes of a biological species. Beyond the point just mentioned—that capital is capable of multiplying itself (of 'bringing forth living offspring')—four further similarities are worth noting. First, capital is what it is—and differs from mere money—by virtue of the specific function it serves, a function that governs its infinitely many individual transactions and unifies them into a single process, much like the multifarious behavior of a living being is determined and organized by the single biological end of reproducing the species to which it belongs. In the case of capital, too, a single aim defines its function: the ceaseless accumulation of surplus value.

A second similarity between capital and life is that both are "self-moving" in the sense that their governing ends 'come from within' rather than being imposed on them from without: The activities through which a species reproduces itself have no purpose beyond the continuation of life itself, just as the constant renewal of capital's circulation serves no end beyond that of its own reproduction and augmentation. Each process is an end in itself rather than in the service of some end outside itself. Hegel would say that this makes them self-sufficient, autonomous processes (moved by wholly internal ends) and that, as such, they approximate Aristotle's general criteria for the (spiritually) highest form of activity, *theoria*, which, superior even to *praxis*, is self-sufficient, continuous, and determined by no ends outside itself.

A third similarity Marx means to draw between the circulation of capital and the reproduction of life is that both processes embody—or come close to embodying—the ontological structure Hegel ascribes to conscious subjects. For Hegel, self-conscious subjects have a characteristic mode of being, different from that of inert things, which takes the following form: A subject exists only insofar as it 'posits contradictions' internal to itself and then consciously negates those contradictions without losing its identity as an individual being. It would take us too far afield to explain here why Hegel takes self-conscious subjects to exhibit this structure; in the case of capital, however, Marx is thinking of its constant need to assume 'contradictory' forms—first as money, then as commodity, then again as money, and so on—in order to be what it is (which is to say, in order to fulfill its defining function). What makes subjects, living beings, and capital structurally similar for Marx is that each exists only as a *sich Reproduzierendes*—that is, only insofar as it is constantly engaged in the activity of reproducing itself. Just as a living being that ceases to actively maintain itself falls out of the domain of the living, so capital that rests and discontinues its self-expansion ceases to exist as capital and becomes instead 'lifeless' value.

Finally, processes of life and the circulation of capital are alike in that, although both approximate the structure Hegel ascribes to subjects, both also fall short of self-conscious subjectivity. The reason life is not fully a subject is that its species reproduce themselves un-self-consciously. This means that even though the processes of life are in some sense autonomous and self-driving, they cannot achieve the self-conscious freedom that is available to spiritual beings by virtue of their capacity consciously to know and determine their activities. Life's ontological 'inferiority' to spirit is due to its lack of self-consciousness, and this is why capital, too, falls short of being fully subject-like. Even if there is a similarity between its motions and those of an autonomously moving subject, capital, in its self-expanding life-cycle, is similar to life in that it is unaware of itself as a unified social process. This means not only that there is no consciousness that oversees or intends the overall process of capital accumulation but also that, when the individual transactions that make up that process are taken as a whole, they have systematic consequences that none of its participants anticipate, intend, or, in many cases, are even aware of.

An important difference between Hegel's treatment of life and Marx's attitude to capital is that Hegel does not interpret life's lack of self-consciousness as a criticism of life, whereas Marx thinks the same lack in the circulation of capital shows it to be an alienated social power and, so, worthy of critique. Life for Hegel may be defective in comparison with self-conscious spirit (because the former is by nature less free than the latter), but this defect is merely part of what it is for something to be life rather than spirit. Even if spirit is 'higher' than mere life, it is not appropriate to expect life to be more than it is or to criticize it for not being what it is not. This is different in the case of capital. For even though the formula for capital's circulation presents its movements as the motions of things (money and commodities), those motions are in truth activities of human beings, and this means that it is fitting to judge capital's motions by the standards of freedom appropriate to spiritual activity and that their failure to be fully subjective is indeed a criticism of them. Activities of humans that appear instead as the motions of things are alienated spiritual powers. As such, they fall short of the normative standards appropriate to the kind of thing they are. I now want to explain what that means.

The first thing to be explained is what it means to say that the motions described by M—C—M'—… are activities of human agents, as well as essentially social. Part of Marx's point is that the formula for the circulation of capital cannot be understood on its own terms alone—as representing a movement of things—without referring to what is not present in the formula: the activities of humans that make those movements of things possible. One obvious point is that any exchange is undertaken by humans who are conscious of what they are doing and for what purpose: in the absence of human agents, things do not simply exchange themselves for one another. A more important respect in which M—C—M'—… masks the social activities on which it depends is related to Marx's claim that the basic unit of that formula—M—C—M'—is mysterious in a way that C—M—C is not: It is easy to understand how one commodity might be exchanged for a different one of equal value when money, as a medium of exchange, mediates the equivalent exchange values of the two commodities. It is not, however, easy to understand, in the formula for capital, how money can increase in quantity through circulation alone, simply by purchasing a commodity and then re-converting it into money. As Marx goes on to argue, M—C—M' sheds the appearance of being an occult phenomenon only when it is expanded so as to make clear that M can become M' only if a process of production (P)—involving an expenditure of human labor—intervenes between the two. In other words, M—C—M' shows itself to be, in truth: M—C … P … C—M', where further investigation reveals that if P is to yield surplus value, it must make use of a kind of activity (human labor) under specific social conditions—conditions that make the *exploitation* of human labor possible—the most important of which is that one class of humans appears in the marketplace only as sellers of labor-power while another appears there as owners of exchange value in excess of what is required to satisfy their life needs.

3 Labor as Cooperative Praxis

It is important to be clear about how the categories of activity and social activity enter the picture here. What makes the capitalist circulation of commodities possible is that they have been produced by labor, which is a human activity, not a movement of things. The reason Marx regards labor as an especially important species of agency derives from a claim about the kind of thing it is at more or less all times and places: Labor is a subjective activity because it engages the subjectivity of those who perform it to an extent that many other human behaviors do not. Unlike digestion, labor requires conscious, intentional direction of the bodily motions it consists in, as well as an awareness of the end those motions are to achieve. Digestion functions best when one is unaware of doing it, whereas the idea of unconscious labor is barely intelligible; in the case of labor, both awareness of the end to be achieved and conscious control of the processes conducing to that end are essential. Unlike strolling in the park, labor—like *poiesis* for Aristotle—is directed at a specific end external to the activity itself, where that end derives from and is answerable to specific needs or desires outside itself that it is meant to satisfy. This explains why labor requires a degree of subjective engagement—a concentration and attention to the specificity of one's objects and environment (and to the needs or desires one is trying to satisfy)—that is not essential to amusement or relaxation. And unlike enjoying a simple meal or shopping for clothes, labor requires deploying specific habits and skills that themselves have been acquired through the discipline of previous labor. This means that labor engages the worker's personal makeup and history—specific habits and skills she has participated in acquiring—in ways that make it plausible to think of labor as an *externalization* of oneself, or as self-expression (which itself can be thought of as a kind of freedom). It is for these reasons that Marx regards labor as an activity that is appropriately judged by the norms of subjectively free agency, and this explains why, when labor is not understood or controlled, or when its consequences are not known or affirmed, by those who perform it, it counts as unfree.

I now want to consider why labor, insofar as it makes the circulation of things in capitalism possible, is a social activity. One reason is that (nearly) all labor is, in Marx's view, *cooperative praxis*. I will return to the idea of *praxis* below, after asking first: In what sense is labor cooperative? While it is true that most laboring processes require the working together of many hands—harvesting crops, building ships, educating children are not easily accomplished by one person working alone—this is not Marx's main point. The type of cooperation most relevant here is to be understood in light of the fact that even in capitalism the productive activities that enable society to reproduce itself materially constitute, whether recognized as such or not, a socially organized scheme of cooperation. This feature of labor does not simply follow from its definition; as the example of Robinson Crusoe shows, it is conceptually possible for there to be labor that is not part of any socially organized scheme. Rather, the cooperative nature of labor in the sense at issue here follows from a fundamental social condition under which the vast majority of human production takes place, namely, that a division of labor, whether simple or complex, renders each of us dependent on the labor of others for our survival and well-being. This interdependence necessitates that individuals' productive activities be organized according to a cooperative scheme of some sort if there is to be even a rough correspondence between the kinds and amounts of labor undertaken within a society and the diverse needs that labor is intended to satisfy. In Hegel's terminology, a laborer in capitalism is an *I* that is a *we* (what she does is determined by how her individual activity fits in with that of all the other members of her society), even if in this case she is unlikely to be aware of the respect in which her individual activity is in reality a "social force". Marx believes that in capitalism, much more so than in other modes of production, the cooperative character of our labor (in this sense) is concealed from us by the atomized way in which production is undertaken when coordinated (unconsciously) by a system of market exchange. It is largely the fact, then, that capitalism is generalized commodity production that explains why labor within it is often not recognized by those who perform it as the social activity it already is.

4 Spiritual Pathologies of Capitalist Circulation

Part of the legacy Marx inherits from Hegel's conception of spiritual phenomena is the view that if human activities are unfree in the sense I just articulated—unknown as the social forces they in fact are—then those same activities will appear, to those who carry them out, as forces that control or dominate the very subjects whose forces they are, thereby inverting the proper relation between agents and their activities. According to this view, a necessary concomitant of the unrecognized social character of labor in capitalism is that the unconsciously coordinated productive activities of individuals manifest themselves as 'objective' laws of the market that dictate (without there being a dictator) everything about production in that society, including what will be produced, how it will be produced, and whether workers will be able to find employment at wages high enough to feed and shelter themselves and their families. While this aspect of the alienated character of market-determined forces is not visible from the formula for the circulation of capital itself, returning to that formula reveals another sense in which productive activity in capitalism escapes the control of its agents.

Seeing this requires focusing on another respect in which that formula reveals the circulation of capital to be unlike movements of life: Capital's motions aim not at the mere reproduction of its species (exchange value) but at its continual increase. As we have seen, this means that there is no stopping point to this process internal to the logic of its own cycle of life, no point at which its striving could be 'satisfied' or completed. But whereas this distinguishes the circulation of capital from the life cycles of individual living beings—an acorn achieves completion when it becomes a healthy oak—it does not distinguish capital from life more generally, regarded as the life of a species (or of a larger system of interdependent species). In the case of Life (capital 'L') there is also no internal reason for reproduction ever to come to an end. The crucial difference between the processes of capital and those of Life, then, lies not in the former's infinite character—that it just goes on and on—but in the fact that its aim is defined solely in terms of quantitative, and hence 'abstract', *growth*. Because capital seeks nothing but quantitative increases, its circulation is subject to no natural or self-imposed constraints with regard to its rhythm or pace, or to any internal limits on the size of what it strives for. The circulation of capital, in other words, is governed by a single, quantitatively-defined imperative that commands not merely its own reproduction, nor merely its continual growth, but even more: the maximization of surplus value. (If only quantity matters to capital, there is no reason for it not to strive for maximization rather than mere increases.) What the formula for the circulation of capital reveals is that capital's cycle of life is subject to an unceasing pressure to find ways to maximize the production of surplus value and to do so single-mindedly, without concern for any extra-economic, or human, costs it might entail. If it is possible, for example, to speed up the phases in which M is converted into C and back again into M', capital will use all means at its disposal to accelerate that cycle, where the 'decision' to accelerate flows simply from the kind of thing capital is, not from the choices of those whose productive activities make its circulation possible. The familiar image of modern life as racing on a hamster wheel—a furious 'going nowhere' the pace of which is beyond control—derives much of its resonance from this feature of capital's pattern of reproduction. To return to the comparison with life, the logic of capital's circulation—unstoppable, uncontrollable, ever-accelerating—makes it look more like cancerous growth than the healthy reproduction of life. Capital is value that just grows and grows, without discernible bounds and without regard for its human effects.

Another respect in which capitalist production escapes the control of those who carry it out is revealed by the 'abstract' character of capital's aim (its being defined exclusively in terms of quantitative units of exchange value). Here, too, capital differs importantly from life. Whereas life achieves its aims only by establishing very specific relations to its world—relations determined by the specific requirements of life and the circumstances of its environment—capitalist accumulation is supremely indifferent to the particular forms the commodities it produces assume, including which use values they possess: In capitalism "use values are produced only because and insofar as they are the material substratum ... of exchange value".[15] This is related to the issue of whether social participants control their own forces because it opens up a nearly unbridgeable gap between the two kinds of value that capitalist circulation depends on: Those whose labor produces commodities enter the economic sphere with aims defined in terms of use values—they sell their labor power in order to satisfy needs and desires they have in virtue of being alive—but their production is organized with a different end in view, the maximization of exchange value. Of course, capitalist circulation achieves this end only if it produces use values of some kind—there must be (effective) demand for its products if increased exchange value is to issue from the process—but it is indifferent to what specifically it produces as long as production serves the end of accumulation. Since satisfying effective demand is not the same thing as satisfying human needs, the motor that drives capitalist production is decoupled from the ends of those whose labor sustains that process. Such labor is still *poiesis* in Aristotle's sense—it aims at creating a product that serves some end exterior to the laboring activity itself—but under conditions of capitalist production, it is radically dissevered from the needs or desires of those who perform it. One of the costs of the autonomous, self-moving character of capital's circulation is that its own criteria for success do not track the needs of those who make the process possible and who enter into it for the purpose of satisfying those needs. Insofar as it strives toward its end independently of the consciousness and wills of the agents who make it possible, capitalist production escapes our control; it functions as an alienated social force that serves first and foremost its own ends (and those of the individuals who own it) and only secondarily, if at all, the ends of the subjects whose labor it depends on.

It is fine for life to be autonomous and self-moving (to serve only purposes internal to itself) but something has gone wrong when the movements of things, which depend on the activities of subjects, serve the sole end of maximizing surplus value. The 'internal' character of capitalist circulation's aim is especially inappropriate when the activity that makes it possible is human labor. For—in every mode of production known thus far—labor is not primarily undertaken for its own sake but for ends external to it, the satisfaction of needs and desires laborers have independently of their laboring. No matter how unalienated it might become, labor retains an ineliminable moment of *poiesis*; it aims, at least in part, at ends external to itself. This means that in order for labor to be subjectively free, it must not only be transparent to, and controlled by, those whose activity it is; it must also satisfy the ends that are the reasons for performing it. Part of what it is for an agent's activity to be 'his own', and therefore free, is for it to satisfy him by achieving the ends for the sake of which he undertook it. In the case of labor, seeing what one has accomplished as good—affirming it—involves seeing that one has achieved the ends that motivated one's activity in the first place, which in this case means, at a minimum, seeing that one's life needs have been satisfied through one's labor. Hence, when Marx charges that capitalism turns our collective labor into an alienated social force, he means not only that our labor is opaque and uncontrolled by us but also that its consequences—what it actually accomplishes in the world—cannot be affirmed by those whose activity it is.

If a laborer in capitalism is fortunate enough to find work that pays her a living wage, it may well be that her labor succeeds in satisfying the needs that led her to labor in the first place. This is to say, in Marx's terms, that if she finds a buyer for her labor power who purchases it at its full value, she can use her wages to purchase the commodities she needs, which are nothing but the products of other laborers whose labor has been coordinated with her own by the mechanisms of the market. To that extent, she may well be able to affirm the results of her productive activity as having enabled her to succeed in what she initially set out to do by selling her labor power. (Of course, there remains the question of whether her activity is transparent to and controlled by her, but I will ignore this issue for now.) Since it is possible for individual workers in capitalism to be fortunate in this respect (and to earn a living wage), the more serious obstacle to their being able to see the results of their activity as good lies elsewhere. It comes into view when one looks at labor not from an individual perspective—with regard to what my activity achieves for me—but as a totality, as constituting a cooperative project (or "social force"). If labor is a cooperative undertaking, then it ought to be collectively affirmable, which it is only if it succeeds at satisfying the needs of all who participate in it. The formula for the circulation of capital explains why, viewed from the perspective of the whole, it is purely a matter of chance whether labor satisfies needs in ways that can be affirmed by more than a few. For the aim that determines the specific forms that production assumes in capitalism—the end of maximal accumulation—is divorced from all consideration of the collective good, even when 'good' is interpreted as thinly as possible to refer simply to the system's satisfying the life needs of its participants.

This helps us to see how Marx understands the claim that human emancipation requires *organizing* our individual laboring activities as social forces. As we have seen, labor in capitalism already exists as a social force in one sense—the labor of each is determined (via market mechanisms) by its relation to the labor and needs of all—but making this labor free requires making it social in a more robust sense. The goal here is not merely to bring to consciousness what is hidden from view in commodity production—that individual forces are in fact socially coordinated—but to *make* our labor social in the sense of organizing it so as to be answerable to standards of the collective good, including the material needs of each member of society. If we are to do this well—in a way that unites the ends of freedom with those of life—our concern must not be merely to satisfy the life needs of all but to do so in a way that our laboring activity is at the same time subjectively free: Collectively transparent, controlled, and affirmable by us not merely in its results but also as an activity itself. In unalienated social activity, *poiesis* is joined with *praxis*, insofar as it is also its own end and not done solely for the sake of what it produces.

Notes

1. Karl Marx, "On the Jewish Question" (MER 46; MEW 1: 370). MER = *The Marx-Engels Reader*, 2nd edn, ed. Robert C. Tucker (New York: Norton, 1972); MEW = Karl Marx, Friedrich Engels, *Werke* (Berlin: Dietz Verlag, 1956–91).
2. Marx, *Capital III* (MER 441; MEW 25: 828).
3. I'm indebted to Rahel Jaeggi for this point.
4. Marx, *Capital III* (MER 441; MEW 25: 828).
5. Georg Wilhelm Friedrich Hegel, *Elements of the Philosophy of Right*, ed. Allen W. Wood, trans. H.B. Nisbet (Cambridge: Cambridge University Press, 1991), §§142–320.
6. I try to do this in Frederick Neuhouser, *Foundations of Hegel's Social Theory: Actualizing Freedom* (Cambridge, MA: Harvard University Press, 2000), ch. 1.
7. Hegel, *Phenomenology of Spirit*, trans. A.V. Miller (Oxford: Oxford University Press, 1977), §§190–6 (pp. 115–9).
8. Ibid., §177 (p. 110).
9. Marx, "The Economic and Philosophic Manuscripts of 1844" (MER 74; MEW 40: 514–5).
10. Marx, *Capital I* (MER 332; MEW 23: 164–5).
11. Marx, *Capital I* (MER 334; MEW 23: 168).
12. Marx, *Capital I* (MER 334; MEW 23: 169; translation amended).
13. Ibid.
14. Marx, *Capital I* (MER 334–5; MEW 23: 168).
15. Marx, *Capital I* (MER 351; MEW 23: 201).

8
Abstract Labor and Recognition

Sven Ellmers

1 Introduction

Recent studies in Marx's theory of value unanimously emphasize that abstract labor is a social quality of the products of labor. However, the meaning of 'social' remains quite ambiguous. In this chapter, I would like to show that Marx, too, already had distinct issues in mind when he underscored the social foundation of the substance of value: (i) its connection to socially necessary labor time, (ii) its connection to social needs, and (iii) the historicity of commodity-producing society. I think we ought to take Marx's argument a step further. His theory of value would be more persuasive still if the aforementioned meanings of 'social' were complemented by yet another one: (iv) social recognition. In conclusion, I shall discuss if or to what extent this proposition might be substantiated by reflections on recognition in Marx's *Capital* itself.

'Abstract labor' is already at first glance a key concept in *Capital*. Right at the beginning of his major work, Marx determines abstract labor as the "substance"[1] of value, from which it follows that his entire theory of value and surplus value can only be developed through a more exact understanding of this substance. Marx emphasized its importance: the distinction between concrete and abstract labor is "crucial to an understanding of political economy".[2]

Within traditional Marxism, the importance that Marx attributed to abstract labor for his entire project was rarely taken into consideration. In the popularizing summaries of *Capital*—such as those by Rosa Luxemburg or Karl Kautsky—the term is not mentioned at all.[3] An awareness of the problem first arises with an interpretative approach that Ingo Elbe,[4] following some of its protagonists, refers to as the *neue Marx-Lektüre* or New Reading of Marx: a discursive context, influenced by the unorthodox-dissident contributions from the early Soviet Union (Rubin, Rjazanov, Paschukanis) and French structuralism (Althusser, Balibar, Rancière), focused upon the scientific discoveries, but also ambivalences and blind alleys, of Marx's critique of economy.

Since the middle of the 1960s, the scientific discussion—not just in Germany, but worldwide—could narrow down what Marx meant with the term 'abstract labor'.[5] Thus, contemporary Marx researchers are largely unanimous (i) in not equating abstract labor with mechanized, meaningless labor. In contrast to Hegel,[6] abstract labor is not for Marx an antonym for sophisticated activities that are then referred to as 'concrete labor'. The conceptual pair of 'concrete/abstract labor' does not indicate differing levels of qualification of labor, but rather two different facets of every type of commodity-producing labor: In its facet as a specific expenditure of labor-power to create useful objects, monotonous assembly line labor is just as much concrete labor as sophisticated, artisan activity; and in its facet of value creation, artisan activity is not qualitatively distinct from assembly line labor. They both count as expressions of abstract human labor. Furthermore, it is largely undisputed in the research (ii) that the abstraction from the concrete-useful side of labor is not to be understood as a *mental* abstraction on the part of *economic actors* who assert the validity in exchange of expended magnitudes of labor. Marx had already criticized the notion that the process of abstraction is a cognitive one in the case of Adam Smith.[7] Commodity exchange is a conscious, intentional activity—participants in the market consider whether they can afford the object, whether they really need it, how to negotiate the best price for it, and ultimately whether or not to buy it—but the reduction to abstract human labor is executed unconsciously during the consummation of exchange. The famous observation from the fetish chapter, alluding to the Gospel of St. Luke, refers to this: "they do this without being aware of it (*Sie wissen das nicht, aber sie tun es*)."[8] Following Alfred Sohn-Rethel, one can speak of a *real* abstraction as distinct from a *nominal* abstraction.[9] Ultimately, in the recent research, there is no dissent concerning the fact (iii) that with the term 'abstract labor', Marx intends to also conceptualize the historical specificity of bourgeois society.

Nevertheless, many questions remain open, and are controversially discussed.[10] To this day there are disputes over which levels of meaning the concept exhibits, whether acts of labor in pre-capitalist societies were also equated as abstract human labor, or what influence supply and demand have upon the magnitude of the value product. I will touch upon many of these questions in my contribution, but the focus will be something else: the question of whether social esteem or recognition of acts of labor should have been taken more strongly into consideration by Marx as a value-creating factor. Before I can address this, I will retrace the argumentative context in *Capital* into which Marx introduces the concept of abstract labor, and how he determines it there.[11]

2 Reconstruction and Outline of the Problem

The term is introduced within the framework of the first chapter, the *analysis of the commodity*. According to Marx, a product of labor that takes the form of a commodity is characterized by two properties. First, it has a useful side, which he calls 'use value', and second, it is exchangeable with other commodities in certain proportions. Marx calls these proportions 'exchange value'. Since at the beginning of his examination, Marx abstracts from the factually presupposed measure of value, money, every commodity has not just one, but many exchange values within this mental construct: Adorno's collected works exchange for a standing room season ticket to Borussia Dortmund matches, 20 short haircuts at the barber's, 100 bars of Marabou chocolates, and so on.

Since the exchange values of Adorno's collected works are also exchangeable with each other in the given proportions—a Borussia Dortmund standing room season ticket for 20 short haircuts, 20 short haircuts for 100 bars of Marabou chocolates—the many exchange values of the collected works are obviously relations of equivalence: They express something qualitatively equal. But this immediately raises the question as to the qualitative unity of the commodities, since equally large proportions presuppose a common measure; the task is to determine a quantifiable quality underlying the exchange values.

This common quality "cannot be a geometrical, physical, chemical or other natural property of commodities"[12]—and in fact, the exchange proportions cannot be explained in terms of weight, physical extension, form, or chemical composition of the commodities. The material qualities, to the extent that they are present, are relevant merely to the use of a product. In societies organized according to a private division of labor, that constitute the subjective occasion for exchanging one's own product for another, but according to Marx, they do not explain the relations according to which they are exchanged. As exchange values, commodities "therefore do not contain an atom of use-value".[13] Correspondingly, in order to determine the common quality underlying exchange-values, one must disregard the use-value properties; and then "only one property remains, that of being products of labour".[14] But by abstracting from the useful side of the commodity, one also disregards at the same time the concrete form of labor expenditure, which is why the labor of a worker at the publishing house Suhrkamp does not exchange for the service of a barber. Acts of labor "can no longer be distinguished, but are all together reduced to the same kind of labour, human labour in the abstract."[15]

2.1 *Socially Necessary Average Labor Time and Solvent Demand*

The metaphors and characterizations Marx uses in the paragraph that immediately follows are among the most frequently quoted, but can hardly be developed from the previous elaborations. The abstract or equal human labor that remains after abstracting from the material properties of the commodity and the labor that creates it is the "social substance, which is common to them all"; a "specter-like objectivity".[16] But what does abstract labor have to do with specters? And in what, exactly, does its social character consist?

What is particular to specters is that they are visible, but without bodies; that which can be seen by the eyes cannot be grasped by the hands. When Marx speaks of a phantom-like or "purely fantastic objectivity"[17] he obviously doesn't mean to say that abstract labor is a mere fantasy or illusion. Rather, his intent is to point out that the quality of possessing value and the magnitude of value cannot be determined in the case of a single commodity. At the beginning of the analysis of the value-form, he expresses this as follows:

> The objectivity of commodities as values differs from Dame Quickly in the sense that 'a man knows not where to have it'. Not an atom of matter enters into the objectivity of commodities as values; in this it is the direct opposite of the coarsely

sensuous objectivity of commodities as physical objects. We may twist and turn a single commodity as we wish; it remains impossible to grasp it as a thing possessing value.[18]

Marx names two reasons in chapter 1.1 for the impossibility of grasping the commodity as a thing possessing value: a) the productive power of labor and b) solvent demand. Both reasons result in the conclusion that value and the magnitude of value cannot be explained from an isolated act of labor expenditure.

With regard to a): According to Marx, the value of a commodity cannot be determined according to an individually expended quantity of labor, since this would have as a consequence that a lazy or unskilled producer who requires an excessively long amount of time to produce his commodity would receive an especially high price. What therefore creates value is *socially necessary average labor time*, meaning the labor time required to: "produce any use-value under the conditions of production normal for a given society and with the average degree of skill and intensity of labour prevalent in that society."[19]

Accordingly, equal human labor is a social substance to the extent that its quantity is not measured according to individual labor expenditure, but rather according to the *productivity of labor* which, disregarding natural conditions—that is, disregarding climactic and geographical conditions—is *socially* determined: by the level and spread of science, technology, and the organization of labor.[20] It emerges from the first edition that Marx primarily had this relatedness in mind when he wrote of the social nature of the substance of value. Similarly succinct as in the second edition, he writes at the beginning of the analysis of the value-form: "Commodities as objects of use or goods are corporeally different things. Their reality as *values* forms, on the other hand, their *unity*. This unity does not arise out of nature but out of society. The common social substance which merely manifests itself differently in different use-values, is—*labour*."[21]

Here, Marx sharply demarcates this common third element from nature. But if one considers the argumentation that directly follows it, which constitutes the largest part of the later part of chapter 1.1, then initially, with the strong assertion that the substance of value is a genuinely social phenomenon, Marx merely has in mind that a primarily technologically determined socially necessary average labor time creates value.

With regard to b): In the last section of chapter 1.1, Marx briefly addresses the relation between use value and value for the first time. First, there are use values, such as air, not mediated by labor and which therefore do not possess value (labor expenditure is a necessary condition for the product of labor to have value); second, there are use values mediated by labor that do not possess value, because, for example, as Marx says, the producer consumes them (expenditure of labor is not a sufficient condition for the product of labor to have value); and third, the property of having use value is a necessary condition for the property of having value: "[N]othing can be a value without being an object of utility. If the thing is useless, so is the labour contained in it; the labour does not count as labour, and therefore creates no value."[22]

Abstract labor, according to Marx, is a social substance to the extent that the products offered correspond to a *social need*. For one thing, abstract labor is determined by the productivity of other producers, and for another thing by the needs and solvency of consumers. Value is therefore a property that cannot belong to the commodity prior to its exchange.[23]

With this, Marx touches upon an eminently important point which he nonetheless still does not grant any increased attention in chapters 1.1 and 1.2: the insight that a society in which the production of commodities predominates is distinguished from other polities by relations of production characterized by the private division of labor. The fact that a society is based not only upon a division of labor, but upon private labor, means namely that decisions concerning the production of goods are not made according to convention, force, or deliberation *in advance*. Rather, producers in societies based upon a private division of labor face each other as competitors: They play their cards close to their chests, which is why supply and demand regularly do not correspond to one another. Products must therefore first *prove* themselves on the market as a part of the total labor of society. For Marx, this retroactive socialization, which already contains the possibility of economic crisis, is for one thing a result of a historical development, and on the other hand can and should be replaced by a planned form of production: With his critique of political economy, he intends to break through the illusory naturalness of its categories.

The historicization of abstract human labor that takes place in the fetish chapter unfortunately does not just slide into the background in chapters 1.1 and 1.2. Rather, Marx operates here with misleading formulations that threaten to thwart his own insights. Thus Marx writes, for example, in the first edition that 'labor' is the substance of value. But if the expenditure of labor is already sufficient for the constitution of value, then social constitution by means of it is a social universal. An alternative to commodity production would be inconceivable.

Excursus: What led Marx to speak of abstract *labor?*
As we have seen, in the second edition Marx no longer speaks of labor *as such* as the substance of value, but rather of *abstract* or *equal* human labor. For what reason? Heinrich surmises that Marx introduced the two adjectives in order to avoid the misunderstanding that his theory of value was an ahistorical theory of labor magnitude, independent of all social validity (in the *neue Marx-Lektüre*, this is frequently referred to as a *substantialist* theory of value).[24] When he speaks of equal or abstract labor, Marx wishes to emphasize that private acts of labor are initially unequal or concrete acts of labor, the equality of which is first forced by exchange: They count as equal in their mutual relationship but *are not* without this relationship. The additions in the second edition, according to Heinrich, were intended to emphasize that the common property of having value is a property that only exists relationally, or more exactly: It is the result of an abstraction consummated in exchange, which a) makes the incommensurable commensurable and b) presupposes very specific social relationships (namely, relations of production based upon a private division of labor).[25]

I wish such considerations would have, in fact, led Marx to insert the adjectives 'equal' and 'abstract' on the spot. However, the fact alone that the substantive fundamental structure does not change in the slightest in the second edition speaks against that: The argument that the substance of value is a *social* substance, since it depends upon socially necessary average labor time, still stands at the center of the elaborations in chapters 1.1 and 1.2. If Marx had really wished to emphasize that the equality of private acts of labor is first created in the course of exchange (that is to say, not based upon non-relational properties of the things), and if Marx had (as in many later passages) the historicity of bourgeois society in focus, then why did he leave things at the insertion of two adjectives? Why didn't he also revise the passages that according to Heinrich also abet a substantialist reading?

The answer is that Marx could have been satisfied with the introduction of the two adjectives, because he had a far less ambitious aim: the aim of pushing even further into the foreground—due to its importance—the dual character of labor, which Marx had already claimed in the first edition to have worked out. This is already indicated by a comparison between the elaborations in chapter 1.1 with the corresponding passages of the first edition. What one initially notices is that in this passage the first edition does not yet explicitly indicate that the abstraction from use value also includes the abstraction from the concrete form of labor expenditure. The corresponding section on page 128 ("If then we disregard the use-value of commodities ... ") is first mentioned in the second edition—and it is precisely in this section that Marx introduces the adjectives *abstract* and *equal*.

Strictly speaking, we are dealing here with a *re*-introduction. Already in *A Contribution to the Critique of Political Economy*, published eight years before the first edition, Marx writes:

> Different use values are, moreover, products of the activity of different individuals and therefore the result of individually different kinds of labour. But as exchange values they represent the same homogeneous labour, i.e. labour in which the individual characteristics of the workers are obliterated. Labour which creates exchange value is thus abstract general labour.[26]

In the first edition of *Capital*, Marx contracts this argument into just two words: The substance of value is "*labor (die Arbeit)*",[27] one could also say, labor *as such*. But the argument condensed in such a way, however, is hardly comprehensible, which ultimately led Marx to the corresponding additions in the second edition. In it (more exactly: in the analysis of the value-form), one finds the following illuminating observation:

> Franklin is not aware that in measuring the value of everything 'in labour' he makes abstraction from any difference in the kinds of labour exchanged—and thus reduces them all to equal human labour. Yet he states this without knowing it. He speaks first of 'the one labour', then of 'the other labour', and finally of 'labour', without further qualification, as the substance of the value of everything.[28]

Whereas Benjamin Franklin does not know what he is saying, in Marx's case—as he will note self-critically—it is the other way round: He does not tell us what he knows, at least not with the necessary clarity. In the second edition, he therefore adds a section emphasizing the dual character of labor, but without—as I would like to demonstrate in the following—following such far-reaching intentions with regard to a theory of validity as Heinrich assumes.

2.2 Complex and Simple Labor: The Problem of Reduction

Marx describes the exchange abstraction consummated behind the backs of market participants as the reduction of different acts of labor to a specific quantity of "*simple average-labour,* the character of which varies admittedly in different lands and cultural epochs, but is given for a particular society. More complex labour counts merely as simple labour *to an exponent* or rather *to a multiple.*"[29]

In the reduction of concrete-useful acts of labor to abstract human labor, according to Marx in *A Contribution to the Critique of Political Economy* and in all editions of *Capital,* the common reference point is culturally specific simple labor, meaning "the expenditure of simple labour-power, i.e. of the labour-power possessed in his ['man' as such; S.E.] bodily organism by every ordinary man, on the average, without being developed in any special way."[30]

The different acts of labor, according to Marx, constitute from the viewpoint of value-creation nothing further than a greater or lesser amount of our basic physiological operations (which are also influenced by the cultural level of each respective country). Marx admits that the acts of labor are "qualitatively different",[31] which is shown in everyday capitalist life already in the fact that switching from one type of work to another "may well not take place without friction", but he immediately adds: "it must take place".[32] One must understand Marx to mean that the acts of labor equated in exchange are *different,* but not *completely heterogeneous*: "Tailoring and weaving, although they are qualitatively different productive activities, are both a productive expenditure of human brains, muscles, nerves, hands etc., and in this sense both human labour. They are merely two different forms of the expenditure of human labour-power."[33]

On the one hand, tailoring and weaving are *concrete,* that is, *different* acts of labor, on the other hand tailoring and weaving are *acts of labor,* that is, particular shapes of that which characterizes labor as labor: The essential characteristic of labor is the— not further qualified—expenditure of labor-power, meaning the expenditure of *some such* physiological energies to fulfill *some such* human need. If in chapter 1.2 Marx demarcates abstract human labor from concrete-useful labor, he also demarcates *what is common to concrete acts of labor* from the *particularity of concrete acts of labor*:

> On the one hand, all labour is an expenditure of human labour-power, in the physiological sense, and it is in this quality of being equal, or abstract, human labour that it forms the value of commodities. On the other hand, all labour is an expenditure of human labour-power in a particular form and with a definite aim, and it is in this quality of being concrete useful labour that it produces use-values.[34]

What is common to the many different acts of labor is that they have a physiological dimension. When a concrete act of labor is discussed not as concrete labor, but rather from this general viewpoint of *all* concrete acts of labor, the specific form of labor expenditure and its specific purpose are disregarded. Carpentry and software programming are not as such related to each other in exchange, but rather as a specific quantity of a common quality of being expenditures of labor power. Regardless of the problem this entails that the commensurablity problematic from chapter 1.1 is now repeated in chapter 1.2 at the level of acts of labor (this is dealt with in further detail below), it seems to me rather obvious that with abstract labor, Marx is theorizing concrete labor in general.

However, concrete labor can also be regarded *as concrete*, this means as "a specific productive activity appropriate to its purpose, a productive activity that assimilated particular natural materials to particular human requirements."[35] Acts of labor then differ from one another to the effect of *which* movements the human organism performs with the help of *specific* tools, in order to alter *specific* external objects of nature with regard to a *specific* need. Labor is then: "determined by its aim, mode of operation, object, means and result. We use the abbreviated expression 'useful labour' for labour whose utility is represented by the use-value of its product, or by the fact that its product is a use-value. In this connection we consider only its useful effect."[36]

Here, concrete labor is determined as *concrete labor in its particularity*, and does not pose any further difficulties. The case is different for the determination of abstract labor in 1.2; it appears problematic to me for two reasons.

A: The assertion that the physiological expenditure of labor-power creates the value of the commodity, if taken literally, amounts to saying that value is not the historically specific unifying characteristic of products created under conditions of to a private division of labor, but rather that *every product*—independent of the relations of production in which it was created—*has value*.[37] Michael Heinrich[38] interprets this passage as a fall back into the ahistorical and individualistic terrain of classical political economy. This is one possible interpretation. Another reading would be that Marx is not vacillating between different theoretical fields, but rather—as in another passage[39]—is making use of a truncated manner of speaking. In its complete form, then, the sentence would be as follows: 'On the one hand, all labour is an expenditure of human labour-power, in the physiological sense, and it is in this quality of being equal, or abstract, human labour that it forms the value of commodities *under the precondition of relations of production based upon a private division of labor and the correspondence of supply to demand*'.

It's possible that Marx dispenses with these additions because in the first two subchapters, his primary aim is to use a labor theory of value as a foundation for his later theories of surplus value and exploitation—especially since subjective theories of value at the time were gaining the upper hand with the decline of the Ricardian school. In this case, the identification of the substance of value with physiologically equal labor would be the misleading side effect of the didactic and theoretical-strategic motive of maintaining—against pure circulation theories of value, which Marx directly criticizes repeatedly in the analysis of the value-form[40]—that exchange relations have an intrinsic relationship to labor expenditure. However one reads the physiology quote, it shows that its de-historicizing effect in the history of *Capital*'s reception could only emerge because the historicity of bourgeois society is also barely a topic in chapters 1.1 and 1.2.[41] Even as Marx establishes in the final paragraph of 1.1 that commodity production not only presupposes the production of use-values, but the production of use-values *for others*, he does not address the historically specific dissociation of private producers and the necessity of real abstraction intrinsic to it, but instead mentions the possibility that a producer can also consume the use-value he has created—thus choosing an example that does not transcend the ahistorical and individualistic discourse of classical political economy. It is ultimately undecidable whether this is to be evaluated as vacillating between scientific revolution and the classical tradition, as Heinrich assumes, or as the conscious deferral of questions and answers that require longer elaborations (ones rather detrimental to the trenchancy of a labor theory of value). Luckily, the question is only of secondary importance, since even if in certain passages of his work Marx falls below the level of insights already attained, that does not affect those insights themselves.

B: What proves to be considerably more important is the question of whether the connection made by Marx between physiology and abstract labor is also still convincing when one brings to account, by means of the corresponding additions, the specificity of bourgeois society. Considering that the process of reduction consummated by means of exchange is rooted in particular relations of production, namely the private division of labor, and for that reason value and the magnitude of value do not already arise from the mere expenditure of labor-power, but rather only inhere to the object through sale, that is, in the course of recognition as a part of the total labor of society—then historically specifically abstract labor (as a result of real abstraction) is still related to *physiological homogeneity*: Through commodity exchange, according to the argument, products of labor are reduced to a specific quantity of a physiological substrate *independent of social validity*—as long as supply and demand correspond. But is the assumption that the qualitative and quantitative equality of private acts of labor is rooted in physiological homogeneity or at least commensurability at all justified? In what, exactly, does their physiological unity consist? What is the *quantifiable quality in common* between a primarily physical and a primarily mental activity? That both are labor as such, that is, expenditure of some kind of labor-power, however determined, is not a satisfactory answer within the framework of the task posed by Marx, since 'purposive activity as such' cannot be sensibly quantified (see below). Physiological units such as calories must also be ruled out as the common third of concrete labor. Nobody would want to assert that the higher value that mental labor usually generates can be traced back to more calories being burned than in the case of more physical labor. An argument rooted in the labor theory of value based upon the training or education of the worker also does not solve the problem: Bank clerks whose average gross monthly income in Germany amounts to 3,879 euro earn 1,400 euro more than daycare workers (2,490 euro) and receive nearly double the wages of cooks (2,016 euro)[42]—although the training periods for all three professions is identical.[43] What remains is the possibility of explaining the difference by means of the level of complexity of the respective acts of labor. But how much more complex is training bank clerks than training daycare workers or cooks? One cannot argue in terms of physiological effort so long as lack of clarity reigns with regard to the physiological unit of measure—and it appears more than questionable whether it can be sensibly determined.

Heinrich therefore draws the conclusion that abstract labor "means a socially *enforced* attribution".[44] In the course of real abstraction, unequal acts of labor merely *count* as equal; ultimately, equality is *constituted* through exchange. He can support this reading with, inter alia, the following quote from *A Contribution to the Critique of Political Economy*: Exchange is an "objective equalisation of unequal quantities of labour *forcibly* brought about by the social process".[45] Abstract labor would thus be the result of a triple reduction.[46] Initially, individual labor-time is reduced to the essential technologically determined socially necessary average labor-time; then, on the market, it is revealed to what extent there exists a liquid demand corresponding to the products (to what extent was the socially necessary average labor time expended also *necessary to society*); finally, qualitatively distinct acts of labor are forcefully equated. The third step leads Heinrich to a convincing—and as far as I know, within the *neue Marx-Lektüre*, singular—position: "[A]lso decisive are processes of social hierarchization that are reflected, for example, in the fact that 'female professions' have a lower status than 'male professions', which in turn influences how activities are considered 'simple' or 'skilled'."[47]

Correspondingly, abstract labor is not just socially determined to the extent that it depends upon the productivity of labor and solvent demand, but also to the extent that social esteem plays a role. To put it differently: Abstract labor exhibits a *dimension of recognition*—which Marx, however, does not explicitly deal with, but which remains concealed behind naturalistic appeals. The formulation that all labor is on the one hand "an expenditure of human labour-power, in the physiological sense" and on the other hand "an expenditure of human labour-power in a particular form and with a definite aim"[48] is therefore rather problematic, regardless of how one understands labor-power as such:

(i) 'Labor-power as such' can mean a mere nominal abstraction, meaning a mentally constructed generic term. Labor-power in this sense, however, can never be expended—in the same way as the general concept 'motorcycle' cannot be driven on the street. Labor-power can only be expended in a particular, purposive form.

(ii) 'Labor as such' is not just a product of the human mind, but as a concept it encompasses a *real commonality of concrete labor-power expenditure, independent of attribution*.[49] During every act of labor, the human organism is set into motion and physiological energy is expended. However, the obvious advantage of being able to state the *common quality* that all products must exhibit so that they can be related to each other in exchange in the first place is obtained dearly, since we are immediately confronted with the problem of how abstract labor, thus determined, can be meaningfully quantifiable: One can either measure the duration of expenditure of 'labor-power as such'—which is not a sensible option, since that would not take adequately into account the distinction between simple and complex labor or the intensity of labor—or one can measure the physical and biochemical processes in the human body common to all acts of labor (such as calorific value), which also does not lead to any sensible results.

(iii) 'Labor-power as such' can be understood as the result of a multilevel act of recognition consummated without the knowledge of commodity owners. But even in this case, it is misleading to speak in a reified manner of expenditure, since relations of recognition cannot be measured with a stopwatch.

2.3 *Marx's Proposal for Solving the Problem of Reduction*

Up to this point it could be established that Marx's search for a quantifiable quality has put us on the trail of a dimension of recognized labor, which Marx, however, does not further pursue. That Marx does not devote much attention to the question of how complex labor can be reduced to simple labor might be rooted in the fact that in his text *The Poverty of Philosophy* from 1847, Marx proceeds from the assumption that industrialization increasingly marginalizes qualified labor:

> If the mere quantity of labour functions as a measure of value regardless of quality, it presupposes that simple labour has become the pivot of industry. It presupposes that labour has been equalised by the subordination of man to the machine or by the extreme division of labour; that men are effaced by their labour; that the pendulum of the clock has become as accurate a measure of the relative activity of two workers as it is of the speed of two locomotives. Therefore, we should not say that one man's hour is worth another man's hour, but rather that one man during an hour is worth just as much as another man during an hour. Time is everything, man is nothing; he is, at the most, time's carcase. Quality no longer matters. Quantity alone decides everything; hour for hour, day for day.[50]

The same train of thought underlies the observation in *A Contribution to the Critique of Political Economy* that the reduction to abstract labor is "an abstraction which is made every day in the social process of production."[51] In the same spirit, Marx writes in *Capital* that

> [t]he distinction between higher and simple labour, 'skilled labour' and 'unskilled labour', rests in part on pure illusion or, to say the least, on distinctions that have long since ceased to be real. ... Moreover, we must not imagine that so-called 'skilled' labour forms a large part of the whole of the nation's labour.[52]

The theoretical problem of how to equate unequal acts of labor is solved according to Marx by the real process of industrial homogenization, which is why in *Capital*, for the sake of "saving ourselves the trouble of making the reduction"[53] he treats all labor-power as simple labor-power—and the expenditure of simple labor-power in turn is "easy to count",[54] namely with the clock.

Although Marx does not regard the problem of reduction as being as urgent as it appears to us today (keyword: knowledge society), a few hints are found in his work that allow us to draw conclusions as far as how he thought about solving:

> We stated on a previous page that in the valorization process it does not in the least matter whether the labour appropriated by the capitalist is simple labour of average social quality, or more complex labour, labour with a higher specific gravity as it were. All labour of a higher, or more complicated, character than average labour is expenditure of labour-power of a more costly kind, labour-power whose production has cost more time and labour than unskilled or simple labour-power, and which therefore has a higher value. This power being of higher value, it expresses itself in labour of a higher sort, and therefore becomes objectified, during an equal amount of time, in proportionally higher values.[55]

On the one hand, Marx chooses here the formulation that certain acts of labor *count* as complex acts of labor with regard to simple average labor, but on the other hand, he does not lend an emphasis to this relation of validity [*Geltungsverhältnis*], but rather assumes that the values expressed in the products correspond to the time of training the respective labor-power. "Marx does not provide ... a reason for why that must be the case."[56] So Marx does not solve the problem; he merely *defers* it. Experience, which Marx takes pains to use to make the process of reduction more plausible,[57] teaches us, however, that the value of the commodity labor-power does not at all correlate with the length of training time. If, however, identical training periods are expressed in labor-power values that strongly deviate from each other, this deviation must have non-temporary reasons.

3 Conclusion: Marx's Form-Analytical Approach and Contemporary Recognition Theory

That Marx does not even take the dimension of recognition into consideration as one factor among many is surprising to the extent that it plays a leading role not only in the early writings such as the Mill excerpts or Paris Manuscripts—which are more frequently the topic of discussion these days—but also, as Michael Quante has demonstrated in detail, in *Capital* at various levels.[58] For example, the entire analysis of the value-form is based upon the notion of the *determination of reflection* borrowed from Hegel:

> In a certain sense, a man is in the same situation as a commodity. As he neither enters into the world in possession of a mirror, nor as a Fichtean philosopher who can say 'I am I', a man first sees and recognizes himself in another man. Peter only relates to himself as a man through his relation to another man, Paul, in whom he recognizes his likeness. With this, however, Paul also becomes from head to toe, in his physical form as Paul, the form of appearance of the species man for Peter.[59]

The relationship of recognition depicted here implies two things. On the one hand, Peter's self-reference presupposes the recognizing external reference to Paul; on the other hand, Paul functions for Peter as a mirror of his existence as a human being, which is why in this relationship it is not the concrete human being Paul with his multiple facets who is taken into consideration, but rather Paul only as an incarnation of the human species. In the terminology of recent theories of recognition: Every act of recognition is at the same time an act of misrecognition.[60]

The relationship between Peter and Paul is an analogy chosen by Marx to illustrate the polar relation between the relative form of value and the equivalent form of value: Analogous to Peter, who relates to himself as a human being by relating to Paul as an incarnation of the human species, in the simple form of value, the commodity linen relates to itself as value by relating to the coat as an incarnation of value. The coat, however, *is not* the incarnation of value, but rather *counts* or *is valid* (German: *gilt*) as the incarnation of value—and only within this relation. The *fetishism* that Marx criticizes consists in conceiving this relational characteristic as an objective characteristic independent of any relation: "Determinations of reflection [*Reflexionsbestimmungen*] of this kind are altogether very curious. For instance, one man is king only because other men stand in the relation of subjects to him. They, on the other hand, imagine that they are subjects because he is king."[61] The objectification of a determination of reflection is a second-level misrecognition: What is misrecognized is that the properties of a person or thing are the result of a recognizing misrecognition.

That Marx calls upon fundamental structures of recognition in the value-form analysis in order to describe money as a relation of validity and the money fetish as a lapse in perception of this relation of validity does not mean, however, that Marx reduces the existence of money and the money fetish to historical-contingent practices of recognition. Rather, relations of production based upon a private division of labor assert themselves with regard to producers as a "silent compulsion".[62] The relations of validity that Marx analyzes are relations of validity under the precondition of economic structures that have taken on a life of their own: *They* are what assign people their places, from which those people then act. This becomes particularly clear at the beginning of the second chapter:

> Commodities cannot themselves go to market and perform exchanges in their own right. We must, therefore, have recourse to their guardians, who are the possessors of commodities. Commodities are things ... In order that these objects may enter into relation with each other as commodities, their guardians must place themselves in relation to one another as persons *whose will resides in those objects*, and must behave in such a way that each does not appropriate the commodity of the other, and alienate his own, except through an act to which both parties consent. *The guardians must therefore recognize each other as owners of private property.*[63]

In contrast to the first chapter, which analyzes the commodity form, in the second chapter commodity *owners* enter the stage—not, however, as the actual subjects of recognition, but rather, as stated a page later, as "personifications of economic relations".[64] The mutual transfer of commodities presupposes mutual recognition as commodity owners, that is, mutual recognition as people who can exclude other people from the use of the item in question, but this recognition is the necessary condition of exchange and a necessary consequence of relations of production that have taken on a life of their own. Marx expresses this with the formulation that on the one hand commodity exchange is an intentional relation, and on the other hand this "will resides in those objects". Marx reflects this structural overhang of bourgeois-capitalist society by initially abstracting from economic participants before he then deals with them in their structurally conditioned roles, that is, as character masks.

However, this methodological procedure does not prevent Marx from thinking about the relative autonomy of relations of recognition in certain passages. Especially relevant for the topic of abstract labor I deal with in this chapter is the indication that the value of the commodity labor-power contains a "historical and moral element": It depends upon the "level of civilization attained by a country"[65] and past labor struggles. If, however, we take into consideration that a) Marx makes use of a theoretical abstraction when he speaks of the value of the commodity labor-power in the singular; b) the preconditions for the implementation of the demands of labor unions are highly variable according to branch; and c) the "level of civilization attained by a country" can also consist in the fact that certain areas of labor are socially recognized, whereas others experience only a low level of esteem or are even stigmatized, it can therefore be assumed that the different values of different acts of labor should also be rooted in a gradient of recognition.

I foresee two possible objections against a recognition-related expansion of Marx's argument; however, I think they are only conditionally sustainable. The first objection says that social esteem as a factor relevant to value cannot play a role, since the *mechanism of competition* between branches leads to an equalization of wages: Why would anyone choose a profession that, due to a lack of social esteem, promises a lower income? This objection overlooks two things. For one thing, it overlooks that income is an essential aspect with regard to choosing a profession, but not necessarily the decisive one. The choice of a profession depends to a considerable extent upon *what a person wants to be*: The current tendency toward self-economizing, which implies a high level of indifference toward the content of one's own labor, is indeed just a tendency; still of great importance are values and aspects of self-realization imparted during one's socialization. But even if we assume that monetary reasons are the clincher in one's choice of profession, the competition argument overlooks that many people, for various reasons, don't have the choice of switching from a poorly paid profession to a better paid one (e.g., because jobs are only available in the poorly paid branches, from a certain age onward chances of finding employment after retraining vanish, refugees frequently can't provide proof of their qualifications).

A second objection might be that taking the dimension of recognition into consideration is not as harmless as it initially appears, but rather undermines the foundation of a labor theory of value: In place of a subjective estimation of how useful a commodity is for me (and as a consequence which price I'm willing to pay for it) comes esteem, dependent upon conventions and normative conflicts, encountering acts of labor at a given point in time. This suspicion is indeed obvious to the extent that Axel Honneth, one of the highest-profile theorists of recognition, advances the view that *Capital* would have been a completely different work if Marx had brought in his pronounced interest in eventful, open-ended, and normatively mediated class conflicts just as productively as in his historical-political writings.[66] In place of a timeless structural theory, which reduces actors to the status of individual utility-maximizers and can only consider history in the sense of a "linear, uneventful progression of submission to the capital-relation"[67] there would be a sociologically saturated—that is to say, sensitive to the cultural situatedness of collective actors—examination of dynamic conflicts. "The surrender of every intention of a synchronic analysis to the capital-relation"[68] does not result from this—so Honneth argues—but he leaves open which aspects of Marx's critique of political economy still appear compatible to him. In his study *Freedom's Right: The Social Foundations of Democratic*

Life, published at roughly the same time, he does not refer at all conceptually to Marx's main work, but rather presents it as an economic theory, the core elements of which are regarded as obsolete even within Marxist discourse.[69] Since Honneth has not provided an in-depth examination of capitalist structural logics in his early writings, the effect is as if he only invokes them in a cursory way as soon as his endeavor to reconstruct the moral grammar of our current economic and political institutions encounters difficulties in light of neoliberal deficiencies (which Honneth himself concedes).

The skeptical objection that the integration of the viewpoints of recognition theory amounts to a fundamental revision of Marx's theory thus appears all too justified. Hence, a question of methodology arises that goes far beyond the correct understanding of Marx: Do we have to *choose* between Marx's form-analysis of bourgeois society on the one hand and a reconstruction of the historical struggle for social freedom grounded in recognition theory on the other hand? Or—alternatively—are they just two different research programs, which both have their justification and which can usefully supplement and correct each other, despite their independence on certain points?

I am of the latter view. If Marx examines those—and only *those*—social relations that constitute capitalism, he remains at a rather high level of abstraction. His fundamental interest in finding out what a commodity is, what money is, and what capital is, is not sociological in the narrower sense—which does not, however, make it less legitimate. If Marx, in contrast to his historical writings, introduces active participants rather late in *Capital*, and then only as the personification of economic structures, this might seem from a sociological perspective to be an early variant of the *homo oeconomicus* model, but from a form-analytical perspective, it merely reflects (mentioned above) the condition that the economic-social basic forms have *taken on a life of their own* with regard to us: The existence of the commodity, money, and capital are mediated by intentional activity, but cannot be traced back to it.[70] A large part of the methodological critique that Honneth expresses with regard to Marx appears to me due to the misunderstanding that both of them are talking about the same object—or more exactly: that they are not just talking about the same *material* object, but also the same *formal* object. The epistemological distinction made with this conceptual pair can be made clear using a simple example. A butterfly can be considered from both an aesthetic viewpoint and a biological viewpoint—and no biologist would ever have the idea of rebuking the aesthetic form of presentation *as* biology. Because it's all too obvious that in both cases, the cognitive faculty is directed toward the same object (*objectum materiale*), but the perspectives of this object (*objectum formale*) are so fundamentally different that a methodological critique is meaningless.

If it's so obvious that the points of view from which an object is examined condition the choice of conceptual means and methods, then how could Honneth succumb to such a simple mistake in his critique of Marx? There are two reasons for this:

1. Marx himself does not observe the limits of his research program. When, for example, at the end of the first volume he predicts the decline of the capitalist mode of production, he leaves the form-analytical terrain in order to derive concrete action

from social structures as necessary. Honneth's critique that capitalist structures follow the inheritance of a substantialist philosophy of history is not new, but completely accurate.[71] The problem, however, is not limited to the end of the first volume; it is of a fundamental nature: On one hand, Marx is certain that in order to elaborate the laws of capitalism he must mentally abstract from many things that play an important empirical role; on the other hand, he assumes that the empirical deviations are merely outmoded traditions whose relevance increasingly fades away in the course of capitalist development. He thus writes in the third volume: "In theory, we assume that the laws of the capitalist mode of production develop in their pure form. In reality, this is only an approximation; but the approximation is all the more exact, the more the capitalist mode of production is developed and the less it is adulterated by survivals of earlier economic conditions with which it is amalgamated."[72] That's why one repeatedly encounters passages in *Capital* in which Marx attempts to prove by means of empirical data how far this conformity to pure theory has flourished; the consideration of non-capitalist logics seems there to be almost window dressing.

2. Whereas in biology and poetry the differences immediately spring to mind, the formal objects of Honneth and Marx exhibit far greater commonalities, since in both cases we are dealing with social theories with a critical intent. That is also the objective reason why both research programs do not stand completely unrelated alongside one another. One aim of my contribution is the intent to show, using Marx's labor theory of value, at least a point of contact: Value theory gains plausibility as long as one supplements (not: replaces) it with the aspect of recognition that Marx neglects. If this is done, the reduction to abstract human labor can furthermore be described, in accordance with Marx, as a triple one: (i) Technological or organizational changes in production reduce or increase the value of the commodity/the socially necessary labor time. If we are dealing with fundamental changes that increase productivity to a high degree, it can deprive some occupations of their basis for existence—even if they previously enjoyed much respect. (ii) A systematic discrepancy between the supply and demand of commodities has an effect on the magnitude of value corresponding to the excess labor-time expended. (iii) With the period of training or education, there is at least one criterion for the distinction between simple and complex labor. However, it was also demonstrated that the period of training or education cannot be a *sufficient* criterion of distinction: Acts of labor cannot be clearly graded on a scale of complexity, but rather *count* as simple or complex. If this is admitted, then it is shown that the dimension of recognition plays a value-theoretical role in other respects. For example, that women frequently may have the same qualifications as their male colleagues, perform comparably, and nonetheless be more poorly paid are connected, among other factors, with the gender stereotype that women are less resilient and less productive. An up-to-date critique of political economy must consider these moments relevant not only to income, but also to self-esteem,[73] just as the economic-philosophical strain of recognition theory can profit from the *neue Marx-Lektüre*. Ideally, both sides would contribute to an intermediary critical economy theory.

Notes

1. Karl Marx, *Capital Vols. I–III* (New York/London: Penguin 1976–81), 128.
2. Marx, *Capital I*, 132.
3. Michael Heinrich, "abstrakte Arbeit," in *Historisch-kritisches Wörterbuch des Marxismus*, Vol. 1, ed. Wolfgang Fritz Haug (Hamburg, Berlin: Argument, 1996).
4. Ingo Elbe, *Marx im Westen. Die neue Marx-Lektüre in der Bundesrepublik seit 1965* (Berlin: Akademie-Verlag, 2010).
5. Jan Hoff, *Marx Worldwide. On the Development of the International Discourse on Marx since 1965* (Leiden: Brill, 2016).
6. Georg Wilhelm Friedrich Hegel, *Outlines of the Philosophy of Right* (Oxford: Oxford University Press, 2008), 191.
7. Karl Marx, "A Contribution to the Critique of Political Economy," in *Marx & Engels Collected Works* (MECW), Vol. 29 (London: Lawrence & Wishart, 1975), 299–330.
8. Luke 23:34: "Father, forgive them, for they know not what they do" (Marx, *Capital I*, 166–7).
9. Alfred Sohn-Rethel, *Intellectual and Manual Labour. A Critique of Epistemology* (London and Basingstoke: Macmillan, 1978), 20.
10. See for example: Karl Reitter, "Der Begriff der 'abstrakten Arbeit'," *Grundrisse – Zeitschrift für linke Theorie und Debatte* (2002); Dieter Wolf, *Zur Konfusion des Wertbegriffs. Beitrag zur 'Kapital'-Diskussion* (Hamburg: Argument, 2004) and Helmut Reichelt, "Zur Konstitution ökonomischer Gegenständlichkeit: Wert, Geld und Kapital unter geltungstheoretischem Aspekt," in *Kapital und Kritik. Nach der neuen Marx-Lektüre*, ed. Werner Bonefeld and Michael Heinrich (Hamburg: VSA, 2011). For the German-speaking world, see inter alia the contributions by Heinrich (e.g., "abstrakte Arbeit"), for the Anglophone world, the debate in *Capital & Class*: Werner Bonefeld, "Abstract Labour: Against Its Nature and on Its Time," *Capital & Class* 34, no. 2 (2010): 257–76; Guglielmo Carchedi, "A Comment on Bonefeld's 'Abstract Labour: Against Its Nature and on Its Time'," *Capital & Class* 35, no. 2 (2011): 307–9; Axel Kicillof and Guido Starosta, "On Value and Abstract Labour: A Reply to Werner Bonefeld," *Capital & Class* 35, no. 2 (2011): 295–305.
11. Marx does not use the term "abstract labor" for the first time in *Capital*, but rather already since the *Economic and Philosophical Manuscripts of 1844*. See the contributions by Michael Quante, *Karl Marx. Ökonomisch-Philosophische Manuskripte. Kommentar von Michael Quante* (Frankfurt: Suhrkamp, 2009) and Ingo Elbe, "Entfremdete und abstrakte Arbeit. Marx' Ökonomisch-philosophische Manuskripte im Vergleich zu seiner späteren Kritik der politischen Ökonomie," in *Paradigmen anonymer Herrschaft. Politische Philosophie von Hobbes bis Arendt*, ed. Ingo Elbe (Würzburg: Königshausen & Neumann, 2015) which place considerably different accents with regard to the relationship of the early and later works.
12. Marx, *Capital I*, 127.
13. Ibid., 128.
14. Ibid.
15. Ibid.
16. Ibid.
17. Karl Marx and Friedrich Engels, "Ergänzungen und Veränderungen zum ersten Band des 'Kapitals'," in *Gesamtausgabe*, ed. Institut für Marxismus-Leninismus beim ZK

d. KPdSU u. vom Inst. für Marxismus-Leninismus beim ZK d. SED (Berlin: Dietz, 1975) II/6, 32.
18 Marx, *Capital I*, 138.
19 Ibid., 129.
20 Ibid., 130.
21 Karl Marx, *Das Kapital. Kritik der politischen Ökonomie. Erster Band. Hamburg 1867*, in *Gesamtausgabe*, II/5, 19.
22 Marx, *Capital I*, 131.
23 In Chapter 1.1, Marx mentions only the case of a completely *useless* and therefore *completely* value-less shelf warmer. But what's the case with a *useful* commodity where the supply exceeds demand? Here, two variants are conceivable. Either only *a part* of the total amount produced can be sold—it is then exchanged in accordance with the technologically determined socially necessary labor time—or the *total* amount produced finds buyers, because the value of every single commodity has decreased: "Let us suppose, finally, that every piece of linen on the market contains nothing but socially necessary labour-time. In spite of this, all these pieces taken as a whole may contain superfluously expended labour-time. If the market cannot stomach the whole quantity at the normal price of 2 shillings a yard, this proves that too great a portion of the total social labour-time has been expended in the form of weaving. The effect is the same as if each individual weaver had expended more labour-time on his particular product than was socially necessary. As the German proverb has it: caught together, hung together" (ibid., 202).
24 Heinrich, "abstrakte Arbeit," 57.
25 Michael Heinrich, *Die Wissenschaft vom Wert. Die Marxsche Kritik der politischen Ökonomie zwischen wissenschaftlicher Revolution und klassischer Tradition* (Münster: Westfälisches Dampfboot, 2006).
26 Karl Marx, *A Contribution to the Critique of Political Economy*, MECW 29: 271.
27 Marx and Engels, *Gesamtausgabe*, II/5, 19.
28 Marx, *Capital I*, 142.
29 Marx and Engels, *Gesamtausgabe*, II/5, 20.
30 Marx, *Capital I*, 135. I don't see any hint for Heinrich's thesis that Marx in *A Contribution to the Critique of Political Economy* and the first edition of *Capital* still identifies abstract labor with simple labor, but "strongly distinguishes" the two (Heinrich, "abstrakte Arbeit," 57) from the second edition on. In neither the *Contribution* nor the first edition of *Capital* does Marx *identify* abstract labor with simple labor—in both texts, simple labor is merely the *measure* of abstract labor.
31 Marx, *Capital I*, 134.
32 Ibid.
33 Ibid.
34 Ibid., 137.
35 Ibid., 133.
36 Ibid., 132.
37 The same consequence follows from the formulation in the analysis of the value-form that "[h]uman labour-power in its fluid state, or human labour, creates value" (ibid., 142).
38 Heinrich, *Die Wissenschaft vom Wert*, 211.
39 In the analysis of the value-form he writes in retrospect: "the value of a commodity is independently expressed through its presentation [*Darstellung*] as 'exchange-value'. When, at the beginning of this chapter, we said in the customary manner that a

commodity is both a use-value and an exchange-value, this was, strictly speaking, wrong. A commodity is a use-value or object of utility, and a 'value'. It appears as the twofold thing it really is as soon as its value possesses its own particular form of manifestation, which is distinct from its natural form. This form of manifestation is exchange-value, and the commodity never has this form when looked at in isolation, but only when it is in a value-relation or an exchange relation with a second commodity of a different kind. Once we know this, our manner of speaking does no harm; it serves, rather, as an abbreviation." (Marx, *Capital I*, 152)

40   Ibid., 152–3, 155 fn. 25.
41   The sole exception is the observation in 1.2 that the division of labor "is a necessary condition for commodity production, although the converse does not hold; commodity production is not a necessary condition for the social division of labour" (ibid., 132).
42   Data from the wage index of the Hans-Böckler-Stiftung (www.lohnspiegel.de).
43   Heinrich, "abstrakte Arbeit," 58. One could object that training as a bank clerk usually presupposes a higher-level secondary school diploma, whereas this is maybe not necessarily demanded for an apprenticeship as a cook. But then how would one explain that university-educated social workers, who at the moment are being desperately sought, earn considerably less than bank clerks?
44   Heinrich, "abstrakte Arbeit."
45   Marx, "A Contribution to the Critique of Political Economy," 299; emphasis mine.
46   Michael Heinrich, *An Introduction to the Three Volumes of Karl Marx's Capital* (New York: Monthly Review Press, 2004), 49–50.
47   Ibid., 52.
48   Marx, *Capital I*, 137.
49   Dieter Wolf, *Der dialektische Widerspruch im 'Kapital'. Ein Beitrag zur Marxschen Werttheorie* (Hamburg: VSA, 2002), 54–5.
50   Karl Marx, *The Poverty of Philosophy*, MECW 6: 127.
51   Marx, "A Contribution to the Critique of Political Economy," 272.
52   Marx, *Capital I*, 305, fn. 19.
53   Ibid., 135.
54   Translator's note: corrected translation of "*einfach zu zählen,*" which is given in the Fowkes translation of *Capital I* as "simply requires to be calculated" (296).
55   Ibid., 304–5.
56   Michael Krätke, "einfache/komplizierte Arbeit," in *Historisch-kritisches Wörterbuch des Marxismus*.
57   Marx, *Capital I*, 134.
58   Michael Quante, "Recognition in Capital," *Ethical Theory and Moral Practice* 16, no. 4 (2013): 713–27.
59   Marx, *Capital I*, 144, fn. 19.
60   Thomas Bedorf, *Verkennende Anerkennung. Über Identität und Politik* (Berlin: Suhrkamp, 2010).
61   Marx, *Capital I*, 149, fn. 22.
62   Ibid., 899.
63   Ibid., 178, emphasis mine.
64   Ibid., 179.
65   Ibid., 275.
66   Axel Honneth, "Die Moral im 'Kapital'. Versuch einer Korrektur der Marxschen Ökonomiekritik," *Leviathan* 39 (2011): 583–94.

67 Ibid., 585.
68 Ibid., 591.
69 Axel Honneth, *Das Recht der Freiheit: Grundriß einer demokratischen Sittlichkeit* (Berlin: Suhrkamp, 2011), 354. Honneth merely refers positively to the normative ideal of the early Marx, primarily the Mill excerpt; see Daniel Brudney, "Community and completion," in *Reclaiming the History of Ethics: Essays for John Rawls*, ed. Andrews Reath, Barbara Herman and Christine M. Korsgaard (Cambridge: Cambridge University Press, 1997), and Chitty, "Recognition and Property in Hegel and the Early Marx."
70 Moishe Postone, *Time, Labor, and Social Domination* (Cambridge: Cambridge University Press, 1993).
71 Whereby Honneth doesn't even go far enough: The historical-political writings that Marx produced between 1846 and 1852 hardly suffice as contrasting foils for *Capital*, since they also have underlying teleological premises; cf. Gerhard Kluchert, *Geschichtsschreibung und Revolution. Die historischen Schriften von Karl Marx und Friedrich Engels 1846 bis 1852* (Stuttgart/Bad Cannstatt: Frommann-Holzboog, 1985).
72 Marx, *Capital III*, 275.
73 Axel Honneth, "Recognition and Moral Obligation," *Social Research* 64, no. 1 (1997).

9

Love Will Tear Us Apart

Marx and Hegel on the Materiality of Erotic Bonds

Federica Gregoratto

Introduction: Modern love

Philosophers (and non-philosophers) have fought over the meaning and implications of love, especially erotic love,[1] since philosophy's very beginnings. Is love better understood as a desire to merge with the beloved, or rather as a form of robust concern for their well-being? Do lovers' feelings depend on an evaluation of the beloved's qualities, or do these feelings rather bestow value on the beloved?[2] Despite the diversity of answers to these and many other questions, most modern conceptions seem nevertheless to share one common assumption: Modern erotic love is usually viewed as different and substantially disentangled from other aspects and domains of social life, especially from politics and economics. Social philosophers and sociologists such as Luhmann, Giddens, and Honneth[3] have largely expounded upon and justified this view by reconstructing the process of differentiation, or "autonomization", of the social sphere of intimate and erotic relationships from other social spheres.[4] According to these theorists, modern individuals fall in love for motives that cannot be convincingly explained by reference to social, economic, or cultural and communal norms and values. Lovers are able to carry on and organize their relationships in ways that do not depend upon, and can contrast with, the habits, rules, and beliefs of the social context in which they live.[5] Popular culture abounds with representations of this conception of love. Consider, as a paradigmatic example, the popular movie *Pretty Woman* (Garry Marshall, 1990): While the affair between the billionaire Edward Lewis and the prostitute Vivian Ward begins as an economic transaction—as an employer–employee relation—we can start to believe in the authenticity of their mutual romantic feelings only as she scornfully refuses the large sum of money he owes her.[6]

The aim of this chapter is to challenge the thesis according to which erotic love should be conceived of as substantially differentiated from other dimensions of social life. The argumentative strategy I pursue here does not intend to merely show how love is de facto influenced or even determined by heteronomous reasons (e.g., money).

Rather, my argumentation hinges upon the fact that erotic love does not simply happen in *intersubjective* relationships. Instead, erotic relationships consist of encounters and interactions between subjects that are *mediated by objects*, namely, by material things that pertain to, and are ordered by, economic and political institutions and norms. Since the objective, material world does constitutively enter and thus shape intersubjective erotic bonds, love cannot be thought of simply as a private phenomenon, disentangled from other modalities of social interaction and retaining a high degree of autonomy in relation to them.

In what follows, I intend to pursue my aim by confronting and discussing two thinkers, Marx and Hegel, whose seminal writings have contributed immeasurably to our understanding of modernity. In their view, modernity is defined, among other things, by its constitutive tendency toward self-criticism. In the context of the present chapter, (the young) Marx and Hegel are interpreted as contributing to the critique of modern love, or at least of that interpretation of modern love as a separated social domain: On their accounts, the things that mediate erotic relationships predominantly assume the shape of commodities and/or private properties. As I will argue, such mediation has a double and ambivalent function: The things of love do not only connect lovers but also separate them. While the connection, under certain sociopolitical conditions (capitalism), can have damaging effects, the separation might moreover represent a positive, namely, empowering condition for lovers and love bonds. Love will thus appear not only as a type of social bond that is shaped and even constituted by other dimensions of social and political life, but also as a lens through which we can critically scrutinize other aspects of society.

Marx on Nondyadic Recognition and Noncapitalist Love

The young Marx is not a proper philosopher of love. A glimpse of love, however, can be caught in the few passages in which, in his early writings, he relies upon an idea of (mutual) recognition for conveying the semantics of social relationships and gives some indications to figure out what these relationships would look like in a nonalienated, namely, noncapitalist society. The full realization of human beings' social or communal nature cannot be understood without reference to loving interactions.

In both "Comments on James Mill" and the *Economic and Philosophical Manuscripts of 1844*, Marx depicts human beings as not individually self-sufficient, as constitutively dependent on others for fulfilling their needs, wishes, and desires.[7] Individuals need the things that others make, but they also need their feelings, passions, experiences, and expectations to be perceived, acknowledged, and confirmed: in one word, recognized by others. Social relations are, in general, relations of interdependence. In capitalism, "the interdependence occurs through our instrumental use of one another in the market."[8] Under capitalist market conditions, we can acquire the things that we need and produce only by buying them, and our emotional relationships are also mediated by money. As a result, our activities are solely, or mostly, aimed at obtaining enough money, the only thing that can guarantee the satisfaction of our wishes and desires. In such a system, the main aim is the accumulation of money, and thus of power over things and over fellow human beings. People who possess more money can slacken their ties of dependence and control the others' wishes and desires—not only in the market but within intimate relationships as well. The division of societies between those who are more dependent (proletarians) and those who manage to acquire more independence (capitalists) corresponds to an alienated system of social bonds, in which producers are structurally detached from the products of their labor, from their labor activities, from their fellow human beings and from the whole human species (from the life of the species).[9] Alienation, in all these facets, consists of a profound distortion of, and damage to, human nature. Producers (and capitalists, who control the production) are still human beings; human beings, however, who structurally, unintentionally, yet continuously betray their nature.

A noncapitalist society might be able, on the contrary, to actualize human nature. Marx's more fully fledged exposition of such human actualization is based on the recognition theory that he sketches out at the end of the Mill excerpt. Marx invites us to imagine a society in which we would produce as human beings, namely, as men and women who make and exchange goods and relate to each other in ways not mediated by money and commodities. We would, in this society, realize ourselves "through transforming the natural world (freely, consciously, and in concert with others)".[10] Human beings would produce and exchange their products because they are moved by a sort of drive of recognition;[11] a drive, that is, to act as subjects of recognition and at the same time to become objects of recognition. Human beings would recognize each other and would be ready to be recognized as vulnerable, dependent beings, namely, as beings who need others on many different levels. The active side of recognition is depicted by Marx as mostly expressed through work: As a subject of recognition, I would recognize my fellow human beings by working and producing things to satisfy their needs and wishes. At the same time, as an object of recognition, I would expect my fellow human beings to work and produce in order to satisfy my needs and wishes. The products of our work would therefore signify and embody our mutual recognition as vulnerable human beings.

Marx points out that this process of recognition brings about individuals' consciousness of being an object of love: "I would know myself", writes Marx, "to be confirmed", namely, recognized, "in your thought and your love".[12] The recognition process would then include manifestations of love: Recognizing you in these ways would mean, among other things, loving you. It is important to stress, following Robyn Marasco's admonition, that Marx is not suggesting here that men and women's human nature can be realized in a society entirely organized on the basis of love relationships. Love is not the only, or fundamental, principle of a noncapitalist society. In other writings as well, Marx clearly argues that a noncapitalist society cannot resemble the early Christian community.[13] As Engels has moreover emphatically remarked in his critique of Feuerbach, communism is not based on the commandment to "fall into each other's arms regardless of distinctions of sex or estate". A non-alienated society cannot be a "universal orgy of reconciliation!"[14]

Love, however, might be considered a useful critical tool. Consider the fragment in which, in the *Manuscripts*, Marx discusses the power of money. In this passage, Marx debunks money's capacity to shape and transform individuals' identities, their interpersonal relationships, and their relation with nature. Such "creative" or constitutive power "confounds" all natural and human qualities and distorts social bonds.[15] Under capitalism, market relations influence and ingurgitate sexual, erotic, and emotional relations as well. For instance, money allows (ugly) men to form intimate ties with (beautiful) women; money transforms love into hate (and, presumably, hate into love). Marx quotes Shakespeare's *Timon of Athens*, where money (gold) is what "makes the wappen'd widow wed again"[16] and concludes the passage with the following words:

> Assume man to be man and his relationship to the world to be a human one: then you can exchange love only for love, trust for trust, etc. ... Every one of your relations to man and to nature must be a specific expression, corresponding to the object of your will, of your real individual life. If you love without evoking love in return—that is, if your loving as loving does not produce reciprocal love; if through a living expression of yourself as a loving person you do not make yourself a beloved one, then your love is impotent—a misfortune.[17]

These lines sketch out considerations that have little, if anything, to do with the Christian notion of love. Marx's main claim is that only in a noncapitalist society, namely, in a "human" society, would love be exchanged for love. Love under capitalism is, then, most of the time, perhaps always, profoundly damaged and distorted. Note that Marx is not arguing that money cannot buy "true" love, or that love relations have nothing to do with market relations. Indeed, in capitalism, money and market exchanges *do* affect love (and sexuality). Marx is arguing, rather, that by trying to outline the anti-capitalist logic of human relationality, we might be able to formulate another—and better—conception of love. At the same time, by trying to outline an alternative notion of love, we might be able to outline the logic of noncapitalist relations.

The idea of love as being exchanged "only for love" constitutes an important element in such an outline. Now, one might wonder whether it is problematic to conceive of anti-capitalist love in terms of exchange. Isn't such a requirement of reciprocity inevitably tied to market logic? Michael Hardt claims that this is indeed the case: Commenting on this passage, he submits that "considering love only in terms of exchange undermines an understanding of love as a power that generates social bonds."[18] Hardt, however, does not consider what exchange, and love, would look like from a noncapitalist point of view.[19] What does Marx intend as undamaged, undistorted, namely, noncapitalist love? Following precisely Hardt's suggestions, we can imagine noncapitalist love as a *powerful and empowering* bond, one that makes human beings flourish, fostering their particular capacities and qualities, their senses and attributes, their "singular human powers".[20] A love of this sort would have the power to transform individuals, enhance their differences, and would avoid unification and sameness. What Hardt overlooks, however, is the role of reciprocity in powerful and empowering love. Empowerment, transformation, and flourishing may occur, in fact, only if loving dispositions and activities are reciprocated.[21] Imagine that A loves B—A, that is, tries to foster B's singularity, specific qualities, and capacities—while B merely wants to profit from A's love, without trying to empower her: The powerful, transformative, creative relation that Hardt has in mind would then very probably not happen.[22] There is obviously no guarantee, neither in a "human" society, that we would find partners willing and able to love us as we love them. The crucial point is, however, that capitalism *does structurally impede a certain kind of reciprocity and empowerment*. How? Unfortunately, Marx does not address this question. We could argue, however, that one of the structural impediments within capitalism consists of the commodification of persons and their powers: If we conceive of and treat our lovers (or friends) like private property or commodities, we would not be able to empower them; at the same time, the lovers who are regarded as our property or commodities would not be able to empower us.

Consider now another point of the previously quoted passage: Marx states that it is the "living expression" of oneself "as a loving person" that makes this person "a beloved one". We can understand this conception of love only by recalling the structure of alienated and nonalienated *labor* that Marx had described previously in the *Manuscripts*.[23] Labor consists, to put it briefly, in an activity that produces, shapes, and transforms the external world. As a result of our labor, we create objects that are not only the products of our labor but that also entail an objectification of ourselves. We, as laborers, have thus also been shaped and transformed by such producing activity. The problem with alienation is that both dimensions of objectivity, the external and the personal, are forcedly separated from the laborer; the laborer loses both her products and herself. By losing herself and her products, she is moreover deprived of those conditions, faculties, and powers that would allow her to recognize other human beings as human beings.

Now, a similar relational structure is also at play in love relationships. In loving someone, I express myself as a loving person: I open myself to others, I show my vulnerability, I disclose my dependence. My emotions acquire an objective dimension, I put myself out in the world and thus I put myself at risk.[24] I expose and dispossess myself.[25] In loving attachments, vulnerability and dependence cease to be scary and become a source of enjoyment and empowerment insofar as the loving person that I am is recognized by my partners as a "beloved one".[26] When my partners reciprocate my love, my being-outside-of-myself, my objectivity, is confirmed in ways that enhance my singularity, empower me, and make me flourish. Citing Simone de Beauvoir, I would then love and be loved not to escape from myself but to find myself—not out of resignation but to affirm myself—and thus love would become a "source of life".[27]

This line of argument is supported by another passage in the *Manuscripts*. Some pages earlier, Marx speaks of the relation "of man to woman" as the most "direct, natural, necessary relation of person to person".[28] The erotic, sexual relationship is mentioned here by Marx as paradigmatic for a type of social bond that has actualized human beings' true communal nature. In the erotic relation, persons need other persons *as persons*; as such, their individual existence realizes itself as a "social being".[29] A communist society corresponds then precisely to this "resolution ... between objectification and self-confirmation".[30] Under capitalism, the objectification of myself as expression of my emotional needs and desires and in the fruits of my labor cannot be recognized in empowering ways. Such objectification, which is also the expression and manifestation of my neediness and vulnerability (and of human beings' constitutive neediness and vulnerability), represents, under capitalist conditions, a leverage for exploitation and domination. The *resolution of the conflict between objectification and self-confirmation*, on the contrary, would mean that such vulnerability is recognized, and our dependence on others becomes a source of flourishing, empowerment, and transformation.

Marx's frugal but precious considerations on love hint at two ways in which love relationships are interrelated with, although not identical to, the broader sociopolitical world, and more precisely with economic relationships. First, it is very far from Marx's intention to depict love as a happy oasis of human self-realization in the midst of alienated relations of exchange. Love could give rise to empowering interactions only in a society in which human beings could relate to each other as human beings, as persons; in a society dominated by an asymmetry between laborers' dependence and capitalists' interdependence, love relationships cannot but resemble alienated relationships. As Brudney rightly argues, erotic relations may be regarded then as the "weathervane for human relations generally",[31] as a critical tool, namely, for diagnosing broader social ills. According to Hardt, a new 'properly political concept of love', inspired by these Marxian considerations, even allows for highlighting the structure of social bonds that would characterize a radically different, noncapitalist, society. Three traits, according to Hardt, would define such love:

> First, it would have to extend across social scales and create bonds that are at once intimate and social, destroying conventional divisions between public and private. Second, it would have to operate in a field of multiplicity and function through not unification but the encounter and interaction of differences. Finally, a political love must transform us, that is, it must designate a becoming such that in love, in our encounter with others we constantly become different.[32]

Hardt's definition perfectly sums up the critical potential of erotic relationships—a potential that cannot be grasped by those modern accounts that theorize the disentanglement of the sphere of love from the broader sociopolitical world. However, Hardt's view runs the risk of establishing love as the sole organizing social principle. Although economic relations would function in a noncapitalist society according to a logic of recognition that entails a loving component, erotic relationships cannot be equated with social relationships *tout court*. Whereas production and exchange relations necessarily aim at the fulfilment of certain needs and wishes, love bonds entail activities that do not have this aim or even any aim at all: Quite often, lovers just enjoy being together, or play or act together without pursuing any goal. Lovers, moreover, can satisfy only a restricted number of their partners' wishes and needs; even in a noncapitalist society, individuals would have to rely on other types of relations to fulfil the needs and wishes that their intimate partners and friends cannot satisfy. While, on the one hand, the considerations outlined so far intend to show a certain intertwinement of love and other relationships, such interconnection does not mean that the (modern) distinction between different kinds of social relations has been completely erased.

The second way in which Marx can help us to challenge the modern representation of love as an autonomous social sphere builds upon the analogy between labor and love. Both are, in fact, relations of recognition that do *not* display a *dyadic* structure. They entail, on the contrary, an objective, material dimension that encompasses—without merging or unifying—the singular lovers or laborers. In labor relations, the things produced and exchanged incorporate and mediate laborers' mutual recognition. In empowering love relations, the lovers' recognizing subjectivities mutually become objects of recognition, thus acquiring an exterior dimension: "Feelings and passions", says Marx, are "*ontological* affirmations of being (of nature)" and they are "only really affirmed because their *object* exists for them as a *sensual* object ... Insofar as man, as hence also his feeling, etc., is *human*, the affirmation of the object by another is likewise his own gratification."[33] When a lover recognizes the exteriorization and objectification of her partner's feelings and passions, she feels herself gratified, confirmed in her (emotional) existence, recognized. The objectification can be conceived of as sensuous not only because subjects and objects of love are material, bodily beings, but also—I would now like to suggest—because relationships between lovers are mediated by things, namely, by objects that are significant to them and that they may produce or exchange, or give to each other as gifts. For instance, lovers may express their care and gratitude for, or attraction to, their partners, thus sustaining and enhancing their senses, qualities, and powers, by cooking and preparing food for them, or by weaving, putting together, giving, or even just wearing certain garments. Lovers' recognition is incorporated in, and enabled, conveyed, or enhanced by, objects of this sort.

It is not difficult to understand, at this point, how broader social structures and norms enter and shape erotic relationships through these things. *Pretty Woman*, and the entanglement of economic and gender norms that build up its social context, can help again to illustrate this point: The fashionable, expensive clothes that Vivian buys with Edward's credit card[34] do not just enable her to enter certain social and cultural milieus; they do not merely alter her physical appearance, but do rather seem to change her 'substance', her 'nature', turning her into a legitimate object of love. When she rejects the comfortable life of a high-class mistress that Edward has offered her and leaves, she does so not as the loud, insolent girl who wears over-the-knee shiny boots and chews gum, but as a chic, sophisticated woman. Gender norms about desirable and lovable bodies are woven within these garments as well.

Marx does not tell us much about the things that mediate love bonds. His only characterization is a negative one: These things cannot be commodities; they cannot be bought and sold. Only the overcoming of the capitalist mode of mediation would guarantee that the things produced and exchanged, including lovers/laborers' subjectivities, are not separated from the persons needing and cherishing them. Such overcoming should guarantee that people would not be deprived of the things and of the recognition they need. Capitalism has structured the materiality that mediates social relationships by commodifying both persons and things, thus regulating, fixing, and disciplining social relationships in ways that advantage some and exploit, oppress, or damage others.

Hegel's thoughts on love might now disclose further possibilities to explore such mediating materiality, which is to be predominantly understood, according to his view, as private property. In the next section, I will argue that for erotic relationships, the role of private property is to be seen in ambivalent terms.

Hegel on Love and the Separating Function of Private Property

According to Hegel, love is a living process in which lovers' independence, their personhood as embodied in things (property), tends to be absorbed in a more encompassing unity. The lovers' individual selves tend to disappear in a *we*. Private property, the seal of the separated person, appears therefore in contrast with the loving spirit of communal relationships. Is the independence of individual lovers, however, so detrimental for erotic relationships? In this section, I intend to problematize Hegel's conception of love—even while relying on Hegelian arguments. The aim is to suggest that lovers' separation, enabled by private property, might foster the modality of empowering and powerful love that I have sketched out in the previous section.

In the fragment "Love" (1797–8), Hegel does not only provide a suggestive definition of love; he also reflects on the relationship between love and property: "Since possession and property make up such an important part of men's life,cares, and thoughts, even lovers cannot refrain from reflection on this aspect of their relations."[35] The fragment's point of departure is the problematic relation between the person and the community, which is here thought of as a religious (Christian) community based on love. By joining such a 'community-of-love', human beings renounce their material attachments to things, to their properties. The love sustaining communitarian relations of this type is characterized by its separation and opposition to the external world, to every kind of objectivity and materiality. Incidentally, this appears to be one of the first formulations of the modern thesis of the autonomization of love.

In the religious community of love, human beings relate to each other by appealing to their feelings, to their innermost nature, and abstract from everything else in the world, especially from their material possessions.[36] Asceticism proves to be, however, in this context, hardly satisfying and sustainable. Without relating to objects, persons cannot determine themselves. Human beings exist only as "something opposed [to the object]". Subject and object, man and matter: "the one exists only for the other"; as a result, the human being "cannot bear to think himself in this nullity".[37] What does he (or she) do then? The 'solution' seems to be that of switching from the kind of religious communitarian love to sexual, erotic love.[38] The erotic relation is described as a "true union", which "exists only between living beings who are alike in power and thus in one another's eyes living beings from every point of view".[39] This "genuine love excludes all oppositions", and "finally" ends up destroying objectivity, even the objectivity enacted by lovers' own matter, by their bodies that is.[40]

(Un)fortunately, lovers' complete, symbiotic fusion does not seem feasible: Lovers longing to annul their differences, for "complete surrender", to make the "consciousness of a separate self disappear",[41] cannot get rid of a "still subsisting independence"[42]: "Part of the individual is severed and held back *as a private property*."[43] Private property, which should have been destroyed at the beginning as a condition for entering the religious community, is now reentering the scene of love. On the one hand, Hegel here describes the act of erotic union, sexual intercourse, which, as it comes to its end, allows the lovers to regain individual possession of their own bodies. On the other hand, Hegel admits that lovers have never really given up their properties (things), thus obstructing complete fusion. "External objects" still "belong to each of them", and "[t]he one who sees the other in possession of a property must sense in the other the separate individuality which has willed this possession."[44]

In this passage of the love fragment, Hegel sees personhood as expressed and sensed in her own property "as a hindrance"[45] to the loving union; the solution he very briefly adumbrates is common property. In the *Outlines of the Philosophy of Right*, common property will be indeed depicted as the material resource of the married couple. In the family, "while no member of the family has property of his own, each has his right in the common stock"[46] (which is controlled and administrated by the husband). When the marriage dissolves, because of natural reasons (death) or divorce, both man and woman are entitled to regain private property.[47]

The conception of love that emerges if we consider Hegel's texts belonging to different phases of his production is rather consistent: Love is seen as the sensuous and emotional process of overcoming lovers' independent selves, thus constituting a unity, a *we* that absorbs all differences and particularities, including material ones, and the things that lovers own and with which they identify. I stress the fact that this is a process—of overcoming, of absorbing, of obliterating—and not a final state in which persons' independence is completely nullified. According to Hegel's central thesis in this context, the individual lover is not annihilated, she rather realizes herself as a true human being precisely within the relation between partners. In *The Spirit of Christianity and its Fate*, Hegel writes: "[i]n love man has found himself again in another."[48] In the *Philosophy of Right*, Hegel provides the following well-known definition:

> Love means in general terms the consciousness of my unity with another, so that I am not in isolation by myself but win my self-consciousness only through the renunciation of my independence (*Fürsichsein*) and through knowing myself as the unity of myself with another and of the other with me. The first moment in love is that I do not wish to be a self-subsistent and independent person and that, if I were, then I would feel defective and incomplete. The second moment is that I find myself in another person, that I count for something in the other, while the other in turn comes to count for something in me.[49]

In his *Lectures on the Philosophy of Religion*, Hegel again writes that love is "consciousness or feeling of the identity of the two—to be outside of myself and in the Other."[50] The condition for this is that the lovers leave behind their particularities and differences, ready to abandon their previous selves, and thus to accept transformation in order to reach a higher, more fulfilling reality:

> Ethical life, love, means precisely the giving up of particularity, of particular personality, and its extension to universality—so, too, with friendship. In friendship and love I give up my abstract personality and thereby win it back as concrete. The truth of personality is found precisely in winning back through this immersion, this being immersed in the other.[51]

Many aspects of Hegel's philosophy of love would deserve consideration here: In particular, more should be said on the transformative quality of the 'finding oneself in the other', which can be interpreted, and has been in fact interpreted, as a relation of recognition.[52] In what follows, I concentrate solely on a circumscribed aspect of Hegel's account, namely, on the alleged aversion of love for the lovers' independence. In the early writings on Christianity, Hegel says that love "recoils if it senses an [exclusive] individuality in the other".[53] Independent individuals are portrayed as unhappy, restless, anxious, incapable of "integration [or completion]".[54] In the *Philosophy of Right*, moreover, the tension between individual independence and merging with the other is called a "tremendous contradiction",[55] which only the process of love can solve.

The aversion to personhood's particularity and independence goes hand in hand with the thesis that lovers should abstract from, forget about, bracket, or destroy their own possessions and thus the "external", material, objective world, namely, everything that does not correspond to a sort of emotional connection of souls or to a sexual union that allegedly overcomes bodies' separateness.[56] According to Hegel, private property elicits and requires from the person determinate actions in objectivity that result in the structuring of the self and the social and political world. Through property, the person attains an objective mode of existence and creates an objective, actual world. As Peter Stillman sharply puts it, "Property contributes to freedom and individuality because it allows and requires man to act in and to shape the objective world."[57] In civil society, the property owner is a concrete individual who is freely determining herself in action, shaping and transforming herself and the world. By recognizing each other as property owners and by recognizing each other's will as objectified, embodied in things, persons can truly *relate* to each other.[58] This is accurately captured by Jeremy Waldron:

> It is no accident that the world of enduring objects on which we work is also the world of public objects and that what is visible and significant to us as the work of our wills on the external world is also perceptible as such by others. By objectifying his will in this sort of world, Hegel's person not only brings that will into a stronger and more mature relation to itself, but also brings it into a relation with the similarly matured wills of other persons.[59]

Marx's idea of recognition as mediated through things, which we have previously discussed, finds here its root. It is clear at this point, incidentally, why Marx cannot think of a noncapitalist society as entirely constituted by love bonds. Despite the fact that the Hegelian conception of love has been important for Marx's critique of private property, commodities, and money, Marx thinks of true communal relations as relations of interdependence between individuals, and not as their amalgam in an indistinct unity.[60]

But should we necessarily embrace Hegel's rather melancholic view according to which differentiation, opposition, and the impossibility of complete symbiosis are to be thought of as a failure of love? Shouldn't we rather regard lovers' relative independence as a resource for a flourishing and empowering modality of love?[61] According to Hegel, oppositions and differences count as fruitful for the process of love insofar as they set this process in motion: They must be constantly overcome and transformed but can never be completely erased and nullified. Hegel senses that lovers' independence, their alterity, might represent an enriching resource when he writes: "The beloved is not opposed to us, he is one with our own being; we see us only in him, *but then again he is not a we anymore—a riddle, a miracle [ein Wunder], one that we cannot grasp.*"[62] Commenting on this passage, María del Rosario Acosta explains: "Love, therefore, takes place in the never-ending passage towards others, a passage always already opened to and by the alterity that traverses it."[63]

Lovers' alterity, the fact that they cannot be completely grasped (understood, seen, recognized), thus always retaining a certain separateness, gives rise to a powerful, empowering, and flourishing modality of love for at least two reasons: First, it maintains the erotic bond as a relationship between subjects, avoiding the complete objectification of one of the partners (or all of them). As subjects, the lovers are endowed with the power to sustain, care for, and support their partners, but also to solicit, push, and influence them in ways that might have transformative consequences. Moreover, this power enables the lovers, and this is the second reason, to detach themselves, if need be, from bonds that might become too demanding, suffocating, or just boring.[64]

In Hegel's thought, one crucial condition for this sense of individuals' independence is provided by private property. According to his view, one might say, private property constitutes a sort of 'safe place' in which persons can build, shape, and transform themselves and the world through work. Is it possible then to find an analogy between love bonds with relations of recognition between property owners in civil society?[65] This is not an argument sustaining a conception of erotic relationships that should resemble market relations. What the Hegelian take on private property might suggest, rather, is that lovers might also need their own things, those enabling and strengthening their individual powers as well as giving them the possibility to back away from the love bond when needed. One might even say that such things represent a condition that prevents lovers from becoming each other's possessions. Furthermore, lovers' things would also allow them to better express their feelings, to more concretely convey their recognition.

More work is needed, at this point, to explore the socio-ontological status and normative-critical meaning of the things interwoven within lovers' bonds. How can we avoid the things becoming a condition of alienation, of individuals' self-loss and loss of the world, as Marx warns us when criticizing the mediating function of money and a certain notion of private property?[66] How can we think of the things of love as mediations that both deeply connect and, if need be, separate lovers? How can these things foster both lovers' alterity and independence, while at the same time ensuring their most intimate encounters?

Unfortunately, these, and other, crucial questions are going to be left open in this chapter. As a conclusion, I would like to come back to the critique of modern love: The previous considerations, if plausible, should have shown that love cannot be conceived of as a worldless, immaterial union, detached from the things of the world. Contrary to Hannah Arendt's conviction, love is not an unpolitical or antipolitical force because it does not destroy "the in-between which relates us to and separates us from others".[67] Rather, such in-between is constitutive for lovers, and is (partially) built up by them;

it consists of the objective, material things that mediate lovers' expression of feeling, attitudes, and concrete acts toward each other, care, recognition, and desire to unite with and separate from the partners. The interrelation between lovers and their things is the material medium in which love unfolds. In one of the rare passages in which Adorno offers a glimpse of good, or at least undamaged, "undistorted" modalities of intersubjective relations, he reflects that in this kind of human interaction, individuals' singularity would flourish "only *in live contact with the warmth of things*".[68] These are relationships, according to Adorno, in which everyone involved gives themselves to others; this devotion implies and brings forth the giving of certain things that, in order to be real gifts, should somehow escape the capitalist logic of the market. As Jean-Luc Nancy put it, love is, at the same time, gift and appropriation of the self; in fact, it puts into question the opposition between gift and property.[69] Is it possible? Under which conditions? In order to answer these and other questions, love relationships cannot be conceived of as completely disentangled from the economic system or from political settings. Objective, material things—things that are perceived, received, interpreted, produced, exchanged, given, and so on, according to a complex network of institutional and cultural patterns and norms—both intimately connect and separate lovers.

Notes

1 Erotic love can be roughly defined as an intimate, passionate bond that brings together adult human beings who are not kin. In the relevant literature, this phenomenon is sometimes designated as 'romantic' or 'sexual'.

2 For a rather complete overview of the numerous debates on love, from Plato and Aristotle onward, see for example Neera K. Badhwar, "Love," in *The Oxford Handbook of Practical Ethics*, ed. H. La Follette (Oxford: Oxford University Press, 2003), 42–69.

3 Niklas Luhmann, *Love as Passion. The Codification of Intimacy* (Cambridge: Harvard University Press, 1986); Anthony Giddens, *Transformations of Intimacy: Sexuality, Love and Eroticism in Modern Societies* (Stanford: Stanford University Press, 1993); Axel Honneth, *Freedom's Right: The Social Foundations of Democratic Life* (Cambridge: Cambridge University Press, 2014).

4 See e.g. Honneth, *Freedom's Right*, 152.

5 Interestingly, this socio-theoretical perspective finds a match in those ethical theories according to which the "reasons of love" cannot be reduced to moral imperatives or ethical–communal values, since love is itself a source of reasons and values; see Henry Frankfurt, *The Reasons of Love* (Princeton: Princeton University Press, 2004).

6 Note the gender asymmetry at play here: The responsibility to disentangle love from the economic sphere, thus declaring it 'authentic' or 'true', is represented as a woman's burden.

7 Karl Marx, "Comments on James Mill *Élements D'économie Politique*," in *Marx & Engels Collected Works* (MECW), Vol. 3 (New York: New York International Publishers, 2005), and Karl Marx, *Economic and Philosophic Manuscripts of 1844*, MECW 3.

8 Daniel Brudney, *Marx's Attempt to Leave Philosophy* (Cambridge, MA: Harvard University Press, 1997), 169.

9 Marx, *Economic and Philosophic Manuscripts*, 276.

10 Brudney, *Marx's Attempt*, 175.
11 Cf. ibid., 156f.; 169f.; cf. also Michael Quante, "Recognition as the Social Grammar of Species Being in Marx," in *Recognition and Social Ontology*, ed. Heikki Ikäheimo and Arto Laitinen (Leiden: Brill, 2011).
12 Marx, "Comments on James Mill," 228.
13 Robyn Marasco, "'I would rather wait for you than believe that you are not coming at all': Revolutionary love in a post-revolutionary time," *Philosophy and Social Criticism* 36, no. 6 (2010): 643–62, at pp. 647–8.
14 Friedrich Engels, *Ludwig Feuerbach and the Outcome of Classical German Philosophy* (New York: International Publishers, 1941), 40. Marx and Engels criticize here in particular the Christian imperative according to which people ought to love their neighbor, in spite of class and gender differences: This principle is not powerful enough to liberate a society from alienated labor and capitalist domination; moreover, it implies a submissive attitude that is incompatible with revolutionary aims. For reasons that will become clearer later, not only Christian love but also erotic love cannot be considered the only form of social interaction.
15 Marx, *Economic and Philosophic Manuscripts*, 325.
16 Ibid., 323.
17 Ibid., 326.
18 Michael Hardt, "For Love or Money," *Cultural Anthropology* 26, no. 4 (2011): 676–82, at pp. 679–80.
19 Hardt does moreover not, consider how love "frustrates the simple opposition between economy and noneconomy". Jean-Luc Nancy, "Shattered Love," in *The Inoperative Community* (Minneapolis: University of Minnesota Press, 1991), 111.
20 Hardt, "For Love or Money," 680. A conception of powerful sexual love in this sense is outlined by Anna G. Jónasdóttir's theory of "love power". Love power is the activity that makes (and remakes) human beings, individuates and personifies them, thus creating human agency and bringing about transformation both at the level of the self and of the collectivity; Anna G. Jónasdóttir, *Why Women Are Oppressed* (Philadelphia: Temple University Press, 1994), 13–4. What distinguishes it from labor is the fact that lovers act without aiming to shape the love object according to their own light: "On the contrary, it is essential that the object in receiving love wins the capability of 'shaping' himself or herself and his or her own goals." Ibid., 73.
21 Marx's conception of love in these passages and the emphasis on reciprocity seem to be inspired mainly by Aristotle's theory of love and friendship (*philia*); Aristotle, *The Nicomachean Ethics* (Oxford: Oxford University Press 2009), 1164a–b. Friends expect, or hope, that their love is reciprocated, according to Aristotle, especially when they find themselves in relationships of "perfect friendship", namely, friendship based on virtue and not on utility and pleasure. The expectation does not mean that our love is conditioned by our friends loving us back; we love them indeed for their own sake, without expecting anything in return. However, as both Marx and Aristotle explain, if our beloveds do not love us in return, and engage in sexual or friendly practices with us with the sole aim of receiving some pleasure or utility, we suffer and cannot thrive; we cannot enjoy a good life.
22 Jónasdóttir delivers an explanation of the systematic, structural failure of reciprocity by identifying two gendered ways to practice love, namely, female care and male eroticism: Jónasdóttir, *Why Women Are Oppressed*. I have, moreover, further explained what mutual loving empowerment could mean in Federica Gregoratto,

23 "Why Love Kills: Power, Gender Dichotomy, and Romantic Femicide," *Hypatia* 32, no. 1 (2017): 135–51.
23 Marx, *Economic and Philosophic Manuscripts*, 270–82.
24 As Judith Butler writes when commenting on Hegel's early conception of love: "Love cannot remain a mute and internal feeling, but requires the presentation of love in some way." Judith Butler, "To Sense What Is Living in the Other: Hegel's Early Love," in dOCUMENTA (13) (Hatje Cantz Verlag: Ostfildern, 2012), 6.
25 Ibid., 11; María del Rosario López Acosta, "An*other* Kind of Community: Hegel on Law, Love and Life in the Frankfurt Fragments," in *Der Frankfurter Hegel in seinem Kontext*, ed. Thomas Hanke and Thomas M. Schmidt (Frankfurt: Vittorio Klostermann, 2015), 191–208, at p. 204.
26 In the *Manuscripts*, Marx explains dependence in a radical ontological sense: Human beings depend on each other because they are created by other human beings. This sort of creation can be intended here both as human labor and as sexual reproductive labor: Marx, *Economic and Philosophic Manuscripts*, 304–5.
27 Simone de Beauvoir, *The Second Sex* (London: Vintage Books, 2011), 725.
28 Marx, *Economic and Philosophic Manuscripts*, 295.
29 Ibid., 296.
30 Ibid.
31 Brudney, *Marx's Attempt*, 181.
32 Hardt, "For Love or Money," 678.
33 Marx, *Economic and Philosophic Manuscripts*, 322.
34 Note that capitalism, in the film, is clearly represented in critical terms as financial capitalism: At the beginning, Edward is depicted as an unscrupulous businessman who does not produce anything but only makes money.
35 Georg Wilhelm Friedrich Hegel, "Love," in *On Christianity. Early Theological Writings*, trans. T.M. Knox and R. Kroner (New York: Harper and Brothers, 1948), 302–8, at p. 308.
36 Ibid., 303–4. Cf. also: "In love's task the community scorns any unification save the deepest, any spirit save the highest … every other tie in other objective activities is alien to the community." Hegel, "The Spirit of Christianity and Its Fate," in *On Christianity. Early Theological Writings*, 182–281, at p. 280.
37 Hegel, "Love," 304. As Hegel will later explain in the *Philosophy of Right*, "A person must translate his freedom into an external sphere in order to exist as Idea." Hegel, *Outlines of the Philosophy of Right*, ed. Stephen Houlgate (Oxford: Oxford University Press, 2008), §41.
38 In her fascinating comment on this fragment, Butler does not hide her puzzlement: "The scene is dyadic, and thus we might well wonder what happened to the community? Did community collapse into coupledom? And what happened to the object world?" Butler, "To Sense What Is Living," 10.
39 Hegel, "Love," 305. The fact that lovers must be "alike in power" sounds like a reference to Aristotle's thesis according to which, in perfect forms of philia, lovers/friends must be equal or similar (e.g. Aristotle, *The Nicomachean Ethics*, 1158b1–10).
40 Lovers' independence and singularity mean, at this moment, only that they "may be separated by death". Hegel, "Love," 305.
41 Ibid., 307.
42 Ibid., 306.
43 Ibid., my italics.
44 Ibid., 308.

45 Ibid., 306.
46 Hegel, *Philosophy of Right*, §171.
47 For a critique of this bourgeois reconciliation of the opposition between love and property, see e.g. Theodor W. Adorno, *Minima Moralia. Reflections on a Damaged Life* (New York: Verso, 2005), 30.
48 Hegel, "The Spirit of Christianity," 278.
49 Hegel, *Philosophy of Right*, §158R.
50 The entire quote reads as follows: "I have my self-consciousness not in myself but in the other. I am satisfied and have peace with myself only in this other—and I am only because I have peace with myself; if I did not have it, then I would be a contradiction that falls to pieces. This other, because it likewise exists outside itself, has its self-consciousness only in me, and both the other and I are only this consciousness of being-outside-ourselves and of our identity; we are only this intuition, feeling, and knowledge of our unity. This is love, and without knowing that love is both a distinguishing and the sublation of the distinction, one speaks emptily of it." Hegel, *Lectures on the Philosophy of Religion*, ed. Peter C. Hodgson (Oxford: Oxford University Press, 2006), 418.
51 Ibid., 428. The equation between friendship and love is noteworthy and should be further discussed.
52 In the Jena *Realphilosophie* of 1805–6, Hegel introduces for the first time the term "recognition" in the marginalia to his discussion of love: Lovers, in this passage, are depicted as natural individuals, with uncultivated selves, who are recognized as such; Hegel, "Jena Lectures on the Philosophy of Spirit (1805/06)," in *Hegel and the Human Spirit*, ed. Leo Rauch (Detroit: Wayne University Press, 1983), 83–183, at p. 107.
In her brilliant book on Hegel and love, Laura Werner argues that the connection between recognition and love constitutes a bridge between Hegel's earlier critique of Kant's moral philosophy through the concepts of feeling, life, and love, and his social and political interests in the Jena period; Laura Werner, *"The Restless Love of Thinking": The Concept* Liebe *in G.W.F. Hegel's Philosophy* (Helsinki: University of Helsinki, 2007), 100.
53 Hegel "The Spirit of Christianity," 278–80.
54 Hegel, "Fragment of a System," in *On Christianity. Early Theological Writings*, 309–20, at p. 317.
55 Hegel, *Philosophy of Right*, §158R.
56 The only form of loving objectivity, which I unfortunately cannot discuss here, is the child, who represents the "objective embodiment" of the lovers' union; Hegel, ibid., §175 A.
57 Peter G. Stillman, "Property, Freedom and Individuality in Hegel's and Marx's Political Thought," in *Hegel's Social and Political Thought*, ed. D.P. Verene (Sussex: Harvest Press, 1980), 135.
58 Ibid., 143.
59 Jeremy Waldron, *The Right to Private Property* (Oxford: Clarendon Press, 1988), 375–6.
60 As already mentioned, Hegel also realizes the impossibility of a community based only on love; Hegel, "The Spirit of Christianity," 278–80.
61 In his innovative reading of *Romeo and Juliet*, inspired by a Hegelian understanding of love, Paul Kottman shows how separation and differentiation are not only a necessary component of Romeo and Juliet's bond, but must also be reclaimed by the lovers themselves as an expression of their individual freedom—individual freedom

that is enabled and can unfold only because of, and within, the love relationship; Paul Kottman, "Defying the Stars: Tragic Love and the Struggle for Freedom in Romeo and Juliet," in *Shakespeare Quarterly* 63, no. 1 (2012): 1–38, at pp. 24–33.

62 Hegel, "Entwürfe über Religion und Liebe," in *Frühe Schriften*, Werke 1 (Frankfurt: Suhrkamp, 1986), 244, my italics.

63 Acosta, "An*other* Kind of Community," 205. Alterity is thus the condition for love to be "rebellious, fugitive, errant, unassignable, and inassimilable … at once the promise of completion … and the threat of decomposition, always imminent." Nancy, "Shattered Love," 93.

64 The feminist meaning of this condition should be intuitively easy to grasp; see Gregoratto, "Why Love Kills."

65 Cf. A.R. Bjerke, "Hegel and the Love of the Concept," *The Heythrop Journal*, LII (2011): 76–89, at pp. 80–1.

66 In the early writings, Marx is rather ambivalent about property: On the one hand, he harshly criticizes the form of Hegelian private property that excludes others from an individual's domain, turns this individual into an egoistic self, and perpetrates privileges; see e.g. Karl Marx, "Contribution to the Critique of Hegel's Philosophy of Law," MECW 3: 3–129, at p. 99. On the other hand, he sees it just as "the existence of essential objects for man, both as objects of enjoyment and as objects of activity". Marx, *Economic and Philosophic Manuscripts*, 322.

67 Hannah Arendt, *The Human Condition* (Chicago/London: The University of Chicago Press, 1998), 242; see also 51–2.

68 Adorno, *Minima Moralia*, 43, my italics.

69 Nancy, "Shattered Love," 95–6.

Part Three

Postcapitalism and Utopia

10

Marx's 'Hegelian' Critique of Utopia

David Leopold

1

Socialism is best understood as a modern phenomenon. As both a political movement and a set of ideas, it was shaped by the emergence of capitalist society; a society dominated, we might say, by an economic system in which immediate producers own only their own labor power, and where production—and much else—is driven by the remorseless pursuit of profit.

Socialism typically envisages an alternative to capitalism so understood; an alternative that embodies a commitment not only to certain values, but also to the institutional and other conditions that might best promote them. Much of the diversity and disagreement that has characterized the socialist tradition reflects division over the content of this alternative.

Socialists disagree about the values here; what they are—'equality' and 'community', perhaps—as well as their further specification, and the relation between them (e.g., priority rules). In addition, socialists disagree over the institutional and other conditions—the forms of ownership, the role of markets, the kind of family structures, and so on—that would best realize these values, and over whether these institutional and other conditions are constitutive of what socialism is.[1]

However, these are not the only areas of disagreements within the socialist tradition. Another concerns, not the content—the values and institutions—of any future socialist society, but rather whether that society needs to be designed. That might seem an unlikely dispute, but there is no consensus around what I shall call the common-sense view. According to that common-sense view it seems obvious that socialists need *both* detailed and persuasive *critical* accounts of what is wrong with capitalist society, *and* detailed and persuasive *constructive* accounts of the social and other arrangements that might replace it.[2] Socialists who embrace the constructive dimension of the common-sense view are typically committed to the necessity of socialist design, to the idea that the socialist future needs to be built, and that such building—at least, if it is to go well—requires prior reflection on its normative, institutional, and other, dimensions. On this account, providing plans and blueprints of the socialist future presumably plays a crucial role in guiding and motivating socialists in their transformative ambitions. (I use the expression 'plans and blueprints' in order to capture the *detail* of these descriptions of the socialist future, and not to suggest that these designs have to be thought of as 'stipulative', as having to be followed to the letter.) Of course, socialists committed to socialist design might disagree, not only about the (normative and institutional) content, but also the status of these plans and blueprints. By 'status', I have in mind disagreements over the thorny question of how 'ideal' these plans and blueprints should be; that is, for instance, whether they should be constructed to reflect considerations of accessibility and feasibility in addition to those of desirability.[3]

It might be thought that all socialists subscribe to this view about the need for plans and blueprints of a socialist future. However, it is a remarkable, and not always noticed, feature of Marxian socialism that it does not endorse the common-sense account. (I use 'Marx*ian*' here to refer to the ideas shared by Karl Marx and Friedrich Engels, and not to refer to those of later Marx*ists*.) In particular, there is an interesting, and not much noticed, *asymmetry* in the attitude of Marx and Engels toward the critical and constructive dimensions of socialism. Simply put, Marx and Engels accept the need for socialists to offer detailed and persuasive account of what is wrong with contemporary capitalist society, but deny the need to offer similarly detailed and persuasive accounts of future socialist arrangements. Indeed, they think of the provision of detailed accounts of the socialist society of the future as paradigmatically *utopian*, and identify their own form of communism as the most steadfast opponent of utopianism so understood.[4]

This remarkable Marxian anti-utopianism, embodied in its hostility to plans and blueprints, is the subject of the present chapter. I attempt to justify its attribution to Marx, evaluate its merits, and consider whether, and to what extent, this rejection of socialist design is connected with certain ideas and arguments found in G.W.F. Hegel's writings, especially in the *Rechtsphilosophie* and philosophy of history.

2

The anti-utopianism of Marx and Engels is perhaps most visible in their hostility toward what—following Marxian nomenclature—we can call utopian socialism, the tradition said to have originated with Charles Fourier, Robert Owen, and Henri de Saint-Simon.

Despite their many differences, it is plausible to group those three writers and activists together. They form a rough age cohort (born within twelve years of each other), the mature form of their work emerges at around the same time (on the cusp of the eighteenth and nineteenth centuries), and they share some intellectual commitments. In particular, what makes the 'utopian' label appropriate—for all that it would have been unwelcome—is that they saw the provision and promotion of plans and blueprints for a future socialist society as an important and legitimate endeavor. This association with an ideal, but not extant, society also respects the concept's etymological origins; the neologism of Thomas More famously connoting both "good place" and "no place".[5] And it also seems central to the Marxian use of the label; Engels, for example, identifies utopianism with the provision of institutional and other detail in an account of precisely how the flaws of existing society are to be overcome.[6]

Helpfully for present purposes, this usage also maintains a distinction between Marxian and utopian socialism. Marx and Engels obviously have some broad vision of the future socialist society, but they never flesh out that vision with anything like the kind of institutional and other detail found in utopian literature. However, no one should imagine that 'Marxian' and 'utopian' exhaust the options here, as if all socialisms fall into one of these two categories. Nor, despite much commentary, was this the view of Marx and Engels; in the *Communist Manifesto*, for instance, they identify utopian socialism as one of five extant varieties of socialism. Finally, it will be apparent that denying that Marx and Engels are *in this sense* utopian does not rule out the possibility of (here unspecified) senses in which they might, coherently and accurately, be so described.

Marxian anti-utopianism is often misunderstood. In particular, Marx and Engels are frequently said to hold an unremittingly hostile view of utopian socialism. This is to confuse the part with the whole. Marx and Engels do, of course, often criticize utopianism, but they also have many more positive things to say, both about the utopian socialist tradition, and about individual utopian socialists. Moreover, this assorted criticism and praise is not contradictory.[7] There is an underlying structure to their remarks, a structure that rests on two distinctions: one chronological; the other substantive. The *chronological* distinction runs between the original triumvirate (Fourier, Owen, and Saint-Simon), on the one hand; and second and subsequent generations of utopian socialists, on the other. The *substantive* distinction runs between the critical part of utopian writings (the portrayal of faults within contemporary society), on the one hand, and the constructive part of utopian writings (the detailed description of the ideal socialist future), on the other.

Crucially for present purposes, both distinctions track a difference in the degree of approval and disapproval accorded by Marx and Engels. Simply put: They are more enthusiastic about the achievements of the first generation of utopians, by comparison with those of second and subsequent generations; and they are more enthusiastic about utopian criticism of contemporary society, by comparison with utopian constructive endeavors. It is the rationale and origins of the second kind of disapproval—the dislike of utopian plans and blueprints—that concerns me here.

3

It is helpful to draw a distinction between foundational and non-foundational criticisms of utopianism. I take this to be an exhaustive distinction; in that all Marxian criticisms of utopianism will, on examination, fall into one of these two categories. *Foundational* criticisms of utopian socialism are those which, if sound, would provide us with a reason to reject utopianism as such; that is, a reason to refrain from engaging in socialist design, a reason not to describe in relevant detail the socialist society of the future. (Of course, that reason might not be decisive, all things considered, but it would still count against utopianism per se.) In contrast, *non-foundational* criticisms of utopian socialism are those which, if sound, would provide us with a reason to reject views which might be held by, or even be characteristic of, utopian socialists, but which are not constitutive of their utopianism. That is, these non-foundational complaints might give us a reason to abandon the relevant beliefs, or to criticize those (including utopians) who held them, but they do not give us cause to reject utopianism as such.

Many familiar Marxian complaints about utopian socialism are non-foundational. Consider the following three examples taken from the *Manifesto*.[8]

Marx and Engels reject the 'paternalistic' view of the proletariat that they attribute to utopian socialists. This is a complicated complaint which involves several threads: that utopians misidentify the proletariat wholly with suffering; that utopians fail to understand that the proletariat is (potentially) a powerful collective agent; and that utopians mistakenly imagine that socialism will be brought to workers from above by non-proletarian others (and certainly not as the result of the *self*-emancipation of the proletariat). This complaint appears non-foundational, in that one could accept both that this paternalistic view of the proletariat is mistaken, and that it is held by many utopian socialists, without thereby having a reason to abandon utopianism as such. A commitment to the necessity and desirability of socialist design does not require one to hold any particular view, either about the character of the class of immediate producers in capitalist society, or its role in any transition to socialism.

In addition, Marx and Engels reject the 'ahistorical' view of social change that they attribute to utopian socialists. The complaint here is that utopians fail to understand that the achievement of socialism depends on conditions which can only emerge at a certain stage of historical development. They might, for instance, recognize that there are strategic preconditions for socialism (for instance, the right plan and sufficient will to put it into practice), but mistakenly imagine that those preconditions could have appeared at any point in time. The charge appears non-foundational, in that one can accept that there are historical conditions for establishing a socialist society, and that the utopian socialists fail to understand this, without thereby having a reason to abandon utopianism as such. A commitment to the necessity and desirability of socialist design does not require one to hold an ahistorical view of social change.

Finally, Marx and Engels reject the 'anti-political' perspective that they attribute to utopian socialists. This complicated charge also involves several threads: that utopians position themselves apart from the class struggles that increasingly characterize modern society; that utopians seek social rather than political change, standing aloof from legal and legislative mechanisms in particular; and that utopians reject involvement with revolutionary activity, not only shunning violence but also embracing gradualist solutions (especially communitarian ones). This complaint appears non-foundational, in that one can accept that socialists should participate in politics and that utopian socialists fail to understand this, without thereby having a reason to abandon utopianism as such. A commitment to the necessity and desirability of socialist design does not require one to reject involvement in class struggle, legislation, or revolution.

Assessing the soundness of these three non-foundational criticisms, and their relevance to the utopian socialist tradition, would be a complicated task.[9] However, even if sound and relevant, these criticisms give us no reason to abandon utopianism *as such*. Consequently, I pursue them no further here.

4

My concern is rather with foundational Marxian arguments. Three of these appear central: a *normative* claim that utopian plans and blueprints are undemocratic; an *epistemological* claim that utopian plans and blueprints are impossible; and an *empirical* claim that utopian plans and blueprints are unnecessary. In each case, I elaborate the relevant reasoning, give some evidence for attributing it to Marx in particular, and comment briefly on its soundness.[10]

The first foundational Marxian objection invokes the *normative* claim that that utopian plans and blueprints are undemocratic. Of course, to be a foundational objection it has to find fault with all plans and blueprints, and not just those recommending undemocratic institutional content. The suggestion here is that utopian plans and blueprints somehow necessarily, and regrettably, foreclose the future; that they inappropriately restrict the freedom of individuals to determine for themselves the kind of society that they want to live in. This 'democratic' thought concerns 'self-determination' or 'autonomy', the attractive but slippery idea that individuals can be 'part-author' of their own lives, making meaningful choices about, and being (partly) responsible for, the shape that those lives take. The democratic objection assumes both that self-determination is of value, and that utopia and self-determination necessarily conflict—that the provision of utopian designs somehow limits the capacity of future generations to be autonomous, to live their own lives in their own way.

This democratic objection appears more popular with commentators than with Marx and Engels themselves, but I do not deny that adjacent claims can be found in Marxian writings. Not least, Marx and Engels often contrast their own emphasis on the 'self-emancipation of the working class' with the utopian endorsement of what is sometimes called 'socialism from above'. For example, Marx commends the Paris Commune because, instead of seeking to establish a "Phalanstère" or an "Icarie"— that is, an intentional community modelled after the utopian designs of Fourier and Étienne Cabet, respectively—the popular mass of the French capital took the "actual management of the revolution into their own hands".[11]

However, this democratic objection to utopias is not persuasive. In particular, providing a detailed description of a future socialist society does not obviously undermine any plausible (subjective or objective) condition for self-determination. As a result of my drawing up socialist plans and blueprints, you (and others) are not, for example, 'brainwashed' in a way which casts doubt on the self-determining character of your beliefs, desires, or preferences. Nor does the mere existence of my plans and blueprints remove or obstruct any meaningful opportunities or options that would otherwise be available to you (and others). Consequently, the suggestion that utopian plans and blueprints necessarily prevent others from determining their future actions for themselves looks implausible. Of course, you (and others) might be rationally persuaded of the merits of my plans and blueprints, and, as a result of the consequent conviction, seek to put them into practice (insofar as that is within your control). However, such an outcome scarcely deprives you (and those others) of self-determination. Indeed, it looks to be an entirely familiar and acceptable form that self-determination (in both individual and collective forms) can and does take.

The second foundational Marxian objection invokes the *epistemological* claim that all these utopian plans and blueprints are impossible. The thought here is not that we are unable to draw up plans and blueprints, but rather that these plans and blueprints presuppose a kind of knowledge that cannot be had (is 'impossible'). It is this epistemological failing which makes them useless (or, at least, useless for strictly socialist purposes). The suggestion is seemingly that plans and blueprints are only useful if they facilitate the construction of a future socialist society, and that they can only do this if they are accurate. However, to be accurate the plans and blueprints would have correctly to predict the precise circumstances relevant to socialist construction, and for mundane but seemingly universal reasons—encompassing certain facts about human nature (including, e.g., our lack of omniscience) and human society (including, e.g., its complexity and contingency)—this kind of knowledge of the future is not available to us.

An example of this kind of objection can be found in Marx's correspondence with Ferdinand Domela Nieuwenhuis, concerning a Dutch proposal that a forthcoming socialist congress in Zurich discuss what economic and other legislation should be passed once socialists had come to political power. Marx maintains that it would be a grave mistake to raise this question; indeed, he suggests that the correct response to it is "a *critique of the question* as such", that is, an exposé of its faulty assumptions.[12] The faulty assumption here concerns the availability of knowledge. Simply put, in order to answer the Dutch question, we would need to know things about the future that we cannot now know. "What is to be done, and done *immediately* at any given, particular moment in the future", Marx remarks, "depends, of course, wholly and entirely on the actual historical circumstances in which action is to be taken."[13] Yet accurate and precise knowledge of those future historical circumstances is something that we cannot now have, because the relevant detail is not discernible at this distance. "We cannot", Marx remarks, "solve an equation that does not comprise within its terms the elements of its solution."[14]

This epistemological objection is not promising. The claim that—given certain human limitations and facts about the social world—we are unable to construct completely accurate plans looks compelling. However, there are reasons to doubt that only completely accurate plans could be of any use in constructing the future socialist society. And that assumption—or something very like it—seems to be needed in order to get from the claim that future circumstances are not completely predictable, to the conclusion that plans and blueprints are useless. The constructive utility of plans and blueprints does not disappear, just because we lack perfect knowledge of the various circumstances that might disrupt their realization. Indeed, it seems likely that less than wholly accurate plans can still help us make our way through the world, forming part of the process whereby we determine the future for ourselves and others (insofar as that is within our control). Plans for social change are not simply predictions of where we will end up, but rather—at least potentially—part of the process by which we help make the future the kind of place we would want to live.

The third foundational Marxian objection invokes the *empirical* claim that detailed plans and blueprints of a future socialist society are redundant. This view builds on some central elements of Marx's theory of history, according to which, at the point when a social order has exhausted its contribution to historical progress, not only is a new order happily available to replace the exhausted one and take progress further, but also that this new order is to be found in the old society itself.[15] In the present case, the basic structure of the future socialist order is growing up within, and will in due course emerge from, the existing capitalist society. Consequently, the design of that future society does not need to be anticipated by thought, since it develops automatically within the existing order.

Perhaps the clearest affirmation of this reasoning is found in the obstetric metaphors that appear throughout the Marxian corpus, especially when utopianism is the critical target.[16] Discussing the Paris Commune, Marx famously insists that the working class "have no ready-made utopias" to introduce by decree, but that their task is rather "to set free elements of the new society with which old collapsing bourgeois society itself is pregnant".[17] (Marx wrote this particular text in English, but Engels was careful to preserve the obstetric metaphor when translating it into German.[18]) The link between the obstetric model of political practice and the redundancy of utopian blueprints is clear. The socialist solution is already being produced by the historical process, but remains hidden, emerging only when the time is ripe. At that moment, the role of the proletarian midwife, to pursue the metaphor, is to deliver and not to design the contents of the historical womb. In short, Marx and Engels disagree with the utopians not about the need for human agency, nor presumably about its intensity (historical midwifery might turn out to be grueling), but rather about its proper scope.

The objection here rests on a complex empirical claim whose plausibility is hard to assess briefly and effectively. I offer two observations. The confidence of Marx and Engels does not seem to be underwritten by a coherent explanation of the social mechanisms which guarantee that the basic structure of the future socialist society will develop without the design efforts of human agency. (Literal babies, we might assume, are designed either by 'nature' or by 'God'—which is why they don't need designing by humankind—but the analogue of either candidate in the case of the metaphorical socialist infant is scarcely obvious.) In addition, the Marxian claim about the redundancy of socialist design does not look to be warranted by the subsequent development of capitalist societies. The complex empirical claim here—that the basic structure of future socialist society develops automatically, needing human agency only to release it from its capitalist integument—has been rendered less, rather than more, plausible by the evolution of capitalist societies since the deaths of Marx and Engels. This foundational Marxian objection that broadly empirical considerations make socialist plans and blueprints redundant looks increasingly implausible.

5

I am interested here in possible connections between Hegel and these foundational anti-utopian Marxian arguments. However, I should emphasize the narrowness of this remit. It excludes discussion of both positive utopian threads and other kinds of anti-utopian arguments that might be found in Hegel's writings. Moreover, since links with the normative claim seem to me much harder to discern, I focus here on the epistemological and empirical threads in Marxian anti-utopianism.

In pursuing possible connections with Hegel, it is helpful to distinguish between affinity and influence. By an 'affinity' between Hegel and Marx's anti-utopianism, I mean that there exists some resemblance, a similarity of character or content, between the relevant views of the two authors. By the 'influence' of Hegel on Marx's anti-utopianism, I mean that an appropriate causal connection obtains between the two authors; that the earlier author shaped, or otherwise had an effect on, the relevant views of the later one.

So understood, one might have examples of affinity but no influence; two authors could have independently come up with the same, or sufficiently similar, ideas. Less obviously, one might also have influence but no affinity; I take it that *negative* influence, in which my views are formed entirely in rejection of yours, might be of this kind. In addition, there are cases of *positive* influence where affinity and influence typically go together; indeed, where influence is usually advanced as, at least part of, the explanation for the affinity. (Henceforth, references to influence are to this positive variety.)

My focus here is on affinity and not influence. I postpone the question of influence, not because of any skepticism about the concept's explanatory power, but because it is so hard to establish. It has been suggested that one would have to demonstrate: that the later author studied the earlier author; that the later author could not have found the relevant ideas in any other writer; and that the later author could not have arrived at the relevant ideas independently.[19] These last two conditions look overly demanding, but even if reformulated into more 'probabilistic' form, meeting them would require more historical work than is attempted here. However, anyone disappointed by this focus might recall the suggested conceptual priority of affinity—with claims about influence typically coming along later, in order to explain, or cast doubt on, affinity—and read what follows as a first step toward answering the question that interests them.

6

In the 'Preface' (dated June 25, 1820) to the *Philosophy of Right*, Hegel discusses the relation between philosophy and the world, between what—with half an eye on Marx—we might call the relation between theory and practice.[20] Hegel does not provide a systematic argument, but elaborates his perspective using three epigrammatic, and elusive, remarks: the much-discussed "*Doppelsatz*", according to which "What is rational is actual; and what is actual is rational";[21] the philosophical insight that "To recognize reason as the rose in the cross of the present and thereby to delight in the present" involves a reconciliation with "actuality";[22] and the claim that "the owl of Minerva begins its flight only with the onset of dusk".[23] The three remarks are connected but I concentrate on the last of them here.

The owl of Minerva—that is, the sacred bird of the goddess of wisdom—is a metaphor for philosophy, and in the 'Preface' Hegel provides us with examples of how philosophers should, and should not, engage with the social and political world.

What philosophy should *not* be doing, is going around "*issuing instructions* on how the world ought to be".[24] Hegel rejects the approach to the world which might be called "utopian moralising".[25] His contemporary critical target here is Jacob Friedrich Fries, which complicates matters a little. Hegel's contempt for Fries was longstanding, personal, and wholly reciprocated.[26] Hegel had long resented Fries's career success (compared to his own); he held a low opinion of Fries's philosophical work (as a shallow reheating of Kant); and there were complicated political differences between the two (revolving around Fries's republicanism, nationalism, and antisemitism).[27] Hegel's timing is also an issue here. Fries had recently been removed from his chair at Jena, as part of the 'demagogue persecutions' that followed the Wartburg Festival.[28] As a result, the fierce criticism in the 'Preface' looked like kicking someone when they were down; an anonymous contemporary reviewer, writing in the *Hallesche Allgemeine Literaturzeitung*, described Hegel's actions as "not noble".[29]

Given my subject matter, I can bracket the question of how unfair or ill-timed Hegel's charges might be, and simply treat Fries as the placeholder for this misguided account of the relation between philosophy and the world.[30] "Herr Fries" represents a subjective railing against the world, a perspective which promotes the contingent products of imagination "in opposition to what already exists [*dem Daseienden*]".[31] It is a standpoint which fails to understand how far, and in what ways, reason is already embodied in established institutions and customs; a standpoint, consequently, in which emotion replaces reason, doing what one pleases replaces the idea of duty, and "subjective conviction" replaces "*Sittlichkeit*".[32] Fries's republican fantasies—Hegel quotes (loosely) from his Wartburg speech—are said to involve "the setting up of a *world beyond* which exists God knows where".[33] (Although as Hegel wryly remarks, we do in fact know where these imaginary worlds reside, "namely in the errors of a one-sided and empty ratiocination".[34])

Hegel also tells us what philosophy *should be* doing: "[T]o comprehend *what is* is the task of philosophy, for *what is* is reason".[35] Less epigrammatically, philosophy is properly concerned with the finite world only because, and to the extent that, the latter is 'actual' or true to its underlying rationality. The 'actual' here is not synonymous with the existent, since the latter can include both particular entities whose existence is wholly contingent, and entities whose underlying rationality is, as yet, inadequately realized. In the social world, the adequate embodiment of reason is the cumulative historical result of its progressive unfolding in both subjective (philosophy, religion, and art) and objective (social institutions and history) forms. The role of philosophy, in this context, is to comprehend the rationality embodied in social institutions and culture. (As embodiments of reason, the form and content of philosophical science, Hegel remarks, are "essentially inseparable".[36])

Hegel identifies Plato's *Republic* as exemplifying the proper role of philosophy. It is a remarkable choice because that text is thought of as a "proverbial example of an empty ideal", an imaginative portrait of a "world beyond" unrelated to actuality.[37] However, Hegel rejects the conventional view that Plato is a "utopian" theorizer, and insists that what looks like an empty ideal is, on closer inspection, "the embodiment of nothing other than the nature of Greek ethical life [*Sittlichkeit*]".[38] The suggestion is presumably not that the *Republic* accurately describes Greek social and political arrangements, but rather that Plato, nonetheless, captures an essential truth about the ancient world. In particular, Plato understood that Greek ethical life was characterized by an immediate, unreflective, harmony between individuals and society. Indeed, his notorious institutional recommendations—concerning property, family, occupational choice, and so on—were designed to resist the nascent forms of subjective freedom, exemplified by Socrates's moral conscience, that were beginning to threaten that harmony. For Hegel, that Platonic political ambition was bound to fail, but the philosophical achievement here remains intact. Hegel advances a claim about both good philosophy, and the historical context which makes it possible. Just as Greek ethical life reached the beginning of the end of its life, Plato came to grasp both its essential characteristic, and the corrosive force that would destroy it. For Hegel, all good philosophy is, like Plato's work, "its own time comprehended in thought", and the condition for that comprehension is that reason has already unfolded in the relevant institutions and culture.[39]

This is also a way of introducing Hegel's own ambition; namely, to comprehend the rational structure embodied in the *modern* social world. This does not, of course, make the *Rechtsphilosophie* a descriptive, *rather than* a normative, project. Since reason creates and governs the world, the relevant normative standards are, in complex ways, embedded in, and not independent of, the institutions and customs of the day. Moreover, since the rationality of the historical process and divine providence are said to be equivalent, these normative standards are also, in some sense, divine standards. As always, there is a lot going on here, but I focus on the broadly epistemological thread in this anti-utopian account of the role of political philosophy.

For Hegel, the task of *Rechtsphilosophie* is not "to construct a *state as it ought to be*", but rather to recognize the rationality of what exists.[40] It seems that philosophy should not go around telling the world how it ought to be, because it cannot tell the world how it ought to be, and it cannot do that because doing that presumes a kind of knowledge that is impossible to obtain. For philosophy to play a constructive role here it would have to grasp a part of the developmental plan of reason that has not yet unfolded in history, and this is something that it cannot do.[41] Philosophy, for Hegel, comes into the world "too late" to give "instruction as to what the world ought to be"; as "the thought of the world, it appears only when actuality is already there cut and dried after its process of formation has been completed".[42] Indeed, by the time that philosophy comes to paint "its grey in grey"—the allusion is to Goethe—the shape of life which gave rise to it "has grown old" and cannot be "rejuvenated but only recognised".[43] Philosophy is a *post-festum* activity—recall that the owl of Minerva only goes to work ("spreads its wings") when the day's non-philosophical labors are over ("with the falling of the dusk")—and the recognition that it provides is only possible because, and to the extent that, reason has already found expression in the world.[44]

Hegel portrays the utopian as analogous to the braggart in the eponymous fable of Aesop, in that they both claim they can do something impossible. Hegel insists that "[i]t is just as foolish to imagine that any philosophy can transcend its contemporary world as that an individual can overleap his own time or leap over Rhodes."[45] The appropriate response in both cases is to call their bluff: "*Hic* Rhodus, *hic* saltus [Here is Rhodes, jump here]."[46] Of course, utopian plans and blueprints do exist, but only as "opinion" ("a pliant medium in which the imagination can construct anything it pleases"), and emphatically not as instantiations of philosophical knowledge.[47]

Lots of questions remain. One might variously wonder about: the extent and kind of social criticism that Hegel's position still allows; the apparent gap between extant 'Germanic' institutions and those rational arrangements endorsed later in the book; the consistency of the 'Preface' with other parts of Hegel's corpus; and the plausibility of the thought that the essential structure of modernity was already embodied in the world, and so available to Hegel, at the time of writing.

Here I would make two points. First, despite appearances, philosophy might still, on this account, play an emancipatory role. However, it must be a liberation founded on our recognition of, and reconciliation with, the rationality embodied in the modern social world. Second, there looks to be an affinity here with the epistemological thread in Marxian anti-utopianism. Simply put, Hegel appears committed to the claim, both that there is a kind of knowledge of future social arrangements (genuine philosophical knowledge) which is not available to us, and that this lack rules out a constructive role for political philosophy (it cannot tell the world how it ought to be).

7

The central claim of Hegel's *Lectures on the Philosophy of World History* is that "reason governs the world, and that therefore world history is a rational process".[48] The suggestion is not simply that we can discern a pattern in the broad sweep of the past, but rather that this pattern consists in the actualization of some purpose or design. Reason creates and governs both the natural and the social world, but only in the latter sphere is there genuine development, "a change in the direction of completion, an impulse of perfectibility".[49] The unfolding of reason—more precisely, the actualization of the categorical system unearthed in the *Science of Logic* (or what Hegel calls *the* Concept)—constitutes both the driving force, and the end, of human history.

This rational unfolding results in a series of four historical epochs, each characterized by a dominant people (that is, a community which shares institutions and customs, but is not necessarily, or even typically, united in a single state): the oriental world, the Greek world, the Roman world, and the Germanic world. Notoriously, large parts of the globe are thereby excluded from world history, which apparently consists in a surprisingly parochial dance, moving from east to west, around the Mediterranean.

Hegel holds that earlier historical stages are very imperfect embodiments of what later stages will embody more adequately. Humankind gets progressively better at realizing reason, but once they have made their particular contribution, the energy and ambition of particular peoples is seemingly exhausted. They fall aside and play no further historical role of any significance.

Progress culminates in 'the Germanic world', a region officially synonymous with modern Europe, although Hegel's detailed descriptions often give it a more narrowly Teutonic cast. Commentators are divided about both the existence and meaning of the idea of 'the end of history' in Hegel's writings. However, these *Lectures* offer both support for, and some clarification of, the idea: textually, he happily talks of world history having "a final end";[50] and philosophically, as a teleological process, it seems that world history "must have a goal, a final end".[51]

Hegel associates his fundamental claim, that reason governs the world, with the Christian idea of providence. Indeed, he maintains that we can think of the idea (the concept as actualized in the world) as equivalent to God's will, and world history as the progressive "unfolding of God's nature".[52] Hegel is, of course, aware of the historical reality of conflict and suffering—the past appears as a "slaughterhouse in which the happiness of peoples, the wisdom of states, and the virtues of individuals are sacrificed"—but insists that it forms a necessary part of the historical unfolding of reason to which we can be reconciled.[53] So understood, the philosophy of world history, he tells us, is also a theodicy.

Redemption, as well as evil, is a part of this rational unfolding. Given the present concern with utopianism, and the widespread (if misleading) association of utopia and perfection, it is worth emphasizing that, on Hegel's account, the goal of history is the *adequate* (and not the perfect) embodiment of reason. Imperfections are a necessary feature of the finite world—only God is truly actual—witness the persistence in the rational state of divorce, war, and poverty. Yet, from the perspective of humankind, we might say that the Germanic world is as good as it gets.

The place of human agency in bringing this rational social world into existence is perhaps best illuminated by Hegel's discussion of 'the cunning of reason'. The teleological structure of world history is realized only through the activity of individuals. However, Hegel does not imagine that any of us, either individually or in cooperation with others, consciously sets out to advance the cause of reason. What motivates us are conflicting passions, interests, and needs, but the resulting actions aggregate in such a way that the relevant outcomes are both unintended and progressively rational.

Hegel remarks that the idea (the concept as actualized in the world) and the passions of individuals "together form the weft and the warp in the fabric that world history spreads before us", but it seems clear that it is the idea that forms the guiding power, whilst the passions of humanity are the vehicle for its realization.[54] In this context, Hegel's language might sometimes mislead. Consider the famous passage in which he describes the idea as keeping itself in the background, safe from "opposition, conflict, and danger". It is, he continues, "what we may call the *cunning of reason* that it sets the passions to work in its service, so that the agents by which it gives itself existence must pay the penalty and suffer the loss."[55] Despite that occasionally instrumental tone, it seems correct to insist that reason is not an external agent, using individuals as a craftsperson uses a tool. Reason is rather an expression of something immanent in, and central to, our individual and collective lives; its purposes are not alien to the kind of beings that we are.

The guiding hand here, however, remains hidden to historical agents. The rational social world, which seemingly forms the end of history, comes about behind their backs. Those rational structures, we might say, are delivered rather than designed by humankind. In pursuing their own passions and interests, individuals are "at the same time the *means* and *instruments of a higher* and wider purpose, which they know nothing of but unconsciously carry out".[56] In human history, the actions of individuals "produce an effect altogether different from what they intend and achieve, from what they immediately know and desire".⁵⁷ They might advance their interests, but "at the same time they bring about something additional that indeed is implicit in their actions but was not present in their consciousness and intention".⁵⁸ There is a parallel here with the idea of providence, which also forms "a veiled inner power [*eingehülltes Inneres*] that achieves its ends and prevails via the recalcitrant volition of the people".⁵⁹

Note that the striking figures—Alexander, Caesar, Napoleon, and so on—usually known as 'world historical individuals' are no exception to this picture. They may possess buckets of commitment and charisma, but these "great historical figures" are still motivated by their own passions and interests.⁶⁰ They act "in order to satisfy themselves, not others"—shunning conventional standards of individual morality in the process—but thereby manage to advance the cause of reason, owing to the overlap between their particular ends and what the evolution of reason requires at that point.⁶¹ This *practical* grasp of what reason requires explains their significant impact on the world.

It is the good fortune of world historical individuals that they get to advance the cause of reason—this is why we can call them 'heroes'—but they are not conscious creators of the future. (Of course, there is another side to this good fortune; they sacrifice everything to the demands of reason, and tend to die young, are murdered, or end up in exile.⁶²) In particular, for all their impact in bringing the future about, they have no particular input into its content. As one commentator remarks, they turn out to be, just like the rest of us, "servants of a larger purpose, not autonomous creators and masters of events".⁶³

Which brings us to the affinity with the Marxian claim that the unfolding of the historical process makes the design approach redundant; there is no need for us to devise socialist solutions to social problems, because satisfactory solutions will themselves emerge from the historical process. Now Hegel is obviously not thinking of socialist solutions, but the rational social order remains the unintended outcome of individuals, great and small, pursuing their own passions and interests. In both cases, individuals deliver but do not design the relevant historical solution.

8

The overlap between these anti-utopian threads is striking. Roughly speaking, for both Hegel and Marx, we can say: first, that a certain kind of knowledge of future social arrangements is not available to humankind, and this lack rules out a constructive role for social theory; and, second, that satisfactory social solutions emerge from the historical process, needing human agency for their delivery but not for their design. The extent of Hegel's responsibility for Marx's anti-utopianism is harder to establish, but, in identifying these affinities, I hope to have made an initial step—no more than that—toward resolving that question of influence.

As will be apparent, I do not share the Marxian hostility to socialist design, and am not persuaded that plans and blueprints are undesirable, impossible, and unnecessary. This hostility strikes me as theoretically unwarranted and politically problematic:

Epistemological limitations do not make our plans and blueprints useless; the evolving historical process shows little sign of rendering socialist design redundant; and a refusal to reflect carefully on its values and institutions seems unlikely to help create a future society that we would want to live in. Indeed, I rather subscribe to the common-sense view that socialists have good reason to reflect on, and clarify, the institutional and other alternatives to capitalism that they admire and hope to introduce. Consequently, insofar as Marxian anti-utopianism is influenced by a vestigial Hegelianism, the latter is to be regretted.

However, I would not want that negative note to be misunderstood. Readers might recall my earlier disclaimer that possible 'pro-utopian' threads in Hegel's writings simply fall outside my remit here. I should also stress that my interest in the anti-utopian connections between Hegel and Marx is not driven by any overarching conviction about the extent, and merits, of the wider relation between these two authors. Both the extent of Hegel's influence on Marx, and whether that influence is a good or bad thing, depends on the issue in hand. There are plenty of issues—the importance of historical context; the complex interconnections between community and individuality; the basic idea of alienation; and so on—where Hegel's influence looks to redound to Marx's considerable benefit.

In addition, and even in the present context, it should be apparent that there are considerations in Hegel's favor. For example, his account of reason creating and governing the world provides a coherent—I do not say plausible—explanation of the hidden hand here. Marx abandons the idealist account of the relation between reason and the world, but does not seem to appreciate the extent to which those elements sustained the 'Hegelian' conclusions to which he continues to help himself. As a result, Marx is left with no warrant for his redundancy claim beyond a brute—and increasingly unconvincing—appeal to complex empirical fact. (This perhaps helps to explain the whiff of something like bad faith that sometimes lingers in this context; Marx can appear to want these anti-utopian conclusions so badly, that he does not always worry unduly about the reasoning that gets him there.)

Finally, the present discussion supports a (quasi-methodological) lesson that can be endorsed even by those skeptical of my substantive conclusions. Namely, that the benefits of this comparison are considerable and bidirectional. Juxtaposing these two authors illuminates not only historical continuities and ruptures, but also philosophical characteristics and strengths. Simply put, reading Hegel and Marx together can benefit our understanding of both authors. That lesson is confirmed by, but goes well beyond, the anti-utopian threads considered here.

Notes

1   "[A]nd other" because culture and ethos might be constitutive of, and/or a condition for, socialism, and yet not be rightly conceptualized as 'institutional'.
2   Readers worried that this label prejudges the merits of the view might note that the pejorative connotations here can go in either direction; that is, while some disparage 'common sense', others disparage those that lack it.

3   For adjacent distinctions, see Allen Buchanan, *Justice, Legitimacy, and Self-Determination* (Oxford: Oxford University Press, 2007), 38 fn. 44, and Erik Olin Wright, *Envisioning Real Utopias* (London: Verso, 2010), 20–5.
4   See Karl Marx, "The Débat Social," *Marx & Engels Collected Works* (London: Lawrence & Wishart, 1975–2005), Vol. 6, 538 [henceforth MECW]/"Der 'Débat social,'" *Marx Engels Werke* (Berlin: Dietz, 1956–68), Vol. 4, 512 [henceforth MEW].
5   *The Complete Works of Thomas More*, Vol. 4: *Utopia*, ed. Edward Surtz and J.H. Hexter (New Haven: Yale University Press, 1965), 21.
6   See Friedrich Engels, "The Housing Question," MECW 23: 384–5/"Zur Wohnungsfrage," MEW 18: 280.
7   See David Leopold, "The Structure of Marx and Engels' Considered Account of Utopian Socialism," *History of Political Thought* 26, no. 3 (2005): 443–66.
8   See Karl Marx and Friedrich Engels, "Manifesto of the Communist Party," MECW 6: 514–7; "Manifest der kommunistischen Partei," MEW 4: 489–91.
9   See David Leopold, "Marx's Non-Foundational Critique of Utopian Socialism," *Reassessing Marx's Social and Political Philosophy*, ed. Jan Kandiyali (London: Routledge, 2018), ch. 3.
10 This section draws on David Leopold, "On Marxian Utopophobia," *Journal of the History of Philosophy* 54, no. 1 (2016): 111–34.
11 Marx, "First Draft of *The Civil War in France*," MECW 22: 498–9/"Erster Entwurf zum Bürgerkrieg in Frankreich," MEW 17: 556–7. See also Marx, "Notes on Bakunin's Book *Statism and Anarchy*," MECW 24: 520/"Konspekt von Bakunins *Staatlichkeit und Anarchie*," MEW 18: 636.
12 Marx, Letter to Nieuwenhuis, MECW 46: 66/MEW 35: 160.
13 Ibid.
14 Ibid.
15 See Gerald A. Cohen, *If You're an Egalitarian How Come You're So Rich* (Cambridge, MA: Harvard University Press, 2001), 69.
16 Discussed with characteristic brilliance by Cohen in *If You're an Egalitarian*, ch. 3–4.
17 Marx, *The Civil War in France*, MECW 22: 335.
18 See Marx, *Der Bürgerkrieg in Frankreich*, MEW 17: 343.
19 Quentin Skinner, "Meaning and Understanding in the History of Ideas," *Visions of Politics*, Vol. 1: *Regarding Method* (Cambridge: Cambridge University Press, 2002), 76.
20 For a commentary, see Adriaan Th. Peperzak, *Philosophy and Politics. A Commentary on the Preface to Hegel's Philosophy of Right* (Dordrecht: Nijhoff, 1987).
21 Dieter Henrich, "Einleitung der Herausgebers: Vernunft in Verwirklichung," *Philosophie des Rechts: Die Vorlesung von 1819–20 in einer Nachschrift* (Frankfurt: Suhrkamp, 1983), 14. G.W.F. Hegel, *Elements of the Philosophy of Right*, ed. Allen W. Wood, trans. H.B. Nisbet (Cambridge: Cambridge University Press, 1991), §12. Except where noted, translations are from this edition.
22 Hegel, *Philosophy of Right*, "Preface," §15.
23 Ibid., §16.
24 Ibid.
25 Michael Inwood, *A Hegel Dictionary* (Oxford: Blackwell, 1992), 222.
26 Fries was a person "whom Hegel detested and who detested Hegel". Terry Pinkard, *Hegel. A Biography* (Cambridge: Cambridge University Press, 2000), 114–5.
27 Hegel, *Philosophy of Right*, "Preface," §8.

28 Allen Wood suggests that Hegel's animus toward Fries was more personal than philosophical, and more philosophical than political. See editorial notes to Hegel, *Philosophy of Right*, 385–7.
29 For the incident, see Pinkard, *Hegel*, 497–8.
30 On Fries, see Gerald Hubmann, *Ethische Überzeugung und politisches Handeln. Jakob Friedrich Fries und die deutsche Tradition der Gesinnungsethik* (Heidelberg: Winter, 1998).
31 Hegel, *Philosophy of Right*, "Preface," §7 addition.
32 Ibid., §17.
33 Ibid., §20.
34 Ibid.
35 Ibid., §13.
36 Ibid., §3.
37 Ibid., §12.
38 Ibid.
39 Ibid., §13.
40 Ibid., §16.
41 As Inwood has it: "A realistic prediction or proposal of some future social state of affairs would involve unravelling the logical idea beyond that segment of it that which is embedded in history so far." Michael Inwood, *Hegel* (London: Routledge, 2002), 505.
42 Hegel, *Philosophy of Right*, "Preface," §16. T.M. Knox translation.
43 Hegel, *Philosophy of Right*, "Preface," §16. See Goethe, *Faust*, part one, li. 2038–9.
44 Hegel, *Philosophy of Right*, "Preface," §16. T.M. Knox translation.
45 Hegel, *Philosophy of Right*, "Preface," §13.
46 Ibid.
47 Ibid.
48 Hegel, *Lectures*, 79/*Vorlesungsmanuskripte*, 140. References are to G.W.F. Hegel, *Lectures on the Philosophy of World History*, Vol. 1: *Manuscripts of the Introduction and the Lectures of 1822-3*, ed. and trans. Robert F. Brown and Peter C. Hodgson (Oxford: Clarendon Press, 2011), 79 [henceforth *Lectures*]. The texts translated there are G.W.F. Hegel, *Vorlesungsmanuskripte II (1816–1831)*, ed. Walter Jaeske (Hamburg: Meiner, 1995) [henceforth *Vorlesungsmanuskripte*]; and G.W.F. Hegel, *Vorlesungen über die Philosophie der Weltgeschichte, Berlin, 1822–23*, ed. Karl Heinz Ilting, Karl Brehmer, and Hoo Nam Seelmann (Hamburg: Meiner, 1996) [henceforth *Vorlesungen*].
49 Hegel, *Lectures*, 108/*Vorlesungsmanuskripte*, 182.
50 Hegel, *Lectures*, 166/*Vorlesungen*, 56.
51 Hegel, *Lectures*, 167/*Vorlesungen*, 57.
52 Hegel, *Lectures*, 145/*Vorlesungen, 23*.
53 Hegel, *Lectures*, 90/*Vorlesungsmanuskripte*, 157.
54 Hegel, *Lectures*, 147/*Vorlesungen*, 26.
55 Hegel, *Lectures*, 96/*Vorlesungsmanuskripte*, 165. Following H.B. Nisbet's rendering of the Johannes Hoffmeister edition.
56 Hegel, *Lectures*, 94/*Vorlesungsmanuskripte*, 162.
57 Hegel, *Lectures*, 94/*Vorlesungsmanuskripte*, 163.

58 Ibid.
59 Hegel, *Lectures*, 462/*Vorlesungen*, 439.
60 Hegel, *Lectures*, 174/*Vorlesungen*, 68.
61 Hegel, *Lectures*, 175/*Vorlesungen*, 70.
62 See Hegel, *Lectures*, 176/*Vorlesungen*, 70.
63 Joseph McCarney, *Hegel on History* (London: Routledge, 2000), 112.

11

Where Are We Developing the Requirements for a New Society?

The Dialectic of Today's Capitalism from a Hegelian-Marxist Perspective

Eva Bockenheimer

In his famous Preface to "A Contribution to the Critique of Political Economy", Marx summarizes the guiding principles of his studies, claiming that

> no social formation is ever destroyed before all the productive forces for which it is sufficient have been developed, and new superior relations of production never replace older ones before the material conditions for their existence have matured within the framework of the old society. Mankind thus inevitably sets itself only such tasks as it is able to solve, since closer examination will always show that the problem itself arises only when the material conditions for its solution are already present or at least in the course of formation.[1]

If we analyze today's capitalism starting consistently from Marxist presuppositions, we therefore have to ask whether we have developed new productive forces that enable us to overcome capitalism and build a new society. From a Marxist point of view, this question is a vital one: In the face of today's capitalism, with the humanitarian and ecological crisis it produces, the political Left has to find an answer to this question in order to become capable of acting instead of simply reacting or 'managing crisis'.

There is a broad consensus that the nature of work has changed fundamentally in the last fifty years, especially in industrial countries. In debates about the future of work and social transformation, democratic and emancipatory approaches often place high hopes on technical developments such as the automatization and digitalization of work, assuming that such new means of production will provide opportunities for non-capitalist relations of production. The Marxist term *productive forces*, however, has a much broader meaning: It does not simply relate to humans' means of production or *technical* capabilities but to their *own* capacities. In this contribution,

I will therefore present an analysis of the new forms of work organization, which systematically emphasizes newly developed human capacities. The starting point for this consideration is the observation that employees in industrial countries are nowadays increasingly expected to undertake entrepreneurial functions. This is often assessed critically, since employees thereby seem to submit themselves entirely to the capitalist imperative of profitability. However, as I will argue, closer examination shows that this development is an expression of a new productive force: the worker's ability to deal with the social meaning of their work *in* their work. This capacity, it will be claimed, is a fundamental requirement—a material condition—for enabling working people to master their relations of production.

Before presenting this analysis in detail, I will, however, go 'from Marx to Hegel and back'. One could ask: Why not just ignore Hegel's philosophy when dealing with today's capitalism and simply relate to Marx's thought? In what follows, I wish to demonstrate that it is wise to go from Marx to Hegel but not to skip over Marx when returning to the present and looking to the future. It is not my concern to recover those thoughts of Hegel that Marx has allegedly forgotten or wrongly rejected. I support the idea of going back to Hegel for another reason: The confrontation with Hegel's philosophy was essential for Marx's development of historical and dialectic materialism—as Marx and Engels frequently pointed out themselves. Marx developed his critique of political economy, and of capital, in the tradition of dialectical thinking. Marxists today, however, often deny the importance of Hegel's dialectical philosophy to Marx's thought. Thus, to clarify my Hegelian interpretation of Marx's thought, I will first discuss what Marx found in Hegel that challenges us to go back to Hegel in order to understand Marx. With this Hegelian-Marxist background, I will finally approach the question: Where are we developing the requirements for a new society?

From Marx to Hegel and Back

According to Marx's Postface to the 2nd Edition of *Capital*, it is the merit of Hegel that he was "the first to present [dialectic's] general forms of motion in a comprehensive and conscious manner".[2] In their translation from 1887, Aveling and Moore translate dialectic's "general forms of motion" ("allgemeine Bewegungsgesetze") as "its general form of working",[3] and thus they do not capture the *Bewegung*, the *movement* that is characteristic for dialectical thinking. From Marx's point of view, the "rational kernel" of dialectic "within the mystical shell" of Hegel's idealism is that "it regards every historically developed form as being in a fluid state, in motion, and therefore grasps its transient aspect as well".[4] This concerns any form of being, social as well as natural: Any form of being is in a fluid state, in motion, and therefore transient. In its rational form, dialectic "includes in its positive understanding of what exists a simultaneous recognition of its negation, its inevitable destruction".[5] And, I may add here, of its passage into something new through this negation. Even though Hegel's philosophy seems to glorify what exists, according to Marx, dialectical philosophy in its essence or rational kernel is critical and revolutionary, since it does not cling to any state of being or any category of thinking. Hegel stresses this aspect of dialectic himself:

> It is of the highest importance to interpret the dialectical [moment] properly and to (re)cognise it. It is in general the principle of all motion, of all life, and of all activation in the actual world. Equally, the dialectical is also the soul of all genuine scientific cognition ... [A] closer look shows that the finite is not restricted merely from the outside; rather, it sublates itself by virtue of its own nature, and passes over, of itself, into its opposite.[6]

Therefore, when Marx refers to Hegel's philosophy affirmatively, he is interested in what one could call the 'heart' of Hegel's thought: his presentation of dialectic's general forms of movement, rather than any other thought of Hegel in particular. Even though, according to Marx, with Hegel, dialectic is "standing on its head",[7] Hegel still develops its general forms of movement correctly because these general forms are nothing but "the ideal of the material world reflected in the mind of man, and translated into forms of thought";[8] in this way, they capture the movement of the material in general, in the form of thought.

Precisely because Marx refers to the heart of Hegel's thinking and not just to pieces of his work, it is difficult to briefly present dialectic's "general forms of movement" as they are developed by Hegel. I would like to call to mind only one aspect of Hegel's dialectic: the *Bestimmte Negation* (determinate negation) and the *Negation der Negation* (negation of negation). For the *negation of negation* is what Marx explicitly refers to in *Capital* when he talks about the maturing of the new society within the old one—and which, therefore, will lead us back to the present day and to issues of the future after returning to Marx.

According to Hegel, the method of any philosophical science can only be "the consciousness of the form of the inner self-movement of the content of logic".[9] Otherwise, the scientific method would be external to its content and therefore could never grasp it. He goes on: "In the *Phenomenology of Spirit*, I have presented an example of this method with respect to a concrete object, namely *consciousness*. At issue there are shapes of consciousness, each of which dissolves itself in being realized, has its own negation for result—and thereby has gone over to a higher shape."[10]

Thus, in the *Phenomenology of Spirit*, Hegel followed the dialectic of the content itself—in this case, of consciousness as part of the *Realphilosophie*. Hegel points out that, in doing so, there is one important thing to understand:

> The one thing needed to *achieve scientific progress* ... is the recognition of the logical principle that negation is equally positive, or that what is self-contradictory does not resolve itself into a nullity, into abstract nothingness, but essentially only into the negation of its *particular* content; or that such a negation is not just negation but is the negation of *the determined fact* which is resolved ... ; that in the result there is therefore contained in essence that from which the result derives ... Because the result, the negation, is a *determinate* negation, it has a *content*. It is a

new concept but one higher and richer than its preceding—richer for it negates and opposes the preceding and contains it, and it contains even more than that, for it is the unity of itself and its opposite.[11]

Consequently, dialectic is not mere skepticism, because due to the *determinate negation*, there is also a *specific result*. In *The Science of Logic*, Hegel uses the term *bestimmte Negation* (determinate negation) for the first time, namely, when we reach *Dasein* (determinate being)[12] as the result of *Werden* (becoming), in which abstract immediate *Sein* (being) and abstract immediate *Nichts* (nothing) vanish. The English translation of *Dasein* as "determinate being" reveals even more that every *Dasein* is a determinate negation and, as such, a mediated immediacy.

While one could call the determinate negation the principle of movement from one notion to another, the negation of negation adds another aspect: self-relation or mediated identity. In his *Logic*, Hegel refers to it for the first time when he addresses *Etwas* (something). In the so-called "Shorter Logic", he states: "[I]n its passing into another, something only comes together *with itself*; and this relation to itself in the passing and in the other is *genuine Infinity*";[13] and in *The Science of Logic*, Hegel expounds: "*Something* is an *existent* as the negation of negation, for such a negation is the restoration of the simple reference to itself—but the something is thereby equally the *mediation of itself with itself*."[14] Therefore, *negation of negation* is not only a simple movement from one notion to another, but self-relation of notion, its negative unity with itself. The process of *determinate negation* is part of the self-negation of the absolute idea.

Hegel presents the logical development of the *determinate negation* and the *negation of negation* right at the beginning of the *Logic*, but since it is a general law of movement, it is present throughout the *Logic* and *Realphilosophie*; for example, in the *Philosophy of History* and in the *Philosophy of Nature*.[15] Engels calls the *negation of negation* the "fundamental law for the construction of the whole system".[16] This is correct, since the whole process of self-positing, becoming other to itself, and self-restoring of the absolute idea, is a negation of negation. In this way, the absolute idea is real infinity. If it was just the opposite of the finite, it would be determined by its other and would thus be finite itself. As real infinity, it is the process of positing its own negation—becoming a finite—and negating this negation to restore itself. This process is the actual content of Hegel's system.

Although Marx acknowledges that Hegel was the first "to present [dialectic's] general forms of motion in a comprehensive and conscious manner", at the same time, he criticizes Hegel strongly and claims that his own "dialectical method is, in its foundation, not only different from the Hegelian, but exactly opposite to it".[17] Marx's critique mainly concerns two aspects of Hegel's philosophy. First of all, he criticizes Hegel's idealism: "For Hegel, the process of thinking, which he even transforms into an independent subject, under the name of 'the Idea', is the creator of the real world, and the real world is only the external appearance of the idea."[18] Secondly, he accuses Hegel of adjusting the real world to the logical forms of thinking. Due to his idealism, Hegel "does not develop his thinking from the object [*aus dem Gegenstand*], but expounds the object in accordance with a thinking that is cut and dried—already formed and fixed in the abstract sphere of logic".[19] So in Hegel's *Realphilosophie*—against Hegel's claim to simply follow the inner self-movement of the content—"not the logic of the matter, but the matter of logic is the philosophical element".[20] Given the many particular and materialistic insights we owe to Hegel, this is quite exaggerated, but still altogether true, and it helps to point out the difference between Marx's materialism and Hegel's idealism. According to Marx, the scientific inquiry has to analyze in detail the concrete forms of development of its material and to "track down their inner connection".[21] If it works to reflect these inner connections in the presentation of the material, it may appear as if it is the development of the idea itself, an "a priori construction".[22] But in reality, it is nothing but the reflection of the life and the development of the material, reflected in thought.

Now, the content of *Capital* is "the capitalist mode of production, and the relations of production and forms of intercourse [*Verkehrsverhältnisse*] that correspond to it".[23] As a materialist, Marx examines human modes of production because, for mankind, the production of the means of subsistence is a fundamental condition for its existence, a "real premise".[24] It is the production of material life itself and therefore—as Marx and Engels point out in *The German Ideology*—their "first historical act",[25] since there is no history of mankind without the existence of human beings. It is Marx's important materialistic insight that human beings are *not free* in *how* to produce their means of subsistence. The modes of production, on the one hand, depend on natural conditions (e.g., geological ones); on the other hand, every new generation finds modes of production as they are passed on from the previous generation. While producing their means of subsistence, humans simultaneously but unconsciously change the way in which they produce and reproduce themselves; they develop productive forces that enable them to satisfy their wants and needs and, at the same time, produce new wants and needs.[26] According to Marx and Engels, it is through this unconscious, reflective way of producing—and not through their consciousness—that human beings distinguish themselves from animals and are able to "make history".[27] Consciousness is just a result of humans' productive forces, not the reason for them.[28] It is important to keep all of this in mind when talking about Marx's materialistic concept of production. Marx does not reduce human life to economy; he is not a narrow-minded economist. When he studies the different modes of production, he works out the foundation for a comprehensive inquiry of society, since these modes of production essentially determine the way in which human beings produce their material life as a whole, how they reproduce themselves and interact with nature. Therefore, the modes of production ultimately determine the social, political, and spiritual life of human beings as well. But that is not to say, of course, that there is no interaction between social, political, and spiritual processes on the one hand and the modes of production on the other—an interaction that Marx and Engels were quite aware of, even though they stressed the fact that economic premises and conditions were ultimately decisive.[29]

The method of presentation in *Capital* is a dialectical one, because Marx presents the "development of the economic formation of society ... as a process of natural history",[30] from the "economic cell-form"[31] of bourgeois society to its complex form. And the economic cell-form of bourgeois society is the "commodity form of the product of labour, or the value-form of the commodity"[32] that Marx consequently begins with. The analysis of this cell-form can therefore reveal "*all* the contradictions (or the germs of *all* the contradictions) of modern society"[33] and of the capitalist mode of production, as Lenin remarked in the fragment *On the Question of Dialectics*.

Briefly summarized, the contradiction of a society that is based on commodity production, in general, is that it is a social formation in which the communality of production is not presupposed in production even though it is the material basis of it. Therefore, "the social character of production is *established* only *post festum* by the elevation of the products to exchange values and the exchange of these exchange values".[34] In commodity production, individuals produce through private labor, with private means of production, socially necessary and useful things, which are their private property. Thus, they produce within an anarchic social division of labor, independently from each other. Since every one of them produces one particular product only, in reality, all private producers are dependent on each other and forced to exchange their products. It is only through exchange that the individual producers get to know whether their product meets an actual demand and whether the work for producing the good will be acknowledged as socially useful and part of the total labor of society.[35] In the exchange process, the various products of different kinds of labor with very heterogeneous *use-values* are equated as *values*. The substance of the value of the commodity is that it embodies abstract human labor, the expenditure of identical human labor power. The magnitude of the value of a commodity is determined by the labor time that is socially (or on average) necessary for its production.[36] Historically, before the production of commodities became the predominant mode of production, one product of labor was exchanged for another and thereby turned into a commodity.[37] In these practices of exchange, one commodity expressed the value of another and served as its equivalent, until eventually, over time, one commodity—money—acquired the function to count as a universal equivalent.

In a society based on commodity production,

> the labour of the private individual manifests itself as an element of the total labour of society only through the relations which the act of exchange establishes between the products, and, through their mediation, between the producers. To the producers, therefore, the social relations between their private labours appear as what they are: i.e. they do not appear as direct social relations between persons in their work but rather as material [dingliche] relations between persons and social relations between things.[38]

Commodities are—and this is an inherent contradiction—*social* things. They "appear as autonomous figures endowed with a life of their own, which enter into relations both with each other and with the human race",[39] what Marx calls their *fetish character*. In a society based on commodity production, humans are not "expending their many different forms of labour-power in full self-awareness as one single social labour force", as they would in an "association of free men".[40] Therefore, it is a social formation "in which the process of production has mastery over man, instead of the opposite".[41]

Already in feudalism—even though it was based on a subsistence economy—some products became commodities. But with capitalism, commodity production is a basic and dominant feature and a particular commodity has to enter the market en masse: the commodity of labor power. The owner of money buys this commodity on the same fair terms and conditions as any other commodity: He buys it at its value, which is the labor time it takes to (re)produce it: in other words, the value of the means of subsistence that the worker needs for the maintenance of his labor power. But labor power is the only commodity that creates value when being consumed. Now, the money owner exploits the worker by letting him work longer than necessary to produce the value that is necessary for the maintenance of his labor power. In this way, he can extort surplus value. With the exploitation of labor power, by extorting surplus value, money transforms itself into capital: It becomes self-valorizing—a value searching for an accretion of value—and appears to be an "autonomous subject".[42]

Now, in capitalism we formally still have a society based on private production and an unplanned division of labor. But inside capitalist factories, we find socialized production with a planned division of labor, since these factories work "with the combined social forces of a collectivity of individuals"[43] according to a definite plan, as Engels pointed out. This is quite different to the petty commodity production of the Middle Ages. The historical mission of capitalism is to organize socialized production. This, of course, again presupposes the possibility to hire people who have to sell their labor force.

In the Middle Ages, at least in England, workers (as immediate producers) had private property in their means of production and, in general, the individual who produced something appropriated this product to him- or herself. With the possibility to buy labor power and to exploit "alien, but formally free labour",[44] this changes. Now, the owner of capital, since he owns the means of production and can buy labor power for a certain amount of time, appropriates the products of alien labor. Of course, he can only buy labor power as a commodity if there are a certain number of individuals who are free in a double sense: free to dispose of their labor power, but also free of any means of production to actualize this power, so that they need to sell their labor power as a commodity.[45] According to Marx, in the process of history, the commodity of labor power arises, on the one hand, due to the "direct transformation of slaves and serfs into wage-labourers"[46] and, on the other hand, through "the expropriation of the immediate producers", small peasants and artisans.[47] The "fragmentation of holdings, and the dispersal of the other means of production"[48] had become a fetter and had to be annihilated. The individualized, scattered, smallish means of production of the immediate producers are replaced by more productive, socially concentrated ones.[49] More and more people are expropriated and forced to sell their labor power and there is an enormous accumulation of capitalistic private property. This development does not stop, however, with the expropriation of the immediate producers. "Through the immanent laws of capitalist production itself, through the centralization of capitals",[50] more and more smaller capitalists are expropriated by the bigger ones. The number of capitalists constantly decreases with the monopoly of capital. Capitalists are forced to raise capital on an ever-increasing scale to win the rat race. This goes so far that they have to establish joint stock corporations to bring together the necessary mass of means of production and distribution. The crisis forces them to establish trusts for the purpose of regulating production.[51] "Along with the constant decrease in the number of capitalist magnates, who usurp and monopolize all the advantages of this process of transformation, the mass of misery, oppression, slavery, degradation and exploitation grows."[52] It is noteworthy that many aspects of this dynamic of capitalism are also examined by Hegel who in his inquiry on *Civil Society*, in his *Philosophy of Right*, once more shows how well acquainted he is with contemporary scientific research. Hegel notices that capitalism creates an ever-growing impoverishment of the masses and at the same time causes "the concentration of disproportionate wealth in a few hands".[53] But, unlike Marx, Hegel assumes that, in the end, the state is able to master, or at least reduce, the emerging problems; therefore, according to Hegel, the *civil society* can also be considered a moment of the realization of free will. Marx, on the other hand, demonstrates that, due to the immanent laws of capitalism, the bourgeois state *cannot* master this dynamic, and that its actual function is to guarantee capitalist production.

Now, if the growing number of people affected by hunger and poverty was all that played a role in this dynamic of capital, it would be nothing but a deteriorating situation. According to Marx, due to the dialectic of capitalism, there is another aspect to it: As the ruling class in capitalist societies, what the bourgeoisie "produces, after all, is its own grave-diggers".[54] It is the historical mission of capitalism to organize social production in the factory with socialized means of production and masses of cooperating workers. But, in this way, the proletarians are "trained, united, and organized by the very mechanism of the capital process of production"[55] itself. Capitalism produces the class that wants to abolish class rule: the proletariat. Proletarians are certainly not only blue-collar workers, but everyone who is forced to sell their labor power to earn their living—Marx mentions teachers as well as actors or clowns, for example.[56] The "*antagonism between the organisation of production in the individual workshop, and the anarchy of production in society generally*"[57]—as well as the contradiction of socialized production in the individual factory and capitalist appropriation—becomes more and more obvious, and finally, "the centralization of the means of production and the socialization of labour reach a point at which they become incompatible with their capitalist integument", that is, with the capitalistic mode of appropriation by only a few capitalists. "The knell of capitalist private property sounds. The expropriators are expropriated."[58]

To grasp this historical process as a whole, Marx refers to the general dialectical law of the negation of negation: The first negation is the negation of feudal, individual private property, based on the labor of its owner, by capitalistic private property:

> But capitalist production begets, with the inexorability of a natural process, its own negation. This is the negation of the negation. It does not re-establish private property, but it does indeed establish individual property on the basis of the achievements of the capitalist era: namely co-operation and the possession in common of the land and the means of production produced by labour itself.[59]

Put this way, we can understand this entire historical process as the development of individual property. For an association of free men, in which "the free development of each is the condition for the free development of all"[60]—as Marx and Engels famously put it in the *Manifesto of the Communist Party*—individual property, thanks to which everyone can satisfy their wants and needs, is essential. But Marx demonstrates that the requirement for individual property for everyone, for the satisfaction of everybody's wants and needs on a *high level*, is conscious social production. Conscious social production is not the abolishment of individual property but is in fact its realization. At the beginning, we had individual property only as the scattered, limited, narrow private property of the immediate producers. Capitalism negates this in favor of planned and socialized production, setting enormous productive forces free, but expropriating masses of people from all means of production. At the same time, it produces the proletariat as a social force that can overcome the capitalist mode of appropriation in favor of individual property: This time not scattered, limited, and narrow as in the beginning, but based on the "possession in common"[61] of the land, of the means of production, and of their own cooperative relations. This process results in what Marx called an

> association of free men, working with the means of production held in common, and expending their many different forms of labour-power in full self-awareness as one single social labour force ... The total product of our imagined association would be a social product. One part of this product serves as fresh means of production and remains social. But another part is consumed by the members of the association as means of subsistence. This part must therefore be divided amongst them.[62]

In contrast to a society based on commodity production, in this association of free men, "*the social character of production* is presupposed, and participation in the world of products, in consumption, is not mediated by the exchange of mutually independent labours or products of labour. It is mediated by the social conditions of production within which the individual carries on his activity."[63]

So according to Marx—as a dialectical thinker—the analysis of capitalism necessarily leads us 'back to the future'. Because, due to capitalism's internal contradictions and its own economic laws, the material conditions and requirements for overcoming it mature in its own womb—unconsciously and unintentionally—until they are so far developed that we can finally recognize them.[64]

From Marx to the Future as Present

If we take this Hegelian-Marxist background seriously and try to get back to the present and the future, we know that we cannot simply ask: What is our *ideal* for the future? Dialectical materialism teaches us that we're not simply free to determine our mode of production as we please. So, the question is rather: Where are we developing the requirements for a new society? Have we developed new productive forces that will allow us to free ourselves from the laws of capitalism? And to establish a socialist society that this time will not deserve to fall? After the legitimate fall of socialism and its failure, it requires courage to even ask these questions. But on the other hand, the humanitarian and ecological crisis of capitalism forces us to do so—and if we are able to seriously ask them and set ourselves this task, maybe Marx and Engels are right and the material conditions to solve them must "already be present", or at least "in the course of formation"?[65] To approach and reinforce this question, I will outline the thesis that Stephan Siemens develops in his book *Das unternehmerische Wir*[66] (The Entrepreneurial We). Based on my analysis of Hegel's and Marx's thoughts above, I wish to demonstrate that Siemens presents a very consistent Hegelian-Marxist examination of our present day.

In current sociological debates on the changing nature of work, it is often noticed that employees today have more and more entrepreneurial responsibilities. Management expects employees to act and think entrepreneurially. Well-known books that discuss this phenomenon are, for example, *The New Spirit of Capitalism* by Eve Chiapello and Luc Boltanski,[67] *From Employee to "Entreployee"* (Arbeitskraftunternehmer) by G. Günter Voss and Hans J. Pongratz,[68] *The Culture of the New Capitalism* by Richard Sennett,[69] and *The Entrepreneurial Self* by Ulrich Bröckling,[70] just to name a few. In spite of their different approaches, they all share a critical assessment of this phenomenon, or at least an evaluation of it, as highly ambivalent. In contrast, in his book *Das unternehmerische Wir* (The Entrepreneurial We), the Hegelian-Marxist philosopher Stephan Siemens elaborates an emancipatory aspect of this development that is usually overlooked. Siemens confirms that workers today are expected to undertake entrepreneurial functions. He claims, however, that capitalists and their managers do not pass the entrepreneurial functions on to the workers of their own free will. In fact, capitalists and their managers have to adapt to a new productive force of the workers, which they have to "skim" in order to "survive" the global rat race.[71] This new productive force is workers' ability to deal with the social meaning of their work *in* their work. They used to do that after work—in church, all kinds of associations or political parties—but not *during* work or *in* work itself.[72] The old way to organize work—early industrial work and so-called 'Fordism'—was based on a system of 'command and control'. Workers were by and large reduced to simple heelers and appeared as a mere "appendage of the machine".[73] For a long time, this was regarded as the most rational form to manage workflow, and it was very productive, even though workers were hostile to it. It seemed inconceivable to organize work without a strict hierarchy and a system of command and control, because in these working conditions, workers seemed to be lazy and simple by nature.

It was not until the 1950s that, in Silicon Valley, it became obvious how productive it could be to organize work differently.[74] In the emerging IT business, work could no longer be organized by command and control, since no one would have known what to command. So, managers had to count on the ability of their employees to decide *what* to do and *how* to do it. They soon recognized the huge productive potential of their employees, especially in team work; over the course of time, other capitalists from all kinds of branches followed this path—advised by management consultants— since they realized how much profit would otherwise slip through their fingers. Thus, capitalists actually didn't have a choice—they had to pass the entrepreneurial functions on to their employees to maximize their profit and according to Siemens, in this way, they adapted to a new productive force.[75]

But how can capitalists actually pass the entrepreneurial functions on to their employees without immediately losing control? How can they ensure that the workers exert their new productive force in their favor, which means that they deal with the social meaning of their work regarding nothing but business profit? To make sure that workers focus on business profits, companies use an instrument that, in the German debate, is called *Indirekte Steuerung* ('indirect steering' or 'indirect control')—a term invented by Klaus Peters and Stephan Siemens. In contrast to 'command and control', with the search for direct control, management nowadays steers workers indirectly by creating an 'environment' and certain 'framework conditions' that make them react just as desired. Part of this 'environment' is the formation of an artificial market within a certain company.[76] Since the so-called free market is mainly characterized by competition, management organizes the cooperation of employees as a form of competition; this cooperative competition is called 'coopetition'—a portmanteau of cooperation and competition. To imitate a market environment within a company, management builds teams, profit centers, business units, and so on, which have to prove their profitability and are compared with other teams, suppliers, or subsidiaries.[77] With Fordism, the wageworkers did not have to worry about the effects of their work or whether the production process kept on running smoothly once they left their place of work. According to Siemens "meanwhile, this has changed fundamentally".[78] "Today, working means that a specific product has to be ready by a specific date and to a determined price with a determined gain."[79] Above all, the team has to decide on its own what it has to do to accomplish this task, since that changes all the time; the team works in a more or less self-organized manner. Managers no longer give instructions but simply check the outcome.[80] Their main task is to create the environment and to set the framework conditions that place the necessary pressure on the team to actually perform the entrepreneurial functions and take on responsibility. There are a number of such framework conditions: Employees are confronted with certain key figures to evaluate their performance and to compare it with the performance of other competing teams. They are provided with a minimum budget and staffing to make them cope with as few resources as possible. Through constant reorganization and restructuring measures, employees are forced to ascertain again and again what they actually have to do and how they can prove their profitability. 'Management by objectives' (MBO) and other management techniques create a feeling of personal 'commitment' to the entrepreneurial tasks.

According to Siemens, employees now have a dual role: As individuals, they have to do their work just like before. Then again, they are part of an entrepreneurial team, and they have to organize their cooperation within this team.[81] Suddenly, they have to prove to themselves, to the other team members, and to their management, that they personally contribute to the entrepreneurial success of the team; furthermore, they are concerned about the entrepreneurial accomplishments of their team and demand excellent work from their colleagues. Employees are often torn between their individual interests, on the one hand, and their interests as team members on the other.[82] Managers, usually informed by organizational psychology, know how to take advantage of the resulting unconscious group dynamics to increase profits. Experiments in organizational psychology have shown, for instance, that a team that has been moderately deprived of human or financial resources will try as much as possible to accomplish its task nevertheless. In such situations of change, the team tends to return to its original activity level to hold what Kurt Lewin would call its "quasi-stationary equilibrium".[83] This means, for example, that team members will stand in for absent colleagues, go to work despite being ill, or take on additional responsibilities to compensate for the lack of resources. For the companies, this dynamic has a high cost-saving potential. For employees, however, it often leads to psychological stress for different reasons: On the one hand, some of the team members, under these circumstances, overestimate and overwork themselves and some cannot cope with the new demands. On the other hand, personal conflicts between the team members emerge systematically in such situations. Therefore, instead of sticking together to criticize the bad working conditions and demand new staff and a larger budget, overstrained employees tend to accuse their colleagues of lacking commitment and team members begin to pressure or even attack each other. Since this dynamic usually remains unconscious, it is a permanent source of stress for the members of the team, and managers as well as employees are often unaware of the fact that it can lead to burnout at worst, as Siemens points out.[84]

Even though Siemens acknowledges that the new organization of work has a negative impact on the health of employees, as a Hegelian-Marxist, he reminds us that these entrepreneurial functions once were the capitalist's actual *productive function*.[85] And indeed, according to Marx and Engels, in the course of capitalism, capitalists gradually lose their productive function—which is to organize social production—since they pass it on to managers, who take care of the organization of work, the administration, and the supervision of workers, while the capitalist maintains ownership for the exploitation of labor. The manager's function in capitalism has a double nature, as Marx points out: On the one hand, he has to act on behalf of the capitalist and therefore represents the supremacy of capital over labor,[86] while on the other hand, he is himself a (highly paid) proletarian, who has a productive function: to organize combined labor. By passing this productive function to the manager, "the capitalist has become no less redundant as he himself ... finds the big landowner redundant".[87]

If today management passes more and more entrepreneurial functions on to the combined workers, this is quite consistent, since these are productive functions and can therefore increase the productivity of workers. For managers as well as workers, this new task has a double nature: On the one hand, it is a new form of what Marx called a *real capitalist subsumption*, since it changes the way of working itself. The personal cooperation of workers now appears to be nothing but a function of capital, since they are burdened with the corporate goals to gain profit.[88] While with Fordism the individual worker was subsumed under capital by his or her single specific activity at the assembly line, he or she is now forced to devote his or her entire individuality to the maximization of profit. Workers become a 'human resource', 'human capital'. They act within the supremacy of capital and thereby reproduce it.

But on the other hand, these functions are, as Siemens points out, productive ones. In capitalism, profitability is the criterion to decide whether a certain labor is socially meaningful and productive. It certainly is quite a confined criterion, since it involves the conflation of productivity and profitability. Nevertheless, it is the way in which, in a society based on commodity production, the social character of production is reflected after all. Through market and profit orientation, the entrepreneur reflects the socially useful character of his company's products, as well as their ability to serve as a commodity and to be acknowledged as a product of abstract labor. To be successful, he constantly strives to improve the forms of cooperation, the means of production, the ways of distributing products, and so on and so forth. So, by appropriating the entrepreneurial functions, workers deal with the social character and meaning of their work in the confined form of profitability. Or to put it in Hegelian terms: They deal with meaningful content in a perverted and confined form. The ability to organize labor and combined cooperation efficiently and economically, and to think about the socially useful character of labor, is useful for mankind and always will be. Even though in capitalism it only serves to intensify work and to exclude people from the working process, in a future society it could actually help us to reduce the amount of work that is necessary and give us time to do other things. Because these abilities are productive, it is a good thing that workers develop them right now and start to appropriate them. Only because they are unconscious of their new productive force does it appear to them as an alien power.

Marx often mocks the narrow-mindedness of the capitalist criterion of profit to decide whether a certain labor is socially meaningful and productive.[89] The ecological and humanitarian crisis produced by capitalism forces us to deal with this capitalist confinement concerning productive labor. In capitalism, the ecological and social impact of the products of our labor and of their production process can only be considered as far as they do not limit profit expectations. Right now, employees are beginning to deal with this confinement, since they are expected to deal with the social character and meaning of their labor. In contrast to a real entrepreneur, they can reflect on the difference between productive work and profitability because, for them, profit is not an end in itself. They are not real entrepreneurs or subsumed under entrepreneurship, but only perform entrepreneurial functions as combined workers who have to sell their labor power. In a certain way, they are interested in the company's success as it secures their job, but far too often, they lose their job when the company booms. Workers increasingly experience that they know how to produce more reasonably with respect to the ecological and social impact of their work, but are hindered by the capitalist mode of production. In this way, they experience the difference between productivity and profitability.[90] This can be quite a crucial test. While the capitalist owes his existence to the confinement to profit and therefore, *as capitalist* (although not as a human being), he has no interest in overcoming it, workers will want to change the mode of production as soon as they understand that it has become—to speak with Marx—a fetter to their newly gained productive force.

To sum up: According to the analysis of Siemens, as wage-earners we presently learn how to deal with the social meaning of our work *in* our work itself—although through the confined criterion of profit. We learn how to jointly and autonomously organize cooperation; due to the global market within major corporations, we do that on an international level. The ability to relate all of our activities to social labor as a whole and to organize our forms of cooperation ourselves is an essential requirement for a new society. In this way—as Hegel would say—the 'working class' (in a broad sense) today learns to produce socially for-itself (*für sich*) not only in-itself (*an sich*).

If we look at the current change of work from this angle, we do not primarily see the decline of bourgeois moral values and achievements, which allegedly had to be stopped to prevent worse—such as fascist barbarism—but we can recognize that it is actually, at the same time, the development of something new: It is the beginning of a new productive force that workers are not yet able to fully unfold, because they have to cooperate within the limits of private companies. If this analysis is correct, it would be the task of the political Left to raise the consciousness of the people for this development and to support the workers to autonomously appropriate this new productive force.

Of course, this is only one aspect of current developments, but from a Hegelian-Marxist perspective, it is a decisive one. For it is to be hoped that the conscious development of this new productive force, besides other current developments, will enable us to establish a social formation through which we can jointly satisfy our wants and needs and have mastery over the process of production. In this new society, this time, not just their representatives but the working people themselves would master the process by relating their many individual activities to the needs of society as a whole.[91] Individuals would not be subordinated to society as a whole but—quite the contrary—would be able to appropriate it jointly and individually. In this way, socially planned production and individual freedom would be compatible, just as Marx had claimed it for an "association of free men", or, to be quite clear, let us say: an 'association of free humans'.

Notes

1. Karl Marx, *A Contribution to the Critique of Political Economy* (New York: International Publishers, 1987), 263 (MECW, Vol. 29).
2. Karl Marx, *Capital. A Critique of Political Economy*, Vol. I, intro. Ernest Mandel, trans. Ben Fowkes (London: Penguin, 1990), 103. In the following, the short-title Marx, *Capital I*, refers to this edition.
3. Cf. Marx, *Capital: A Critique of Political Economy*, Vol. I, ed. Friedrich Engels, trans. Samuel Moore and Edward Aveling (MECW 35: 19).
4. Marx, *Capital I*, 103.
5. Ibid.
6. Georg Wilhelm Friedrich Hegel, *The Encyclopaedia Logic*, trans. Theodore. F. Geraets, Wallis A. Suchting, and Henry S. Harris (Indianapolis: Hackett, 1991), §81A 1, 128–9.
7. Marx, *Capital I*, 103.
8. Ibid., 102.
9. Georg Wilhelm Friedrich Hegel, *The Science of Logic*, ed. and trans. George Di Giovanni (Cambridge: Cambridge University Press, 2010), 33.
10. Ibid.
11. Ibid.
12. I use *determinate being* as a translation for *Dasein*, since this translation is widely accepted; please note, however, that in his new English translation of *The Science of Logic*, Di Giovanni has decided to translate *Dasein* as *existence* (see ibid., lxviii).
13. Hegel, *Encyclopaedia Logic*, §95, 151.
14. Hegel, *Science of Logic*, 89.

15 Most prominent is Hegel's example of a flower; cf. Hegel, *The Phenomenology of Spirit*, trans. A.V. Miller, with Analysis of the Text and Foreword by J.N. Findlay (Oxford: Oxford University Press, 1977), 2. This is also cited by Friedrich Engels in his *Dialectics of Nature* (MECW 25: 502), and in his *Anti-Dühring* (MECW 25: 126).
16 Engels, *Dialectics of Nature*, 356.
17 Marx, *Capital I*, 102.
18 Ibid.
19 Karl Marx, *Contribution to the Critique of Hegel's Philosophy of Law* (MECW 3: 14).
20 Ibid., 18.
21 Marx, *Capital I*, 102.
22 Ibid.
23 Ibid., 90.
24 Cf. Karl Marx, Friedrich Engels, *The German Ideology* (MECW 5: 31).
25 Ibid., 42.
26 Cf. ibid.
27 Ibid., 41, cf. also ibid., 31.
28 Cf. ibid., 43–5.
29 Cf., for example Friedrich Engels, *Letters 1893, Engels to Mehring, July 14 1893* (MECW 50: 164) and Friedrich Engels, *Letters 1890, Engels to Bloch, 21–22. September 1890* (MECW 49: 35).
30 Marx, *Capital I*, 92.
31 Ibid., 90.
32 Ibid.
33 Vladimir Ilyich Lenin, *On the Question of Dialectics* (Moscow: Progress Publishers, 1976), 358–9 (LCW, Vol. 38).
34 Karl Marx, *Outlines of the Critique of Political Economy* (MECW 28: 108).
35 Cf. Engels, *Anti-Dühring*, 292.
36 Cf. Marx, *Capital I*, 129.
37 Ibid., 181.
38 Ibid., 165–6.
39 Ibid., 165.
40 Ibid., 171.
41 Ibid., 175.
42 Ibid., 255.
43 Engels, *Anti-Dühring*, 257.
44 Marx, *Capital I*, 928.
45 Cf. ibid., 272.
46 Ibid., 927.
47 Cf. ibid.
48 Ibid., 928.
49 Ibid.
50 Ibid., 929.
51 Cf. Engels, *Anti-Dühring*, 639.
52 Marx, *Capital I*, 929.
53 Hegel, *Hegel's Philosophy of Right*, trans. and with notes by T.M. Knox (Oxford: Oxford University Press, 1967), §2.
54 Marx and Engels, *Manifesto of the Communist Party* (MECW 6: 496) and Marx, *Capital I*, 930, Footnote 1.

55 Marx, *Capital I*, 929.
56 Cf. ibid., 644, and Karl Marx, *Economic Works 1861–63* (MECW 31: 13).
57 Engels, *Anti-Dühring*, 261.
58 Marx, *Capital I*, 929.
59 Ibid.
60 Marx and Engels, *Manifesto of the Communist Party*, 506.
61 Marx, *Capital I*, 929.
62 Ibid., 171–2.
63 Marx, *Outlines*, 109.
64 Cf., for example Marx, *A Contribution to the Critique of Political Economy*, 263–4.
65 Ibid., 263.
66 Cf. Stephan Siemens with Martina Frenzel, *Das unternehmerische Wir: Formen der indirekten Steuerung im Unternehmen*, 2nd edn (Hamburg: VSA Verlag, 2014).
67 Luc Boltanski and Eve Chiapello, *The New Spirit of Capitalism* (London, New York: Verso, [1999] 2007).
68 Hans J. Pongratz und G. Günter Voß, *Arbeitskraftunternehmer: Erwerbsorientierungen in entgrenzten Arbeitsformen* (Berlin: edition sigma, 2003). "Arbeitskraftunternehmer" can be translated as 'entreployee' or as 'self-entrepreneurial work-force'. An overview of their ideas in English can be found in: Hans J. Pongratz and G. Günter Voß, "From employee to 'entreployee': Towards a 'self-entrepreneurial' work force?" *Concepts and Transformation* 8, no. 3 (2003): 239–54.
69 Richard Sennett, *The Culture of the New Capitalism* (New Haven: Yale University Press, 2007).
70 Ulrich Bröckling, *The Entrepreneurial Self: Fabricating a New Type of Subject* (London: SAGE Publications, 2016).
71 Cf. Siemens, *Das unternehmerische Wir*, 131–56.
72 Cf. ibid., 12–3.
73 Ibid., 133.
74 Cf. ibid., 16–8.
75 Cf. ibid., 131–56.
76 Cf. ibid., 20–1, and 139–42.
77 Cf. ibid.
78 Ibid., 12.
79 Ibid., 13.
80 Cf. ibid., 13–4.
81 Cf. ibid., 21.
82 Cf. ibid., 22–3.
83 Cf. ibid., 100–2.
84 Cf. ibid., 157–8.
85 Cf. ibid., 14–5 and 131–3.
86 Cf. Marx, *Capital. A Critique of Political Economy*, Vol. III (MECW 37: 384).
87 Ibid., 385; see also the following paragraphs.
88 Cf. Marx, *Economic Works 1861–63* (MECW 30: 260).
89 For a prominent example cf. Marx, *Economic Works 1861–63* (MECW 34: 128).
90 Cf. Siemens, *Das unternehmerische Wir*, 152–6.
91 Cf. ibid., 148–56, and Marx, *Capital I*, 171.

12

Social Freedom beyond Capitalism

Three Alternatives

Hannes Kuch

How is it possible today to regain a sense of real alternatives to our current economic order? This is obviously a pressing issue, given the growing discontent with capitalism that we have witnessed during the past two decades, spurred by the fact that capitalism proves itself to be increasingly crisis-prone. It is also clear, however, that there is a gap—a disproportionate gap even—between our knowledge of the flaws of capitalism on the one hand and our knowledge of any viable, desirable alternative to it on the other. The various criticisms of capitalism are well known, and were developed and updated by generations of Marxist, Critical, Feminist, and other theorists. The most important arguments are that the capitalist order is entrenched with unjust class structures; that it comes with a structural tendency to increase social inequality; that it threatens democratic self-determination; that it spurs the maximization of profits, making the pursuit of ever more profits a never-ending rat race; that it is marked by an expansionary drive to commodify ever wider spheres of social life; and that it erodes public solidarity and promotes social anomie. The list of criticisms could be extended. So we do know how to criticize capitalism, but we have much less knowledge about how to replace it.

On closer inspection, the situation is less desperate than at first glance. In recent years, a growing number of institutional proposals and social practices are being explored that might help us guide the way to a postcapitalist society. My aim in this chapter is to examine three of the most prominent alternatives to capitalism debated in contemporary critical thought, and I will do this building on ideas developed by Hegel and Marx. The first, immediate question, then, is: Is it even possible to carry out this task following these two thinkers? Even if it turns out to be possible, is it a promising and fruitful thing to do? These questions lead me to the first part of the chapter. In each of the subsequent three parts, one distinct economic practice that may count as an alternative to capitalism is examined: *Commons economies*, where people make productive contributions to satisfy the needs of others voluntarily, without coordination mechanisms such as markets or state planning (Part II); *democratic planning*, with a special focus on attempts to institutionalize planning procedures respecting the value of personal choice and without the need for overly centralized institutions (Part III); and *market socialism*, where goods are bought and sold in markets, but where these goods are produced within enterprises that are collectively owned in one way or another (Part IV). These alternatives are connected to reflections in Marx, and more controversially also in Hegel, and then discussed within the context of systematic debates in contemporary political philosophy. It goes without saying that in what follows, I can offer no more than a sketchy map of a large territory; but I think it is of vital importance to consider which alternatives there are in the first place. Moreover, we will see that we can only really assess each of these alternatives by comparing them with one another.[1]

I. Hegel, Marx, and the Alternatives to Capitalism

Hegel and Marx were opposed to drawing blueprints of future societies. Marx gave some vague indications as to how a communist society should look, yet he never went into detail.[2] He scorned the idea of inventing "recipes" for the "cook-shops of the future".[3] Among the major reasons for Marx's reticence is that he thought construing concrete alternatives to capitalist society to be more or less superfluous: He was certain that a postcapitalist society would simply work better, by freeing human productivity from its capitalist "fetters".[4] According to him, modern capitalism, while on the brink of collapsing, was already "pregnant"[5] with real alternatives to it, so that theorists could leave open the task of inventing concrete institutional alternatives to the spontaneous action of social movements. Nor *should* theorists interfere in the creative process of social change; the reason being that Marx considered proposing concrete blueprints of a postcapitalist society from the safety of the philosopher's armchair to be undemocratic and paternalistic—as if theorists "had the solution of all riddles lying in their writing-desks, and the stupid, exoteric world had only to open its mouth for the roast pigeons of absolute knowledge to fly into it".[6] Thus the latter argument is a normative one about the undemocratic, paternalistic nature of concrete proposals, while the former is an empirical argument about the superfluity of such proposals.[7]

Both the superfluity argument and the paternalism argument are flawed, however. Historical materialism holds that truth—in the words of Adorno and Horkheimer—has a "temporal core";[8] that is, truth crucially depends on concrete historical and social contexts. What was true in the nineteenth century might be wrong today, and in fact, the conditions have radically changed: There are hardly any utopian socialists left today; quite to the contrary, many people have given up hope of *any* alternative to capitalism, not least because the 'actually existing socialism' proved to be a dismal failure. We have not only lost faith in the idea that a postcapitalist society would be as productive as a capitalist society, we also have reasons to worry that any alternative to capitalism might turn out to be a totalitarian nightmare. Thus, the critique of capitalism would be much more convincing today if we were to face the task of making explicit what concrete alternatives to capitalism might look like. Vague references to a completely different, intangible world are unpersuasive. Once this argument is conceded, it implies an acknowledgment of the institutional challenges to be faced: It urges us to take into account that in construing alternatives to capitalism, we are confronted with various problems of social feasibility, of unintended social consequences, of coordinating economic action under conditions of social complexity and at least moderate forms of scarcity, and so forth. All of these challenges are serious and have to be addressed accordingly.

The normative argument about the undemocratic character of theoretical proposals articulates a more troublesome concern. Construing institutional proposals might easily give the impression that the theorist assumed the superior position of the army general on the commanding hill, or that individuals and social relations could be engineered at the drawing board, just like the architect manipulates stones, walls, and rooftops. From this real danger it does not follow, however, that utopian abstinence and a resort to pure negativity are the appropriate responses. The negative dimension of Marxist and Critical Theory is surely indispensable, yet a relapse from any kind of utopianism risks playing into the hands of the status quo: Regardless of how radical the critique of capitalism might be, it can always be countered by the argument that—to rephrase Churchill—capitalism is indeed the worst economic system, except for all the others. Attempting to tame capitalism might then appear more realistically feasible and desirable than any other option. Thus, the response must be to acknowledge the indispensability of exploring alternatives to capitalism in a concrete and sufficiently detailed way. It is true, however, that this cannot mean coming up with an ultimate solution that would have to be implemented only through a top-down process. Any institutional proposal is nothing more than that: a proposal to be discussed and amended in an ongoing learning process, in dialogue with social movements, practitioners, and the broader public.[9] Hence, developing institutional proposals is not necessarily undemocratic. But one can even go a step further and turn the tables: The truly undemocratic attitude may, in fact, be to remain vague and reticent. This is because there are surely people who raise questions and doubts; in this situation, it is overbearing not to respond. To decline the discussion and resort to one's uncompromised vagueness is to invite undemocratic dogmatism where, ultimately, some sectarian vanguards claim to be in exclusive possession of a superior, yet inaccessible, knowledge. Being responsive to doubts and queries of skeptics means leaving the free-floating stance of utopian reticence and get involved in the democratic process, by trying to face up to the challenges posed in this process; gradually, one will thereby begin to work out one's proposals ever more concretely.[10]

Despite all these critical revisions of Marx's approach, his critique of capitalism is indispensable for any constructive exploration of alternatives to capitalism. Real utopian proposals have to cope with the challenges that Marx's analysis poses, especially with regard to the dynamics that markets, money, labor, capital, and so on unleash. And even if Marx's indications of a postcapitalist society are rare and vague, they provide fertile grounds for envisioning an alternative form of life.

So much about "Marxian Utopophobia",[11] but what about Hegel's? Isn't it even more difficult to theorize alternatives to capitalism following him? His explicit statements are known well enough. He insisted that political philosophy "must be removed as far as possible from any attempt to construct a *state as it ought to be*",[12] since he claimed that the "actual" is already "rational".[13] To many readers, this seemed to tie Hegel to a conservative defense of the current state of his days, the Kingdom of Prussia, but there is also a progressive reading, claiming that Hegel rather meant that certain core institutions of modern society already embody some degree of rationality. It is important to note that the rational form of society Hegel envisions in the *Philosophy of Right* does not conform to any of the existing societies of his time, and it has never actually existed in the precise form outlined by Hegel.[14] In addition, as we will see in the fourth and final part of the chapter, elements of Hegel's institutional proposals stand in opposition not just to the empirical reality of his own time, but to market capitalism as such. It might also be worthwhile to recall the subversive utopianism of the young Hegel: "Once the realm of imagination is revolutionized, actuality will not hold out."[15] In other words, ideas do matter when it comes to bringing about social change. I would not go so far as to read Hegel's statement in a naively idealistic way, as claiming that a few good ideas will suffice to change a bad reality. Surely and crucially, this also depends on the strength of social movements and the proliferation of heterodox social practices. But with Hegel's claim in mind, it is possible to see that the strength of social movements is itself not independent from the availability and cogency of alternative visions to the prevailing social conditions.[16]

Now, even if it is possible to think about alternatives to capitalism with Hegel and Marx, it remains to be clarified why we *should* do so. The main reason is that both Hegel and Marx shared the same highly attractive idea of social freedom, which serves us well in guiding the construction and assessment of institutional alternatives to capitalism. Hegel and Marx agreed that true individual freedom can be attained only in social relations. When we think of freedom as social freedom, then the other is not an obstacle or a limitation to our freedom; she is rather a precondition of it—or even an enlargement of our own freedom.[17] To think of freedom as essentially social in nature, to think of it as involving dependency, community, and attachment to others, is certainly a radical thought. For in the everyday use of the term 'freedom,' others often appear as barriers to our own freedom: If you are stuck in a traffic jam, the other car drivers are indeed an obstacle to your freedom. In contrast to this, for Hegel, the paradigmatic case for explaining the social nature of freedom is friendship: Here, individuals realize their selves and their individual freedom precisely in being related to others, in being committed to them, in caring for them; in a true friendship, all these determinations and obligations are not experienced as limitations; they rather constitute the framework within which friends realize themselves *as friends*.

Without going into further detail, I only want to hint briefly at the normative justification of social freedom in Hegel and Marx. Marx's justification of this notion of freedom is grounded in a particular ethical ideal, which in turn rests on his anthropology of species-being.[18] On my reading, Hegel's justification is less demanding: He puts forward a stability argument that attempts to spell out the minimal stability conditions of liberal freedom, comprising negative freedom, moral autonomy, and collective self-rule. In Hegel's political philosophy, these various dimensions of liberal freedom are shown to be dependent on institutionalizing freedom as *social* freedom in the three fundamental social spheres of modern society that are indispensable for social reproduction: the family, the economy, and the state. Hegel's basic idea is that in all these three spheres, a vivid sense of solidarity, particularly solidarity in our economic practices, is necessary in order to realize the various dimensions of liberal freedom.[19]

II. Commons Economies

In one of Marx's early unpublished works, in the "Comments on James Mill"—a text that for a long time stood in the shadow of the much more famous *Economic and Philosophic Manuscripts*, both of which were written in 1844—Marx sketches a fascinating picture of communal relationships in a postcapitalist society.[20] Marx's vision is centered on the idea that, in producing for others, individuals can be genuinely concerned with satisfying the needs of others. Here, producers would not produce instrumentally as a means to a self-interested end, for the sake of getting something in return, for example money or goods; rather, individuals would be genuinely responsive to the other's needs. The needs of others would be the reason for the individual to produce a particular good, and the other's use of the product would be part of the realization of one's own ends in engaging in productive activity.[21] It would give me the pleasure of knowing that I have satisfied a vital human need: "In your enjoyment or use of my product I would have the *direct* enjoyment ... of being conscious of having satisfied a *human* need by my work."[22] In the society Marx envisions, individuals would be responsive to each other's needs; they would not be indifferent to one another.[23] This means that in the communist form of production, producing for each other would be a way of recognizing one another: In producing for others, I would "become recognised and felt by you yourself as a completion of your own essential nature and as a necessary part of yourself, and consequently would know myself to be confirmed both in your thought and your love".[24]

Marx is quite explicit in that his ideal of communal relationships can be realized only in the absence of private property, money, legal rights, and the contractual form.[25] In Marx's early vision of a postcapitalist society, social interaction is built on the model of an unmediated, non-instrumental, horizontal relationship between peers. Communal relationships as envisioned by Marx are incompatible with the social indifference and instrumental attitudes associated with market exchanges. According to the early Marx, neediness characterizes our human essence, and thus recognition means recognizing one another as essentially needy human beings. In effect, this implies that recognizing the particular needs of others gives us sufficient reason to produce things that may satisfy these needs. As Andrew Chitty explains, people would produce for others "just because they recognise each other as fellow human beings with needs, in the sense that they identify each other as such, and are thereby disposed to produce things so as to satisfy each other's needs and to make these things unconditionally available to each other".[26] Marx considered these communal production–consumption patterns to be the main activities in which human beings could realize their freedom as dependent, needy beings. Since this freedom can be achieved only in a social context that is interpersonal, voluntary, and horizontal in nature, Marxian freedom essentially is social freedom.

If we try to think of Marx's vision as a real-world practice, it certainly sounds 'merely' utopian in a pejorative sense, but on a second look, it is much less so. Consider, for example, the success of digital gift communities such as the online encyclopedia Wikipedia.[27] Here, people contribute articles simply for the reason that they see the need for them to be written, without conditioning their contribution upon any reward or service in return. Certainly, the writers of articles are also readers of other texts on Wikipedia, but their own production of a text is not directly contingent upon others also contributing texts. On Wikipedia, a vast number of people contribute voluntarily and freely to produce a new form of knowledge, while simultaneously enjoying the fruits of their common effort. Thus, Marx's vision of a truly human form of production is not merely utopian; it is already accomplished in our actual social practices; in fact, it is effective to such an extent that it could largely crowd out the market for commodified encyclopedias. We can also leave the domain of the digital world and see that there are real-world *material* practices functioning along the same lines: Just think of the domain of care work in a household context; feminist scholars have argued that this domain has been excluded from our dominant conception of 'economy' for a long time, with the effect that care work and housework have become invisible as valuable forms of economic practice.[28] But this kind of work is, in fact, carried out as a voluntary, unpaid, non-marketized activity, where the satisfaction of the needs of others is the very reason for carrying out the activity.[29]

What these diverse activities in the digital and the material world have in common is that through them, people make productive contributions to satisfying the needs of others, without directly receiving payment, and without coordination mechanisms such as markets or state planning. Theorists of the commons coming from a social democratic tradition hold commons economies to be a third sector beyond the market and the state.[30] There are, however, also critics of capitalism, such as David Graeber, Silvia Federici, and Michael Hardt and Antonio Negri, who consider commons economies as something that could be the basis for the transcendence of capitalism.[31]

Yet there are several reasons for doubting the optimism of some of the proponents of commons economies. To begin with, there is the problem of coordination. It may be no surprise that commons economies function so well in the digital world, for here, products can often be completed step by step, in a modular way: Online encyclopedias can already be used in the fairly early stages of development; in addition, they can always be improved, whereas many products and services in the material world need to be completed in a determinate form before they can be used. One cannot live in a house unless the windows, doors, and roof have been completed. This implies that the cooperative production of material goods has to be coordinated in a fairly complex way, yet precisely the coordination of the productive activities of a large number of people is a very difficult thing. It is questionable whether this can be possible without coordination mechanisms such as markets or economic planning.[32]

A *second* problem is the question of how to ensure *cooperation*. How can we rely on communal production–consumption patterns being reciprocal in the long run, so that the production of a certain good by someone is sooner or later reciprocated by the production of others? This difficulty stems from the fact that in Marx's ideal, reciprocity must not be conditioned upon contracts, a barter product, money, or legal sanctions. Reciprocity has to be realized freely and voluntarily. Marx seemed to think that fully human work would be a means to the creative self-realization of humans as productive beings, so why people should be motivated to reciprocate the services of others would not really be a question. But not all human needs can be satisfied by creative, fulfilling work. This leads to the problem of who does the 'dirty work', that is, unsatisfactory, exhausting, or boring work, like cleaning toilets? In order to ensure a form of cooperation that is not too lopsided, some form of social coordination might be inevitable.[33] It is only through an institutionalized practice that we can decide what social needs exist to be satisfied, which working activities are to be carried out, and an assignment of responsibilities along a common plan. Yet, if this is true, we would have already left Marx's ideal of a horizontal form of voluntary cooperation. Instead, we would have entered the realm of economic planning through the medium of social institutions, with vertical relations between individuals and institutions, and with the institutional platform of self-determination having enforcement rights upon individuals.[34]

A *third* problem is that commons economies often require strong communities to function. It is true that *when* close communal ties obtain, commons economies often do work well without institutionalized forms of coordination, so that voluntary cooperation can be upheld even where dirty or boring work has to be carried out. This is made possible, to a large degree, because these economies are embedded in local communities, neighborhoods, families, and networks of friendships. Whatever the differences between these various forms of communality, their shared characteristic is to be limited in terms of range and confined in their nature. For this reason, these communities tend to limit individual freedom, by subjecting the individual to parochial norms and traditions, just as they are in danger of excluding outsiders.

Despite the three problems outlined, Marx's ideal of social freedom in its interpersonal form is, as such, an appealing ideal, which spells out social freedom in an attractive way. Even if it might not be viable to fully realize this ideal on a larger scale, it is, in itself, an ideal that is good and valuable. It is a matter of debate to what degree this form of social cooperation could be—and should be—extended; but it is much less debatable that human beings have much greater powers of voluntary, non-instrumental cooperation than many conservative or liberal thinkers acknowledge.

III. Democratic Planning

The early Marx spelled out social freedom in an interpersonal, horizontal way, whereas the later Marx gradually turned to another vision of social freedom: social freedom in its *holistic* form. In the first form, social freedom is realized in the free, cooperative interaction with others, while in the second form, social freedom is realized through the collective autonomy of a social whole. Here, individuals attain their freedom through determining their selves in the medium of a self-determining collective.[35] We might experience this kind of freedom when, for example, collaborating in a team: Facing a particular task that can be solved only collectively, the team members sit down, discuss the work to be done, and then assign responsibilities among themselves. If all goes well, every team member has good reason to recognize herself in the joint action and the collaborative achievement.[36]

Now, the most important issue for the present purposes is that the holistic form of social freedom is, in principle, capable of dealing with the problem of coordinating economic action and ensuring fair cooperation among members. In this vision of social freedom, economic action might be organized by a conscious and deliberate process of collective planning. What could this process look like? At some points in his work, notably in the *Communist Manifesto*, Marx encouraged the idea that it would suffice that the masses take over centralized state power and bring all means of production under their control.[37] The state would then figure as the central planning authority. In later works, particularly in his writing on the Paris Commune, Marx gradually shifted toward a more decentralized, participatory approach: Here he argued that the planning process should be based on decentralized, self-governing bodies of producer assemblies. The historical experience of the Paris Commune demonstrated, according to Marx, that the "old centralized government" could be replaced by "the self-government of the producers",[38] and indeed Marx even considered the Paris Commune as an attempt at "a Revolution against the *State* itself".[39] So the hope was that the decentralized democratic self-government would eventually lead to a 'withering away of the state'.[40]

Obviously, with these claims, Marx aimed at saying that a communist society would have overcome the bourgeois state in its oppressive form. But overcoming the capitalist state is not tantamount to getting rid of all forms of centralized institutional platforms that stand in a vertical relation to individuals and that have some kind of enforcement rights over them—which is precisely the minimal definition of nothing else but the state. At times, Marx acknowledges this problem, for example, when he pointed to the requirement that the "united cooperative societies" would have to "regulate national production upon a common plan".[41] This is an important issue: Without such a centralized harmonization of production, the allocation of goods and services could not be fair and just, and it might not even function at all. It can be expected that sectarian attitudes among producers would then proliferate, encouraging the various groups of producers to pursue their own particular projects at the expense of the needs of other groups of society; for example, people living near the coast might see no need to fish above their own immediate consumer demand, resulting in a neglect of the society-wide demand for fish. The need to coordinate the planning process at higher and more centralized social levels implies that social relations will be *vertical* to some degree, with social relations moving from individuals up to the coordinating institutions and then top-down again. Unfortunately, Marx did not see the need to provide a more detailed account of how such planning procedures could be organized democratically; to some extent, he even gave the impression that one could evade the problem entirely.[42]

At any rate, one can still argue that as long as the collective institutions are ruled democratically, and as long as they are least based on participatory self-governing local assemblies, they may be rationally endorsed by everyone, with everyone acknowledging the determination of his or her own individual action by the collective institutions as an expression of his or her own free self-determination. Yet in effect, this would mean that a large part of our lives would be governed by binding instructions from higher-level boards, committees, and assemblies telling us what do. Thus, vertical relations such as these, crucial for realizing social freedom in its holistic form, run into the danger of being experienced by individuals as petrified and alien, hence eventually undermining precisely the value of social freedom itself. So, the result is this: We've seen that commons economies have the virtue of being structured horizontally while having problems with securing comprehensive cooperation and coordination. Democratic planning faces the reverse problem: It is holistic—and in this sense comprehensive—from the outset, but it now turns out that it is in danger of giving rise to overly vertical relations.

Instead of reassessing the disputes between state-socialist and council-communist approaches on this issue, I shall take a closer look at a contemporary, highly sophisticated proposal that aims to steer clear of all these problems: Michael Albert and Robin Hahnel's 'Participatory Economy'.[43] Its most remarkable ambition is to function precisely without the need for a central planning office that would have to be vested to set up a comprehensive plan and entitled to issue binding instructions. Hahnel, an economist, and Albert, an activist, propose a nested structure of worker and consumer councils mandated to democratically develop and decide a comprehensive consumption and production plan. Instead of a central planning office, a highly particular quasi-market is built into the center of the participatory economy. Effectively, this means that bare figures, that is, prices, will do much of the coordinating work between the councils. Still, what Hahnel and Albert propose is not an ordinary market as we know it, with ad hoc pairs of buyers and sellers attempting to push through their private interests at the expense of transaction partners, unrelated third parties or competitors who are driven out of the market. Instead, the quasi-market of a participatory economy would be thoroughly embedded in a fundamentally democratic framework, with everyone having the same voice in shaping the benefits and burdens of economic cooperation.

At the basis of the model are worker and consumer councils, complemented by federations of councils at higher levels.[44] Personal consumption requests are submitted at the level of neighborhood consumer councils that merely gather the information, with no ultimate rights of disapproval. The planning process begins with consumers articulating their consumption requests, by announcing what he or she plans to consume in the year to come. Everyone has free choice in his or her consumption decisions, with the only limit to one's budget being individual work offers; hence, one simple way to expand one's budget is to work longer hours. Work offers, on the other hand, are articulated within the context of worker councils making production proposals for the coming year. They declare what inputs they want to employ in order to produce a particular output.

What prices do the consumer and worker councils use when deciding production pledges and consumption requests? This is where the so-called "Iteration Facilitation Boards" enter the scene.[45] They provide councils with "indicative prices",[46] signaling the estimates of the opportunity costs of the various inputs, including natural resources, labor, and capital stocks, as well as the estimates of the social costs of production.

The latter costs include the negative and positive externalities caused by producing or using a good or a service. Opportunity costs, on the other hand, reflect how much benefit society has to forgo when deciding to produce a particular good requiring a particular mix of labor power, natural resources, and capital goods instead of the next best alternative good.[47] So, for example, if an IT expert whose talents are very scarce decides to work in another sector with a higher work supply, say the baking business, then his decision would imply very high opportunity costs. Typically, with every additional good or service of a particular type, the opportunity costs increase while the social value of the good or service decreases. In our scenario, with every additional baker, the social value of providing bread decreases while the lost benefit increases, due to the fact that there is one additional baker who decides against providing his services in branches with an undersupply of work pledges, say the IT sector; in other words, the opportunity costs go up.

At the outset of the planning process, the indicative prices are based on the prices of the previous year. When the planning process begins, the major function of the indicative prices is, of course, to approximate supply and demand. Given the consumption requests and production pledges, the facilitation boards calculate updated indicative prices by aggregating the total consumer requests and work pledges. Initially, there will probably be an excess demand for goods and services, and too few production offers, particularly in undesirable fields of work. This is where indicative prices come in to do their work, signaling excess demand or supply shortages, thus helping to balance the disparity between overall supply and demand.

From the perspective of worker councils, indicative prices make transparent to everyone the relationship between the estimated social benefit of a production pledge and the estimated social and opportunity costs. If the ratio is less than 1, this signals that another use of the resources (land, labor, capital) would be socially more useful. In that case, the other councils are entitled to disapprove of a particular production proposal. The higher the ratio between benefits and costs, the better for society as a whole.[48] The crucial point of all this is to provide all members of society with an opportunity to form an educated judgment about what a socially responsible decision requires in regard to their consumption and work activities: "Unless I know the opportunity costs of resources a work proposal requires, unless I know the social costs of producing the intermediate inputs needed, and unless I can compare these costs to the social benefits of the outputs the workers propose to deliver, how can I sensibly decide if a work proposal is socially responsible?"[49] Concretely, this means that if it turns out that the ratio between the benefits of a proposal and its costs is too low, the individuals have reason to change their plans (and the other councils the right to disapprove of a particular proposal). The worker council can then either decide to try to economize on the inputs, or else shift the production proposals toward more beneficial outputs.[50]

In Hahnel and Albert's scheme, another iteration round in the planning process begins with the goal of bringing supply and demand even closer. The data of the consumption requests and production pledges are computed again by the facilitation boards, which will probably notice that the overall work supply and the overall consumer demand are now better balanced. The planning procedure goes on for a few iterations—Hahnel and Albert expect that there will be five rounds altogether—until supply and demand correspond. In the final round of the planning procedure, the facilitation boards present several comprehensive production and consumption plans, either of which would achieve a viable equilibrium. Between these competing plans, a democratic vote decides.

What are we to make of Hahnel and Albert's proposal? To begin with, their proposal is admirable for making the systematic effort to meet the tough issue of democratic planning head on, and in sufficient detail. Most notably, the merit of Hahnel and Albert's participatory democracy is that it allows all producers and consumers to freely articulate, and even to form, their consumer choices and their work pledges in conscious consideration of the wishes and offers of the other members of society. For this reason, the participatory economy would come quite close to realizing social freedom in its holistic version, without the need for a centralized authority and vertical relations.

Despite these ethical and institutional virtues, there are, however, a number of problems: The first one—which immediately springs to mind to many people—is inconvenience and complexity.[51] Just think of the task of announcing a list of every single consumer wish you might have during the coming year, and think about being called to go through the long list and revising it over and over again during the various iterative rounds of decision-making. The more fine-grained the categories among which to choose from, the better one's personal choice can be taken into account—but the more complicated the process. Yet the more abstract the selectable categories remain, the larger the disparities between real demand and supply in the year to come, and the greater the frustration on the part of consumers.[52]

A second problem is that there are several reasons why the higher-level federations and the iteration boards need to have a great deal of power. Federations not only make decisions about public goods at higher levels,[53] they also have to decide ongoing economic adjustments during the year.[54] In addition, they have to decide on investment in research and development as well as all larger credits regarding risky production proposals.[55] These are numerous and substantial decisions to make. To be sure, Hahnel emphasizes that it is important "to design appeals procedures federations can use to handle unusual cases where 'the numbers lie'".[56] But it remains unclear how the procedures are designed in detail, and here details do matter. Similar problems pertain to the iteration boards: They have to decide the precise quantification of the qualitative information that should be taken into account by calculating the indicative prices. Yet qualitative decisions about positive or negative externalities of particular goods or services are a highly conflict-laden issue. This is a huge challenge, and the fact that Hahnel and Albert seem to underestimate it might stem from their partial complicity in cherishing the economist's illusion of solving social problems with the help of bare numbers and allegedly neutral mechanisms. But numbers and mechanisms will not do the work, at least not to a sufficient degree; instead, an entire range of contested issues have to be solved in a democratic way. The fundamental problem here is that the more there is at stake to decide, and the more substantial the conflicts over qualitative assessments are, the greater the need for a centralized institution that may legitimately claim to have the final say. The danger, then, that lingers in the background is that there are quite a few occasions for top-down decisions in the end, going from the highest-level federations all the way down to local councils and individuals, while at the same time, the democratic legitimacy of these enforcement claims remains unclear at best.[57]

Another problem stems from the absence of direct market competition. It is important to see that when worker councils make production proposals, the ratio of benefits to costs crucially depends on the number of similar proposals in that sector. If there is an oversupply of proposals, the opportunity costs of each of the 'competing' enterprises are high. In case the number of competing enterprises were to decrease in the next planning round, the benefit to cost ratio of the remaining enterprises would automatically increase, all else being equal. Thus, in the absence of direct market competition, each enterprise is tempted to hope that the competing enterprises withdraw to other sectors first. This might induce worker councils to start 'gambling': They might place a bet on being capable of holding out the longest among the competing enterprises, for example by only cosmetically modifying their original proposal in the next planning rounds. Obviously, this would gravely undermine the spirit of participatory planning. Yet I do not see how the problem is solved in Hahnel and Albert's scheme. It is certainly laudable that the participatory economy aims to eschew the coercive forces of market competition. But this absence leaves a gap: How are enterprises induced to shift to sectors that are socially more beneficial? My worry is that this is yet another factor that increases the need for top-down instructions from higher-level federations. Considering this objection in conjunction with the previous one, it becomes clear that Hahnel's proposal is in danger of realizing participation only superficially while, in effect, having to rely quite heavily on vertical relations with a strong tendency to ossify.

IV. Market Socialism

Let us now turn to the third alternative to capitalism. According to the concept of 'market socialism', there is a world beyond capitalism where markets still play an important role, yet have been transformed so fundamentally that this would amount to a transcendence of capitalism. If capitalism, according to Marx, means a market economy with the means of production in private ownership, then, in principle, it is possible to think of an economic system that is non-capitalist in the sense that enterprises are collectively owned in one way or another while these enterprises still sell goods in consumer markets. The market-socialist idea has a long tradition, going back as far as the 1930s, and was partly put into practice in Yugoslavia in the postwar period; as a theoretical concept, it was widely discussed and further developed in the 1990s, and it resurfaces now in a variety of philosophical contexts.[58] When we include the nineteenth-century cooperative movement in the concept of market socialism, then the idea is even older.

From the perspective of social freedom, the market-socialist option is only the third best one, as we shall see later. Commons economies and democratic planning are at least in some respects superior in realizing the value of social freedom; the difficulties these models face partly stem from problems of feasibility and partly from their conflict with other essential values, be it personal choice or democratic legitimacy. The market, on the other hand, is in some fundamental ways inimical to the value of social freedom itself. But still, its potential for social freedom is greater than some might expect. Market-socialist models can be taken to aim at realizing the implicit potential for social freedom that lies dormant in the capitalist market, by fostering social freedom *internally*, and not primarily by way of external regulation or *ex post* redistribution. In fact, the crucial point is that welfare capitalism aims to tame the market from the outside, through state regulation and redistributing economic incomes merely after the fact, while leaving the basic structure of the market untouched, namely, the privatized structures of property ownership. Market-socialist approaches, in contrast, aim to alter the market in terms of its *constitutive* rules; they aim to transform the market from within, through its most basic rules and institutions.

But why hold on to markets at all? In the previous discussion of the participatory economy, it became clear that markets have an important *functional* role to play: They are decentralized coordination mechanisms balancing supply and demand, with prices functioning as information signals for buyers and sellers. From a Hegelian perspective, markets also allow for the realization of some *ethical* virtues: First, they are, essentially, a form of free association between individuals; there is no superior institution instructing individuals what to do. Second, markets are based on *horizontal* relations between peers, at least in principle. It is true that these horizontal relations come in the form of contractual agreements, yet, precisely for this reason, market relations are horizontal relations between independent equals. Finally, markets cultivate freedom as *social freedom*, if only tacitly and to some degree; for in a market context, you can only freely satisfy your own needs and wishes if you contribute to satisfying the needs and wishes of others.[59] By acting in the market, individuals experience—again, at least implicitly—their freedoms as interdependent, that each can only realize his or her individual freedom in a common, cooperative endeavor.[60]

Hegel is often viewed as someone arguing for a "capitalism with a human face",[61] as a kind of inventor of social democratic welfare capitalism. That's surely not far wrong. It is, however, also possible to read Hegel as suggesting that a rational form of economic cooperation rather points in the direction of market socialism, and this is mainly because of the fundamental role that 'corporations' play in Hegel's theory of ethical life: They can be viewed as cooperative associations.[62] Of course, as is often the case with Hegel, rather than a definitive answer to a problem, this proposal can only count as an inspiring framework for it. In any case, it would be wrong to belief that Hegel, with his institution of the corporation, simply wanted to restore the old, pre-modern guild system, which had just been abolished in Prussia in Hegel's time. Rather, Hegel construed corporations as genuinely *modern* institutions, for example, comprising, among others, the free choice of one's profession. Most importantly, what Hegel had in mind were small enterprises of craftspeople who carry out their businesses on an associated, cooperative basis—Hegel literally speaks of the 'cooperative' (*die Genossenschaft*)[63]—which makes it clear that corporations are hardly compatible with the division between property owners and wage-laborers characteristic of the capitalist firm.[64] In the ideal cooperative, all employees are also the owners of the firm, and all owners are its employees. While the cooperative excludes the hierarchy between capitalist and wage-laborer, the only acceptable hierarchy within the cooperative enterprise is the one between master craftsman and apprentice, where the latter is expected to start his own business with his fellow craftsmen on an equal footing sooner or later. The members of Hegelian corporations are also collectively organized in more encompassing associations within the branch of their discipline, allowing for agreements on shared norms and standards in regard to the work process and product. We have now reached the point where it becomes obvious that Hegel himself participated in outlining a rationally construed social arrangement that stands in sharp opposition to market capitalism.

It is beyond doubt that Marx was always deeply critical of attempts to establish socialist institutions that leave any space for the institution of the market. He was a hardnosed critic of the predecessors of twentieth-century market socialism, most explicitly Robert Owen and Pierre Proudhon's proto-market-socialist proposals, and he surely would have rejected contemporary market-socialist approaches. There are at least two reasons for Marx's criticism: The first is that, in his view, there cannot be any market without capitalist structures and dynamics emerging sooner or later. Even if a system of generalized commodity exchange could be established that would not allow for a class division between capitalists and wage-laborers, it would be impossible for this economic system to not, at some point, begin to exhibit precisely those dynamics that are characteristic of capitalist economies—namely, an autonomization of profit imperatives that start to lead a life of their own, subjecting individuals to their dictates. That is, I think, how the transition from commodity to money to capital in the first volume of *Capital* has to be read.[65] Marx's second argument against the market is that even if a completely non-capitalist form of the market were possible, it would still, *as a market*, fundamentally impede the realization of social freedom. This claim is more clearly articulated in the early Marx.[66] Here, the major argument is that markets dissolve the social bond, pitting us against one another, inducing each of us to push through our own interests at the expense of our transaction partners, our competitors, or unrelated third parties.[67]

I think market-socialist approaches are well advised to take Marx's critique of the market very seriously, and in fact there are contemporary market-socialist approaches that can be criticized along the lines of Marx's arguments. At the same time, it would be wrong to locate Marx's critique on such a fundamental, categorical level, that every analysis of market-socialist institutions would always already be decided from the start. Before making generalized assessments of market-socialist proposals, we should take a very close look at the specific arrangements of particular institutional designs.

This is surely not the place to go into detail about how market-socialist institutions would look if they were robust enough to do justice to Marx's objections. But I would like to at least hint at what it principally means to transform the constitutive rules of the market, in contrast to merely regulating the market more rigidly. Consider a market socialism based on producers' cooperatives, where the producers working in an enterprise also own and manage the enterprise themselves. Here, the exploitation of workers by private capitalists is ruled out from the start. There is no longer a capitalist maximizing profitability by squeezing labor power. This stands in stark contrast to welfare-state capitalism, where the profit-maximizing behavior of capitalists has to be held in check by numerous labor regulations and mitigated by ex-post redistribution. From the capitalist's perspective, these regulations mainly appear as limiting obstacles; hence, he tries to strain or to sidestep these regulations wherever possible, which in turn necessitates even more control and regulation. In a producer cooperative, on the other hand, such exploitative dispositions are ruled out from the start, and at the same time, working within such cooperatives establishes—as the name suggests—a *cooperative* framework of thinking and acting within the enterprise.

Another example of what it means to transform the market in terms of its most basic rules is an unconditional basic income, which is a social benefit great enough to satisfy one's material, social, and cultural needs, categorically awarded to every citizen. It is afforded irrespective of the other incomes one accrues, and it is not conditional on productive contribution—and not even the willingness to do so.[68] The basic income changes the constitutive rules of the market in a very specific sense: It radically transforms the material entry and exit options for market participation, so that failure in the market or unemployment is completely detached from the question of individual survival. This means that the basic income ensures that people can opt out of relations where competitive pressures force them to take advantage of the vulnerabilities of others, for they will no longer have to fear losing their means of subsistence.

With these two institutional transformations, I only intend to give an impression of what it could mean to transform the market *from within*, through its constitutive rules. From the perspective of the Marxian critique of capitalism, there are at least two crucial issues that need to be addressed before market-socialist proposals could even claim to be satisfying. Without going into detail, I shall briefly mention two challenging problems: The first is how the producer cooperatives would be financed in a market-socialist scheme, and the second issue is how the external, alien pressure exerted by competition could be sufficiently transformed. As long as these two problems remain unsolved, it will be quite certain that a market-socialist arrangement elicits the problematic dynamics of capitalism as we know it. Yet, again, the market-socialist tradition offers a variety of different proposals that aim to solve these two problems. As regards the external financing of enterprises, the classical market-socialist solution is to introduce public ownership of all means of production, with capital being lent to the enterprises for a fee.[69] If, however, cooperative ownership should remain the basic corporate form, then the problem of funding might be tackled by requiring shareholding by the state in each enterprise, or additionally allowing for external, private shareholding, where the power of the shareholders might be curtailed by granting external private parties only non-voting shares.[70] Concerning the regulation of competition, there are proposals to strengthen the role of civil associations in order to expand the discursive negotiations on decent work standards and fair trade arrangements between market actors.[71]

In conclusion, one can say that it is difficult to consider how commons economies could ever be capable of functioning on a larger scale; nevertheless, this vision is vital for providing a guiding ideal in times when we might be too caught up in muddling through the challenges of piecemeal reforms. Democratic planning as well as market socialism provides different accounts of feasible and desirable alternatives to capitalism: As long as vertical relations in a democratic form of planning are sufficiently participatory and deliberative both upward and downward, the demands of collective autonomy might be met. Market-socialist proposals are able to demonstrate that markets can be transformed in their constitutive institutions to a satisfying degree, so that the implicit potential of market relations to realize horizontal relations of social freedom comes to the fore. Even if market socialism might only be the third best alternative, it embodies a real alternative to capitalism. To some degree, it even integrates the merits of the other two models, without buying into their downsides: The horizontalism of commons economies, opposed to the verticalism that planning models imply, is preserved in the form of the peer-to-peer connectedness embodied in market exchange. Moreover, the aspect of non-instrumental voluntarism also characteristic of commons economies receives appropriate room and resources for its partial realization by means of a basic income. Collective autonomy, on the other hand, embodying the fundamental value of democratic planning, is also incorporated—in virtue of the democratic cooperativism in the enterprises, which are, in turn, embedded in an associative democracy built on egalitarian civil associations. Still, I would not go so far as to claim that market socialism is the only option in which to place our resources in thinking about alternatives to capitalism; but market socialism is *one* significant alternative. To be sure, our studies of the alternatives to capitalism should be as diverse and wide ranging as possible; I have presented merely an overview of three major possibilities. There are certainly more.

Notes

1. I leave aside John Rawls's proposal of a 'property-owning democracy', which he sees as an "alternative to capitalism"; John Rawls, *Justice as Fairness* (Cambridge: Belknap Press, 2001), §41. By equalizing the 'predistribution' of social wealth, a property-owning democracy could largely overcome one important dimension of capitalism: its class structure. But it would leave in place private ownership in the productive means. Thus, despite its abolition of class domination, it would still give room to the structural dominance of capital over work.
2. The most detailed reflections—comparatively speaking—can be found in the "Critique of the Gotha Programme," *Marx & Engels Collected Works* (London, 1975–2005), Vol. 24: 75–99. A helpful recent study is Peter Hudis's *Marx's Concept of the Alternative to Capitalism* (Chicago: Haymarket, 2013).
3. Marx, *Capital I*, Afterword to the 2nd edn, MECW 35: 17 (translation amended).
4. Marx, *A Contribution to the Critique of Political Economy*, MECW 29, "Preface," 263.
5. Marx, "The Civil War in France," MECW 22: 335.
6. Marx, "Letters from *Deutsch-Französische Jahrbücher*," Marx to Ruge, September 1843, MECW 3: 142.
7. According to David Leopold (in this volume), these are two of Marx's 'foundational' charges against making concrete proposals for a communist society. Another foundational charge, which I bracket here, is an epistemological argument about the impossibility of knowing what a postcapitalist society might look like.
8. Adorno and Horkheimer, *Dialectic of Enlightenment: Philosophical Fragments*, Preface to the New Edition (1969) (Stanford: Stanford University Press, [1944] 2007), xi.

9   This is where I would situate Erik Olin Wright's idea of 'real utopias', which is close to the thrust of my overall argument; see Wright, *Envisioning Real Utopias* (London: Verso, 2010).
10 I have dealt here mainly with Marxian arguments; for a similar critique that focuses more strongly on Adorno, whose anti-utopianism is even more radical than Marx's, see Bini Adamczak's brilliant epilogue in *Communism for Kids* (Cambridge: MIT, 2017), 71–101.
11 David Leopold, "On Marxian Utopophobia," *Journal of the History of Philosophy* 54, no. 1 (2016): 111–34.
12 Georg Wilhelm Friedrich Hegel, *Outlines of the Philosophy of Right*, trans. T.M. Knox; rev. and ed. Stephen Houlgate (Oxford: Oxford University Press, 2008), 15.
13 Hegel, *Philosophy of Right*, 14: "*What is rational is actual, and what is actual is rational.*"
14 See Frederick Neuhouser, "The Idea of a Hegelian 'Science' of Society," in *A Companion to Hegel*, ed. Stephen Houlgate and Michael Baur (Hoboken: Blackwell, 2011), 281–96.
15 Hegel to Niethammer, October 28, 1808, in *Hegel: The Letters*, trans. Clark Butler and Christiane Seiler (Bloomington: Indiana University Press, 1984), 179 (translation amended; H.K.).
16 See also Nick Srnicek and Alex Williams's *Inventing the Future* (London: Verso, 2015) on the need for developing long-term goals and institutional proposals on a larger scale. Their role model is how neoliberal ideas attained cultural hegemony in an enduring struggle spearheaded by a network of neoliberal think tanks.
17 See Neuhouser, *Foundations of Hegel's Social Theory: Actualizing Freedom* (Cambridge, MA: Harvard University Press, 2000), and Axel Honneth, *Freedom's Right: The Social Foundations of Democratic Life* (New York: Columbia University Press, 2014), for an articulation of this particular idea of freedom in Hegel and Marx. This notion of freedom is condensed in Hegel's claim that to be truly free is 'to be with oneself in an other' (Hegel, *Philosophy of Right*, §7A). Acting freely means to relate to others in a way that they become part of my projects; in a way that I can identify with them. In this way, "we restrict ourselves gladly in relating ourselves to another", Hegel explains, and only "in this restriction [we] know ourselves as ourselves" (ibid.). Marx likewise criticizes a notion of freedom that "makes every man see in other men not the *realization* of his own freedom, but the *barrier* to it" (Marx, "On the Jewish Question," MECW 3: 163).
18 See Andrew Chitty, "Freedom and Community in Hegel and Marx," in *Freiheit. Stuttgarter Hegel-Kongress 2011*, ed. Gunnar Hindrichs and Axel Honneth (Frankfurt: Vittorio Klostermann, 2013), 567–80.
19 For further reflections, see Hannes Kuch, "Ökonomie, Subjektivität und Sittlichkeit: Hegel und die Kritik des kapitalistischen Marktes," in *Warum Kritik? Begründungsformen kritischer Theorie*, ed. Sven Ellmers and Philip Hogh (Weilerswist: Velbrück 2017), 134–63.
20 Marx, "Comments on James Mill's *Éléments D'économie Politique*," MECW 3.
21 This idea is explored more thoroughly in Brudney, "Community and Completion," in *Reclaiming the History of Ethics: Essays for John Rawls*, ed. Andrew Reath et al. (Cambridge: Cambridge University Press, 1997), 388–415.
22 Marx, "Comments on James Mill," 228.
23 Karl Marx, *Grundrisse. Foundations of the Critique of Political Economy* (Harmondsworth: Penguin, 1973), 157.

24 Marx, "Comments on James Mill," 228.
25 Marx, "Comments on James Mill"; for an interpretation along these lines see Chitty, "Recognition and Property in Hegel and the Early Marx," *Ethical Theory and Moral Practice* 16, no. 4 (2013): 685–97, and Quante, "Recognition," 265.
26 Chitty, "Recognition and Property," 692.
27 See also Dave Elder-Vass, *Profit and Gift in the Digital Economy* (Cambridge: Cambridge University Press, 2016, ch. 7) and Wright, *Envisioning Real Utopias*, 194–203.
28 Cf. J.K. Gibson-Graham, *The End of Capitalism (As We Knew It): A Feminist Critique of Political Economy* (Cambridge, MA: Blackwell, 1996).
29 The Marxian idea of voluntary contributions certainly does not imply that serving others is always gratified by pleasure. This is especially clear when it comes to care work within the household. But given that the patterns of "communal caring" (Cohen, *Why Not Socialism*? Princeton: Princeton University Press, 2009, 39) often hold despite the absence of immediate gratification makes the underlying logic even stronger: that the neediness of the other is the very reason for providing a particular contribution.
30 Cf. *The Wealth of the Commons: A World beyond Market and State*, ed. David Bollier and Silke Helfrich (Amherst: Levellers Press, 2012).
31 Silvia Federici and George Caffentzis, "Commons against and beyond capitalism," *Community Development Journal* 49, no. 1 (2014): 92–105; David Graeber, *Debt: The First 5,000 Years* (New York: Melville House, 2011), ch. 5: "A Brief Treatise on the Moral Grounds of Economic Relations"; Michael Hardt and Antonio Negri, *Commonwealth* (Cambridge, MA: Harvard University Press, 2009).
32 At this point, I bracket too optimistic assumptions regarding the prospects of automation, digitalization, and 3D printing, and their social potential to render human work more and more redundant. None of these technologies will make human work superfluous in various fields of the manufacturing industry, the service sector, or the knowledge economy: Think of the production of shoes, machines, or trains; or the service provided by hair-dressers, bartenders, and chefs; or the knowledge generated by journalists, IT experts, or engineers in research and development departments. Some recent studies go quite far in their techno-optimism; see, for example, Paul Mason, *Postcapitalism: A Guide to Our Future* (London: Allen Lane, 2015); Peter Frase, *Four Futures: Life after Capitalism* (London: Verso, 2016); and Srnicek and Williams, *Inventing the Future*.
33 Jerry Cohen is too negligent in tackling the problem: He mentions that the "commitment to socialist community does not require me to be a sucker who serves you regardless of whether (if you are able to do so) you are going to serve me" (Cohen, *Why Not Socialism?*, 43). But he evades the question of how reciprocity can really be ensured. At one point, he says in passing that the "mutual giving" characteristic of socialism might be "planned" (ibid., 10), but he doesn't go into detail on what this kind of planning would require.
34 Federici and Caffentzis, for example, clearly see the need for "*regulations*, stipulating how the wealth we share is to be used and cared for"; they acknowledge that this requires "collective decision making," but emphasize an allocation of "power from the ground up" (Federici and Caffentzis, "Commons against and beyond Capitalism," 102). They neglect, however, that vertical relations from the regulatory body to the individuals are to some degree unavoidable when it comes to asserting collectively decided rules. In their recent proposal on 'commoning', Meretz and Sutterlütti pay

more attention to finding ways to resolve conflicts between general agreements and individuals by relying on practices of mediation and fostering empathy. But such proposals still remain quite opaque. See Simon Sutterlütti and Stefan Meretz, *Kapitalismus aufheben* (Hamburg: VSA, 2018), ch. 6.3.
35 On this idea, see Neuhouser, *Foundations of Hegel's Social Theory*, following, however, not Marx, but Hegel and Rousseau.
36 Diane Elson, "Market Socialism or Socialization of the Market?," *New Left Review* 172 (1988): 3–44, at p. 12.
37 "The proletariat will use its political supremacy to wrest, by degree, all capital from the bourgeoisie, to centralise all instruments of production in the hands of the State." Marx and Engels, *Manifesto of the Communist Party*, MECW 6: 504.
38 Marx, "The Civil War in France," MECW 22: 332.
39 Marx, "Drafts to the Civil War," MECW 22: 486.
40 It was Engels who originally coined the phrase; see Engels, *Anti-Dühring*, MECW 25: 268, translated here as 'dying out'.
41 Marx, "The Civil War in France," 335.
42 For example, by describing communism in a hyper-elliptical way, as in the "Critique of the Gotha Programme". This creates the appearance that certain problems will simply not occur—say, a mismatch between the needs to be satisfied and the abilities people wish to realize.
43 Michael Albert, *Parecon: Life after Capitalism* (London: Verso, 2003); Robin Hahnel, *Of the People, by the People* (Portland: Soapbox, 2012). For a different approach to democratic planning, see Pat Devine, *Democracy and Economic Planning: The Political Economy of a Self-Governing Society* (Cambridge: Polity, 1988). The topic of council democracy resurfaces in contemporary political theory: *Council Democracy: Towards a Democratic Socialist Politics*, ed. James Muldoon (London: Routledge, 2018).
44 See Hahnel, *Of the People*, particularly ch. 9 and 14.
45 Hahnel, *Of the People*, 91.
46 Ibid.
47 Albert, *Parecon*, ch. 8: "Allocation".
48 In deciding a production proposal, the other councils also take into account the extent to which the particular enterprise lived up to its promises in the previous year; that is, to what extent the actual costs were higher or the actual social benefits lower (or the other way round respectively) than the estimated figures at the beginning of the previous year (cf. Albert, *Parecon*, ch. 8). This is important in order to prevent worker councils from making hollow promises.
49 Hahnel, *Of the People*, 103.
50 One frequent objection is that the incentives for supplying socially beneficial outputs are too weak in a participatory economy. A major reason is an additional feature not mentioned up to now: On the level of each enterprise, Hahnel and Albert propose remunerating employees not according to social contribution but according to effort (where individual effort is assessed by the enterprises' worker councils). Rewarding effort instead of contribution leads, however, to some efficiency losses, because it may give people too few incentives to offer work where society might benefit more. Yet I am not sure how grave the effect would be. This is because the social contribution of each enterprise *as a whole* actually *is* taken into account, whereas *within* each enterprise, contribution is disregarded. This would lead to some efficiency losses for the particular enterprise and, as a result, also for society as a whole. Still, all things considered, these losses might be acceptable.

51 See Wright, "Participatory Economics: A Sympathetic Critique," in Hahnel and Wright, *Alternatives to Capitalism: Proposals for a Democratic Economy* (London: Verso, 2016), 17–46, esp. 25–8, and also Seth Ackerman, "The Red and the Black," *Jacobin*, December 20, 2012, https://jacobinmag.com/2012/12/the-red-and-the-black (accessed June 12, 2018).

52 It is a bit unfair of Hahnel to belittle this concern as the "size 6.5 purple women's high heeled leatherless shoe with a yellow toe problem" (Hahnel, "In Defense of Participatory Economics," in Hahnel and Wright, *Alternatives to Capitalism*, 48–70, at p. 51). The problem is reduced to some extent—but only slightly—if one takes into account that one can simply reenter the consumer choices of the previous year in the planning list.

53 Hahnel, *Of the People*, 49.

54 Hahnel, "In Defense of Participatory Economics," 56–7.

55 Hahnel, *Of the People*, 111–2.

56 Ibid., 99.

57 A related problem is that the participatory economy is much less deliberative than it might seem. Even though Hahnel subscribes to the ideal of a "deliberative democracy" (Hahnel, *Of the People*, 101), he considers it an advantage that there isn't all too much need for deliberation: He underlines that "councils never have to argue over someone else's ideas about what they should do" (ibid.); deliberation occurs only *within* the councils. The major reason is that numbers, or precisely prices, do a lot of the coordination work between councils. But as we've just seen, there are many more occasions where higher-level federations or iteration boards have to issue binding instructions than Hahnel and Albert try to make the reader believe. Yet if deliberation is largely absent, the sense of cohesiveness that deliberative processes are typically able to engender will be weak. But in this case, the problem of top-down decisions from higher-level institutions becomes even more pressing. In the end, it seems to me that a market socialism with very strong civil associations might well be more deliberative.

58 The most important studies of the 1980s and 1990s are Alec Nove, *The Economics of Feasible Socialism* (London: George Allen & Unwin, 1983); David Miller, *Market, State, and Community: Theoretical Foundations of Market Socialism* (Oxford: Clarendon, 1989); Joseph Carens, *Equality, Moral Incentives, and the Market: An Essay in Utopian Politico-Economic Theory* (Chicago: University of Chicago Press, 1981); David Schweickart, *After Capitalism* (Lanham: Rowman & Littlefield, 2002); John E. Roemer, *A Future for Socialism* (Cambridge, MA: Harvard University Press, 1994). In recent years, the idea of market socialism has enjoyed a revival in different strands of political philosophy: in Political Liberalism (see Hunt, *Liberal Socialism*, Lanham: Lexington Books, 2015), in Analytical Marxism (Cohen, *Why Not Socialism?*), and in Critical Theory (Honneth, *The Idea of Socialism: Towards a Renewal*, Cambridge: Polity, 2017).

59 This is a major insight we owe to Axel Honneth's reading of Hegel; see *Freedom's Right*, ch. 6.2.

60 Even Marx himself clearly acknowledges this potential: "The fact that this need on the part of one can be satisfied by the product of the other, and vice versa, and that the one is capable of producing the object of the need of the other, and that each confronts the other as owner of the object of the other's need, this proves that each of them reaches beyond his own particular need etc., as a *human being*, and that they relate to one another as human beings; that their common species-

being [*Gattungswesen*] is acknowledged by all." Marx, *Grundrisse: Foundations of the Critique of Political Economy*, transl. by Martin Nicolaus (New York: Vintage, 1973), 243.

61   Cf. Richard Dien Winfield, "Economy and Ethical Community," in *Hegel and Capitalism*, ed. Andrew Buchwalt (Albany: State University of New York Press, 2015), 133–46, at p. 145.
62   Hegel, *Philosophy of Right*, §§250–6. See also the recent volume *Korporation und Sittlichkeit*, ed. Sven Ellmers and Steffen Herrmann (Paderborn: Fink, 2017).
63   Hegel, *Grundlinien der Philosophie des Rechts*, in *Werke*, ed. E. Moldenhauer and K. M. Michl, Volume 7, §251.
64   I am following Sven Ellmers's inspiring interpretation of Hegel here; see Ellmers, *Freiheit und Wirtschaft. Theorie der bürgerlichen Gesellschaft nach Hegel* (Bielefeld: Transcript, 2015), 71–90.
65   Marx, *Capital I*, 157–66. See also his critique of time-chit (or labor voucher) proposals in the *Grundrisse*, 136–58.
66   Marx, "Comments on James Mill."
67   A further objection is alienation in virtue of the instrumental character of market relations. As we have seen, this problem is offset to some extent by the implicit potential of social freedom embodied in market relations. Another criticism is the commodity fetishism that characterizes market societies on Marx's account. This problem should be considered with caution, however; there are good reasons to relate it primarily to the uncontrolled, rampant free-market capitalism of the nineteenth century, whereas twentieth-century capitalism broke "the spell of liberal-capitalist commodity production", since virtually "all participants have become, more or less, good practitioners of value theory." Jürgen Habermas, *Legitimation Crisis* (Boston: Beacon Press, 1975), 68. For a Marxist critique of the concept, see Marco Iorio, "Fetisch und Geheimnis. Zur Kritik der Kapitalismuskritik von Karl Marx," *Deutsche Zeitschrift für Philosophie* 58 (2010): 241–56.
68   The classical proposal is formulated in Robert Van der Veen and Philippe Van Parijs, "Capitalist Road to Communism," *Theory and Society* 15 (1986): 635–55. A recent book-length elaboration is Philippe Van Parijs and Yannick Vanderborght, *Basic Income: A Radical Proposal for a Free Society and a Sane Economy* (Cambridge, MA: Harvard University Press, 2017).
69   See David Schweickart, *After Capitalism*, 2nd edn (Lanham: Rowman & Littlefield, 2011).
70   The first suggestion moves in the direction of a recent proposal by Giacomo Corneo, "Public Stock Ownership," *Annals of Public and Cooperative Economics* 89, no. 1 (2018): 11–24; Elster discusses the second suggestion, see Jon Elster, "From Here to There; or, If Cooperative Ownership Is So Desirable, Why Are There So Few Cooperatives?" *Social Philosophy and Policy* 6, no. 2 (1989): 93–111.
71   See Joshua Cohen and Joel Rogers, *Associations and Democracy* (London: Verso, 2005).

13

Honneth's Democratic *Sittlichkeit* and Market Socialism

Michael Nance

§1. Introduction

In *Freedom's Right*, Axel Honneth offers a nuanced and historically rich discussion of the moral possibilities and limits of market society. Building on Hegel, Polanyi, and Durkheim, Honneth argues that market society is not inherently morally objectionable if economic markets are 'embedded' in a system of other social institutions that rein in the market's pathologies and excesses. In fact, Honneth argues that economic markets can provide a site for recognitive interactions in which agents experience what, following Frederick Neuhouser, he calls *social freedom*.[1] Thus there is a redeemable moral core of market society that anchors Honneth's detailed immanent critique of contemporary economic life. Honneth uses this moral core to reconstruct twentieth-century European social democracy as a site of social freedom. Honneth's arguments thus serve a dual purpose. *Freedom's Right* aims both to reconcile us to our social world by showing how its institutions, including the market, can embody social freedom, and at the same time to use the values embedded in those institutions as a yardstick against which to measure and criticize social reality. Like Hegel's *Philosophy of Right*, Honneth's book is at once a work of theodicy and a work of immanent critique.

My chapter makes two contributions to our understanding of Honneth's view of markets and social freedom as he develops it in *Freedom's Right*. First I aim to reconstruct his accounts of social freedom and legitimacy as these relate to market institutions. This strictly conceptual work occupies §§2–4. Second, in a more social-theoretic mode, I argue in §§5–9 that the trajectory Honneth describes in his normative reconstruction of the constellation of institutions that he calls 'organized capitalism' ultimately requires for its completion the rejection of private ownership in favor of some form of market socialism.[2] According to this hypothesis, the failure of social-democratic capitalism to maintain its mid-century advances in social freedom can be explained in part by the labor movement's failure fully to socialize ownership rights in the means of production. My argument for this claim centers on an account of the differing expressive properties of market capitalist and market-socialist economic institutions. Both parts of the chapter draw on Honneth's own commitments; my critique is thus meant to be internal to his project. The overall aim is to show that structures of capital ownership can either support or destabilize the achievement of social freedom in the market.

§2. Two Interpretations of the Market

According to Honneth, the history of struggles for workers' and consumers' rights in Western capitalist countries can be seen as the site of a conflict between two interpretations of the kind of freedom realized in the market.[3] On the first notion of negative or legal freedom, markets are "conceived of in terms of strategically calculating economic actors"[4] engaged in "exclusively purposive-rational, self-interested calculations".[5] From this point of view, the market is a space for the pursuit of individuals' private goods. There are no "pre-contractual, ethical norms" in place on such a conception that could constrain the self-interested activity of market participants.[6] One recognizes others only insofar as such recognition is necessary for successful strategic interaction in which one achieves one's ends, which are defined individualistically.

On the second, *social* interpretation of freedom, the marketplace offers sites for recognitive interaction in which individuals can cooperate freely and respond to each others' desires, needs, and abilities. Importantly, if it is to be a site of social freedom, the market must provide a system of complementary role obligations to which all could freely consent.[7] The free consent requirement rules out non-reciprocal relations of economic domination, in which the freedom of one becomes the *un*-freedom of another.[8] The market, on the social freedom interpretation, is an effective way of coordinating economic activity to make sure that individuals' ends are complementary, so that all can realize their freedom together.[9] And markets are more efficient than other economic arrangements. But beyond these explicitly recognized social purposes of coordination and efficiency, market interactions are not viewed as opportunities for the unfettered pursuit of individuals' private interests. Instead, participants understand the market as existing for the sake of cooperatively realizing the interests of all, who stand in relations of solidarity with one another that transcend the social sphere of the marketplace.[10] These relations of solidarity are anchored in social institutions such as labor unions and consumer cooperatives that 'embed' the market. Embedded markets allow individual workers and consumers to define and to achieve common aims through social cooperation with other citizens and firms, mediated by civil society institutions.[11]

§3. Two Legitimacy Criteria for Market Institutions

The distinction between the social freedom and legal freedom views of the market provides Honneth with the material for an account of the legitimacy of economic institutions. We can analyze Honneth's legitimacy criterion for market society in terms of two connected requirements. First, markets must actually serve the interests of all participants.[12] Call this the 'common good' requirement. Although it is perhaps most natural to conceive of participants' interests in strictly economic terms, Honneth instead analyzes the idea of 'the interest of all' in terms of mutual recognition: Market arrangements that do not allow each participant to receive equal recognition of her particular needs, desires, and abilities, and to reciprocate such recognition in cooperation with others, will be to that extent illegitimate.[13] This is the essence of Honneth's democratic *Sittlichkeit*: Institutions should be judged according to whether they allow citizens to recognize each other as equal partners in cooperation. In such a scheme, each individual holds that her freedom would be impoverished in the absence of this form of institutionally mediated cooperation; one's cooperation partners are thus constitutive moments of one's own freedom. Legitimate markets provide us with scripts for actions that are inherently cooperative in this sense, for given the complexity of modern economies, acts of production and consumption cannot be completed by isolated individuals.

The second part of Honneth's legitimacy criterion holds that market participants must be able to *know* or *see* that the social function of markets is to serve the interests of all participants, understood as equal partners in cooperative interaction, and that their society's market economy in fact serves this function. And market participants must "remain aware" of these facts over time.[14] Call this the 'epistemic transparency' requirement. What, precisely, the epistemic transparency requirement entails is not immediately clear in *Freedom's Right*. Honneth has in mind more than mere epistemic *accessibility*, for a fact could be epistemically *accessible* to me without my ever *accessing* it. Used as a criterion for market legitimacy, epistemic accessibility would hold that, as long as it is possible for participants to know that the market is a system of social freedom, then markets are legitimate. In principle, then, everyone could go through their entire lives conceiving of the market legalistically, and the epistemic accessibility requirement could still be satisfied.

But given the nature of social freedom, it is, in fact, not possible that the market could be a sphere of social freedom without market participants knowing it. There is an internal connection between the way individuals conceive of their interactions in the market and the nature of the market itself.[15] For conscious awareness of one's reciprocal relation to others as an equal participant in mutually agreeable, complementary role obligations—that is, conscious awareness that one is cooperating with others to advance the common good—is built into the structure of the recognition relations that, for Honneth, constitute social freedom.[16] In a system of social freedom, market agents' actual background knowledge about the social role and limits of the market economy gives interaction in the market a distinctive, cooperative character in comparison with legal freedom conceptions. This is the reason, I take it, that Honneth claims that individuals must *in fact* "remain aware" of the function of their economic institutions in promoting the common good: Social freedom involves cooperative relations, and it is part of the structure of such relations that those who cooperate with one another must be consciously aware *that* they are cooperating with one another. It follows that, for the market to be a sphere of social freedom, not only must knowledge about the market system's function in promoting the common good be *accessible* to all, it must in fact be at least periodically *accessed* by all. Mere epistemic accessibility does not suffice for the kind of epistemic transparency necessary for social freedom.[17]

Honneth's theory of legitimacy provides a way to evaluate the system of market institutions in a democratic *Sittlichkeit*. For economic institutions to function well requires that they meet both the common good and the epistemic transparency requirements. There are two kinds of cases in which the epistemic transparency requirement might fail: first, cases in which the system of political economy also fails to meet the common good requirement of being in the interest of all participants; and second, cases in which the common good requirement is satisfied, but market participants believe, due to a lack of epistemic transparency at the institutional level, that the common good requirement is *not* satisfied. In the second kind of case, the false beliefs about the function of the market would have real effects on the actual behavior of participants in the economic sphere, with the result that the market economy would soon also fail to meet the common good requirement—believing the market economy to be a sphere of self-interested behavior, citizens would defect from cooperative economic behavior, and the market would cease to be a space in which all participants can receive equal recognition as partners in pursuing the common good. Thus the common good requirement and the epistemic transparency requirement are, in practice, closely intertwined: A society that fails to meet one of the requirements will soon fail to meet both.[18]

§4. Two Views of Capital

Whether market agents interpret market interactions in terms of legal or social freedom has implications for agents' understanding of the proper function of patterns of capital investment. When individuals interpret economic life through the solidaristic lens of social freedom, capital is viewed as a social asset that should be subject to democratic norms and thereby directed toward the common good in the socially embedded marketplace. Consider the following example from *Freedom's Right*. In his discussion of the development of 'organized capitalism', Honneth approvingly mentions the attempts of governments in the early twentieth century to structure securities markets in such a way as to "obligate powerful joint stock companies to serve the public interest and the common welfare".[19] In this example, a non-market democratic institution constrains the functioning of capital markets to promote the common interest. This is one of the primary functions performed by the cluster of state and civil-society institutions that, on Honneth's account, are supposed to 'embed' the marketplace: These institutions restrain the profit motive and influence investment decisions in such a way that patterns of capital investment promote the public interest.[20] Thus in Honneth's account, capital investment is supposed to promote the common good, and he argues that we need an institutional framework to make sure that capital does not stray from its proper public function.

If market participants take up the standpoint of social freedom, then, they regard capital as a social asset that should be subject to democratic constraint to promote the common good. Capital's proper function is to provide the material conditions for a free community of equals who recognize each other as such. If participants in economic life take up the perspective of legal or negative freedom, by contrast, the notion of the common good drops out of sight entirely. From this fact it follows, trivially, that legal or negative freedom cannot understand capital as a tool for the promotion of the common good; instead, agents who adopt the legal/negative freedom framework for understanding economic life must view capital as a private asset for the promotion of individuals' private goods. In making the claim that the legal/negative freedom perspective cannot allow for the possibility of the public good, I am relying primarily on Honneth's remarks that characterize the legal/negative freedom view of the market as a site for strategic self-interested behavior.[21] If all market agents construe themselves and others as rational agents concerned only with their own narrow interests, then the only goods that are in view for any market agents are their own private goods and the private goods of other market agents. The very idea that economic markets could be legitimate only to the extent that they serve the common interest falls by the wayside on such a conception. From the standpoint of market participants who conceive of the market in terms of negative/legal freedom, there are only private, individual purposes, from which it follows that from this point of view, the social function of capital can only be to serve private, individual purposes.

§5. Social Freedom and Economic Democracy

The mere fact that the social freedom interpretation views capital as a social asset does not decide any of the important questions with respect to concrete economic institutions or forms of capital ownership. It is still an open question whether the best way to treat capital as a social asset is to subject it to state ownership; or whether it would better serve the public interest to allow capital to be privately owned; or whether perhaps some third alternative would do better than either of these.[22] To make the case for a specifically market-socialist reading of Honneth's democratic *Sittlichkeit*, then, more argument is required. As a first step, I give a brief exposition of Honneth's reconstruction of the rise and fall of economic markets as sites of social freedom in European social-democratic countries during the twentieth century. This section focuses on the *rise* of the social freedom understanding, arguing that the demand for the socialization of capital ownership was already part of workers' struggles for social freedom in labor markets.

In Honneth's account of labor market struggles, the 'social' interpretation of the market was the predominant view among workers and consumers in western European countries in the decades following the Second World War, during the period of what Honneth, following Rudolf Hilferding, calls "organized capitalism".[23] Honneth's normative reconstruction narrates the steady progress made by the labor movement in western European countries up until the 1970s. Honneth summarizes his account in the following passage, which is worth quoting at length:

> In our idealizing reconstruction ... we have not only seen how much resistance such attempts to realize social freedom have encountered in the profit interests of capitalist enterprises, but also that with each victory in the struggle for social

freedom, the extent of the normatively required measures seems to grow. The establishment of social rights that were to protect workers from the most severe risks of wage labour was followed by the realization of the necessity of educational reforms to improve equality of opportunity; soon after, it became clear that even monotonous and purely routine activities had to be eliminated because they prevented any experience of cooperation in a division of labour; and finally—now we are in the middle of the twentieth century—there arose the belief that only the active involvement of wage labourers in decision-making processes within the firm could tame the profit interests of the company and lead to the cooperative restraint of the market.[24]

Drawing on a wealth of historical, economic, and sociological literature, *Freedom's Right* elaborates each step of this historical progression in great detail. But for my purposes, the summary I just quoted suffices to convey the main ideas of Honneth's account. The last point Honneth mentions in this passage, "the active involvement of wage labourers in decision-making processes within the firm", is especially important for him. Honneth is referring to the institution called *co-determination*. The general idea of co-determination is that workers should be able to exercise some agency in determining 'matters of wages and working conditions', as well as in broader issues such as the appointment of managers, the making of decisions regarding the allocation of profits accruing to the firm, and setting priorities for social investment.[25]

Honneth has no illusions that the codetermination rights actually achieved in mid-century social democracies were sufficient to realize the economic democracy that was the goal of progressive unionism for much of the nineteenth and twentieth centuries; these rights were, at most, a quite modest step in that direction.[26] Still, co-determination *is* a step in the direction of social freedom, for co-determination strengthens the sense of solidarity and cooperation among workers. Because they have the capacity collectively to assert their common interests, workers are able to actualize their freedom in their social world; and because their capacity to assert their common interests depends on antecedent norms of social solidarity, workers are able to recognize each other as collectively enabling the freedom of all. Lastly, the institution of co-determination expresses a sense of social respect for the contributions of workers to the productive process.[27] For all of these reasons, worker co-determination as it actually existed in the social democracies created a limited, yet nonetheless important, recognitive space in which workers could experience social freedom. Although Honneth implies that a more radical expansion of institutional opportunities for co-determination would have been required for the full realization of social freedom in economic life, it is important for him that actually achieved co-determination rights show the potential of market economies as spaces of social freedom.

What does all of this have to do with capital ownership? The demand for democratic codetermination in the workplace and the broader economy is at its core a demand that workers gain control over at least some of the functions previously performed by the ownership class. To see why, consider the bundle of rights traditionally included in private property in the means of production in capitalist societies. Following Thomas Weisskopf's analysis, we can decompose capitalist ownership rights into *control rights* and *income rights*. Capitalist forms of ownership, according to Weisskopf, "are characterized by the bundling of control and income rights into comprehensive ownership rights".[28] In a system of capitalist ownership, capitalists have the legal right to control the means of production that they own, and the legal right to the profits of the firms that they control. Control rights include especially the right to appoint managers and thus indirectly to run the operations of the firm, and more generally the right to hire and fire employees; the right to control the conditions under which means of production may be used (when, by whom, for what purpose, etc.); as well as the right to make strategic decisions regarding the long-term direction of the firm. Income rights are self-explanatory: If the firm makes a profit, it accrues to the owners. Both control rights and income rights are included in private property in the means of production. Depending on the precise form of co-determination at issue, workers may take over aspects of either control or income rights, which, although they are bundled together in capitalist ownership, are both conceptually and really separable.

Since these functions are part of the bundle of rights that have historically constituted private ownership of the means of production, it follows that the demand for co-determination rights is a demand for the restructuring of ownership rights in the means of production. As Honneth recognizes in *Freedom's Right*, the demand for co-determination was regarded by labor activists in the twentieth century as a first step on the path toward economic democracy, which implies the socialization of control rights and income rights in the means of production.[29]

§6. Misdevelopment of the Market

According to Honneth, progress in the realization of social freedom in the labor market has broken down in recent decades. The social interpretation of the market has given way to a more individualist, negative understanding of market freedom. Honneth refers to this recent shift toward individualism as a "misdevelopment", that is, a regression from the historical promise of the marketplace as a sphere of social freedom.[30] As Honneth acknowledges, this misdevelopment poses a clear challenge to his progressive narrative. He catalogues the recent negative trends in the labor market, which include a "continuous fall in wages", "growing precariousness of employment", and "fatalistic feelings of powerlessness".[31] Honneth proposes the following as among the complex set of causal factors responsible for these changes: the "increasing pressures of globalization" and global competition, which have led to financial deregulation; a "dramatic" alteration in the "composition of the stock exchange" toward large, ruthless institutional investors; and, beginning in the 1970s, the "comprehensive re-composition of 'proletarianness'" away from traditional industrial wage labor toward low-level salaried employees and service workers.[32]

Further compounding the challenge to Honneth's narrative, he acknowledges that workers in the social democracies have for the most part not countered these misdevelopments with collective resistance.[33] As one possible explanation, Honneth speculates that "over the last few decades the responsibility for success in the market economy has been strongly individualized".[34] This psychological shift toward individual responsibility, in turn, was caused by the colonization of non-market social institutions by market values beginning in the 1990s.[35] What this means, in practical terms, is that the set of values and psychological attitudes characteristic of market actors came to be applied in social contexts that were not previously conceived as spheres of competitive market interaction—for example, in public educational institutions, or in the sector of public health, two spheres which in recent decades have been subject to privatization and market reforms. As a consequence of this colonization, individuals increasingly came to view themselves and others as self-interested strategic actors (i.e., as agents of legal freedom) in all aspects of social life, which in turn led to the breakdown of cooperation and the corresponding individualization of responsibility for market outcomes.[36]

§7. Dual Function of Economic Institutions: Instrumental and Expressive

Organized capitalism ultimately proved to be an unstable economic formation. There are reasons for thinking that, had workers been able to achieve it, market socialism would have proved to be a more stable vehicle for the achievement of social freedom than organized capitalism. One main reason is this: Market-socialist institutions would have expressive properties that are lacking in capitalist economic institutions. The institutions of market socialism would effectively announce to all citizens that: (1) capital is a social asset, not a private asset; and that (2) the marketplace is an instrument in the service of economic cooperation that treats all citizens as equals. These expressive properties would have a stabilizing effect on the socioeconomic structure of market socialism, for they clearly express both the purpose and the limits of market society. Citizens' consciousness of the proper social function of economic markets as instruments of social freedom would counteract the tendency for market values to colonize other social spheres. Thus an additional explanatory factor in the decline of the social freedom interpretation of the market in social-democratic countries is the failure of the workers' parties to fully socialize ownership of the means of production. To make a case for these claims, I first need to briefly sketch, by way of some examples, what it is for a social institution to have an expressive property.

I take it to be intuitively plausible that social institutions can express a society's values. Examples might include a constitution or other major body of law, a welfare-state program, a specific tradition of family or civic life, or an environmental-protection bureau. Each of these kinds of institutions expresses a set of values affirmed within a society—the value accorded to certain rights and statuses, a commitment to value the natural environment, and so on. A clear illustration of the expressive power of institutions is the case of national constitutions.[37] As the most basic legal document that governs a nation's affairs, we look to a nation's constitution to see what values are regarded as paramount by the citizens of that nation. A constitution does its expressive work by formally announcing to each citizen that her country has recognized certain basic rights and liberties as essential and, in some cases, inalienable, and specifying the class of individuals to whom these basic rights and liberties apply. Clearly the views and values expressed by a constitution can be either affirming or degrading; but regardless of the content of the specific messages it expresses, the fact that the document plays a visible and agreed-upon public role in establishing basic rights means that it expresses to the citizens a picture of what it is to be a citizen of that country.

Some economic institutions clearly have an expressive function in addition to their instrumental function in achieving strictly economic ends, such as promoting economic growth.[38] Consider, as one possible example among many, Norway's "Oil Fund".[39] Income from taxes and fees on Norway's oil resources is deposited into the public Fund, which invests these deposits in various ways to get a stable return.[40] The idea is that the Fund, which is collectively owned by the citizens of Norway, will be available for future generations once oil revenues start to fall and Norway's pension system begins to need supplementation. Norway's decision to set up the Fund expresses its citizens' commitment to treat the country's natural resource wealth as a public asset, as well as its concern for the welfare of future generations.

§8. The Expressive Function of Socialist Institutions

This section explains why the expressive properties of market socialism would differ from those of market capitalism in such a way as to make the former more legitimate than the latter according to Honneth's criteria. The market-socialist program can be summarized as consisting of two key changes in the structure of capitalist ownership.[41] First, it involves the socialization of control rights over capital by means of instituting labor-management in firms and democratic oversight of social investment priorities. On such a program, the private sector in capitalist economies would be transformed into a sector of publicly financed, socially owned firms. Banks would be publicly owned, though as much as possible independently and professionally managed on a day-to-day basis, and would be the primary institution that finances firms that compete in the market.[42] Second, the market-socialist program socializes profit and interest income from capital by establishing a (roughly) equal 'social dividend' payment for each citizen. The right to profits (the income rights component of the capitalist ownership bundle) would be distributed (roughly) equally, either among all of the nation's citizens, or among the worker-owners of specific firms or economic sectors, or some combination of both.[43] On the models of Roemer and Weisskopf, for example, each citizen is permanently endowed with a portfolio of stock in the nation's socially controlled and publicly financed firms. Citizens cannot sell their portfolio for cash, but they can trade their shares for shares in other companies, and draw dividend income from the firms in their portfolio.[44] Regardless of the precise institutional details, the main point is that there would not be a small class of citizens who control the vast majority of corporate profits, as in capitalist economies.

From the standpoint of social freedom, two institutional features of this framework have special positive expressive value. First, the fact that investment capital is treated as a public asset through the socialization of the financial sector makes clear to all citizens that capital is a tool for the promotion of the common good, and that overall patterns of capital investment will take into account the interests of all citizens. Such an economic framework effectively expresses the view that capital is a public resource. Second, the fact that each citizen receives a roughly equal stake in the profits of firms in the form of what I have called a 'social dividend' payment expresses the view that the competition of firms in the marketplace is *instrumentally valuable* for the sake of the interests of *all participants*, for when the economy does well, each citizen benefits as an equal partner.[45] Taking together these two expressive features of market social institutions, it is clear that, whatever other virtues or vices they may have, these institutions do a good job of publicly expressing a particular understanding of the status and social role of capital as an instrument of social freedom. Now, given that part of Honneth's principle of legitimacy for market institutions is that such institutions should make the proper function of the market epistemically transparent to citizens, and that market-socialist institutions would, in comparison with market capitalism, do a better job of announcing the proper social function of the market to all citizens, it is likely that market-socialist institutions would be more legitimate than market capitalist institutions. For by clearly expressing the function and limits of market society so that these facts remain visible to all citizens, market-socialist institutions would change the character of individuals' interactions in the market.

Organized capitalism, by contrast, sends an equivocal message regarding the proper social function of capital and economic markets. Some elements of the institutional framework of organized capitalism appear to confirm the social freedom interpretation. For example, the institution of co-determination and the state regulatory apparatus both express a society's commitment to the view that capital ought to be regarded as a social asset for the good of all. But on the other hand, the fact that private individuals possess capital income rights and substantial control rights over capital might be taken to express the view that the actual social function of capital is to enrich the ownership class, which lends credence to the legal-freedom interpretation of the market. In the struggle over how to understand the proper function of the market system, organized capitalism sends 'mixed messages' that provide some expressive support for both legal freedom and social freedom interpretations.

The hypothesis I want to propose is that part of the explanation of the destabilization of organized capitalism described by Honneth is that the institutions of organized capitalism failed to express to citizens that the primary social function of economic markets is to enable the social freedom of all market participants. If the private ownership of productive resources gives a foothold for legal-freedom interpretations of the market, and legal-freedom interpretations of the market in turn give rise to social pathologies in which the public good falls out of view, then it is unlikely that all citizens will be able to hold both the private and the public functions of the market in view, at least not in a stable way over time. And when citizens in organized capitalism conceive their social interactions with others in terms of legal freedom, their adoption of this interpretative framework will be reinforced by readily available evidence from economic life that other citizens have adopted a similar stance, particularly (but not only) in economic affairs. This evidence of the behavior and social expectations of others reinforces the rationality of adopting the legal-freedom view of economic life, that is, of defecting from cooperation. Because from the viewpoint of legal freedom the public good cannot constrain the pursuit of private interests, market values will then tend to colonize non-market spheres, for citizens will lose sight of the proper function and limits of such values.

If something like this line of argument is correct, then the persistence of private ownership of means of production in organized capitalist societies will have a destabilizing effect on the social-democratic compromise between capital and labor. In particular, allowing a private ownership class to control profits sends the message to market participants that the social function of capital is to serve the private interests of self-interested market agents, and that more broadly the marketplace is a sphere for the strategic pursuit of self-interest. This lends credence to the legal-freedom interpretation of the market. As a result, individuals more and more came to view themselves as self-interested strategic actors (i.e., as agents of legal freedom), which in turn led to the breakdown of solidarity and the corresponding individualization of responsibility for market outcomes under neoliberal conditions.

An example of this phenomenon can be drawn from the history of Swedish social democracy.[46] The solidaristic wage policy that characterized the Swedish model of social democracy through the 1970s relied on strong worker solidarity to maintain national wage equality. As Meidner puts it, one key principle of the policy was that "equal work should be equally paid, regardless of the profitability of the firm, the size or location of the workplace. What matters is the kind and nature of work, and the skills which are needed to perform it."[47] Local unions in highly productive sectors were tempted to negotiate higher wages for themselves, but to do so would depart from the norm of solidarity with workers in less productive sectors, who would be unable to negotiate equally high wages, thus violating the principle that "equal work should be equally paid". Maintaining national wage uniformity in accordance with the solidaristic wage policy therefore required some workers to accept less than they could in principle receive in the market, were they to set aside norms of cooperation and solidarity with their fellow workers. This is one aspect of the ethos of solidarity that was central to Swedish social democracy, and it is an instance of social freedom. This ethos was eroded by the persistence of private ownership rights in the means of production. For workers saw correctly that their commitment to solidarity enlarged corporate profits in high-productivity sectors by allowing firms in such sectors to pay lower wages than they would have had to pay in the absence of solidaristic national labor contracts. The unions' solidaristic wage policy thus allowed capitalists to reap higher profits than they otherwise would have.[48] Workers in the solidaristic unions thus encountered models for agency in the market that differed a great deal from their own: On the one hand, their own members traditionally viewed the labor market as a field for the cooperative achievement of collective aims, in which each member voluntarily limits her freedom for the sake of the other, and each member benefits as an equal from the cooperative arrangement, in the form of equal wages for equal work. On the other hand, capitalists pursued more individualistic aims in the market place, unfettered by the norms of solidarity and cooperation that constrained the pursuit of workers' individual self-interest. Owners of firms were able to exploit the solidaristic wage policy to increase their profits. In other words, workers were faced with conflicting evidence as to whether the market was a sphere for the pursuit of social freedom or for the pursuit of negative/legal freedom. Under such conditions, it was understandably difficult to maintain the cooperative ethos that underpinned the solidaristic wage policy.

Had Swedish workers been able to achieve the full socialization of capital ownership rights via the creation of wage-earner funds, as Meidner proposed and was fiercely debated in the 1970s, the profits accruing to capital would (eventually) not have been captured by a small group of agents of legal freedom, but rather would have been treated as a social asset that benefited all workers equally. Such an institutional arrangement would no longer have given mixed messages regarding the function of the market. The achievement of a form of market socialism, in other words, would have contributed to the legitimacy and stability of Swedish social democracy, according to Honneth's principles. So the failure to achieve the full socialization of the market should be added to Honneth's list of causes of the decline of the social freedom interpretation of the market.

§9. Objections

One might object that we need not go all the way to market socialism to satisfy the epistemic transparency requirement. For example, perhaps more emphasis in the education system on the social virtues and limits of capitalist markets could stabilize social-democratic capitalism without fully socializing ownership of the means of production. One can imagine various proposals along similar lines.

Although I cannot definitively refute this objection, there are several considerations that count against it. First, consider again the Swedish example discussed in the previous section. Unless the educational program proposed in the objection could induce capitalists not to profit from workers' solidaristic wage policy, then workers would still be faced with the same situation, in which self-interested market agents take advantage of their solidaristic behavior. This is just to say that the educational program would solve the problem only if it could induce private owners of capital to cease to be agents of legal freedom and instead to adopt the social freedom interpretation of the market. If capitalists adopted socialist values of reciprocity and solidarity, it is true that advocates of social freedom would have little reason to complain about a capitalist political economy, but this seems unlikely, to put it mildly. Second, note that epistemic transparency is a matter of degree, and that there is no contradiction in adopting *both* a market-socialist political economy *and* the kind of educational program suggested by the objection. Having multiple institutions promote epistemic transparency is more likely to result in a system of institutions that meets Honneth's demanding legitimacy criterion. Lastly, one could fall back on the common good requirement. On my analysis, satisfying the common good requirement is a necessary condition for satisfying the epistemic transparency requirement. Thus one could argue that the institutions of organized capitalism failed to express the right message to citizens, not because of a failure of epistemic transparency by itself, but rather because of a failure to serve the common good, which in turn entails a failure of epistemic transparency. This line of argument, however, would require much more development, focused on the relationship between economic institutions, patterns of wealth distribution, and the role of such patterns in recognition relations.

A second objection holds that there is an internal conflict between the two elements of Honneth's legitimacy criterion.[49] For one could argue, with some plausibility, that markets function to promote the common good only if agents within the market conceive themselves as agents of legal freedom who pursue their self-interest.[50] Thus if the common good requirement is satisfied, the epistemic transparency requirement is necessarily not satisfied.

By way of response, first note that the objection relies for its plausibility on a narrowly economic notion of the 'common good' as something like 'aggregate economic output' or 'maximal preference satisfaction'; if the common good is rather understood along Honneth's lines as consisting in socially free relations to others, it is not clear that the objection gets any traction. But let us leave that point aside and grant the premise of the objection for the sake of argument: Markets promote the common good most effectively when market agents aggressively pursue their self-interest. One argument available to a defender of the market-socialist project would be to argue that individuals can hold *both* the legal freedom *and* the social freedom views of the market more or less simultaneously. Considering precisely this issue, David Miller writes:

> It is not difficult to think of relationships that can sustain such a dual character. Typically these are cases where the underlying objective can only be achieved by indirect (and apparently contrary) means, or at least can be achieved most effectively by such means. Consider, for example, a game of tennis between two friends, each of whose main objective is to give pleasure to the other. Since what each most enjoys is battling hard on the tennis court, the only way to achieve the objective is for each to play as hard as he can. On the surface the relationship is competitive, each trying his best to win; underneath the game is a co-operative enterprise for mutual enjoyment. Both players understand this, and understand the other's point of view. Here the co-operative character of the relationship seems well able to survive its immediate competitive quality.[51]

Similarly, Miller argues, market relations could, under market socialism, be simultaneously competitive and cooperative, since the competition would be known by all to serve a well-defined cooperative purpose. The expressive properties of the background institutions of market socialism would presumably aid market actors in maintaining this form of dual-consciousness over time.[52]

§10. Conclusion

The argument I have presented has a lot of moving parts. Hence, I want to provide a brief overview of the main points. First, I explained Honneth's account of legal and social freedom and the divergent interpretations of economic life implied by these two concepts of freedom. I also explained Honneth's account of the legitimacy of economic institutions, which relies on his theory of social freedom. This part of the chapter was strictly a matter of conceptual clarification. Second, I showed how Honneth uses this theory to analyze the rise and fall of economic markets in social-democratic countries as spheres of social freedom. I argued that the struggle between legal and social freedom interpretations of the economic marketplace was at the same time a struggle between two views of the proper social function of capital. Third, I argued that market-socialist institutions would be more stable than organized capitalist institutions due to differences in the expressive properties of the two institutional frameworks. Market-socialist institutions would do a better job of publicly expressing the proper function of economic markets, and would therefore better meet Honneth's epistemic transparency requirement. On this basis, I proposed that, in addition to the explanatory factors Honneth identifies, the destabilizing features of the persistence of private capital ownership were partially responsible for the fall of markets in organized capitalist countries as sites of social freedom.

Honneth offers a suggestive argument that the colonization of non-market spheres by market values and the 'strategic rationality' of the economic sphere results in the individualization of responsibility for market outcomes and a corresponding loss of solidarity and social freedom. What I have tried to show is that, in comparison with organized capitalism, market-socialist institutions would do a better job of fulfilling the *epistemic transparency* requirement by keeping the proper function of the market in view for all citizens. A system of market institutions that meets the epistemic transparency requirement will be more stable and legitimate than a system that does not. Hence market socialism would be less prone to the colonization of non-market spheres by market values that has resulted in the pathologies of neoliberalism. In other words, a market-socialist society would allow for the virtues of market-mediated social cooperation that Honneth emphasizes in his defense of the market while lacking some of the destabilizing features of market capitalism implicated in the regression of social freedom Honneth describes.[53] Thus there is good reason for Honneth and other advocates of the social freedom interpretation of the marketplace to endorse a market-socialist political economy. *The Idea of Socialism*, published after *Freedom's Right*, makes clear that Honneth agrees with this latter claim, although his supporting arguments differ from those offered in this chapter. However, I have not tried to establish that social freedom is the right normative metric for evaluating market relations. I have instead taken this point for granted in order to mount an immanent critique of Honneth's account of economic life. Thus my argument appeals only to someone who agrees with the presuppositions of Honneth's democratic *Sittlichkeit*. Still, I hope my reflections may at least prove useful in elaborating the political-economic commitments of Honneth's left-Hegelian social theory.[54]

Notes

1   See, e.g., Axel Honneth, *Freedom's Right* (New York: Columbia University Press, 2014), 199–200, for an interpretation of market exchange as mutual recognition. For Neuhouser's account of Hegelian social freedom, see his *Foundations of Hegel's Social Theory: Actualizing Freedom* (Cambridge, MA: Harvard University Press, 2000), ch. 1.

2   Honneth has moved explicitly in the direction of some form of socialism in his more recent work *The Idea of Socialism* (Cambridge: Polity Press, 2017). I focus on the analysis in *Freedom's Right*, but make references at points to *Socialism*.

3   For this contrast, see *Freedom's Right*, 177, 192, 228, 249–50. Two further clarificatory notes: First, it is not always clear whether Honneth analyzes this interpretation in terms of negative freedom or legal freedom, which is a specific kind of negative freedom. Hence I use the 'legal or negative freedom' locution, or sometimes 'legal/negative freedom.' Second, Honneth gives very rich analyses of both labor markets and markets for consumer goods in *Freedom's Right*, but does not include a comparable analysis of capital markets. Thus the issue of capital ownership does not feature prominently in *Freedom's Right*'s normative reconstruction (but see *The Idea of Socialism*, 67–70). I focus primarily, but not exclusively, on labor markets in this chapter, but with an eye toward the implications of social freedom in the labor market for forms of capital ownership.

4   Honneth, *Freedom's Right*, 177.
5   Ibid., 179.
6   Ibid., 184.
7   Ibid., 183–4.
8   Ibid., 189.
9   See ibid., 191: "different markets must be able to reflect the rules prevailing outside the market to a certain degree in order to be able to fulfil their function of coordinating economic action."
10 Ibid., 192.
11 These institutions function for Honneth as updated versions of Hegel's corporations. See ibid., 193.
12 Ibid., 191.
13 Ibid., 194.
14 Ibid., 192.
15 Thanks to Frederick Neuhouser for pushing me to clarify this point.
16 In *Freedom's Right*, 192, Honneth writes of the "necessary consciousness of shared cooperation", which "must be seen as anchored within the market economy". The idea of self-conscious reciprocity that is central for Honneth is reflected in various formulations of Hegel and Marx. See Honneth's discussion of Hegel on recognition (ibid., 44–7), and his discussion of Marx in *Socialism*, 18–19. Again, the point Honneth makes is that "individual intentions must be so clearly interlinked that we can only achieve our aims cooperatively, conscious of our dependence on each other."
17 It is still somewhat unclear how frequently and in what contexts one must consciously conceive one's agency in the market as a form of cooperation in order to maintain relations of social freedom. Presumably at least some of the time, one can act simply as a self-interested market agent (Honneth, *Freedom's Right*, 192). This leads to the broader question of the *motivational* requirements of social freedom relations in the market: whether market relations of social freedom are compatible with self-interested motivations for market transactions, or whether such relations require a more demanding form of motivation in which we produce and consume *for the sake of the other*, as in Marx's account of communism, or something in between. For helpful discussion of this question, see Timo Jütten, "Is the Market a Sphere of Social Freedom?," *Critical Horizons* 16, no. 2 (2015): 187–203, at pp. 190–2. Honneth's formulations of social freedom in the economic sphere in *The Idea of Socialism* point toward the more demanding, altruistic motivational requirement (see, e.g., *Socialism*,

23–4), whereas the formulations in *Freedom's Right* are more ambivalent (see, e.g., *Freedom's Right*, 189, 192–3). Honneth has suggested to me in conversation the idea of a motivational division of labor between institutions and individuals, whereby individuals agree to design economic and political institutions in such a way that the institutional background does some of the work in expressing the values and motives of agents in the marketplace. This suggestion fits well with the expressivist account of economic institutions I develop below.

18 In effect, this means it is not possible to fulfill the common good requirement in the absence of epistemic transparency, due to the internal connection between the two requirements discussed in the previous paragraph. The reverse case, in which epistemic transparency is met but proper function is not, is also not possible, for a presupposition of epistemic transparency is that the relevant facts about the economic institutions—that they promote the common good—in fact obtain. But it is theoretically interesting to consider a related possibility based on ideological consciousness, in which individuals *believe* that it is epistemically transparent to them that the common good requirement is satisfied, when this is, in fact, *not* the case. I do not know how widespread such cases are, but their possibility is surely relevant for social theory.

19 Ibid., 232–3.

20 See also Honneth's discussion of the normative and functional priority of the sphere of democratic will formation over the other social spheres (ibid., 329–32). This directly implies that economic relations, including ownership structures, are ultimately legitimate only to the extent that they serve democratic purposes.

21 Ibid., 251.

22 Rawls recognizes a similar point when he says that the decision regarding specific economic arrangements is not solely determined by his theory of justice. The choice between what he calls "liberal socialism", which I here call market socialism, and "property-owning democracy" will depend on additional factors. See Rawls, *Justice as Fairness: A Restatement* (Cambridge, MA: Harvard, 2001), 138.

23 Honneth, *Freedom's Right*, 233.

24 Ibid., 249.

25 Ibid., 238.

26 Ibid., 240. For discussion of German union ambitions for economic democracy in the postwar period, of which factory-level co-determination rights are actually a fairly minor plank, see Diethelm Prove, "*Ordnungsmacht* and *Mitbestimmung*," *Between Reform and Revolution: German Socialism and Communism from 1840 to 1990*, ed. David E. Barclay and Eric D. Weitz (New York: Berghan Books, 1998), 397–420.

27 As Hegel would put it, the social recognition of the value of workers' role in the economy gives workers a secure sense of "honor" in occupying a valuable and socially important role. Cf. Georg Wilhelm Friedrich Hegel, *Elements of the Philosophy of Right*, ed. Allen Wood (New York: Cambridge University Press, 1991), §207, where Hegel discusses the "*honor of one's estate*."

28 Thomas E. Weisskopf, "A Democratic Enterprise-Based Market Socialism," in *Market Socialism: The Current Debate*, ed. Bardhan and Roemer (New York: Oxford University Press, 1993), 122.

29 Regarding the failure of the postwar labor movement in Germany to achieve any of its goals related to the full socialization of ownership rights in the means of production, see Prove, "*Ordnungsmacht* and *Mitbestimmung*," 409–10.

30 "Measured against the institutional achievements of organized capitalism in terms of the expansion of social freedom during the 'social-democratic era' (Ralf Dahrendorf), the current state of the labour market must be regarded as the result of a misdevelopment" (Honneth, *Freedom's Right*, 246).
31 Ibid., 245–6.
32 Ibid., 244–5.
33 Ibid., 247.
34 Ibid., 250. See also Honneth and Hartmann, "Paradoxes of Capitalist Modernization: A Research Programme," in Honneth, *The I in We: Studies in the Theory of Recognition*, trans. Joseph Ganahl (Cambridge: Polity, 2014), 169–90, esp. 182–3.
35 See, e.g., Honneth's comments in *Freedom's Right*, 251, regarding the "generalization of strategic self-optimization", which "increases tendencies to perceive society as a network of actors concerned solely with their own benefit. And it seems obvious that we should regard this as the cause for the individualization of responsibility, which we previously saw to be the decisive factor in the return to a de-socialized view of the economic market." On the topic of "colonization" and neoliberalism, see also Honneth and Hartmann, "Paradoxes of Capitalist Modernization," esp. 175–81.
36 Honneth, *Freedom's Right*, 251.
37 For an excellent discussion of expressivism in constitutional theory, see Elizabeth S. Anderson and Richard H. Pildes, "Expressive Theories of Law: A General Restatement," *University of Pennsylvania Law Review* 148, no. 5 (2000): 1503–75. See also Wibren van der Burg, "The Expressive and Communicative Functions of Law, Especially with Regard to Moral Issues," *Law and Philosophy* 20, no. 1 (2001): 31–59.
38 An institution may have an expressive function even if no one intended that the institution should have such a function. The expressive properties of an institution are not necessarily connected to the intentions of individuals; see the discussion of Anderson and Pildes at ibid., 1513.
39 The socialization of ownership rights in a natural or social resource is not by itself a sufficient condition to generate epistemic transparency, since in cases where political corruption is rampant, socialized resource wealth can be used—or can be perceived as being used—primarily for the benefit of the politically well connected. One could quibble and claim that such resources are not genuinely 'socialized' if they are used for political figures' private benefit, but this merely points to the difficulty involved in *genuine* socialization of ownership rights, a problem I do not tackle in this chapter.
40 See http://www.nbim.no/en/ for more information.
41 For detailed discussions of the political economy of market socialism, see John Roemer's *A Future for Socialism* (Cambridge, MA: Harvard University Press, 1994); *Market Socialism: The Current Debate*, ed. Pranab K. Bardhan and Roemer (New York: Oxford University Press, 1993); *Equal Shares: Making Market Socialism Work*, ed. Erik Olin Wright (London: Verson, 1996).
42 For a useful discussion of the problems with the politicization of investment decisions in a public finance system, and some proposed remedies, see Bardhan, "On Tackling the Soft Budget Constraint in Market Socialism," in *Market Socialism*, 145–55. The classic discussion of this nest of issues is Janos Kornai, "The Dilemmas of a Socialist Economy: The Hungarian Experience," *Cambridge Journal of Economics* 4, no. 2 (1980): 147–57. For discussion of various indirect planning mechanisms that allow for both some degree of democratic control over investment decisions and the independence of the professional financial sector, see Roemer, *A Future for Socialism*, §12, "A Digression on Investment Planning."

43 See Roemer, *A Future for Socialism*, 49–50, 55.
44 The existence of a working stock market would provide the public banks with useful information for monitoring the performance of firms, although Roemer has since backed off of this claim: see Roemer, "Thoughts on Arrangements of Property Rights in Productive Assets," *Analyse & Kritik* 1 (2013): 55–63, at p. 57.
45 The diffusion of capital income rights has the added benefit that no citizen is able to profit greatly from the production of public bads, thereby disincentivizing such undesirable behavior. See Roemer, *A Future for Socialism*, §7.
46 The argument of this paragraph draws on Rudolf Meidner, "Why Did the Swedish Model Fail?," *Socialist Register* 29 (1993): 211–28.
47 Ibid., 216.
48 Ibid., 217.
49 Thanks to Hannes Kuch for raising this worry, and for the David Miller reference discussed below.
50 This point was famously noted by Adam Smith in Book IV, Chapter 2 of *Wealth of Nations*.
51 David Miller, *Market, State, and Community* (Oxford: Oxford University Press, 1989), 221.
52 For a rich discussion of this point in connection with Hegel's account of *Sittlichkeit*, see Hannes Kuch, "Ökonomie, Subjektivität und Sittlichkeit: Hegel und die Kritik des kapitalistischen Marktes," in *Warum Kritik? Begründungsformen kritischer Theorie*, ed. Sven Ellmers and Philip Hogh (Weilerswist: Velbrück 2017), 134–63.
53 It is also worth emphasizing that embedding market-socialist institutions in the framework of Honneth's democratic *Sittlichkeit* gives market socialists resources to respond to some of the important critiques of earlier market-socialist economic models, such as that proposed by Roemer. Mieke Meurs, for example, criticizes Roemer's model for failing to take into account the cultural preconditions of economic cooperation; but placing market-socialist institutions in the context of Honneth's comprehensive social theory helps us to see market-socialist institutions as part of a larger cultural formation based on reciprocal recognition. See Mieke Meurs, "Market Socialism as a Culture of Cooperation," in *Equal Shares*, 110–21. And Debra Satz argues that Roemer's focus on economic equality fails to address equally problematic "status inequalities" (Satz, "Status Inequalities and Models of Market Socialism," *Equal Shares*, 71–89); but again, Honneth's recognition theory is designed precisely to make such inequalities salient.
54 An earlier version of this chapter was presented at the 2014 conference on "Anerkennung und Sozialismus" at the Goethe-Universität, Frankfurt. I thank the audience members at the conference for their feedback. For encouragement and detailed discussion at key points in revising the chapter, I especially thank Axel Honneth. For written comments and discussion, I am grateful to Frederick Neuhouser, Hannes Kuch, Victoria Fareld, Steve Yalowitz, and Johannes Röss. For research funding during the writing of this chapter, I thank the Alexander von Humboldt Stiftung and the CAHSS Dean's Office at UMBC.

Index

abolition 65, 99, 204, 205, 225
abstract domination 12, 84
abstraction 47, 97, 100, 146, 150–1, 154–5
  exchange abstraction 142, 147
  real abstraction 142, 148–9
abstract labor 19, 141–5, 148–51, 153, 157 n.11, 158 n.30, 209
abstract rights 2, 81, 88 n.11
accumulation 67–8, 90 n.41, 116, 118, 124 n.89, 132–4, 138–9, 162, 203
Acosta, María del Rosario López 171
action
  economic 215, 220, 249 n.9
  instrumental 11
  joint 11, 220
  political 68
  revolutionary 67–8
  social 10, 30 n.75, 74
  theory of 55
actuality ('*Wirklichkeit*') 6, 18, 26 n.32, 58, 60–1, 67, 71 n.31, 82, 93, 112, 118, 123 n.78, 186–8, 216
actualization 18, 58, 60–2, 65–6, 115–16, 119, 163, 189
Adorno, Theodor W. 4, 8, 19, 58, 69, 109–12, 120 n.7, 121 n.16, 121 n.23, 123 n.75, 142–3, 172, 214, 229 n.10
agency 4, 80–1, 126–7, 131–2, 135–6, 173 n.20, 185, 190–1, 240, 245, 249 n.17
Albert, Michael 221–4
alienation 1, 3–4, 12, 37, 40, 42, 56–7, 69, 86, 116, 119, 126, 130–1, 163, 165, 171, 192, 233 n.67
Althusser, Louis 8, 17, 27 n.48, 37, 56, 98, 103 n.6
anachronism 63
analytical Marxism 9
antagonism 68
anti-Hegelian philosophy 8–9
anti-utopianism 20, 180–6, 188–9, 191–2
  foundational 181–5, 228 n.7
  non-foundational 181–2

Aristotle 2, 56
Aufhebung. *See* sublation
authority 2, 13, 74, 80, 86, 89 n.24, 128, 130, 220, 223
autonomy 5, 47, 86, 153, 162, 183
  collective 21, 219, 228

Bachelard, Gaston 8
Backhaus, Hans-Georg 19
Badiou, Alain 94–5
Bataille, Georges 9
Bauer, Bruno 57, 63
Benhabib, Seyla 117
Bensaïd, Daniel 93
Bernstein, Jay 111, 121 n.23
Bloch, Ernst 91
Blumenfeld, Jacob 18
Bockenheimer, Eva 20
Boltanski, Luc 206
bondsman-lord relation 19, 128–30. *See also* master-slave dialectics
bourgeois 7, 30 n.76, 40, 44, 51 n.14, 52 n.16, 77, 99–100, 111, 117–18, 142, 146, 148–9, 153, 155, 175 n.47, 185, 201, 204, 210, 220, 231 n.37
bourgeoisie 44
Brandom, Robert 114
Bröckling, Ulrich 206
Brudney, Daniel 166

capital 9, 21, 48–9, 82, 117, 119, 123 n.70, 154–5, 183, 198, 208, 215, 221–2, 226–7, 228 n.1, 231 n.37, 238–9, 242–6, 252 n.45
  capital accumulation 67, 134, 138, 203
  capital ownership 13, 236, 239–40, 246, 248, 249 n.3
  centralization of 67–8, 203–4
  circulation of 19, 90 n.40, 131–9
capitalism 2–5, 10–13, 16—21, 28 n.63, 29 n.67, 38, 42, 45–50, 52 n.16, 66–9, 72 n.51, 82–5, 87–8, 90 n.36, 90

254   *Index*

n.38, 90 n.40, 90 n.41, 100–1, 109,
    111, 116–19, 123 n.75, 123 n.86, 124
    n.91, 125, 130–3, 135–9, 142, 147,
    151, 153, 155–6, 162–7, 170, 172,
    173 n.14, 174 n.34, 179–80, 182,
    185, 192, 197–8, 201–9, 213–18, 220,
    224–8, 228 n.1, 233 n.67, 235–6,
    238–46, 248, 251 n.30
Capital (Marx) 4, 8–9, 11, 19, 57–8, 65–8,
    85, 116–19, 126, 131, 141–2, 146–7,
    151–2, 154–6, 198–9, 201, 226
Castoriadis, Cornelius 12
Celan, Paul 96
Chiapello, Eve 206
Chitty, Andrew 217
Cieszkowski, August 58
citoyen 7
civil society (*bürgerliche Gesellschaft*) 6–7,
    13, 16, 25 n.29, 26 n.34, 29 n.71, 31
    n.87, 61, 80, 84, 109, 127, 170–1,
    204, 236, 238
The Civil War in France (Marx) 65
class 14, 16, 44, 66–8, 84, 98–100, 109, 117,
    129, 135, 154, 173 n.14, 182–3, 185,
    204, 209, 213, 243–5
    class domination 7, 47, 228 n.1
    class struggle 7, 14, 44, 66, 98–100, 182
The Class Struggles in France (Marx) 65
co-determination 240–1, 244, 250 n.26
Cohen, Gerald A. 8
Comay, Rebecca 16
"Comments on James Mill" (Marx) 15, 162
commodity fetishism 12, 30 n.75, 117–18,
    153, 202, 233 n.67
commons economies 21, 213, 217–19
communal 2, 7, 14–15, 26 n.32, 41, 129,
    161–2, 165, 168, 170, 172 n.5, 202,
    217–19
communal being (*Gemeinwesen*) 15
communication/communicative 10–11,
    45–6, 96, 98–9
communism 6, 13, 15–16, 65, 68, 116, 163,
    180
The Communist Manifesto (Marx and
    Engels) 44, 57, 66, 181–2, 205, 220
communitarianism 15
community 15–16, 24 n.15, 74, 83–4, 90
    n.31, 96, 104 n.33, 127–8, 131, 163,

    168, 174 n.36, 175 n.60, 179, 183,
    189, 192, 216, 230 n.33, 238
competition/competitive 46, 48, 84–5, 87,
    90 n.38, 123 n.70, 154, 207, 224, 227,
    241–2, 244, 247
concrete freedom 13, 87
Conflict of Faculties (Kant) 94
confrontational modality 13–14
constructive modality 14–15
consumption 13, 15, 19, 129–30, 205,
    217–18, 221–3, 237
contradiction 5, 10, 17, 26 n.34, 58, 61–3,
    65–7, 110, 113–15, 119, 134, 170,
    175 n.50, 202, 204–5, 246
*A Contribution to the Critique of Political
    Economy* (Marx) 146–7, 149, 197
cooperation 15, 21, 31 n.82, 39–41, 43, 46,
    50, 127, 136, 190, 207–9, 218–21,
    225, 236–7, 240, 242, 244–5, 248,
    249 n.17, 252 n.53
cooperative
    consumer cooperative 236
    enterprise 21, 214, 224–8, 231 n.48, 231
        n.50, 239, 247
    ownership 227
    praxis 4, 61, 133, 135–6, 139
    producer cooperative 45, 227
coordination 213, 218–19, 221, 225, 232
    n.57, 236
corrective modality 12–13
costs
    opportunity 221–2, 224
    social 221–2
councils 14, 221–2, 224, 231 n.43, 232 n.57
crisis 1, 5, 124 n.90, 145, 197, 204, 206, 209,
    213
Critical Theory 1, 3–4, 7, 10, 24 n.15, 24
    n.17, 56, 58, 67, 69, 70 n.14, 75–6,
    109–11, 121 n.16, 122 n.62, 215, 232
    n.58
critique
    of capitalism 11, 17, 19–20, 117, 123
        n.75, 125, 131, 133, 214–15, 217
    defetishizing 117–18, 123 n.78
    immanent 4–6, 15, 19, 24 n.15, 56, 64,
        69, 109–19, 122 n.34, 235, 248
    negativist 19, 109–12, 114, 116, 118–20,
        121 n.16

of political economy 1, 8, 18, 20, 33 n.116, 37, 47, 50, 58, 145, 154, 156, 198
social 5, 17, 19, 56, 62, 69, 125
Critique of Judgment (Kant) 94
Crusoe, Robinson 136
The Culture of the New Capitalism (Sennett) 206
cunning of reason (*List der Vernunft*) 190

Das unternehmerische Wir (Siemens) 206
democracy 13, 69, 228, 232 n.57
　council 231 n.43
　economic 239–41, 245–6, 250 n.26
　participatory 223
　property-owning 228 n.1, 250 n.22
　social 37, 100–1, 235
democratic
　life 111–12, 154
　planning 13, 21, 219, 221, 223–4, 227–8, 231 n.43
Derrida, Jacques 8
desire 1, 7, 9–10, 28 n.57, 43, 64, 81–2, 102, 110, 132, 135, 138, 161–3, 165, 172, 183, 191, 236–7
Dewey, John 55, 69
dialectics 1, 3–4, 7–10, 16, 20–1, 26 n.34, 28 n.62, 28 n.64, 37, 56–8, 69, 70 n.10, 92, 109–14, 116, 119, 198–201, 204–5
　dialectical method 9–10, 26 n.34, 37, 69, 113–14, 200, 205
difference 16, 146, 149, 164, 166, 168–70, 173 n.14
differentiation 161, 170, 175 n.61
　functional 49
　social 7, 49, 52 n.16, 53 n.40
disruptive readings, and Hegelian Marxism 6–9, 17
division of labor 12, 30 n.76, 123 n.70, 136, 143, 145, 148–9, 153, 159 n.41, 202–3, 250 n.17
Doctrine of Right (Kant) 79, 87
domination 18–19, 28 n.64, 46, 50, 87, 112–13, 120, 129–30, 173 n.14, 236
　abstract 12, 84
　class 7, 47, 228 n.1
　and exploitation 6–7, 166
　ideological 7

over nature 40
social 44
of things over persons 12, 29 n.75
dynamics 38, 62, 66, 111, 207, 225–7
　of capitalism 18, 48, 204, 227
　expansionary 18, 47–8

economic
　order 46–7, 49, 213
　relations 7, 42, 77, 119, 123 n.75, 153, 166, 250 n.20
　reproduction 42, 86
　sphere 18, 47–9, 130, 138, 172 n.6, 238, 248, 249 n.17
　system 20–1, 46–9, 172, 179, 215, 224, 226
Economic and Philosophic Manuscripts (Marx) 8, 37, 56–8, 116, 162–4, 217
Elbe, Ingo 141
Elements of the Philosophy of Right (Hegel) 7, 38, 47, 58–64, 77, 87, 109, 127, 169–70, 217, 235
Ellmers, Sven 19
Elster, Jon 9
emancipation/emancipatory 1, 10–11, 20–1, 24 n.17, 37, 40, 63, 66, 69, 91, 93, 97, 100, 102, 109, 117, 119, 120, 126, 139, 182, –183, 189, 197, 206
empower/empowerment/empowering 162, 164–8, 170–1, 173 n.22
Encyclopedia (Hegel) 57, 59–60
Entfremdung. *See* alienation
entrepreneurial
　function 198, 206–9
　we 21, 206
The Entrepreneurial Self (Bröckling) 206
epistemic transparency 237–8, 246–8, 250 n.18, 251 n.39
epistemological break 8, 37
equality 7, 100, 118–19, 145–6, 149, 179, 240, 245, 252 n.53
ethical life (*Sittlichkeit*) 9, 13, 15, 18, 26 n.34, 31 n.82, 45–6, 49–50, 77, 80, 86, 169, 187–8, 225
ethos 9, 192 n.1, 245–6
exchange 42, 47, 84–6, 89 n.24, 90 n.40, 126, 131–2, 145–50, 153, 158 n.23, 163–4, 166–7, 172, 202, 205, 217, 226, 228, 241, 248 n.1

exchange value 118, 123 n.70, 135–8, 142–3, 146, 158 n.39, 159 n.39, 202
exploitation 6–7, 47, 43, 66, 68, 84–5, 117, 119, 124 n.89, 135, 148, 166–7, 203–4, 208, 226–7, 245

family 8, 26 n.34, 31 n.82, 45–6, 49, 80, 91, 126–7, 169, 179, 188, 216, 242
Federici, Silvia 218
fetishism of commodities/fetish character. *See* commodity fetishism
feudal 28 n.63, 45, 62–3, 77, 83–4, 203–4
Feuerbach, Ludwig 8, 37, 39, 56–8, 64
Fichte, Johann Gottlieb 39, 77, 152
flourishing, human 20, 78, 164, 166, 170–1
force
    driving 25 n.25, 26 n.34, 43, 189
    emancipatory 11
    forces of production 28 n.64, 90 n.38, 124
    moving 38, 44, 46
    normative 111, 119
    own 25 n.19, 126, 138
    political 84, 171
    productive 10, 21, 28 n.63, 40, 43–5, 197–8, 201, 205–7, 209–10
    social 4–5, 126, 136–9, 203, 205
Foucault, Michel 8
Fourier, Charles 180
Frankfurt School 4, 10, 58, 109–10
freedom 2, 5–6, 9, 14–15, 18–19, 21, 25 n.25, 30 n.76, 31 n.82, 31 n.84, 31 n.90, 39–50, 51 n.8, 52 n.30, 58, 73–87, 89 n.12, 89 n.20, 89 n.26, 95, 100, 102, 111–14, 118–20, 125–32, 134, 136, 138–9, 155, 170, 174 n.37, 175 n.61, 183, 203–7, 210, 214, 229 n.17
    concrete 13, 87
    individual/personal 13, 45–8, 77–8, 80–1, 85, 87, 175 n.61, 210, 216, 219, 225
    liberal 216–17
    negative 13, 216, 239, 249 n.3
    social 1, 14, 21, 44–5, 80, 155, 216–21, 223–6, 228, 233 n.67, 235–48, 249 n.3, 249 n.17, 251 n.30
    subjective 188

Freedom's Right (Honneth) 154, 235, 237–8, 240–1, 248, 249 n.2, 249 n.3, 249 n.16, 250 n.17, 251 n.35
French Revolution 7, 62, 65, 94–5
Freud, Sigmund 16, 99, 128
From Employee to "Entreployee" (Voss and Pongratz) 206
Fukuyama, Francis 28 n.57
Furet, François 95

Gattungswesen. See species-being
Geist. See spirit
Gemeinwesen. See communal being
The German Ideology (Marx) 57–8, 65, 77, 201
Giddens, Anthony 161
goods 14, 21, 45, 47, 73, 84, 144, 163, 214, 217–18, 220, 222–4, 249 n.3
good
    collective 139
    common 237–9, 243, 246–7, 250 n.18
    conceptions of the 127
    distribution of 45
    economic 14, 47
    good life 111–12, 173 n.21
    private 223, 239
    production of 127–8, 145, 202, 214, 218, 220, 222
    public 223, 239, 244–5
Graeber, David 218
Gregoratto, Federica 20
Grundrisse (Marx) 57, 77, 83, 96

Habermas, Jürgen 10–11, 28 n.62, 28 n.64, 41, 233 n.67
Hahnel, Robin 221–4, 231 n.50, 232 n.52, 232 n.57
Hardt, Michael 164, 166, 218
Hegelianism 3, 58, 62, 110, 192
Hegelian Marxism 1–4, 11, 17–20, 23 n.7, 37, 56–8, 91, 109, 119, 192, 198, 205–6, 208, 210
    and disruptive readings 6–9
    helical approach 2, 11–17
    and progressive readings 4–6
    and reverse readings 9–11
Hegel's Rabble (Ruda) 16
Heinrich, Michael 19, 124 n.90, 145–6, 148–50, 158 n.30

helical approach 2, 11–17
  confrontational modality 13–14
  constructive modality 14–15
  corrective modality 12–13
Hess, Moses 56–8
Hilferding, Rudolf 239
historical materialism 2, 8, 11, 18–19, 46, 50
history
  philosophy of 2, 5–6, 9, 11, 38–40, 46, 51 n.8, 58, 60–2, 65, 156, 180
  and progress 25 n.25, 40, 95, 185
History and Class Consciousness (Lukács) 4
Honneth, Axel 3, 10, 14, 17–18, 21, 32 n.94, 69, 110–12, 114, 121 n.16, 121 n.29, 154–6, 160 n.69, 160 n.71, 161, 235–41, 243–4, 246–8, 249 n.2, 249 n.3, 249 n.16, 249–50 n.17, 250 n.20, 251 n.35, 252 n.53, 252 n.54
human flourishing 20, 78, 164, 166, 170–1
human nature 76, 126, 163, 184
idealism 1–2, 42, 50, 58, 77, 98, 125, 130, 198, 200–1
The Idea of Socialism (Honneth) 248

identity 8, 15–16, 26 n.34, 30 n.76, 111, 115, 134, 169, 175 n.50, 200
ideology 7–8, 47, 84, 100, 118, 250 n.18
immanent critique 4—6, 15, 19, 24 n.15, 56, 64, 69, 109–19, 122 n.34, 235, 248
immediate 5, 18, 59, 62, 80, 83–4, 99, 130, 179, 182, 188, 200, 203, 205, 220, 230 n.29, 247
Indirekte Steuerung ('indirect steering') 207
individual
  activity 136, 210
  freedom 13, 45–8, 77–8, 80–1, 85, 87, 175 n.61, 210, 216, 219, 225
  production 202
  property 204–5
  rights 2
institutions 2, 4–7, 15–16, 18–19, 30 n.76, 31 n.82, 39–50, 62–3, 75–7, 83, 89 n.24, 91, 93, 97, 109, 111, 113–15, 120, 127, 155, 162, 172, 179–81, 183, 187–9, 192, 213–16, 219–20, 223, 225–8, 229 n.16, 232, 246–7, 249 n.11, 250 n.17, 251 n.30, 251 n.38

centralized 21, 214, 220, 223
economic 236–9, 242–3, 247, 250 n.17, 250 n.18
expressive properties of 242, 247–8
institutionalism 2, 12–13, 40–1
market-socialist 226, 242, 244, 248, 252 n.53
social 2, 6, 12, 20, 40–1, 44–5, 76, 80, 187, 219, 235–6, 242, 244
interaction 7, 12–13, 28 n.62, 28 n.64, 42, 55, 86, 118, 128, 162, 166, 172, 201, 235–6, 238, 242
communicative 10
cooperative 219, 237
social 41, 44, 162, 173 n.14, 217, 244
strategic 236
interest 7, 9–10, 25 n.25, 37, 44, 190–1, 207, 237–8, 243–4
common 12–13, 238–40
particular 81
private 12–13, 46, 221, 236, 245
public 238–9
self-interest 87, 217, 236, 238–9, 242, 245–7, 249 n.17
Iteration Facilitation Boards 221

Jaeggi, Rahel 30 n.79, 111, 114
justice 12, 30 n.76, 47–8, 69, 75, 87, 109, 111, 114, 119–20, 226, 250 n.22

Kant, Immanuel 2, 4, 9, 18, 37, 39, 51 n.1, 51 n.8, 59, 73, 77–9, 81–8, 90 n.28, 94–5, 122 n.42, 126, 175 n.52
Kautsky, Karl 141
knowledge
  absolute 27 n.47, 214
  of the present 55, 60, 69
Kojève, Alexandre 9–10
Kuch, Hannes 21

labor 5, 7, 9–10, 12, 24 n.17, 28 n.62, 39–40, 42, 45, 68, 73, 76, 83–5, 87, 89 n.24, 123 n.70, 126–9, 131–2, 146, 158 n.23, 163, 165–7, 173 n.20, 174 n.26, 188, 204, 208, 215, 221, 227, 236, 241, 243, 245, 249 n.3, 250 n.17
abstract 19, 141–5, 148–51, 153, 157 n.11, 158 n.30, 209

alienated 116–18, 123 n.71, 130, 173 n.14
complex and simple 147–51
concrete 142, 147–50
as cooperative praxis 135–7
division of 12, 30 n.76, 123 n.70, 136, 143, 145, 148–9, 153, 159 n.41, 202–3, 250 n.17
labor expenditure 143–4, 146–8
labor market 239, 241, 245, 249 n.3
labor power 18, 21, 117–18, 135, 138–9, 142, 144, 147–52, 154, 158 n.37, 179, 202–3, 205, 209, 222, 226
labor theory of value 47, 148–9, 154, 156
movement 235, 239, 250 n.29
wage labor/laborer 18, 20–1, 47–8, 50, 67, 87, 116, 139, 203, 209, 225–6, 240–1, 245–6
Lacan, Jacques 9, 16
law 11, 38, 68–9, 71 n.31, 79–80, 87, 96, 123 n.70, 137, 156, 200, 242
(general) laws of motion 66, 90 n.38
immanent laws (of capitalism) 67–8, 203–4
natural 29 n.67, 61–2, 66
positive 76–7
rule of 47, 85
'tendential' 18, 66–7
Lectures on the Philosophy of Religion (Hegel) 169
Lectures on the Philosophy of World History (Hegel) 189
Left Hegelians/Left Hegelianism 4–5, 10, 109–10, 248
legitimacy 49, 59, 61, 224–5, 235–8, 244, 247
Lenin, Vladimir 3, 18–19, 91–4, 96–102, 103 n.4, 103 n.6, 103 n.7, 104 n.39, 104 n.45, 105 n.55, 202
Leopold, David 20
Levinas, Emmanuel 8
liberalism 1, 2, 15
liberal freedom 216–17
liberty 14, 39, 46
life 6–7, 12, 14, 16, 19, 26 n.32, 30 n.77, 39, 47–8, 82–6, 94, 103 n.4, 120 n.6, 125–35, 137–9, 147, 153, 155, 162, 164–5, 167–9, 173 n.21, 175 n.52, 199, 201–2, 226, 235, 238–40, 242, 244, 247–8
democratic 111–12, 154
ethical 9, 13, 15, 18, 26 n.34, 31 n.82, 45–6, 49–50, 77, 80, 86, 169, 187–8, 225
form of 43, 80, 109, 111–12, 114–15, 118–19, 123 n.75, 215
good 111–12, 173 n.21
rational 109, 119–20
social 2, 4, 11, 18, 20, 41, 49, 63, 77, 117, 125, 127–8, 161, 213, 242
spiritual 19, 125
Logic (Hegel) 11, 48
lord 19, 84, 116, 128–30
love 8, 10, 15, 50, 96, 100, 121 n.27, 128, 161–72, 172 n.2, 172 n.5, 172 n.6, 173 n.13, 173 n.14, 173 n.19, 173 n.20, 173 n.21, 173 n.22, 174 n.24, 175 n.47, 175 n.50, 175 n.51, 175 n.52, 175 n.60, 175 n.61, 176 n.63, 217
erotic 20, 161–2, 168, 172 n.1, 173 n.14
love relationships 20, 163, 165–6, 172, 176 n.61
noncapitalist 162–7
Luhmann, Niklas 161
Lukács, Georg 3–4, 19, 56
Luxemburg, Rosa 141

'management by objectives' (MBO) 207
management/managers 183, 206–8, 240–1, 243
Manifesto of the Communist Party (Marx and Engels). See *The Communist Manifesto* (Marx and Engels)
markets 2, 13, 26 n.36, 29 n.72, 30 n.76, 45, 50, 76, 84–8, 90 n.35, 135–7, 139, 142, 145, 150, 153, 158 n.23, 162–4, 172, 179, 203, 207, 209, 213, 215–18, 221, 224, 245, 249 n.9, 249 n.17, 251 n.30, 251 n.35, 252 n.44, 252 n.53
capitalist 18, 46–7, 49, 52 n.16, 118, 162, 225, 244, 246
labor market 239, 241, 245, 249 n.3
market-dependency 85
market economy 6, 127, 224, 237–8, 240, 242, 249 n.16
marketization 48–9

market participants 12, 147, 236–9, 244–5
market relations 30 n.76, 164, 171, 225, 228, 233 n.67, 247–8, 249 n.17
market socialism 21, 214, 224–8, 232 n.57, 232 n.58, 235, 242–3, 246–8, 250 n.22, 251 n.41
market society 7, 52 n.16, 78, 83, 235–6, 242, 244
Marx
  appropriation of Hegel 3, 4, 9, 20, 23 n.5, 37, 40, 57–8, 64, 69,109, 116, 130–39, 198–200
  critique of Hegel 1, 4, 6–7, 45, 47, 63, 65, 116, 200–201
  early Marx 7–9, 20, 30 n.77, 37, 62–5, 162, 217, 219, 226
  mature Marx 1, 8, 18–19, 30 n.77, 56–8, 65
  relation to Hegel 1–3, 37–40, 56–8, 62, 125–26, 133, 136, 152, 170, 186, 191–92, 216
Marxian Hegel. *See* Hegelian Marxism
Marxism/Marxist 1–2, 18. *See also* Hegelian Marxism
  analytical 9
  historical materialism 2, 8, 11, 18–19, 46, 50
  history of 1–6, 8–12, 18–20, 23 n.7, 37, 56–8, 91, 96–98, 100, 102 n.1, 109, 141, 179–82, 192, 198, 213–5, 226, 245–6
master 84, 112. *See also* bondsman-lord relation
  dialectic of master and slave 9
materialism 2, 8, 11, 18–19, 46, 50
MBO. *See* 'management by objectives' (MBO)
Mead, George H. 55, 69
means of production 2, 11, 44, 67–8, 117, 197, 202–5, 209, 220, 224, 227, 235, 240–2, 245–6, 250 n.29
means of subsistence 18, 83, 90 n.32, 201, 203, 205, 227
mediate/mediation 12, 30 n.77, 80, 83–4, 110, 119–20, 162, 167, 171–2, 200, 202, 231 n.34
Meidner, Rudolf 245–6
Mill, John Stuart 38

Miller, David 247
Minima Moralia (Adorno) 109–12
Mitsein 15
mode of production 28 n.63, 66–9, 72 n.51, 90 n.41, 117, 138, 155–6, 201–2, 205, 209
modern societies 7, 13, 17, 38–40, 44–6, 49–50, 77, 83, 182, 202, 216
money 12, 30 n.76, 73, 86, 131–5, 142, 153, 155, 161–4, 170–1, 174 n.34, 202–3, 215, 217, 219, 226
moral 4–5, 11, 14, 28 n.62, 28 n.64, 43, 68, 74, 80, 111, 113, 118, 121 n.23, 154–5, 172 n.5, 175 n.52, 188, 210, 235
movement 2, 5, 7, 9, 12, 14, 17, 21, 25 n.26, 26 n.34, 28 n.62, 57, 65, 68–9, 92, 97, 100, 113–14, 124 n.90, 133–5, 137–8, 148, 179, 224
  dialectical 26 n.34, 113–14, 198–201
  labor 235, 239, 250 n.29
  social 1, 10, 120 n.10, 214–16

Nance, Michael 21
Nancy, Jean-Luc 15–16
naturalism 39–41, 50, 116–17
nature 7, 9, 11, 15, 18, 24–5 n.19, 29 n.67, 39–45, 50, 75, 79–83, 85–7, 90 n.43, 116–18, 123 n.71, 125–6, 144–5, 148, 162, 165, 167–8, 185, 201, 206, 217, 221–2, 243, 251 n.39
  human nature 76, 126, 163–4, 184
needs 18, 24 n.15, 29 n.71, 30 n.76, 30 n.77, 44, 49, 52 n.16, 59, 73, 79–83, 87, 89 n.20, 132–3, 135–6, 138–9, 145, 162–3, 165–6, 179, 190, 201, 203, 205, 210, 213, 217–20, 225, 227, 231 n.42, 236–7
  emotional 165
  historically determined 18, 82
  material 21, 82, 125–7, 139
  natural 41, 81, 126
  neediness 125–6, 165, 217, 230 n.29
  needs-abilities principle 30 n.76, 30 n.77
  social 19, 85, 141, 144, 219
negation 26 n.34, 29 n.67, 63, 102, 115, 120, 198
  determinate 110, 113–14, 119, 199–200
  negation of 199–200, 204

Negative Dialectics (Adorno) 111
negativity 9, 16, 28 n.57, 110, 114–16, 119, 215
Negri, Antonio 218
neoliberalism 48, 155, 229 n.16, 245, 248
'neue Marx-Lektüre' 19, 141, 145, 150, 156
Neuhouser, Frederick 19
The New Spirit of Capitalism (Chiapello and Boltanski) 206
normative
　claim 179–80, 183, 186, 188
　commitment 112–15, 118, 125
　criteria 4, 18–19, 21, 49, 64, 77–8, 109–19, 118, 121 n.16, 134, 160 n.69, 188, 214–16
　expectations 4, 14, 73–4, 76–83, 85, 90 n.28
　foundations 11, 41–7, 49, 59, 61–2, 125, 128, 131, 134, 154, 160 n.69
　political philosophy 61–2
　reconstruction 235, 239–40, 248, 249 n.3, 250 n.20
norms 4–5, 9–13, 18, 28 n.64, 30 n.76, 31 n.83, 40, 42, 49–50, 82, 84–6, 111, 115, 118–20, 121 n.23, 127, 129, 136, 161–2, 167, 172, 219, 226, 236, 238, 240, 245
　gender norms 167
　social norms 2, 12, 18, 40–1, 48, 84

objectification 116, 153, 165–7, 171
objective spirit 38, 41–2, 48, 52 n.16
"On the Jewish Question" (Marx) 118, 126
On the Question of Dialectics (Lenin) 202
ontology 18, 27 n.50, 39, 55, 60–1, 69, 96, 134, 167, 171, 174 n.26
　processual ontology 60–1, 67
　social ontology 15–16, 66
Outlines of the Philosophy of Right (Hegel). See *Elements of the Philosophy of Right* (Hegel)
Owen, Robert 180, 226
owl of Minerva (*Eule der Minerva*) 186, 188
ownership
　capital 13, 236, 239–40, 246, 248, 249 n.3
　cooperative 227
　private 2, 67, 224, 228 n.1, 235, 241, 244–5
　public 227
　socialized 13, 21, 31 n.89, 235, 239, 242, 246, 250 n.29, 251 n.39
ownership rights 245–6
　and control rights 241, 243
　and income rights 241, 243, 252 n.45
　socialization of 235, 239, 242, 246, 250 n.29, 251 n.39

Paris Commune 66, 183, 185, 220
Parisian Manuscripts (Marx). See *Economic and Philosophic Manuscripts* (Marx)
participatory economy 221, 223–5, 231 n.50, 232 n.57
paternalism 214
Phenomenology of Spirit (Hegel) 5, 9–10, 48, 56, 59, 92, 99, 109–10, 112, 114–15, 128, 199
Philosophy of Right (Hegel). See *Elements of the Philosophy of Right* (Hegel)
plans and blueprints 20, 179–81, 183–5, 188, 191–2
Polanyi, Karl 42
politics/political 1–2, 4, 6–8, 11, 13, 15–16, 18, 20, 26 n.32, 33 n.116, 37–8, 42, 46–8, 50, 55, 58, 61–9, 74, 76, 80, 84, 91–102, 103 n.2, 109–11, 113, 115, 117–19, 141, 145–9, 151, 154–6, 160 n.71, 161–2, 166, 170–2, 175 n.52, 179, 182, 184–9, 191, 194 n.28, 197–8, 201, 206, 210, 214–16, 230 n.28, 231 n.37, 231 n.43, 232 n.58, 238, 246, 248, 250 n.17, 251 n.39, 251 n.41, 251 n.42
Pongratz, Hans J. 206
Postone, Moishe 12
poverty 16, 190, 204
The Poverty of Philosophy (Marx) 57, 151
power 2, 5, 12, 39, 44, 46–7, 50, 66, 81, 86, 90 n.40, 116, 163–5, 167–8, 171, 173 n.20, 174 n.39, 184, 186, 191, 220, 223, 227, 230 n.34
　labor power 18, 21, 117–18, 135, 138–9, 142, 144, 147–52, 154, 158 n.37, 179, 202–3, 205, 209, 222, 226
　social power 12, 134
pragmatism 55
praxis 4, 61, 133, 135–6, 139
pre-capitalist 18, 42, 83–5, 142

presentism 18, 55–69
  ontological 55, 67
  primacy of the present 58–62, 69
production
  commodity production 136, 139, 145, 148, 159 n.41, 202–3, 205, 209, 233 n.67
  economic 44
  forces of 28 n.64, 90 n.38, 124
  of goods 127–8, 145, 202, 214, 218, 220, 222
  material 126
  means of 2, 11, 44, 67–8, 117, 197, 202–5, 209, 220, 224, 227, 235, 240–2, 245–6, 250 n.29
  mode of 28 n.63, 66–9, 72 n.51, 90 n.41, 117, 138, 155–6, 201–2, 205, 209
  relations of 43, 47–8
  socialized 203–5
productive force 10, 21, 28 n.63, 40, 43–5, 197–8, 201, 205–7, 209–10
profit 21, 47–9, 67, 73, 116, 118, 123 n.70, 156, 164, 179, 198, 206, 238–41, 243–6, 252 n.45
  -maximization 85, 90 n.38, 208, 213
  profitability 49, 198, 207–9, 226, 245
  tendential fall in the rate of 66
progressive readings, and Hegelian Marxism 4–6, 17
proletariat 2, 4, 10, 14, 16, 44, 66, 68, 93, 98–9, 101, 109, 117, 182, 204–5, 231 n.37
property 2, 11–12, 18, 40, 79, 88 n.3, 88 n.4, 88 n.10, 88 n.11, 89 n.12, 89 n.20, 89 n.24, 89 n.25, 142–6, 172, 175 n.47, 176 n.66, 188, 202–5, 225, 228 n.1, 235, 242–3, 247–8, 250 n.22, 251 n.38
  individual 204–5
  -owning democracy 228 n.1, 250 n.22
  private 12, 20, 30 n.76, 68, 75, 77–8, 81–5, 87, 90 n.36, 90 n.41, 117–18, 123 n.70, 123 n.71, 153, 162, 165, 167–71, 176 n.66, 217, 240–1
  property relations 73–5, 77–8, 80, 83, 85–7, 89 n.25, 90 n.38
  property rights 73, 76–7, 84 (See also ownership rights)
Proudhon, Pierre 226

rabble 2, 16, 89 n.14
rationality 18, 25 n.25, 45, 49, 59, 63, 71 n.31, 111–12, 116, 187–9, 216, 244, 248
Rawls, John 9, 228 n.1, 250 n.22
Realphilosophie (Hegel) 175 n.52, 199–201
reconciliation 27 n.47, 59, 62, 103 n.4, 163, 175 n.47, 186, 189
Reichelt, Helmut 19
reification 37, 101, 115, 123 n.75, 150
relations
  bondsman-lord 19, 128–30
  economic 7, 42, 77, 119, 123 n.75, 153, 166, 250 n.20
  horizontal 217, 225, 228
  market 30 n.76, 164, 171, 225, 228, 233 n.67, 247–8, 249 n.17
  of production 10, 42–5, 47–8, 82, 145, 148–9, 153, 197–8, 201
  property 73–5, 77–8, 80, 83, 85–7, 89 n.25, 90 n.38
  social 10, 14–15, 28 n.63, 30 n.77, 45, 50, 74, 77, 83, 118, 129, 145, 155, 162, 166–7, 202, 215–16, 220
  vertical 12, 219–21, 223–4, 227, 230 n.34
Renault, Emmanuel 18
reproduction 49, 67, 78, 82–7, 127–8, 130, 133, 137, 216
  economic 42, 86
reversive readings and Hegelian Marxism 9–11
revolution 4, 7, 18, 38, 59, 65, 67–8, 77, 91–102, 104 n.45, 105 n.55, 124 n.90, 149, 173 n.13, 173 n.14, 182–3, 199, 216, 220
rights
  abstract 2, 81, 88 n.11
  equal 46
  individual 2
  innate 82, 86, 118
  legal 7, 12, 30 n.76, 83–4, 217, 241
  liberal 13, 23, 45–6
  natural 76
  ownership rights (*See* ownership rights)
  property rights 73, 76–8, 80, 82, 84–6
Roemer, John 9
roles, social 45, 80, 82, 237, 244
Ruda, Frank 16–17, 18
Ruge, Arnold 63–4

Index

Saint-Simon, Henri de 38, 180
Sartre, Jean-Paul 9
Schumpeter, Josef 38
The Science of Logic (Hegel) 57, 59, 92, 99, 189, 200
Searle, John 42
Second International 11
Second World War 37, 239
secularization/mundanization 64
self-consciousness 134, 169, 175 n.50
self-determination 6, 45–6, 50, 95, 183, 213, 219, 221
self-realization 4, 39, 43–4, 154, 166, 219
Sennett, Richard 206
Siemens, Stephan 206–9
Sittlichkeit. See ethical life
slave/slavery 5, 9, 68, 203–4
Smith, Adam 12, 50, 142
social critique 5, 17, 19, 56, 62, 69, 125
social democracy 37, 100–1, 235
social freedom 1, 14, 21, 44–5, 80, 155, 216–17, 219–21, 223–6, 228, 233 n.67, 235–48, 249 n.3, 249 n.17, 251 n.30
 holistic form of 220
 horizontal form of 219
socialism 20, 45, 100, 192 n.1, 205, 221, 230 n.33, 239, 249 n.2, 252 n.53
 future socialist society 179–81, 183–5
 market socialism 21, 214, 224–8, 232 n.57, 232 n.58, 235, 242–8, 250 n.22, 251 n.41
 and socialist design 179–82, 185, 191–2
 and socialist proposals 21, 226–8
 utopian 180–2
social order 4–6, 43–6, 49, 58, 126, 129, 185, 191
social philosophy 11, 15, 62, 125–6
social theory 2, 5, 7, 8, 11, 18, 37, 38, 40–50, 110, 191, 248, 250 n.18, 252 n.53
society
 burgeois 7, 30 n.76, 40, 44, 51 n.14, 52 n.16, 77, 99–100, 111, 117–18, 142, 146, 148–9, 153, 155, 175 n.47, 185, 201, 204, 210, 220, 231 n.37
 capitalist 3–4, 12, 15–16, 20, 38, 42, 66, 83, 87, 142, 153, 162–4, 166, 170, 179–80, 182, 185, 204, 213–15, 217, 240, 245
civil society (*bürgerliche Gesellschaft*) 6–7, 13, 16, 25 n.29, 26 n.34, 29 n.71, 31 n.87, 61, 80, 84, 109, 127, 170–1, 204, 236, 238
 communist 13, 15, 30 n.76, 30 n.77, 165, 214, 220, 228 n.7
 human 2, 40, 128–9, 164–5, 184
 market society 7, 52 n.16, 78, 83, 235–6, 242, 244
 modern 7, 13, 17, 38–40, 44–6, 49–50, 77, 83, 182, 202, 216
 noncapitalist 162–4, 166, 170
 socialist 179–85, 205, 248
Sohn-Rethel, Alfred 142
solidarity 213, 217, 236, 240, 245–6, 248
species-being 2, 26 n.32, 116, 216
speculative 18, 92–3, 97–8, 100, 102, 116
spirit (*Geist*) 5–7, 9–10, 12, 25 n.25, 28 n.62, 29 n.71, 37–42, 44, 48, 50, 61, 63, 92, 115, 125–6, 128, 131, 134, 151, 168, 174 n.36, 224
 objective 7, 12, 38, 41–2, 48, 52 n.16
spiritual life 19, 125, 201
The Spirit of Christianity and its Fate (Hegel) 169
state 2–3, 5–7, 12–13, 26 n.32, 26 n.34, 30 n.76, 31 n.82, 31 n.87, 45–6, 49, 52 n.30, 59, 61–3, 65, 80, 87, 99, 127, 188, 213, 215, 218, 221, 225–7, 231 n.37, 238–9, 244
 bourgeois 77, 204, 220
 constitutional 5, 46, 61–3
 sphere of the 7, 26 n.32, 26 n.34, 31 n.87, 236
 welfare state 226
State and Revolution (Lenin) 100
structure
 normative 42, 114
 social 40, 45–6, 48, 67, 109, 156, 167
struggle, social 6–7, 24 n.17, 49
Struggle for Recognition (Honneth) 14
sublation 4, 9, 175 n.50
subsumption 49
 real 47, 208
supply and demand 142, 145, 149, 156, 222–3
symptomatic reading 16

Taylor, Charles 14, 37
technological progress 44
teleology/teleological 20, 39, 51 n.8, 160 n.71, 190
'tendential' laws 66–7
The 18th Brumaire (Marx) 65
Tocqueville, Alexis de 38
totalitarianism 1, 214
totality 4, 8, 15–16, 37, 41, 43, 83, 92, 123 n.75, 132, 139, 214
truth 2, 5, 11, 61–4, 92–6, 98–100, 102, 111–14, 119, 131–5, 169, 188, 214

universal/universalism/universality 2, 6, 15, 18, 26 n.32, 31 n.87, 61, 77, 79–80, 82, 84, 86, 96, 98, 102, 109, 117, 128, 145, 163, 169, 184, 202
utopia
  real utopia 20, 215, 229 n.9
  utopianism 20, 180–2, 185–6, 189–92, 215–16
  utopian socialism 180–2

value
  exchange value 118, 123 n.70, 135, 137–8, 142–3, 146, 158 n.39, 159 n.39, 202
  labor theory of 47, 148–9, 154, 156
  surplus value 47, 67, 132–3, 135, 137–8, 141, 148, 203
  use value 118, 132, 138, 142–4, 146–8, 159 n.39, 202
  value-form 143–4, 146, 148, 152–3, 158 n.39, 202
Vergegenständlichung. See objectification

Voss, G. Günter 206
vulnerability 20, 165–6

wage 47, 50, 66–7, 73, 87, 97, 123 n.70, 137, 139, 149, 154, 159 n.42, 207, 240, 245–6
wage labor, laborer 18, 20–1, 47–8, 50, 67, 87, 116, 139, 203, 209, 225–6, 240–1
Waldron, Jeremy 88 n.4, 170
The Wealth of Nations (Smith) 50
Weber, Max 38
Weltgeist 58
Wirklichkeit 60
work 10, 13–14, 18, 24 n.15, 40, 64, 66, 75, 83–4, 87, 110, 113–14, 119–20, 125–6, 128, 139, 147, 163, 170–1, 188, 190, 197–8, 202–3, 206–10, 212 n.68, 218–23, 226–7, 228 n.1, 230 n.29, 230 n.32, 231 n.50, 245
worker 12, 21, 28 n.59, 68, 90 n.40, 90 n.41, 105 n.55, 117, 123 n.71, 130, 136–7, 139, 143, 146, 149, 151, 159 n.43, 182, 198, 203–4, 206–10, 221–2, 224, 226, 231 n.48, 236, 239–43, 245–6, 250 n.27
working class 10, 67–8, 183, 185, 209

Young Hegelians 8, 18, 27 n.45, 27 n.47, 56–8, 62–3, 69, 77
The Young Hegel (Lukács) 4

Zambrana, Rocío 19
Žižek, Slavoj 3, 16, 98

www.ingramcontent.com/pod-product-compliance
Lightning Source LLC
Chambersburg PA
CBHW070024010526
44117CB00011B/1703